THE LETTERS OF BERNARD SHAW TO *THE TIMES* 1898–1950

Collected and Annotated by
RONALD FORD

Foreword by
MICHEL W. PHARAND

D1336249

IRISH ACADEMIC PRESS
DUBLIN · PORTLAND, OR

First published in 2007 by
IRISH ACADEMIC PRESS
44, Northumberland Road, Dublin 4, Ireland

and in the United States of America by
IRISH ACADEMIC PRESS
c/o ISBS, Suite 300, 920 NE 58th Avenue
Portland, Oregon 97213-3786

www.iap.ie

British Library Cataloguing in Publication Data
An entry can be found on request

ISBN 978 0 7165 2918 7 (cloth)
ISBN 978 0 7165 1919 4 (paper)

Library of Congress Cataloging-in-Publication Data
An entry can be found on request

Typeset by ForDesign
Printed by Creative Print and Design, Gwent, Wales

CONTENTS

FOREWORD

What is astonishing about Bernard Shaw is not that he wrote so many letters, but that he found the time and energy to produce any at all. Yet Shaw the playwright and director, reviewer and critic, essayist and lecturer, vestryman and borough councillor, managed to write many thousands of letters. Moreover, they are often as scintillating and provoking as his plays, even though most were written for a readership of one. *The Times*, however, presents a special case: a venue in one of the most respected and widely read newspapers of Shaw's day.

The five decades of letters collected in this volume evidence not only Shaw's tireless productivity – he often seems to incarnate his own idea of the 'Superman' – but the interest he took in current events of all kinds, from medicine and theatre to politics and economics. Nothing, it appears, was unimportant for Shaw, and his views on topical matters as they appeared in *The Times* form a fascinating portrait of the socio-political and literary controversies and debacles of the first half of the twentieth century.

This new collection of Shaw's correspondence is especially valuable because the majority of these letters have surfaced for the first time since their initial publication. Of the 169 letters in this volume, 109 have never before been published beyond the pages of *The Times*, while those which have appeared in print elsewhere are in volumes not readily available or long out of print. Thanks to the work of editor R.E. Ford, who has assembled and annotated them, we are now able to trace Shaw's progress through *The Times* as he tackles the newsworthy issues of his day: smallpox and vaccination, flogging in the navy, woman suffrage, capital punishment, dramatic and film censorship, copyright law, foreign policy, taxation of income, BBC English, the atomic bomb, the slaughter of animals, 'Slovenly Speech on the Stage' and many more. Shaw cast his intellectual net very wide indeed.

In these pages we discover Shaw at his wittiest and most outrageous, declaring that 'the suggestion, gratification, and education of sexual emotion is one of the main uses and glories of the theatre', advocating 'State-contrived euthanasia for all idiots and intolerable nuisances', suggesting that 'instead of wasting our energies in abusing Stalin, we must take a leaf out of his book and organize our agriculture on modern lines, as he has done', and asking 'Why should a marriage licence be held more sacred than a driving licence?' While readers of *The Times* must have bristled at such pronouncements, with the benefit of hindsight we can appreciate, enjoy and marvel at the legacy of an incisive mind struggling to improve the world.

Michel W. Pharand
January 2007

ACKNOWLEDGEMENTS

My grateful thanks to the Society of Authors, on behalf of the Bernard Shaw estate, for permission to reproduce the letters of Bernard Shaw, and a personal thank you to Jeremy Crow for his helpful assistance in answering my numerous queries.

Some of Shaw's letters to *The Times* were also reprinted in other English and American periodicals and newspapers (notably *The New York Times*). Appendix B ('Previously Published Letters to *The Times*') lists the location of 60 letters in nine published collections, many of them out of print. Further details are found in *Bernard Shaw: A Bibliography* (1983) by the eminent Shaw scholar Dan H. Laurence. It should be noted that Laurence's four-volume edition of Shaw's *Collected Letters* were published between 1965 and 1988 (not 1898 and 1950, as stated in the Introduction).

As the Editor of this book, I am grateful for the assistance, advice and encouragement I have received from many helpful and knowledgeable people around the world. Any remaining errors or omissions in this volume are my own.

Ron Ford
June 2007

INTRODUCTION

This volume collects all of Bernard Shaw's letters to *The Times* from 1898 to 1950. Although on several occasions certain Shaw enthusiasts have 'dipped into' *The Times* letters columns to quote from some of Shaw's letters, this is the first time that they have been edited and annotated. This lively compilation covers a wide range of subjects, from music, law and order, politics, phonetics, art, literature and medicine, to the theatre, economics, censorship, Shakespeare and much more.

These letters also show another side of Shaw. From his first letter in 1898 he was endeavouring to find a 'voice' in the columns of *The Times* that was distinct from his other personae of critic, socialist and playwright. *The Times* was, after all, a powerful medium not just in England but throughout the empire, and in its heyday the views aired in the main articles and the letters columns were noted by those in high places.

The Times, therefore, was a pulpit from which Shaw could pontificate or adjudicate to an audience of the great and powerful. In the columns of *The Times* Shaw took on the world of scholars, politicians, critics and the medical profession. He had no hesitation in offering advice on economics to different Chancellors, (it was he, after all, who was a co-founder, with the Webbs, of the London School of Economics) or to get involved in the campaign for women's rights, and was always ready to tackle the assumptions of eminent people in any profession. Not for nothing did Bertrand Russell (one among many) label him as an iconoclast. Once Shaw established himself in the august columns of The *Times* letters page, there were many who were willing to cross swords with him, but he parried all the attacks with his rapier wit.

When *The Times* published his first letter in 1898 Shaw was already 42 years old. He could look back on the previous twenty years of circumscribed success that by his high standards were akin to failure: an unsuccessful novelist, a not too well-known art and book critic in the mid-1880s, an increasingly noticed and unconventional music critic in the late 1880s and early 1890s, and then in the mid-to-late '1890s a trenchant *avant garde* drama critic. Still, Shaw was nowhere near where he wished to be: centre stage. He had of course already written seven plays, two of which, *Widowers' Houses* and *Arms and the Man*, had been produced amid controversy, while three others, *Mrs Warren's Profession, You Never Can Tell* and *Candida,* had received scant attention. However, several London and provincial papers were beginning to notice him, over and above his regular appearances as theatre critic for the *Saturday Review*. He married Charlotte Payne-Townshend in 1898 and retired as theatre critic while publishing *The Perfect Wagnerite* and *Plays Pleasant and Unpleasant*. He had also been elected as a 'Progressive' to the St. Pancras Vestry, where he soon displayed his ability as a committee-man. Though Shaw was an emerging figure, the pages of *The Times*, the foremost newspaper of the day, had eluded him.

Eventually of course, *The Times* became for Shaw the best platform for attracting the attention of and influencing the people who ran the institutions of the country – the Church, Parliament and its Ministers, the Armed Forces, the Civil Service. For, as a slogan of a later age put it, '*Top People Take The Times*.' If Shaw's name appeared in its pages, these very people would be sure to read him. And the fact that eventually *The Times* reported on him and published his letters almost as a matter of course was another measure, not merely of his celebrity, but of the force of his presence in contemporary affairs. As will be seen from these pages, much of the correspondence illustrates this.

Between the time of his first foray into the hallowed columns of *The Times* and his death in 1950, Shaw had corresponded for fifty-two years and contributed a total of 150 letters, many of great length. As he became more widely known, Shaw also published a number of articles in this foremost newspaper that are not included in this collection.

It has to be added, for those who are not familiar with Shaw's genius, that during his lifetime he wrote some fifty-two plays, many of which he also directed. He became an international celebrity and was awarded the Nobel Prize for Literature for 1925. During his long life Shaw penned many thousands of letters to individuals and friends, many of them collected by the eminent Shaw scholar Dan H. Laurence in his monumental four-volume edition, the *Collected Letters* (1898–1950). It should be noted that *Bernard Shaw: Agitations, Letters to the Press, 1875–1950* (1985), edited by Dan H. Laurence and James Rambeau, now out of print, included some twenty-eight of the letters published herein, and that *George Bernard Shaw on Language* (1963), edited by Abraham Tauber, included four letters.

I am indebted to the late Professor Leon Hugo for his guidance in the layout of this compilation and for some background information to a number of my annotations. I am also grateful to my daughter Candida, who spent many hours assisting in the location and extraction of these literary gems, and to my brother Eugene, who first planted the idea in my mind to undertake the long but enjoyable task that became in the end, an obsession.

R.E. Ford
July 2006

LETTERS

Although Shaw may well have written prior to 27 September 1898, this is the first letter published by *The Times*. He was prompted to write in the course of a debate that was being conducted through the press on the role of juries, which had become quite a public issue, Shaw's letter being one among several that appeared on the subject. His incisive comments focus, in characteristic Shavian fashion, not on the 'inhumanity' of the sentences but on the failure of the juries to return verdicts that found both defendants 'not guilty of wilful murder.'

The circumstances that prompted Shaw to write are clear enough. Ellen Shoesmith had been found guilty of the murder of her 2-year-old daughter by drowning her in a pond, but at her trial she had pleaded that it had been accidental. The jury found her guilty but strongly recommended mercy. In another case, William Viney killed three of his sons after his wife left him and his defence lawyer pleaded insanity. The jury also found him guilty, but because of what they termed extenuating circumstances, recommended mercy. A verdict of 'guilty of wilful murder' having been returned in both cases, the Judge, Sir Matthew White Ridley, had no option but to abide by the requirement of the law and condemn both to death.

～ *1898, September 27* ～

MURDER JURIES AND THE HOME SECRETARY.

Sir, – Two recent cases of severity in the operation of the criminal law, those of William Viney and Ellen Shoesmith, have produced the usual outcry against the cruelty of the Home Secretary, with the accompaniment, now quite common, of letters from members of the jury protesting that they returned a verdict of guilty only because they did not believe that the Home Secretary would permit it to be acted upon.

It is clear that neither the average juryman nor the average humanitarian journalist understands the constitutional function of a jury or the meaning of a verdict. A jury has two separate and perfectly distinct points to decide. First, whether the accused did or did not perform the action in respect of which he is alleged to be guilty; and second (if they conclude that he has performed it), whether the circumstances were such as to make the action a guilty one. For example, a man is indicted for murder. Obviously the jury must first be satisfied that somebody has been killed, and then that the man in the dock is the slayer; otherwise the case falls to the ground, and, in fact, ceases to be a case at all. But suppose the jury to be fully convinced on those two points, a verdict of guilty by no means follows. The jury may consider that in slaying his victim the prisoner was not only not guilty, but was performing an innocent, beneficent, and highly laudable action the omission of which would have deserved capital punishment: for instance, the prevention of a murder by shooting the assassin in the act. If under such circumstances the jurors were to bring in a verdict of guilty, and then write to the papers declaring, in effect, that they did not mean guilty, but used that word improperly to express their conclusion, in itself void of moral significance, that the alleged slaying had actually taken place at the hands of the prisoner, and that they trusted to the judge or the Home Secretary to save him from the consequences of their verdict, then the reasonable course would be to prosecute every one of the 12 for perjury.

I need hardly point out that every attempt to conceal this distinction, and to save our Courts trouble by working our criminal law mechanically upon facts instead of upon the moral interpretation of human intention, tends to make government by law inhuman, abhorrent, and finally impossible. The practice so prevalent of late years of putting a string of questions of fact to the jury, and then permitting the judge to interpret their replies as a verdict, is disgraceful to our constitutional lawyers, by whom it should have been rebuked instead of connived at, as it has been. That it should have been encouraged by Judges is only natural, since its effect is to transfer the really eminent part of the jury's function and power to the judge, who, with his wide experience of jurymen, can hardly help believing himself to be better fitted to exercise it than they are. The result is now before us. Jurymen have lost all sense of moral responsibility; ninety nine citizens out of a hundred, if examined as to the meaning of guilty or not guilty, will explain without hesitation that it means did he do it or did he not do it. In dealing with the lighter offences, the judge, having induced the jury to leave their duty to him, practically does as he pleases by his power of determining the sentence. But the gravest crimes involve fixed penalties which the judge has no power to reduce or modify. When the charge is one of wilful murder and the verdict is 'Guilty' he must sentence the prisoner to death. Certain other crimes are punishable by not less than ten years' penal servitude. In such cases the jury cannot transfer their responsibility to the judge. Consequently it passes on to the Home Secretary. This is how we have reached a state of things in which jurymen openly and shamelessly avow that in murder cases they leave the whole question of guilt to this unfortunate Minister and content themselves with deciding the facts.

Consider the situation of Sir Matthew White Ridley today. It has been proved that a man has taken his children out on a marsh and there slaughtered them. A woman has thrown her child into a pond and drowned it. If all this slaying was guiltily and wilfully done, the culprits are guilty of wilful murder and can claim no further consideration from any official whose duty it is to administer the law. If, on the other hand, they were crazy when they killed the children, and are in their normal state harmless and reputable people, then they are not guilty of wilful murder at all; and it was the duty of the jury to say so. Instead of doing their duty the jury return a verdict of wilful murder, coupled with a recommendation to the Home Secretary not to believe it. Can any constitutional situation more absurd, more unsound, more anarchical than this be imagined? Yet it has become quite the usual upshot of a murder trial. Twenty years ago, in the Penge case, a jury found several persons guilty of wilful murder. They were condemned to death. The Home Secretary released one of them immediately, whilst another remained in prison until the other day. Possibly that may have met the justice of the case as justice is commonly conceived; but it brought the law and the jury system into contempt. What would be said if a jury acquitted a prisoner and the Home Secretary insisted on hanging him? Yet there have been cases in which that would have been quite as satisfactory a solution as some reprieves have been.

I venture to urge, then, that whilst we retain the jury system juries should be taught to act as jurors and not merely as investigators. I am quite aware that those who know most about jurymen will see in this proposal nothing but a reductio ad absurdum of the whole institution of trial by jury as now practised, and that a judicial conspiracy to neutralize the jury is inevitable under present conditions. But it is time to face that conclusion, even if it leads us to tear up Magna Charta. If a juryman were an elected person, if he incurred even as much responsibility as the publication of his name and address would carry, if any sort of qualification, however slender, were exacted from him, something might be said for putting him in the enormously responsible position which he detests and abuses. As it is, I should be glad to hear what any rational person has to say in his defence.

Yours truly,
G. BERNARD SHAW.

Three years elapsed before Shaw returned to *The Times*. He had in the interim published three more plays in *Three Plays for Puritans*, one of which, *The Devil's Disciple,* was a hit in America, while some of the other earlier ones, notably *You Never Can Tell,* enjoyed brief runs in London and elsewhere. In 1901 there was an outbreak of smallpox in London, which spread to Essex. In the event there was no widespread epidemic, although anyone with memories of the 1881 and 1891 epidemics, in which some 30,000 people died, would have had good cause for alarm. Shaw was one such. Though vaccinated in his youth, he had contracted smallpox in 1881. The opinion that this experience coloured his view of the efficacy of vaccination is fairly widespread. However, as his letters to *The Times* on this subject show, it was in his capacity as a councillor serving on the Health Committee in the newly formed Borough of St. Pancras that he acted throughout, arguing strenuously in the cause of public health, against a policy that persisted in treating the symptoms rather than the cause – which he considered to be unsanitary housing and unhygienic living conditions.

It was as a member of the Health Committee that Shaw would have taken note of the letter in *The Times* of 16 September 1901 from the Reverend J.J. Coxhead, whose parish was in St. Pancras, reporting on the number of children who had not been vaccinated against smallpox and on the unsanitary housing conditions in the borough. He was already aware of the situation, having written to his friend and colleague on the Health Committee, the Reverend Ensor Walters, two days previously, declaring: 'I see 8 more cases of smallpox today. This means that we must act . . . everything points to a devastating epidemic next spring if things are left as they are. It is better to frighten London now than to bury it next year' (letter of 14 September 1901, in Laurence, ed., *Collected Letters*, 1898–1910, p. 237). He sprang into action and the letter that follows was the first among many critiques he delivered on the way the health authorities were handling (or not handling) the situation. In all, over the next two years he wrote ten letters on this theme to *The Times*, two to the *Saturday Review*, four to the *British Medical Journal* – a battle royal this was – as well as articles for such journals as the *Vaccination Inquirer.*

Certain themes recur in this correspondence: that Shaw was not opposed to vaccination as such (though they thought he was) but against a policy that persisted in treating the symptoms rather than the cause – unsanitary housing and unhygienic living conditions; that health authorities were falling hopelessly short of their bounden duty in neglecting the science of statistics, which in his view- would have pointed the way to a more accurate and dependable assessment of the situation; that reliance on the opinion of doctors, themselves ignorant, amounted to superstitious veneration; in a word, that the 'witchcraft' surrounding the practice of vaccination had to be exposed to the light of scientific scepticism.

SMALLPOX IN ST PANCRAS.

Sir, – Since it is better to frighten London in September than to bury it in April, it is as well to inform Mr. Coxhead and all others whom it may concern (to the number of four or five millions of people) that St. Pancras, and with St. Pancras all London, is heading straight for an epidemic of smallpox next year. The borough is, as Mr. Coxhead says, illegally overcrowded. It contains unsanitary areas which have been frankly given up by the sanitary inspectors. Its long list of houses registered for inspection is a delusion, since they have never been inspected. Underground dwellings abound and are tolerated. And the remedy urged on all hands is vaccination.

Now there are certain cast iron facts which have to be firmly held in view both by vaccinationists and anti-vaccinationists. Vaccination did not prevent the disastrous epidemic of 1871 in St. Pancras. In spite of the stringency with which vaccination was enforced after that alarm there was another epidemic in 1881, in which I myself, with satisfactory marks on my arm to certify me a vaccinated person, was one of the sufferers. It is not now possible to enforce the law as it was enforced then, owing to the loophole of escape recently opened; and it is still less possible to rehabilitate the credit formerly enjoyed by vaccination as an infallible prophylactic. The vaccinationist may contend that vaccination will at least mitigate the epidemic; and the anti-vaccinationist may contend that it will aggravate it. But the ordinary Londoner, who does not quite know what to think about vaccination, wants neither an aggravated epidemic nor a mitigated one; he wants no epidemic at all. And the only chance of that now lies through energetic action by the sanitary authority, which has nothing to do with vaccination. Vaccination is the business of the guardians; the borough council must concentrate all its energy on an attempt to remedy, in a single winter, the neglect that has been accumulating at compound interest since, terrible as epidemics are, they are the golden opportunities of the sanitary reformer; and at this moment the demands of the medical officer of health and of the health committee, contemptuously disregarded at ordinary times, are likely to be listened to. For it must be understood that in St. Pancras the fault does not rest with the medical officer nor with the health committee at least not in late years. But the neglect of earlier times has left London a legacy of overcrowded tenements, overground and underground. If the local authority carries out the law it must turn numbers of these poor people into the streets. From the popular point of view such a proceeding is so harsh and ruthless that a popularly elected body simply will not face it unless it is forced from above by the Local Government Board. And the Local Government Board is a body which neglects its duty so disgracefully, whether under Conservative or Liberal Ministries, that it is impossible for any one interested in municipal government to speak or write calmly of its inefficiency for every useful purpose or its jealous activity for every obsolete and mischievous one. It has no idea on the subject of smallpox except that the newspapers will find no fault with it as long as it urges larger supplies of calf lymph.

The closing of the schools is an excellent means of preventing smallpox from spreading inside the school buildings. The demolition of the school buildings would be equally effectual. But if it is desired to prevent the spread of smallpox in the borough I fail to see how that can be done by driving the children back into their overcrowded, unsanitary homes out of schools which are up to public standards of sanitation, and in which cases are carefully watched for and detected and isolated at the earliest possible stage. There is, I am sorry to say, no measure too foolish to be adopted in times of danger provided it is called 'a precaution'. Once the cry is raised of 'Something must be done,' people become reckless as to what the something is. As a matter of fact, no special precautions are needed. What is needed is simply to carry out the existing law; and this is the last thing that seems to occur to the citizens and public representatives who have for years connived at the neglect of the law. For years past the County Council has been calling attention to the state of St. Pancras. The medical officer of health, Dr. Sykes, has become widely known as an authority on the subject by his unavailing reports, remonstrance's, and suggestions.

The health committee has again and again recommended not adequate staffing, but at least a decrease of understaffing so as to render house-to-house inspection possible in the worst districts; but the late vestry was proud of St. Pancras as it was (and is) and declined to appoint even two additional inspectors when last the County Council demanded the appointment of seven.

The health committee and the medical officer are energetically seizing the opportunity to return to the charge. They are demanding a sufficient number of inspectors for house-to-house work to bring the borough up to the legal standard of sanitation and ventilation before the spring with its danger is upon us. It is probable that the new borough council will not, like the late vestry, hesitate to grant the medical officer all the money and the staff he needs for the coming fight with pestilence. But public opinion, which is seldom versed in the history of epidemics, and is apt to think that when the winter creeps along with eight cases one week and only seven the next, may easily take the situation too comfortably. London had better know that this creeping along through the winter is the usual preliminary to a formidable explosion in the spring. And it cannot be too carefully borne in mind that the enforcement of sanitary legislation is always unpopular with those whom it touches personally, and that nothing but strong pressure both from above and below – that is, from both the better class of borough voters and the Government departments – can nerve the borough councils to go through with costly precautions the very success of which will afterwards be urged against them as a proof that they were unnecessary. We, the councillors, must do our duty at the risk of our seats unless we are vigorously supported by the Press.

The problem would be simplified if the Local Government Board would do its duty and leave us no alternative but to carry out the law, whether our overcrowded constituents like it or not. That, I take it, is just what the Local Government Board is for. But it never does it. There are ways of making it do it. One is to allow me to edit *The Times* for three weeks.

But I think that without going to that extreme, you, Sir, may still find it possible to wake up the President to an astonished consciousness that there is something else to be done to avert smallpox than to urge revaccination at a moment when the power of compelling even vaccination has been given up by the Government.

I need hardly say that what I have said above is true not only of St. Pancras, but of every borough in the metropolis to some degree, greater or less. We have none of us put our house in order; and we have but a few months left to do it in.

Yours truly,
G. BERNARD SHAW.
29, Fitzroy Square.

In a letter of 5 October 1901 to *The Times*, a medical doctor, Mrs. E. Garrett Anderson, raised the question of the reduced effectiveness of prophylaxis by vaccination when the time-lapse increased between initial treatment and re-vaccination. This apparent resting of the problem of smallpox control by a member of the medical profession on a hit-and-miss statistic based on whether and when was enough to provoke the following letter from Shaw in which he makes the point that there had never been a scientifically conducted statistical survey. One may note his references to 'vaccine lymph containing pathogenic germs' and the question of adequate sanitation, issues he would return to time and again.

Talks with Mr. Gladstone, was by Lionel Tollemache (1883–1919). The doctors mentioned – Sydney Copeman, Charles Bond, Walter Hadwen and Edward Collins (a former chairman of the London County Council) – were prominent practitioners of the time. Professor Bowley (1869–1957) was the author of Elements of Statistics. 'Jennerians' were those who accepted the principles of Edward Jenner (1749–1823), the English doctor who introduced the smallpox vaccine.

VACCINATION STATISTICS.

Sir, – The letter of Mrs. Garrett Anderson in your issue of the 5th is sound in its contention that the fact that the majority of deaths in the present outbreak of smallpox are deaths of vaccinated persons does not discredit the modern vaccinist position. But it shows that the writer, like many other eminent members of the medical profession, does not understand the way in which such statistics really affect the public mind. The death of a single vaccinated person from smallpox does not prove that vaccination is either dangerous or useless; but it does shatter the confidence of the public in a propaganda which began by declaring that vaccination was a lifelong protection, and which still maintains that vaccination at least ensures that any subsequent attack of smallpox will be a very mild one. The Tollemache conversations with Gladstone bring out this effect very clearly. Gladstone became indifferent to the pretensions of vaccinism, not because he had examined the statistics or read anti-vaccination tracts, but because he had been repeatedly misled by the Jennerians. Within his recollection vaccination had dwindled into, at most, decennial revaccination. What is still more disquieting to us, the possibility of vaccine lymph containing pathogenic germs and so transmitting disease from arm to arm (and the lancet, if not the lymph, goes from arm to arm still), though it was once angrily denied by the vaccinists, is now not only admitted, but insisted on, in the advertisements of glycerinated calf lymph and in the lectures of its best known inventor, Dr. Copeman. How can the ordinary citizen witness without misgiving these step-by-step retreats from the old thorough-going Jennerian position? He may be as incapable of dealing with statistics as the ordinary doctor; and he is heartily tired of being pelted with figures which either Dr. Bond or Dr. Hadwen, Dr. Copeman or Dr. Collins, will triumphantly refute next day. But every return of the Registrar-General and every advertisement of the calf lymph manufacturers, with its sensational photograph of the leprous mass of corruption (the unvaccinated child) dying on the bed which the smiling and pretty vaccinated child is leaning over, stirs in him the reflection that, since half of what the vaccinists have too sanguinely told him is admittedly erroneous, perhaps the other half may presently share its fate.

Besides the ordinary citizen who has never seen any harm come of vaccination, there are not only the parents whose children have been killed outright by it, but those who, rightly or wrongly, date a decay in their children's health from the day when they were vaccinated. I am quite willing to grant, for the sake of argument, that these people may be as wrong in their generalizations from their own cases as they are undoubtedly passionate and personal in their feeling on the subject. Still, they have to be reckoned with politically. In 1898 the Government, having then no more intention than Mrs. Garrett Anderson of abolishing compulsory vaccination, and no more suspicion than an average country gentleman that anti-vaccination was anything more than the safely negligible craze of a handful of foolish and ignorant labourers, suddenly found the political ground rocking under its feet. It is not often that Whips come to Ministers quite unexpectedly on the eve of a division to say that their forces are about to bolt; but when it does happen no sensible public man trifles with the public feeling such an event reveals. Compulsory vaccination went by the board the moment the Government realized the situation; and it would be extinct now if it were not that our magistrates are trueborn Protestant Englishmen; that is, ingrained Anarchists who care for no law that is in conflict with their private judgement. And yet there are people who dream that the Government can be persuaded to reimpose compulsion without further investigation!

Finally, there is the fact that has forced me, as a member of a local sanitary authority, into the controversy, namely, that the vaccinists are not only denouncing anti-vaccinism, which they are perfectly welcome to do as far as I am concerned, but vehemently attacking sanitation. And I confess I do not see how they can help themselves. When an anti-vaccinist town is free from smallpox, the anti-vaccinists claim its freedom as a triumph for sanitation. When it is attacked by smallpox, they denounce its sanitary condition. Naturally the vaccinists set to work to prove that the town was a model of sanitation, and that vaccination and nothing but vaccination can avert smallpox. That is to say, the vaccinist propaganda allows itself to be carried away into anti-sanitation propaganda. I am forced to fight against vaccination in council, because if I do not do so all the energy that is wanted to fight the diphtheria and scarlet fever now raging in our insanitary districts, with their cellar dwellings and their illegal overcrowding, will be diverted to vaccination, which does not profess to touch diphtheria.

This state of affairs satisfies no intelligent citizen. One doctor publicly assures St. Pancras that all smallpox epidemics begin with vaccinated people, and that smallpox kills the vaccinated and spares the unvaccinated. Another doctor informs the borough council that a woman covered with smallpox pustules may safely suckle her child provided the child is vaccinated. One popular newspaper describes vaccination as 'a filthy fraud'; another gets angry if vaccination is disparaged even to the extent of suggesting that good drainage and fresh air might help to keep a neighbourhood clear of smallpox. For my own part – and I believe I represent in this matter almost every educated person under 40 in London who has given any thought to the question – I no longer believe that the vaccinist case has been either proved or disproved. It has never been scientifically investigated by experts, because it has been assumed that the science involved is the science of therapeutics, whereas what is at issue is not a therapeutic theory but the two simple statements that (1) people cannot have two attacks of smallpox, whether in its human, vaccine, or equine modification, within a period of x years, and (2) that everybody who is unprotected by a previous attack is so sure to suffer from smallpox that the admitted risks of vaccination are infinitesimal in comparison. The only science which can verify these two statements, if they be verifiable, is statistical science. Of this most doctors, and almost all vaccinist and anti-vaccinist controversialists, are so ignorant that they do not know that such a science exists, and assume statistics to be a natural faculty of man, like English political public speaking. Anybody can prove by the statistical methods used by the disputants, and even by our Royal Commissioners, that typhus fever has been extirpated by the introduction of hair brushing by machinery, or that the alarming increase of child mortality from measles and adult mortality from cancer is due to the spread of teetotalism, to the use of the telephone, to vaccination or anti-vaccination or any other contemporary phenomenon you please. I therefore propose and this must be my justification for troubling you with this long letter that the London University be invited to undertake a purely statistical investigation of the question, and to publish the result.

Professor [Arthur] Bowley, whose work on statistics is, as far as I know, the latest book on statistical methods, lectures on them at the London School of Economics and Political Science, which, as a school of the University specialized for the study of public problems, is obviously the proper department for such an investigation. If University College could spare Professor Karl Pearson or Oxford Professor [Francis] Edgeworth to co-operate, I imagine they would find the work congenial. But neither Oxford nor University College is specialized for the investigation as the London School of Economics is; and if its Principal, Professor [A.W.S. Hewins], will take my proposal into consideration, I will contribute £25 towards the expenses, or more in the event, which seems hardly credible, of insufficient additional support forthcoming. I may explain that what I desire is not an attempt to repeat the work of the Royal Commission by collecting fresh evidence, which would be expensive and endless, but simply to examine the existing data by expert methods, so that we may know whether Sir Michael Foster and Sir James Paget on the one side, or Dr. Alfred Russell Wallace on the other, would have drawn the conclusions they did if they had been as highly qualified in statistics as they were in physiology, medicine, and natural history.

I should perhaps add that, though I happen to enjoy the privilege of being personally acquainted with the four professors named in this letter, I have not the faintest suspicion of what their opinions may be on the subject of vaccination.

Yours truly,
G. BERNARD SHAW.
29, Fitzroy Square

In his next letter, Shaw reacts to what he terms 'a very curious statement'. It is not clear – whether he was quibbling or whether his query was based upon the stern logic of a Borough Councillor who would not be fobbed off with imprecise reporting. One is inclined to believe the latter.

~ *1902, February 18* ~

VACCINATION.

Sir, – In your issue of the 17th you quote a correspondent as informing you that: 'Before smallpox broke out in the Mile end (Stepney) Infirmary 35 of the 43 nurses in the establishment were revaccinated. Of the eight who were not revaccinated seven have already contracted smallpox, while not one of the 35 who were revaccinated has caught the disease.'

This is a very curious statement. Does your correspondent mean that the eight nurses he mentions had never been revaccinated? If so, how did they come to be employed as smallpox nurses? It is usual to insist on the revaccination of nurses and all other professional 'contacts' on their engagement to cope with an outbreak, unless they can show that they have recently undergone revaccination. How did these eight out of the 43 escape? Were they exempted as unfit to bear the operation; or were they the permanent staff of the infirmary, supported in the anti-vaccinist persuasion by sympathetic guardians? If the latter, were they of the same class and age as the 35 extra nurses, or were they pauper nurses? Can we not have some details in explanation? It seems possible that what your correspondent meant to convey was that 35 of the nurses had been revaccinated since the outbreak in London, before it reached the infirmary, and that eight relied on previous revaccination. If so, the dates of such previous revaccinations would help us to settle the open question as to the duration of the alleged immunity.

Yours, &c.,
G. BERNARD SHAW.
10, Adelphi Terrace, W.C.

On 20 February 1902 a Medical Superintendent, J. Harley Brooks, answered some of the questions raised by Shaw in his letter of 18 February. This is Shaw's response, and it sparked – an argument between the two that ran over several weeks. The fact that *The Times* was by now giving Shaw as much space as his letters demanded indicates both the editorial realisation that the vaccination issue was of grave public concern and that Shaw himself, for all the highly personal colouring he gave his letters, was no crank in his insistence on probity and precision in matters of public health.

VACCINATION.

Sir, – The letter of Dr. Harley Brooks concerning the Mile End nurses does not answer the most important of my questions. He admits that three of the seven nurses attacked were not revaccinated. I want to know and I believe the public wants to know why they were not revaccinated. He admits that the other four, though revaccinated, were allowed to take up their duties before the revaccination had taken effect. Again I ask why? Were these seven unprotected nurses exposed to contagion as a 'control experiment', with their own consent? The revaccinated four were clearly not anti-vaccinists; so these at least were allowed to take what they and the medical superintendent believed to be a serious and preventable risk. It seems to me that though the theoretic scepticism as to vaccination may be all on my side, the practical scepticism is all on Dr. Harley Brooks's. He professes to believe that revaccinated nurses are immune. He acts as if it did not matter whether nurses are revaccinated or not. At least, that is how he stands pending some further explanation of the exception made in the case of the three unrevaccinated nurses and the four who were revaccinated after contagion.

I will not quarrel with his opinion that the statement of your anonymous correspondent was 'marvellously near the truth', since there is no serious discrepancy involved. But it is gravely unsatisfactory that the controversy should have come to such a pass that doctors have to confess that an approximately complete and precise statement is a marvel. The difficulty of precision in the present case is not apparent. Your correspondent said that seven out of eight unrevaccinated nurses were attacked, implying that one (no doubt the one absent on sick leave) escaped. Dr. Harley Brooks says that there were only seven unrevaccinated nurses at work; that they were all attacked; and that four of them were revaccinated too late. On any other subject the similarity of the two statements would hardly be described as marvellous.

I wish I could convince Dr. Harley Brooks that what is 'unpalatable' to me on this question is, first, anonymity and irresponsibility; secondly, inaccuracy; and, thirdly, exaggeration of the degree of immunity conferred by vaccination and revaccination. The recently revaccinated soldier who was attacked at Horsell a month ago would probably have escaped if he had been warned that revaccination did not justify him in discarding all caution and exposing himself recklessly to contagion. Revaccination of doctors and nurses in hospital is only part of an elaborate system of precaution applied by trained persons in specially designed buildings; so that the class which is exceptionally exposed to infection is also exceptionally guarded against it. The object of my intervention is not to pick a quarrel with the vaccinists; it is to remind the public that revaccination should not be treated as a substitute for ordinary sanitary precautions, but as an addition to them. The public danger of persuading an ignorant and insanitary housed labourer that he is, when revaccinated, as safe as a doctor or a hospital nurse, is, I hope, obvious.

Yours truly,
G. BERNARD SHAW.
10, Adelphi Terrace, W.C.I.

Dr Harley Brooks replied at length on 27 February refuting some of Shaw's comments but endorsing others. He pointed out that the original infection came from a patient who was admitted and died before smallpox was diagnosed and that one of the nurses had been in contact with him. In his correspondence he also defended revaccination as a generally successful procedure.

~ *1902, March 1* ~

VACCINATION.

Sir, – I hope Dr. Harley Brooks will not think that I am abusing his patience if I suggest that there is another possible explanation of the fact that the seven nurses who had not anticipated involuntary smallpox by voluntary vaccine variola were promptly attacked. That explanation is simply that the unrevaccinated nurses were inoculated with the smallpox lymph which has been coming into use ever since its production was reduced to a commercially practicable routine, and that the presence in the infirmary of a number of nurses suffering from variolous eruptions on the arm produced not only the outbreak among the unrevaccinated nurses, but also among the patients.

I am aware that there is a consensus of opinion, both popular and professional, that vaccine variola is not infectious. But I am old enough to remember when there was the same consensus with regard to diseases so obviously infectious as pneumonia and consumption; and I am sufficiently versed in clinical history to know that the view that smallpox itself is infectious is comparatively modern. Even if we could quite comfortably feel sure that Jenner's belief in the non infectiousness of his equine cowpox was any better founded than the common belief of his day that phthisis 'ran in families', the introduction of a new lymph produced by inoculating a series of calves with human smallpox changes the situation. A glance at the additions made of late years to the lists of diseases classed as infectious and made notifiable will show that our notions as to infection need constant revision, and that the revision goes steadily in the direction of shifting diseases formerly considered safe into the 'catching' category.

On the whole, the question seems to me worth raising. I am still unanswered as to whether the differential between the revaccinated nurses and the seven attacked consist solely in revaccination versus anti revaccination; and I should like to add a question as to extent of disablement (as distinct from quarantine) suffered by the nurses who got smallpox and those who were revaccinated. May I, however, assure Dr. Harley Brooks that in putting these questions I am not trying to pick an antivaccinist quarrel with him, but simply taking advantage of his very instructive and temperate letters to test his position in every possible way? As he has, so far, come off triumphantly, he will probably not grudge the public a further criticism of my doubts.

Yours truly,
G. BERNARD SHAW.
10, Adelphi Terrace, W.C.

The following long, highly charged letter, another reply to Dr Harley Brooks, covers a good deal of ground that now belongs to the footnotes of medical history, but it is as well to bear in mind that a hundred years ago there remained considerable uncertainty about the effectiveness of vaccination and, as one may gather here and in subsequent letters, the difficulty of differentiating between smallpox, general vaccinia and syphilis. This letter gives one pause to note Shaw's fluent expertise in a field in which he had received no formal training, and also his overriding concern for the victims of smallpox and the failure of the health authorities really to contain the outbreak. He confesses himself 'perplexed' by the apparently hit and miss methods of control being undertaken and, for good measure, sums up his stance *vis-à-vis* his adversary in terms that may be read as defining his role in the controversy: 'I can only envy Dr. Harley Brooks his freedom from "the shadow of doubt". He has been dogmatically educated; I have been controversially educated. He, as a physician, belongs to the most credulous profession in the world; I, as a critic, to the most sceptical one. It is natural that I should be somewhat less sanguine and dithyrambic than he.'

The physician Thomas Sydenham (1624–89), known as the 'English Hippocrates' for his pioneering work in medical research, failed to identify the nature of infectious disease, hence Shaw's reference to him.

VACCINATION.

Sir, – Dr. Harley Brooks has now arrived at my own position, as defined by me in the *British Medical Journal* a few months ago. I said then that if people are bound to have smallpox (and a hospital nurse may reasonably regard herself as so bound) they had better take it from my fellow vegetarian, the cow, than from a human subject, And I may add that they had better take it when they are well and presumably best able to resist it than at the weak moment on which smallpox seizes. The more excellent way of not getting smallpox at all is, I admit, not fairly open to professional contacts under existing conditions.

Now let us see where this conclusion, which Dr. Harley Brooks claims as 'a most triumphant victory for vaccination', leaves us. To begin with, we are agreed that what has happened at Mile End is not that the revaccinated nurses have escaped smallpox and the unrevaccinated ones caught it, but that the revaccinated nurses have had it by inoculation in a mild and practically non-infectious form, involving at worst four days' disablement, whereas the others have had it in the ordinary form. Dr. Harley Brooks does not give the disablement for this form; he speaks rhetorically of horrors, agony, and delirium. But this does not affect the main point namely, that we have now got back admittedly to the old practice of inoculation. After a whole century of apparently conclusive proofs that cows could not be successfully inoculated with human smallpox, and that Jenner's smallpox of the horse infected cow must therefore be distinct from human smallpox, we have found out how to do the thing that was found impossible; and we now vaccinate with lymph obtained from a vesicle induced by inoculating a series of calves with smallpox crusts from the hospital ship. The results seem to resemble those claimed for direct inoculation when that practice was in its heyday in the 18th century. The eruption is confined, in most cases, to the spot on the arm where the lymph is inserted; and the practitioners stoutly maintain that it is not infectious. Dr. Harley Brooks will probably agree with me that lymph obtained frankly from human smallpox should be more acceptable to the educated public as being more in line with the modern series of anti toxins than the lymph of casual cowpox or Jennerian horse grease. Of the forgotten fact that 18th century inoculation was finally brought to a point at which the eruption was localized to the point of insertion, and was defended as non-infectious by the inoculators, he can easily convince himself. As to the protective efficacy of inoculation there never was any serious dispute among those who believe that people cannot have smallpox twice. During the present epidemic I have heard of only two cases of the same person suffering twice; and although when the odds laid by the insurance companies are 2,000 to 1 against a single attack, the odds against a second would be greater on the mere chances, still, most of us, including myself, are inclined to admit that people of only normal susceptibility may exhaust that susceptibility, for a while at least, by a mild attack induced by inoculation. It is true that when direct inoculation had given way to vaccination it was repudiated by the medical profession, and made a criminal offence on the ground of its infectiousness, but that was a full generation after the practice had fallen into disuse. In any case, an eruption confined to a spot on the arm covered constantly by a dressing is not likely to be so infectious as the general eruption of a fever stricken patient And it may be that the calf transmits the disease in so benign a form that it is no longer infectious. (Dr. Harley Brooks's dates bear out this reassuring possibility.) It may even be that smallpox is not an infectious disease at all. Were Sydenham to return to life at present he would certainly find abundant evidence in the erratic course of the present epidemic to support his scepticism on that point. But no matter; we are agreed that vaccination, as now advocated is really inoculation with smallpox, and that the vaccinated and revaccinated are not persons who have been rendered 'immune'; they are persons who have had smallpox.

In short, the vaccinists will say, 'You admit, after all, that vaccine smallpox protects against epidemic smallpox.' It will perhaps surprise them when I add that such an admission will not decide the controversy or even greatly affect it. Otherwise I should perhaps be less ready to make it, for I do not possess that abstraction in which Dr. Harley Brooks so very unscientifically believes, 'an unbiased mind', which he further defines as a mind which regards the whole question as 'settled by experience and placed beyond the shadow of a doubt'. Without being 'unbiased' to this remarkable but not uncommon degree, I have learnt at least one thing by political experience as an elected person; and that is that compulsory vaccination does not really go to the poll on its efficacy or inefficacy as a prophylactic. Here inefficacy would hurt vaccination no more than it hurts bread pills. An absolutely inert pseudo prophylactic would be as popular as any harmless remedy is, because nobody would be angry with it, and all those who escaped smallpox would give it credit for their immunity. What, then, is the explanation of the fanatical opposition which has arisen to vaccination? The answer is, simply, general vaccinia. But as that answer conveys nothing to the general public, I must explain at greater length.

If any investigator will take the trouble to canvass our ordinary Anti vaccinist voters, excluding those who belong to leagues, and write to the papers and compile statistical tracts, he will find them just as ignorant about vaccination in general as the ordinary vaccinist is, and obviously passionate and prejudiced in their hatred of it. But he will find in every such case that there is a relative, usually a pet child, in whom vaccination has induced general vaccinia. It may be that this general vaccinia has been diagnosed as syphilis, in which case the complaint of the parent that the doctor must have vaccinated from a syphilitic vaccinifer is pretty sure to have been met by the infuriating medical countercharge that the syphilis must have come by inheritance from the parents themselves. Still more common is the case of the child who was the picture of health before vaccination, and 'never was the same afterwards'. We have no record of the majority of these cases, as general vaccinia is not a notifiable disease and, even if it were, many cases in which illness or disease dates from vaccination and is attributed to it (rightly or wrongly) by the parents, would not be diagnosed as general vaccinia. When death ensues, and the cause of death is certified without prevarication, we get a record from the Registrar General. For example, we find in the Report of the Royal Commission that in the decade 1881/91 vaccination killed one child per week. We also get glimpses of this side of the question through the heated controversy on vaccinal syphilis which arose when the *Encyclopaedia Britannica* startled the medical profession by the view that vaccine variola was not smallpox of the cow but syphilis of the cow.

Let me now, instead of arguing about the real scientific significance of these facts, consider their effect on the minds of voters who know nothing about science. Take the case of a man whose first child has been unluckily killed or made seriously ill or permanently injured in a way suggesting a reflection on his own good name, Imagine that man being forced to submit his second child to the same risk. Imagine him quoting medical statistics to his wife to gain her consent. Imagine him being bullied by an ignorant magistrate, who assures him that vaccination cannot possibly hurt his child. Imagine the feelings of his married brothers and sisters and their whole circle of gossips who, to say the least, will not let the tale weaken in the telling. You will then understand why even so strong a Government as the present is intimidated by the political force of anti-vaccinism, and why the anti vaccinist orators are frantically cheered for declaiming against compulsion in terms which few of us would care to apply to the decree of Ferdinand and Isabella ordering all their Jewish subjects to be baptized. And you will see that, though the anti-vaccinist denial of the mitigative effect of vaccination on smallpox is for the most part as purely vituperative as most of the counter-assertions, a conclusive refutation of them would not save the vaccinist situation in a single one of these centres of anti-vaccination which have for their nucleus a bad case of general vaccinia.

And now, finally, is the new smallpox calf lymph any safer in this respect than the old cowpox strains that went from arm to arm? I do not know, because I have not ascertained whether the lymph that killed Mr. Essex the other day was smallpox lymph or one of the old strains. But I sit on a public health authority in the instructive company of several doctors, all convinced vaccinists, and all excellent and honourable gentlemen. We find that revaccination, with stringent soap and hot water, applied literally tooth and nail, and with resolute baking of clothes, produces wonderful results, as does also the cleansing and baking process when applied to recalcitrant dossers who refuse revaccination because they cannot afford the temporary disablement. But the other day there was a hitch. One of our doctors revaccinated a patient who was next heard of on her way to the hospital ship. The doctor was indignant; a revaccinated smallpox patient was to him a contradiction in terms. The authorities of the wharf agreed, and the case was sent back as one of general vaccinia. Thereupon our medical officer asked the wharf authorities, for the guidance of our medical referees, how they discriminate between general vaccinia and smallpox.

He found that they cannot discriminate; all they can say is that they believe that general vaccinia is not infectious and that smallpox is.

Now, in 1895, Mr. Jonathan Hutchinson gained the assent of his colleagues on the vaccinist majority of the last Royal Commission to his conclusion that the apparently contradictory evidence before them to the effect that syphilis had followed vaccination from sound vaccinifers to the children of sound parents, whilst doctors who had submitted to vaccination from syphilitic vaccinifers had not been infected, was explained by the simple fact that general vaccinia was so like syphilis that the one could easily be diagnosed as the other. It appears, then, that both syphilis, the one disease we dread more than smallpox, and smallpox itself are indistinguishable from general vaccinia. It also appears that a case indistinguishable from ordinary smallpox may be diagnosed as general vaccinia, and consequently not notified, if the patient has been revaccinated so recently as to make the wharf authorities incredulous. The wharf authorities may be perfectly right in doing this; but the anti-vaccinists will inevitably say that the alleged immunity of the revaccinated means no more than the refusal of the authorities to diagnose revaccinated cases as smallpox. I do not say so myself, because two revaccinated cases have already been admitted.

And so the matter remains as perplexing as ever, in spite of the Mile End nurses on the one side and the revaccinated ambulance attendant who has just been attacked on the other. I profess no conviction either way. I can only envy Dr. Harley Brooks his freedom from 'the shadow of doubt'. He has been dogmatically educated; I have been controversially educated. He, as a physician, belongs to the most credulous profession in the world; I, as a critic, to the most sceptical one. It is natural that I should be somewhat less sanguine and dithyrambic than he. But I assure him I have had no object in this correspondence except to induce him to complete a statement which, in its original form, proved absolutely nothing, and in its satisfactorily completed form is already contradicted by that unlucky revaccinated ambulance attendant aforesaid. Nature should have kept the lists clear of fresh cases until the end of our argument. The problem is still too hard for me. I confess I do not know what to think.

Yours truly,
G. BERNARD SHAW.

The controversy continued and in his next letter Shaw makes more of his primary contention, citing his associate in the borough, Dr J.J. Sykes, as setting the desired example, that improved sanitation and hygiene can go a long way in preventing the spread of smallpox. Here and in the letters that follow Shaw goes off on a slightly different tack, presenting facts and figures that point to the health authority's continuing inability to contain and control the disease whilst insisting that the cost of periodic re-vaccination of the entire population would be exorbitant. His stance remains constant throughout, stoutly reiterated in the last letter on this topic (22 January 1904) that 'The tendency of modern sanitary regulations is to mitigate and confine smallpox epidemics, and all other epidemics as well. It is therefore quite possible, without the smallest scepticism as to the possibility of preventing smallpox epidemics by inoculation, to prefer the disease to that particular remedy, both on economic and hygienic grounds.'

~ 1902, August 19 ~

The Imperial Vaccination League.

Sir, – Will you allow me to correct an error into which the writer of your article on the Imperial Vaccination League of the 12th Inst. has fallen? Glycerine is a convenient and economical vehicle for the smallpox lymph used in vaccination (or inoculation, as it would now be properly called but for the rash statute which made direct inoculation a criminal offence), but the risk of general vaccinia is just as great with glycerinated calf lymph as with the old stocks that went, and still go, from arm to arm. One of the most eminent of the signatories of the Imperial Vaccination League, Mr. Jonathan Hutchinson, convinced the Royal Commission that general vaccinia is indistinguishable from syphilis, and that the alleged cases of syphilis conveyed from arm to arm by vaccination were really cases of general vaccinia. General vaccinia is also indistinguishable from smallpox itself. Case after case of a disease diagnosed as smallpox has been sent to the hospital ships during the late epidemic; but whenever the authorities at the wharf found marks of recent revaccination on the patient the case was promptly sent back as one of general vaccinia. One of the leading metropolitan medical officers of health, himself an ardent vaccinist, asked the wharf authorities, for the guidance of his medical referees, how they distinguished smallpox from general vaccinia. They replied that they knew of no diagnostic except that general vaccinia is not infectious. No steps, as far as I am aware, were taken to follow up the rejected cases with a view to tracing infection from them; nor indeed could such steps have been conclusive in view of the apparently hopeless incompatibility of the course and decline of the epidemic with the ordinary view of infection. As I have before pointed out, the real popular objection to vaccination is the possibility of general vaccinia ensuing; and as no known process of treating the lymph, whether by glycerine or anything else, can separate the power of inducing local vaccinia (itself sometimes a by no means inconsiderable ailment) from the possibility of inducing general vaccinia, any attempt to persuade the public that glycerinated lymph is absolutely safe must be classed with those over-sanguine assurances which, as your article very justly remarks, have done more than all the efforts of the anti-vaccinists to discredit the Jennerian propaganda.

Incidentally it will be noticed that, if a public body like the Metropolitan Asylums Board starts with the assumption that a recently revaccinated person cannot catch smallpox, it is quite easy to substantiate that assumption by refusing to diagnose smallpox in revaccinated cases and declaring the case one of general vaccinia or some other indistinguishable alternative. The difficulty of diagnosis is now admitted by the costly new institution of official medical referees, whose reports are very instructive as to the number of complaints which pass as smallpox until there is some strong reason for, or interest in, challenging the diagnosis.

A further significant change is the admission, after a century of sturdy resistance and denial, of the fact that many cases cannot be confidently classed as either vaccinated or revaccinated. We now have a 'doubtful' column, which, as might have been expected, often exceeds in number the ascertained cases. The sort of person who does not know whether he was vaccinated or not is obviously likely to suffer more from smallpox, and every other 'filth' disease, than those who at least know that they were not vaccinated, not to mention the comparatively well nourished, cleanly housed, and educated people who read *The Times* and observe the custom of vaccination among the other customs of ladies and gentlemen. But what is to be said now of the old statistics which would not admit that a doctor could be in doubt about anything? Yet it is on those statistics that the faith of the founders of the Imperial League is based; for they can hardly have been newly convinced, as their manifesto so comically suggests, by the occurrence of a smallpox epidemic.

However, the Imperial Vaccination League is perfectly welcome to do its best for the 'have it and get it over' method of dealing with smallpox, provided only it does not act as an anti-sanitation league also. Of the anti-sanitation danger you allowed me to give early warning in your columns. Let me now give an example of what I feared. In the borough of St. Pancras, Dr. J.J. Sykes, the medical officer of health, a distinguished authority on public health, and a very pillar on vaccinism, promptly recognized that he would have to deal with 'contacts' who could not afford to be revaccinated, since, though we revaccinate for nothing, we give no compensation for temporary disablement by a bad arm. Dr. Sykes induced the borough council to establish a disinfecting station where people could be vigorously washed, including their teeth and nails, whilst their clothes were being baked. The process proved quite as effectual as revaccination. Meanwhile at the hospital ships moribund patients were being visited daily by relatives. One would suppose that, in view of the obvious danger of these relatives carrying infection and the certainty that some of them would refuse revaccination, the visitor would be disinfected as our contacts were in St. Pancras. As nobody could reasonably object to a bath and temporary change it could be made compulsory, whereas there are circumstances under which compulsory vaccination is too atrocious to be enforced without great trouble. Yet, as far as I have been able to ascertain, nothing was done but to offer the visitors revaccination and to call attention quite triumphantly to the cases when refusal was followed by infection. Nor does it seem to have been considered that a revaccinated person's clothes are not revaccinated, and that the disease may consequently be carried by people who themselves escape. If I am wrong in assuming that disinfection was not practised, the public will be glad to have an authoritative assurance to that effect. If I am right, the public will see how untrustworthy a public health authority may become when its officials become men of one idea, and that idea vaccinism. I venture to submit that a league to discover an unobjectionable method of extirpating smallpox is much more urgently wanted than an Imperial Vaccination League, the very title of which is already an anachronism.

Yours truly,
G. BERNARD SHAW.

In a brief reply, W. McM. Wanklyn (Medical Superintendent of the River Ambulance Service) stated that vaccinia was very rare and could reasonably be distinguished from smallpox.

~ 1902, September 1 ~

THE IMPERIAL VACCINATION LEAGUE.

Sir, – The letter of the Medical Superintendent of the Smallpox River Ambulance Service is interesting as a contradiction by an expert of the medical authorities cited by me in your issue of the 19th – May I now beg him to render the Health Committee of the St. Pancras Borough Council the public service of describing, for the instruction of the medical referees, the diagnostics by which general vaccinia can be distinguished from smallpox? The wharf authorities did not say that 'no diagnostic characters exist,' nor did I use that phrase (and I here earnestly plead with Dr. McC. Wanklyn not to use inverted commas when he is neither quoting verbatim nor even accurately paraphrasing the passage he refers to, especially when he places immediately after the inverted commas the sentence, 'Such a statement is not in accordance with facts'). No doubt such diagnostics exist if the diseases are distinct; the point is that the persons authorized at the wharf to correspond with local sanitary authorities do not know them, and, when they diagnose general vaccinia in the case of a revaccinated patient sent to the ships as suffering from smallpox and are then asked for diagnostics to guide local medical referees in future cases, have none to offer except that smallpox is infectious and general vaccinia is not. It now appears that they had only to consult their own 'final medical referee' to ascertain that 'general vaccinia . . . presents no special difficulty in being distinguished from smallpox'. This means that the practitioners who sent the cases to the ships did not know their business; that the distinguished Medical Officer of Health who applied for guidance for his referees was raising a difficulty that does not exist; and that the wharf authorities do not take the trouble of referring questions of diagnosis to their own principal referee. And so I leave Dr. Wanklyn to fight it out with his own profession and his own department. When doctors differ, observant laymen come to their own. It is noteworthy, by the way, that my suggestion that vaccination is treated on the hospital ships as a substitute for thorough disinfection, and that visitors who refuse revaccination are therefore left practically unprotected, has not yet been contradicted.

Yours truly,
G. BERNARD SHAW.

Dr Garret Horder again wrote on 29 August 1902, repeating that he had never encountered a disorder known as vaccinia in his twenty-five years of carrying out vaccinations in Cardiff.

~ *1902, September 16* ~

THE IMPERIAL VACCINATION LEAGUE.

Sir, – In your issue of August 29, Dr. Garrett Horder, of Cardiff, invited a comparison of vaccination in Cardiff and in London in the following terms: 'I have been in the habit of vaccinating more than 1,000 children yearly for the period I have named (25 years) and I can truthfully say that beyond a few cases of popular eruption (and that only existing for a few days) I have never seen any rash which approached in the slightest degree to anything resembling the marks produced by vaccination. Of course it is just possible that the children of the great metropolis differ in constitution from those living in Cardiff; on such a point the voices of my brother vaccinators in London might well be heard.'

Although the above statement has no bearing on the letter from me which elicited this communication from Dr. Garrett Horder, who seems to consider that general vaccinia is 'a rash resembling the marks produced by vaccination', yet his letter conveys an impression of the results of vaccination so very different from that which we get from the reports of his 'brother vaccinators in London', performing the operation with modern lymph according to the latest standards of 'efficiency,' that I have taken the trouble to procure one such report for his information and that of the public. It was made by Dr. W.J. Stewart on the vaccination of workmen at Gore Farm Lower Hospital to the Hospitals Committee of the Metropolitan Asylums Board. It is dated June 13 last, and is printed as No. 150 of August, 1902. From it Dr. Garrett Horder may learn that the sick list of more or less disabled workmen was 28.1 per cent. of the number (587) of men who attended the station between March 10 and June 7, Of this 166, 35 were cases of fever and general illness, and the sufferers lost, on an average, 5,5 days' work each; 125 had septic inflammation at or near the incisions, they lost 8 days' average per man. Of the remaining six, three were cases of abscess, involving no less than 34.6 days' disablement per patient; and the other three were 'general pustular eczema', causing 23 days' disablement per patient. 'The total number of working days for which these 1.6 men on the sick list were incapacitated from work was 1,238, or an average of 7.4 days per man.' As to the cost, 'the grand total of all expenses incurred in carrying out the scheme of vaccination during the 13 weeks the station was open amounts to £1,029 10s. 2d. The average cost per head for the 587 men who attended there is, therefore, £1.15s. 0d.' This total includes a tip ('bonus' is the official term) of 5s. a head to 503 men to induce them to be vaccinated, £278 0s.5d. paid to the contractors for loss of work, and £463 4s. 7d. sick pay to the sufferers. To prevent malingering, the men on the sick list 'were made to attend daily, or, if the state of the arm demanded it, twice, and in some instances thrice daily'. No man could be placed on the sick list without a certificate from Dr. Stewart. The vaccination was not of the severe kind prescribed by those who doubt whether the four incisions which are now de rigueur are sufficient. 'Each man,' says Dr. Stewart, 'was vaccinated in two places, except in the case of men who had not been previously vaccinated, in which case the number was three.' Dr. Stewart suggests that if he had been able to provide the vaccinated men with night nurses, the cases of septic inflammation might have been reduced or avoided.

I leave the two pictures – the Cardiff one and the London one – to speak for themselves. I can add nothing to the force of Dr. Stewart's figures, which enable us to measure the proposals of the Imperial Vaccination League accurately in their financial aspect.

What the league aims at is the revaccination of the entire population every ten years at a cost of £70,000,000 per decade.

The lectures of the late Dr. Cory, whose hereto devotion to Vaccinism is well known, will give Dr. Garrett Horder the clinical information he desires as to general vaccinia. The book contains a coloured picture of the disease which should not be left in the way of mothers bringing children to be vaccinated.

Yours truly,
G. BERNARD SHAW.

The controversy over smallpox control had been running for over two years by now and would soon die away, the threat of a widespread epidemic having been avoided. Shaw's contribution was significant, partly because he kept sundry burning issues alive by his insistence on responsible administration and treatment on the part of the health authorities and partly because the controversy allowed him regular access to the pages of *The Times*, access which may have been denied him had the issue been other than public health.

He had also kept his name in the public eye – an important consideration in view of his continued failure to make significant headway as a playwright. There had been occasional minor productions of his plays, notably by the Stage Society, whose *Mrs Warren's Profession* in 1902 was, in Shaw's opinion, a landmark in his career. In Germany his newly appointed translator Siegfried Trebitsch (1869–1956) would soon be promoting Shaw's drama, while in New York Arnold Daly, following the American actor-manager Richard Mansfield's success with *The Devil's Disciple* in 1897, would within a year or two create a triumph with *Candida* and *You Never Can Tell*. At the beginning of 1903, however, Shaw's career seemed in a cul de sac and in fact it was a quiet year for him in *The Times* as much as in other papers.

~ *1903, January 15* ~

IMPERIAL VACCINATION LEAGUE.

Sir, – I am sorry to be troublesome, but has not Dr. Bond overlooked the report made by Dr. W.J. Stewart on June 13 last to the Hospitals Committee of the Metropolitan Asylums Board, and officially numbered 150 of August, 1902? Dr. Stewart vaccinated the workmen at the Gore Farm Lower Hospital, exactly as the Imperial Vaccination League wants to vaccinate all of us (twice) that is to say, with modern lymph according to the latest standard of efficiency, unless, indeed, this standard has changed in seven months. The results, as reported by Dr. Stewart, were as follows:

Five hundred and eighty seven men attended the vaccination station between March and June, in consideration of a bonus of 5s. per man, without which they refused – reasonably enough, as the event proved – to submit to revaccination. Out of the 587 28.1 per cent., or 166 men, went on the sick list. Of these 125 35 were cases of fever and general illness involving the loss of 5.5 days per man average; 125 had septic inflammation at or near the incisions, losing 6.8 days per man average. Three were cases of abscess, involving 34.6 days disablement per patient. The other three were 'general pustular eczema', causing 23 days' disablement per patient. The vaccination was not performed with special severity. 'Each man', says Dr. Stewart, 'was vaccinated in two places, except in the case of men who had not been previously vaccinated, in which case the number was three.'

I shall make no statement on the contrast between this record of the results of an experimental test and the column and three quarters of promises which Dr. Bond and Dr. Smith have sent you, promises which have now so often been broken that there is little danger of their making much impression. But although I greatly dislike hitting the vaccinists when they have knocked one another down, it is too much to expect the public to allow them to leave so startling an experimental contradiction of their optimism unanswered, and; after waiting four months for the sensation it made to blow over, to calmly return to the old familiar patent medicine advertisements (for really that is what this 'pure and efficient lymph' nonsense has now come to) as if Dr. Stewart's report had never existed.

There is no such thing as 'pure and efficient lymph'. Efficient lymph is lymph which produces modified smallpox; and as nobody knows as yet what smallpox is, the implication that the Local Government Board can supply an article guaranteed to contain nothing but attenuated variolous germs in glycerine has no foundation except in very unscientific imaginations inflamed by vaccinist propaganda.

It is to be noted that the Imperial Vaccination League, having just enjoyed an exceptional opportunity of trying revaccination on the citizens of London, are openly begging the Government not to make the borough councils or the County Council the vaccination authority, but to place the administration of the Acts in the hands of the indirectly elected Metropolitan Asylums Board, a notoriously vaccinist body over which the public has virtually no control. The significance of this is obvious. The league knows perfectly well that what it has to fear at the polls is not the arguments of the anti-vaccinators, but the fury of those who have been disabled by revaccination like Dr. Stewart's workmen at Gore Farm Lower Hospital.

Yours truly,
G. BERNARD SHAW.

A Standing Committee on Trade had been set up by Parliament to consider, *inter alia,* legislation restricting the employment of children on the professional stage. Shaw did not once throughout his long career cast juveniles in his plays.

The popular actress Ellaline Terriss had written to *The Times* on 18 May 1903 defending the practice. She was, incidentally, the daughter of William Terriss, the well-known exponent of melodrama, who had once paid Shaw the compliment of falling asleep while Shaw was reading *The Devil's Disciple* to him.

Terriss was murdered by a lunatic at his stage door not long afterwards. Henry Irving, the most prominent actor of his day, was noted for his productions of Shakespeare and melodrama, which Shaw frequently criticized in his essays for the *Saturday Review*. Irving had been knighted in 1895. Lena Ashwell became a great friend of the Shaws. Shaw described Ashwell to Ellen Terry as 'a fascinating squawker'. (letter of 8 December 1896, in Laurence, ed., *Collected Letters*, 1874–1897, p. 712) She created the role of Lina Szczepan-owska in *Misalliance* (1910).

Arthur Collins, Herbert Campbell and Dan Leno were popular personalities of the London stage.

$\sim$ *1903, May 25* $\sim$

THE EMPLOYMENT OF CHILDREN ON THE STAGE

Sir, – May I venture to express a hope that when the proposals of the Standing Committee on Trade become law the new authorities will use their licensing powers in such a way as to put an end to the sordid exploitation of children on the stage which has disgraced the theatre for so many years? I do not propose to occupy your space with any criticism of the pretensions of the theatre as a perfect school of character and manners for children. I have no doubt the little girls who are fortunate enough to be in the same theatre with Miss Ellaline Terriss, and who intend to be exactly like her when they grow up, are the better for it, and are a source of innocent comfort and pleasure to her. They are also a source of considerable saving to managers who, if the magistrates did their duty, would have to employ adult dancers and figurants to fill up the stage with moving masses of glittering costumes. As to the parents who are not ashamed to live on the labour of children under 13, their indignation when it is proposed that they shall actually support their children instead of their children supporting them may be imagined. These people feel no shame when little children are described as 'breadwinners'; they would willingly belong to a nation of such breadwinners; and the view that such a nation would deserve nothing better than extermination, and would probably get what it deserved in the international struggle for existence, would seem to them fantastic and indeed unintelligible.

But my present purpose is to protest against this infamy being thrown on the shoulders of the public. No doubt the public is thoughtless enough at best; and the playgoing section of it becomes almost mindless from the total disuse of its brains in the theatre. But the public never asked for children on the stage. When Mr. Rosslyn Bruce, in his otherwise excellent letter in your columns, despairingly concludes that 'the British public must have its children's chorus', he is allowing Miss Ellaline Terriss to hypnotize him, just as Miss Ellaline Terriss, with equally innocent intentions, is allowing her feelings to be worked on by what is at bottom pure commercial bluff. I assert as a matter of common knowledge that the presence of children on the stage is as unwelcome to the thoughtless playgoer, whom they bore, as to the thoughtful and public-spirited playgoer whose conscience they disturb. I assert that the child 'professional' is not only a social horror and a national scandal, but an artistic nuisance. I assert that if any theatrical employer of child labour were precise enough in his protests to pretend that if he substituted adults for children in his choruses and dances the attendance at his theatre would fall off he would be laughed at; everybody would know that he was simply pleading against an increase in his salary list. No manager puts children into the parts on which the drawing power of the piece depends. As much nursery sentiment has been worked up for the little princes in the tower as for the babes in the wood; but when Sir Henry Irving revives Richard III he takes care to engage Miss Lena Ashwell for his little prince instead of coaching a child in the part. Mr. Arthur Collins would not engage children even for the babes in the wood; he knows that the public would prefer Mr. Dan Leno and Mr. Herbert Campbell. The last time I witnessed that most revolting of social outrages, the exhibition of a baby in arms on the stage late at night as a joke in a farcical comedy, I am glad to say that the solemn, wondering, shrinking, reproachful stare of the baby at all that vulgarity and folly put the audience so completely out of countenance that it killed the comedy; and if it had killed the magistrate who licensed the transaction as well I cannot pretend that I should have mourned him long or deeply. No doubt he, too, was moved by sympathy for the parents who were depending for a few extra glasses of beer on the sweet little breadwinner, and was convinced that the child's mind would be elevated later on by a precocious initiation into the gossip of the stage, and its taste moulded classically by those masterpieces of English poetry which it would be taught to sing in pantomime choruses.

But it is useless for me to pursue the subject. There are extremities of humbug and depths of baseness with which decent citizens do not stop to argue, and of which statesmen who are worthy of their position make short work. Everything that is now being said for the theatres was formerly said for the Manchester cotton factories when they, too, professed to be teaching and training little children though even they stopped short of children in arms. And when the country would stand no more of it the parents raised the same cry against being deprived of their breadwinners. Though we did stop that, yet it is but a few years since we were shamed in the face of Europe by the fact that we were behind all the neighbouring nations in fixing the age up to which children are protected from exploitation for commercial profit by employers and parents. Why that most grossly commercial of all our institutions, the theatre, should be exempted from the regulations to which our factories and workshops are subject does not appear. I hope the Bill will be amended by an iron rule against the employment of children under 14 in theatres. The managers have been warned over and over again that, if they persisted in abusing their powers of applying for magistrates' licences as they have done, total unconditional prohibition would be the result. They have disregarded the warning; now let them take the consequences.

Yours faithfully,
G. BERNARD SHAW.

The Mayor of the Borough of St Marylebone had called a public meeting to discuss whether the Council should follow the example of St Pancras and invest in publicly funded electric lighting. Several prominent speakers had spoken against the idea and the meeting voted against it. Miss Octavia Hill had written to *The Times* in support of that decision.

Shaw had retired from the St Pancras Borough Council at the end of 1903. In his six years in office, first as a vestryman, then as a councillor, he had served twice on the Subcommittee on Health, once on the Officers' Subcommittee and once on the Subcommittee for Electricity and Public Lighting. He would have known what he was talking about and, as a dedicated Fabian, was committed to the municipalisation of such services as electric lighting, as against conferring it on private, that is capitalistic, enterprise. It goes without saying, although Shaw scarcely hints at this, that vested and financial interests were involved.

ELECTRIC LIGHTING IN MARYLEBONE.

TO THE EDITOR OF *The Times*.

Sir, – May I suggest another view of the matter to Miss Octavia Hill? It is precisely the 'quiet, unadventurous policy, less likely to burden future years,' that has done all the mischief. The neighbouring borough of St. Pancras was active and adventurous enough to undertake its own electric lighting whilst Marylebone was still asleep, borrowing for that purpose a capital – or, as Lord Rosebery would probably put it, incurring a municipal debt – of considerably more than £300,000. The ratepayers of St. Pancras are now supplied with electric light and power as cheaply as the customers of any private company, and their payments for current cover, not only interest, but sinking funds, so that the whole concern will soon be their property without any burden of debt whatever. The enterprise has never added a farthing to the rates, and occasionally makes substantial contributions to them; and though it aims at supplying current as nearly as possible at cost price, it makes profits in spite of itself. The credit of St. Pancras is so good that it finds that it can borrow money in the ordinary money market on lower terms than from the County Council.

All that might have been achieved by Marylebone but for the very arguments that Miss Octavia Hill is now impressed by. Marylebone shirked its business, and now has to pay a million and a quarter for what has cost St. Pancras nothing but a little foresight and business aptitude on the part of its ratepayers and vestrymen. If it takes the lesson to heart it will not make such a bad bargain after all.

As to management, the borough councils conduct their businesses much as joint stock companies do. The ratepayers are the shareholders; the council represents the small number of shareholders who ever attend general meetings; the electric lighting committee is the board of directors; and its chief clerk and engineer, in command of an expert business and technical staff, are the municipal secretary and manager. But they are all, of course, much more highly selected and jealously criticized than if they were private men in private bodies. Marylebone, it is true, is suffering not for being 'quiet and unadventurous;' but that is at least better than the sort of thing some of our private companies are at present suffering for rather conspicuously.

Miss Octavia Hill's prescription really comes to this – that Marylebone should take a hair of the dog that bit it. As an ex-member of the St. Pancras Electric Lighting Committee I venture to suggest that it would be safer to profit by the experience of a neighbour and take care not to be caught napping by the companies next time.

Yours truly
G. Bernard Shaw.
10, Adelphi Terrace

This was Shaw's last letter to *The Times* on the question of smallpox control in the Edwardian years. The issue had fizzled out by now but Shaw was determined to pursue it when other correspondents remained unconverted to his views, as long as he had the last word. And his last word here was to re-emphasize his rubric that 'both on economic and hygienic grounds' modern sanitary regulations would 'mitigate and confine smallpox epidemics, and all other epidemics as well'.

$\sim$ *1904, January 22* $\sim$

SMALLPOX.

Sir, – Your correspondents are missing the real point. Let it be granted that by taking out our smallpox in periodic inoculations instead of in epidemics we can save the whole cost of smallpox hospitals. The question still remains, which plan is the cheaper? The cost of inoculation, both in lymph and in fees to the operator, is heavy and constant; its cost in indisposition and disablement is heavier still, not to mention the chances of serious disease. The tendency of modern inoculation practice is too insist on greater severity in the operation, and consequently in its immediate and inevitable consequences. The tendency of modern sanitary regulation is to mitigate and confine smallpox epidemics, and all other epidemics as well. It is therefore quite possible, without the smallest scepticism as to the possibility of preventing smallpox epidemics by inoculation, to prefer the disease to that particular remedy, both on economic and hygienic grounds.

Yours truly,
G. Bernard Shaw.
10, Adelphi Terrace. W.C.

Shaw stood for election to the London County Council in 1904 as a Progressive in South St Pancras. The most contentious issue was the Tory-backed London Education Bill, engineered by Fabians Sidney and Beatrice Webb, which proposed to extend state control, thus financial control, over Church schools. It was a complicated matter made more so by progressive Shaw's support of a Tory bill and his highly individualistic style of campaigning. His nominal supporters, the predominantly non-conformist voters of the constituency, were suspicious and withdrew their vote. He and his associate, Sir William Geary, lost. This did not silence Shaw and his letter to *The Times* was one among several with which he peppered the press with explanations of his defeat. The Churches had not, in his opinion, been as honest and above board as they had pledged themselves to be; the actions of some clerics were, as he said, 'not cricket'.

~ *1904, March 11* ~

The Failure of the Church's Electioneering for the L.C.C.

Sir, – The Church of England will never be a successful electioneering body until it can answer for the political action of its own officials. In the late election the Bishop of Stepney asked me and my colleague, Sir William Geary, for a certain pledge in return for the neutrality of the Church. We gave it. The Bishop very faithfully remained neutral. But the vicar of St. John's, who represents the Church in one of the wards of the division we contested, signed an appeal to the electors to vote against us, which they accordingly did. In other constituencies the pledge was refused, and the Bishop denounced the Progressive candidates; but the Radical and Christian Socialist clergymen worked for them none the less. I do not complain of this. It is, no doubt, quite Protestant and independent, and proper; but, regarded as electioneering, it is not cricket. If the Bishop of Stepney were able to say to every candidate, 'Unless you give me such and such a pledge, every clergyman in London will work against you,' he would be a formidable political power in the county. At present all he can say is, 'I should like to receive such and such a pledge from every candidate; but whether it be given or not the action of the clergy will not be affected; the Conservative parsons will back the Moderate candidates, and the Radical and Christian Socialist parsons the Progressive, without the smallest regard to any recommendation I may make.' Is it surprising that the Progressives paid no serious attention to the Bishop? It was the prospect of the Government grants that induced the Progressives to pledge themselves to administer the Act, not any hope that the clergy would subordinate their private political opinions to their Church during the election. And what a pledge it was–! Virtually the Progressives said, 'We pledge ourselves to administer this Act because we believe it to be an infamous one.' I was in the unfortunate position of having to say, 'I pledge myself to administer the Act because I believe it to be one of the best ever placed on the Statute-book.' Whereupon the *Westminster Gazette* accuses me of having thrown away the seat for the sake of a paradox, and the *Daily News* politely accuses me of 'tomfoolery.' But the fact remains that, with the exception of Mr. Sidney Webb, whose seat was not contested, I and Sir William Geary were the only candidates whose pledge was convincing, with the result that the Church combined with the Catholics to defeat us, and succeeded triumphantly, to the undisguised delight of the opponents of the Act.

In short, the Bishop most effectually deprived us of the support of the Free Churchmen without screening us from political excommunication by the vicar of one of the most important parishes in the constituency.

Naturally the impression made on me is that the Free Church minister, though utterly wrong about the Act, is a man to be reckoned with because he is loyal to his denomination, even to letting his political champion be defeated for its sake, whereas the clergyman of the Establishment is as likely as not to be simply a private gentleman in a peculiar waistcoat and collar, who has no more sense of solidarity with his Church than a stockbroker. Under such circumstances, and notwithstanding my sense of the scrupulousness with which the vicar of St. Pancras and the vicar of St. Jude's made good their Bishop's guarantee by a neutrality so generously emphasised that it probably won some votes for me, I must say that I regard my case as a conspicuous example of the fact that the Church comes upon the electoral exchange with empty hands, the power to bind and loose being a private matter with the local parson. Again I say I do not complain of this fact; I simply point it out, leaving the Free Churchmen to congratulate themselves on it, and the Establishment to draw what moral it thinks best.

Yours truly,
G.- BERNARD SHAW.
10, Adelphi Terrace, W.C.

In the following letter, the former music critic is allowed to express his views. *The Times* had been through lean years, – its circulation dropping to an alarmingly low level, and Shaw had been proving himself good copy. An article by the music critic of *The Times* criticised the omission of the finale in Mozart's opera *Don Giovanni*. That Shaw thought it one of the greatest works ever composed would have added to the satirical thrust of his comments regarding 'revised versions' of masterpieces of art. Throughout his career he refused to countenance excisions or 'revisions' of his plays other than those he personally approved.

On 25 May 1904, Mr H.V. Higgins wrote to *The Times* to answer a music critic who had praised the performance of *Don Giovanni* but commented that the audience expected to hear the performance without cuts. Mr Higgins, Musical Director of the Royal Opera House, Covent Garden, defended his presentation on the grounds that it was universally omitted and therefore represented a revised version.

Further letters over whether certain cuts were justified caused Mr Higgins to write again and at this point Shaw, who was in Rome at the time- (but obviously kept up with *The Times*) joined in the debate. The unnamed critic apologised to Mr Higgins at the end of his next article but agreed with Shaw that cuts that are not sanctioned fall short of perfection.

Dr Hans Richter (1843–1916) was the renowned conductor who first conducted Richard Wagner's Ring cycle of operas at Bayreuth.

∽ 1904, May 31 ∽

ROYAL OPERA.

Sir, – I am loth to say a word that could hamper Mr. Higgins in his plucky, but hopeless, duel with your critic. When a gentleman explains that in announcing *Don Giovanni* without cuts he meant *Don Giovanni* with cuts, he makes his position clear; and there is nothing more to be said except to apologize for having misunderstood him.

But I have a protest to record against the implied doctrine that when a composer or dramatist is driven by circumstances to allow his work to be performed with cuts, or even to make the cuts himself sooner than trust the scissors to somebody else, he thereby publishes the mutilated score or prompt book as a revised 'version' of his work. When the Deutsches Theater of Berlin accepted for production my play entitled *Caesar and Cleopatra*, I myself proposed the total omission of the third act in order to bring the performance within the customary limits of time. But I shall be greatly surprised if the Deutsches Theater announces the performance as 'without cuts,' and unspeakably staggered if Dr. Richter describes, or allows it to be said that he describes, the performance without the third act as 'the correct version'. A cut score or book is not a 'version' at all; for instance, there are two versions of Beethoven's *Leonore* overture, No. 2 and No. 3 (No. 1 is virtually an independent work); but the old mutilation of No.3, made at a time when it was considered too long for performance, is not a third version.

Take again Meyerbeer's *Les Huguenots*, always outrageously mutilated, and now performed at Covent Garden without the last act. Meyerbeer was forced to let the earlier mutilations pass because of the Procrustean tyranny of the fashionable dinner hour. But I venture to say that if he were alive now, and compelled to cut the same number of bars, he would cut the work in a very different way, sacrificing such dragged in irrelevancies as the chorus of bathers in the third act for the sake of restoring the dramatic coherency of the third. What is performed of any opera at the opera house is only that part of it which survives from the composer's struggle with the public, always ten years behind the composer, and the impresario, always twenty years behind the public. To call the result 'the correct version' is – well, it is what Mr. Higgins accuses Dr. Richter of.

No doubt the finale to *Don Giovanni* is 'an anti-climax'. To the many people who do not wait even for the statue scene, that is an anti–climax too. And the third part of the *Messiah* is an anti-climax after the Hallelujah chorus. And Bach's *St. Matthew Passion* should end with the thunder and lightning chorus. For all who sit out the mutilated last scene of *Don Giovanni* simply because they want to see the ghost, not only should the finale be cut, but the preliminary pages also; in fact, a surprisingly compact selection from the opera would satisfy them better than what they get at present. But for those to whom an impresario pretends to appeal when he announces *Don Giovanni* without cuts, and takes it out of the hands of the third- rate conductors by whom this great work has been outraged and insulted for so many years past at Covent Garden, the finale is not only indispensable to its integrity, but contains, in its last ecstatic fugato, one of the most delightful and intensely characteristic of all Mozart's personal outbursts. We never expected its restoration from Mr. Higgins; why should we? But we did expect it from Dr. Richter; and I hope that, if his authority is again brought into question in this correspondence, it may not be offered at second-hand.

Yours truly,
G. BERNARD SHAW.
Rome.

June 1904 was pivotal in Shaw's career, although he may not have realized it at the time. In April, Shaw's friend and Fabian associate, actor and director Harley Granville Barker, had successfully produced Shaw's *Candida* in a series of matinées at the Royal Court Theatre on Sloane Square, London. Encouraged, Barker began to promote the idea of matinee performances at the 'Court' of *avant garde* plays which would not normally be staged in the commercial theatre. Shaw, initially sceptical, grew to support the idea. With some twelve largely unperformed plays to his credit, he may well have seen opportunity beckoning. He began work on a new play, *John Bull's Other Island,* with which the newly formed management of Barker and John E. Vedrenne (the other business manager) hoped to initiate the enterprise. As this was not possible, the legendary Vedrenne–Barker seasons at the Court opened on 18 October 1904 with six matinée performances of Gilbert Murray's translation of *The Hippolytus of Euripides.* Shaw meanwhile, on holiday in Scotland, worked feverishly to complete, – revise, and then, back in London, direct *John Bull* as the second play on the bill. It opened at the Court on 1 November 1904. The critics were stuffily critical but the public was delighted and it rapidly became one of the standbys of the Court repertoire.

It was in the context of the demands this made on him (including the writing of the one act play *How He Lied to Her Husband*, written in four days for the American actor Arnold Daly), that Shaw involved himself in the controversy surrounding the question of flogging in the Royal Navy. It is no exaggeration to see him as possibly instigating the controversy.

The issue, entitled 'Corporal Punishment in the Navy' in the following letter and, in ensuing letters, headed more baldly as 'Flogging in the Navy,' was not new to Shaw. He had published five letters on the subject in the *Saturday Review* from August to November 1897. His stance then, as now in 1904, was the basic Shavian one: strenuous opposition to – unyielding disgust at – a vicious custom and the mindset that approved of flogging as a necessary discipline. It was a disgrace to the nation; as he puts it: '. . . there are certain practices which, however expedient they may be, are instinctively banned by the humanity of the highest races; and corporal punishment is one of them'.

He was prompted to enter the debate (and promote controversy) by remarks a correspondent who signed himself 'In Partibus Maris' ('partly of the Sea') made in a letter to *The Times* that quoted full details of the King's regulations applicable to men serving in the navy.

∽ 1904, June 14 ∽

Corporal Punishment in the Navy.

Sir – The letter of your correspondent, *'In Partibus Maris'*, inspires a hope that the Government will lose no time in abolishing corporal punishment in the Navy unconditionally and at once, before there is any chance of our finding our seamen under the strain which the Japanese and Russian fleets are now enduring.

According to *'In Partibus Maris'*, whose letter bears the stamp of that combination of direct practical knowledge and straightforward statement with unsuspicious simplicity which survives only in remote villages and in partibus maris, the effect of corporal punishment in the Navy is to retain in the service a percentage of ill-conditioned youths, lazy, dirty, foul-mouthed, incapable of subordination, deaf to exhortation, callous to rebuke, and consequently useless to the ship until the incentive of earning their wages, serving their country, and taking their share with their comrades is replaced by the terror of being cut across the back with the corporal's cane. The birch has an even more important function, Without it, it seems, we should have to expel from our ships all the liars, the thieves, and the offenders against decency and common morality. Thanks to its application, we have now in our Navy, as your correspondent vouches from his personal knowledge, a member who was habitually filthy, one whose leisure was given to telling foul stories to his mates, and one who had been grossly cruel to a monkey who was the pet of the ship. And to keep these heroic tars in countenance we use the same instrument to secure for them the congenial society of the unfortunate wretches who, being too weak morally to refrain from mean and low offences, are too weak physically to refrain from 'howling like curs' when they are birched for them. Finally, we have the cat, which some of us supposed to have been abolished, but which we now find to be still a cherished institution of the British Navy. Its use is to enable us to retain the services of persons addicted to mutiny, to brutal assault on their officers; and to unnatural crime. It is for the sake of these persons that the respectable and manly men and boys in the Navy are paraded to contemplate their bare breeches (I quote the regulations) whilst the ship's police administer not more than 24 cuts with a birch. And the medical officer, a humanitarian by profession, and presumably a gentleman of culture and delicate habits, is compelled to superintend this indecency.

Your correspondent's conclusion is altogether what might be expected. 'If a vote,' says *'In Partibus Maris'*, 'were taken for and against the retention of the cat as a possible punishment for crimes against country and humanity, the British sailor would uphold the custom of the service and the regulations of his King.' I do not quite see why the King should be dragged into this unsavoury business. If the matter were in his hands its settlement might possibly take *'In Partibus Maris'* aback quite as much as the vote of the seamen most assuredly would. But suppose it be true that the spectacle of a flogging is popular in the Navy! Could a better reason be given for abolishing it? One of the most popular entertainments in London in former times was the public fustigation of the street-walker by the beadle. The defence of the practice was precisely the defence now offered by *'In Partibus Maris'* of its remnant in the Navy. It was abolished not because it was unpopular, and not because it hurt the women (imprisonment is much crueller), but because it was degrading to the spectators and dishonourable to the nation. If our seamen really enjoy flogging and caning parades, and would vote for their continuance, the sooner we discharge them all and replace them by really manly men without any percentage of ill-conditioned, lazy, foul-mouthed, insubordinate liars, thieves, &c., the safer I, for one, shall feel, if we are ever unhappily engaged in a business that makes so tremendous a demand on the character of the combatants as a modern naval war.

In the police force, in signal cabins, and in cordite factories, where the least breech of discipline may entail consequences no less disastrous than on a battleship, discipline is maintained by making the employment worth the while of men of good character, and promptly discharging them if they do not do their duty. I do not believe for a moment that the British Fleet is manned by a horde of intimidated blackguards who cannot be trusted with the liberties of a tramp in a casual ward; but I am, of course, aware that in ships, as on shore, a man's character, like his constitution, may break down and leave him practically a criminal. This might occur on a battleship clearing for action as easily as in a liner overtaken by a typhoon. The same remedy is available for both cases; put the man in irons until it becomes possible to put him ashore at the nearest port. The only difficulty peculiar to the Navy is the case of the man who refuses his duty, or the boy who strikes his officer, because he hates the service and wants to be discharged. It is held that, if the man or boy were free to go when he liked on reasonable notice, as in civil employment, and the commander equally free to sack a man who was not worth his salt, the officers would lose all their authority, and the men would instantly give a month's notice and leave England at the mercy of her enemies. The most charitable explanation of this delirious absurdity is that the isolation which discipline imposes on the higher grades of naval officers produces some of the familiar effects of solitary confinement on land, and makes them morbidly apprehensive of results which the common experience of civil life shows to be wildly impossible.

In conclusion, may I say that I am sincerely sorry that '*In Partibus Maris*' thinks me 'a well intentioned but mischievous person.' At the same time, I am resolved that he shall never have an opportunity of reforming me by the hands of the ship's police. Not that I have any overwhelming dread of being flogged; I have survived worse physical sufferings than that. But nothing would induce me to enter a service in which I could be either compelled to flog another man or paraded to see it done by any one else. I am not prepared to argue about it; it is an elementary point of honour with me, just as it is an elementary point of honour with me not to pick '*In Partibus Maris's*' pocket, though I could give a column and a half of excellent reasons for believing that I could spend his money much more beneficially to the nation than he could himself. In short, there are certain practices which, however expedient they may be, are instinctively barred by the humanity of the highest races; and corporal punishment is one of them. I should blush to offer a lady or gentleman more reasons for my disgust at it.

Yours truly,
G. BERNARD SHAW.

Some weeks later, on holiday in Scotland and working full tilt at *John Bull's Other Island*, Shaw took up the cudgels again, this time on behalf of a 'boy of the first class' who had been found guilty of stealing a couple of postal orders and been dismissed from the navy 'as an objectionable character'. The boy also appears to have been flogged, being administered the 'most severe flogging the regulations permit namely, 24 strokes of the birch'.

This incident, which came to be known as the Archer-Shee case, was the source of Terence Rattigan's play The Winslow Boy. The famous barrister Edward Carson, KC, took the case on Archer's behalf in 1910, accepting a nominal fee, and won. Arthur was rehabilitated. – Rattigan, researching his play and paging through back copies of *The Times*, most likely read Shaw's letter, given his prominent role – in the controversy.

~ 1904, September 2 ~

FLOGGING IN THE NAVY.

Sir, – In a recent correspondence in your columns on this extremely disagreeable subject, I pointed out that the effect of flogging in the Navy, on the showing of its advocates, was to retain in the service lads of weak or vicious character, who had much better be put out of it.

Accordingly, it appears from a recent report that a boy of the first class in the cruiser Berwick, having stolen a letter containing two postal orders from the ship's post-box, has been dismissed from the service 'as an objectionable character'. Nobody with any sense and knowledge of the world will fail to appreciate the severity of this proper and inevitable result of the boy's dishonesty. It bars all public employment to him, and all responsible private employment. It condemns him to the grade of labour in which character is not important enough to be worth inquiring into, or in which the absence of it is taken as a matter of course. It hits him harder than a sentence of imprisonment for petty pilfering hits an office boy; for many people would give the office boy 'another chance' who would be merciless to a person dismissed from the Royal Navy for stealing a comrade's money.

Now here one can conceive a sentimentalist, moved by the boy's hard case, pleading that he should be let off with a flogging sound enough to keep his hands from picking and stealing for the rest of his life. Such a plea would show little regard for the honour of the service and the dignity of English manners and customs, and still less enlightenment on the general question of crime and its treatment; but it would at least show a sort of rough and ready consideration for the boy.

Will it be believed by any person, not a member of the Royal Navy or an inmate of a lunatic asylum, that the actual sentence passed by the Court martial was dismissal from the service as aforesaid and the most severe flogging that the regulations permit: namely, 24 strokes of the birch, the ship's company being compulsorily paraded to witness the flaying of the unfortunate wretch's 'bare breech' (see regulations,) and the ship's police, or the ship's corporal, or whoever the official executioner may be, being compelled to flay it.

Let us, as our custom is in England, leave out of the question the possibility of this being a case of flogging for the mere lust of flogging, not forgetting, however, that we do not leave that view out in our own judgement of Russian and Oriental floggings, and that those of us who travel enough to value Continental public opinion are painfully aware of the popular European belief that all Englishmen are addicted to physical cruelty and to the coarse vices which are usually associated with it: a belief for which our public schools are even more largely responsible than our naval Courts martial.

What reason, then, can there be for this apparently senseless heaping of physical torture on social ruin for a theft of 40s. by a lad? The old plea for reformation of the offender, of a sharp punishment that will be a lesson to him not to do it again, is here frankly given up; for if the flogging is to reform the boy, why dismiss him from the service, and, if not, why flog him? Is it not clear that the object of the flogging is to intimidate the other boys, and that this constitutes an admission that the brutalities which they are called on to witness week after week, the stupid, ill-tempered canings on the most trivial provocation – canings for such offences as smoking and backwardness in learning to swim (why not flog the instructors, by the way?) – have so destroyed their self-respect and esprit de corps that they have come to regard dismissal from the service as a stroke of good luck instead of a punishment, and have no conception of loss of character as a disadvantage at all? And the only remedy proposed is more flogging. The real remedy is more brains. When the quarter-deck is adequately supplied with this commodity the cane and the birch, which are essentially a fool's implements, are not tolerated.

But really, when we have the Government itself justifying the caning of backward swimmers on the ground that it is better that boys should be caned than drowned – which is a false issue, would not be true if it were the right issue, and would be just as good a reason for caning every yachtsman in the House of Commons as for caning lads in the Navy – it seems a heartbreaking waste of time to struggle against the flagellant epidemic.

The intellectual contrast between Mr. Balfour at the British Association and some of his colleagues on the front bench is so stupefying that I have hardly sufficient courage or hope left to ask you to insert this protest. It seems as though the determination with which the Humanitarian League is forcing these naval floggings on the notice of the public will end, not in the abolition of corporal punishment in the Navy, but in the refusal of every decent and high spirited lad to enter the service, and consequently an actual increase of mere brute coercion as a means of driving refuse-recruits through their duties. Which, I submit, is not the way to rule the waves.

Yours truly,
G. BERNARD SHAW.
Rosemarkie, N.B.

Shaw's outspoken comments on the topic aroused a good deal of anger. A certain Vice Admiral C.C. Penrose-Fitzgerald (1888–1940) was goaded into firing a veritable broadside of words at Shaw and his like, '. . . the pseudo-philanthropists and effeminate doctrinaires who compose all the ranting brotherhoods and shrieking sisterhoods which are responsible for humanitarian leagues, anti-vivisection leagues, and numerous other anti-commonsense leagues, supported by feeble minded . . ..' This was typical if rather extreme. Shaw's meek and mild (and sarcastic) response showed that he could argue the case from the Bible a good deal more knowledgeably and effectively than his 'amphibious' adversary.

~ 1904, September 14 ~

FLOGGING IN THE NAVY.

Sir, – Will you allow me to thank Admiral Penrose FitzGerald in your columns for his invaluable letter on this question? It is conclusive both as to the temper in which corporal punishment is administered in the Navy and the fitness of our naval commanders for powers which civilians in situations of equal and sometimes much greater difficulty have discarded as unnecessary and barbarous. It will no doubt be vigorously circulated by the Humanitarian League, with what effect on our naval recruiting may be imagined.

On the admiral's kind recommendation, I have gone carefully through the history of Solomon and his presumably well birched son. I find that Solomon himself was the son of David, a successful warrior and ruler, who spoiled his children, as the case of Absalom shows. Solomon introduced the flogging system, which grew more severe in the family until scorpions were substituted for whips. And, as might have been expected, Solomon's children lost the kingdom his father had built up, and scattered the nation he had welded together. To this day the remnant of that nation, reverting to the sentimental practice of David, spoils its children, with the result that in dealing with them our grown-up public school boys are as clay in the hands of the potter.

As to Solomon himself, unrestrained authority, and the practice of flogging other people, had such an effect on him that, on reaching the age of an admiral, he turned to the worship of Ashtaroth, and never could be reclaimed. A more impressive warning against governing empires on Solomonic principles, and governing navies on the principles of Captain Kidd's boatswain, is not to be found in the Scriptures.

I quite appreciate the implication that the reverend head of a public school either could, or, if he could, dare, administer such birchings and canings as are given on board ship by able bodied seamen to boys who have neither social influence nor legal remedy to protect them. Perhaps the admiral will be good enough to pass it on to that amphibious branch of His Majesty's forces at sea which is reputed to be specially susceptible to presentations of this character. Finally, may I point to a recent article in the Boston Transcript, arising out of this correspondence, and showing how our retention of flogging in the Navy, and especially of that degrading and obscene form of flogging officially called birching, convincing other nations that our Navy is recruited from the lowest and most worthless classes among us?

Yours truly,
G. BERNARD SHAW.
Edinburgh.

Shaw, now in North Berwick and still on working on *John Bull's Other Island*, wrote this, his fourth letter on the subject, in more serious vein, although he was not above depicting his opponents as stage stereotypes and sarcastically echoing Vice-Admiral Penrose-Fitzgerald's character-isation of him and other humanitarians as 'feeble minded cranks.' As he says, 'I submit to your correspondents, without the smallest respect, that all this is claptrap', and then proceeds to demolish their arguments in a series of incisively telling paragraphs. The controversy as reflected in *The Times* languished after this.

~ *1904, October 11* ~

FLOGGING IN THE NAVY.

Sir, – This correspondence has been so fertile in quick changes that even my professionally trained dramatic powers make it difficult for me to follow it. We have had all the familiar stage conventions of the Navy, the breezy, choleric, landlubber- despising, rope's-ending old salt; the pious, simple seaman with his Bible open in his hand at the Proverbs of Solomon and his thick-rimmed spectacles on the binnacle; and the rough seadog who bites on a bullet and takes his two dozen as a civilian takes a cold bath, scorning alike the 'morbidly hysterical and sensitive' lads who do not revel in a flogging and the feeble-minded civilian cranks who have always supposed that the whole point of flogging lay in the floggee's objection to it. And now we have the Cornish fisherman whose lads would scorn an unflogged Navy, and who regard the difference between a village loafer and a smart seaman as due solely to the difference in poignancy between the parental strap or boot toe and the ship's corporal's cane.

I submit to your correspondents, without the smallest respect, that all this is claptrap, good enough, perhaps, for a nautical melodrama in an inland booth, but out of place in a serious discussion in the columns of *The Times*. Let me try to formulate a few propositions which are, at least, worth arguing.

The radical objection to flogging is not its cruelty, but the fact that it can never be cleared from the suspicion that it is a vicious sport disguised as reformatory justice. Imprisonment is much crueller, so atrociously cruel, in fact, that it is endlessly amazing to any humane person that it should not only be tolerated, but dealt out wholesale in periods of years at a time without shocking any one. But, cruel as it is, it is at least free from the taint of corrupt passion. It does not gratify even the vilest of us to look at Pentonville Prison. When the police raid a disorderly house they never find there the convict cell and the tin of skilly. They always find the implements of the ship's corporal.

In ordinary civil life it is possible to be too particular on this point. But on board ship, and in prison, the moral conditions are morbid, especially in modern navies, which are physically unhealthy, our battleships being incipient consumption hospitals. When a Cornish lad is cuffed by his mother, or when he provokes his father to give him a trouncing which no ship's corporal could improve on, there may be no great harm done; and there is certainly no question of the transaction being a disguised debauch. But any one who will argue from this that it is wise or decent to take a ship's crew, consisting of adolescent lads and men who are cooped up for long periods together without the society of women, and parade them to witness the operation which has already been sufficiently described in your columns, must be a person either utterly ignorant of the real difficulties of the situation, or else so coarsened and hardened by the results of disregarding them as to care very little what a sailor is, provided he has been thrashed into technical efficiency and prompt obedience.

The Chinese, inveterately democratic and logical, flog their admirals as well as their humbler heroes. And certainly, if flogging is all that our admirals say it is, the quarter deck should be strenuously kept up to the mark by the cat and the birch; for an admiral can send a battleship to the bottom when a boy can only hurt his own digestion by a clandestine cigarette. But does the public realize that we actually do allow the captain of a ship to be condemned, without any misconduct on his part, to the cruellest of all tortures – solitary confinement? So absurd and inhuman are the superstitious rites which we call discipline, that the attainment of command practically makes the captain a solitary prisoner in his cabin, and forbids any man in the ship to treat him as a fellow creature. I submit quite seriously that this is the simple explanation of the fact that whereas men who command railways, who direct great engineering works, who lead political parties, who edit newspapers, who organise industrial combinations, show in their conduct and utterances all the mental superiority which their functions involve, naval officers who have passed through the ordeal of command write and talk like short tempered nurses or common sailors. This is not often brought into public notice; but we do not forget the appalling catastrophe of the sinking of the *Victoria* by the *Camperdown*. Such milder lights as have twinkled occasionally since then on the quarter deck intellect from letters to the press are not reassuring.

It must be remembered that it is in time of peace that all this so called discipline produces its worst effects. In time of war discipline keeps itself; and the stupidest officer is nerved to extraordinary efforts by the tremendous stress of battle. But in time of peace and fine weather, when there is nothing to do but housemaid your ship, scrubbing clean boards, polishing speckless metal, and driving sulky and bored officers and men through factitious struggles with sham emergencies, the strain on every one's temper is very great; and it is then that the flogging system does its worst.

Unfortunately flogging can always depend on the support of timid people who pass their lives in terror of children, of servants, of soldiers, of sailors, of tramps, of labourers, of dogs, of anybody or anything that can strike or bite or rebel. These people call themselves lovers of discipline, and clamour for whips and muzzles and complete systems of intimidation. I am sorry for them. The bravest of us are only brave relatively; and none of us can afford to despise a coward. But the cowards would be the first to suffer from the reign of terror they are always clamouring for. They had better continue to be terrified by shadows than get something real to fear.

There are only two possible methods of keeping order in a ship or anywhere else. One is to give everybody a status, with a certain responsibility and respect attached to the status, as well as fair pay and honourable conditions. Under such circumstances 99 out of 100 men and lads will keep themselves in reasonable order without further pressure than that of public opinion and their own self respect. The hundredth, who will not, can be discharged, and, in the last social extremity, killed. The other system is intimidation. Under it half your forces are wasted in coercing the other half; and the loss through friction and bad blood is enormous, without counting the horrible unhappiness of it. It is also politically impossible to carry it out with any thoroughness nowadays. But perhaps the main objection to it from the point of view of the subordination is that any fool can keep order (of a sort) with a whip in his hand, whilst under the other system the officer must govern by character, or rather make his men govern themselves by character, so that the officers become a highly selected class. The flogging system would never have flourished but for the old practice of giving commands to men of family, officers neither born nor made, who could not, like Paul Jones, do without the cat, because they were not Paul Joneses, and should never have been placed in command of anybody. The case against flogging is thus seen to be exactly parallel with the case against industrial sweating. It is true that some officers cannot command without flogging, just as some employers cannot make profits without sweating. The effect of the abolition of flogging or the passing of a Factory Act is to force these officers and employers into retirement or into subordinate positions to make room for those who are able to succeed under the raised conditions. That is how the national standard of character and conduct goes up from time to time. The opposition of many officers and employers to the process is natural enough. When they tell us that they cannot succeed without the cane, the birch, and the 'Song of the Shirt', there is no reason to disbelieve them. Abler men can and will – that is enough for us.

Finally, let us not suppose that what is called 'perfect discipline' is possible under any system. The officers in a ship cannot have things all their own way. Sailors die inconveniently; captains go melancholy mad inconveniently; men give way to momentary flashes of temper; scurvy, smallpox, fogs, typhoons, and other unlooked-for things upset the routine of a ship and interfere with the plans of her commanders. It is of no use to say that we will not stand these things – we have to stand them; and even if among them must be included so unnerving and cataclysmic an upheaval of all order as 'a young monkey cocking a snook' at an undignified admiral, the admiral had better pretend not to see it, and the nation had better replace him with a dignified admiral as soon as possible.

Yours truly,
G. BERNARD SHAW.
North Berwick.

Shaw's silence in The Times for some nine months after his campaign against flogging in the navy may be ascribed in part to his heavy involvement in the Vedrenne–Barker season at the Court where *John Bull* was followed by a revival of the April 1904 production of *Candida,* then *How He Lied to Her Husband* in a triple bill, then *You Never Can Tell* (another popular success) and then, as a grand finale to the season, in May 1905 *Man and Superman.* Theatre critics continued to carp at him, but there could be no denying his success with theatregoers who sought intellectual stimulation from the stage. He had 'arrived' at last, he had become 'fashionable' and, thanks to a Royal Command Performance of *John Bull,* which Shaw refused to sanction, he had gained immense prestige.

He was quoted everywhere, often on the most unlikely of subjects. and even featured in March 1905 in an interview (self-drafted, like almost all of his 'interviews') in the fashion magazine *The World of Dress.* His criticism here of Edwardian dress codes for males and females as a vile and unhygienic reflection of a Capitalist society is echoed in the letter that follows. Similarly, his reaction to the headgear (the 'pitiable corpse of a large white bird') of the 'lady' who sits down in front of him reflects his loathing of the cruelty this gave evidence of and his lifelong abhorrence of vivisection.

One notes Shaw's reference to a 'matinée hat' at a performance at Drury Lane. Amusingly, the 'matinee hat' became quite a talking point, not always amused, at the Court matinées, attended as they were by predominantly female audiences.

This letter is similar in content to one Shaw had written to the Star some years before under his music-critic pseudonym of Corno di Bassetto. 'Statue music' refers to an episode in Mozart's Don Giovanni. Enrico Caruso (1873–1921) was one of the most famous tenors of his day.

~ 1905, JULY 3 ~

Sumptuary Regulations at the Opera.

Sir, – The Opera management at Covent Garden regulates the dress of its male patrons. When is it going to do the same to the women?

On Saturday night I went to the Opera. I wore the costume imposed on me by the regulations of the house. I fully recognize the advantage of those regulations. Evening dress is cheap, simple, durable, prevents rivalry and extravagance on the part of male leaders of fashion, annihilates class distinctions, and gives men who are poor and doubtful of their social position (that is, the great majority of men) a sense of security and satisfaction that no clothes of their own choosing could confer, besides saving a whole sex the trouble of considering what they should wear on state occasions. The objections to it are as dust in the balance in the eyes of the ordinary Briton. These objections are that it is colourless and characterless; that it involves a whitening process which makes the shirt troublesome, slightly uncomfortable, and seriously unclean; that it acts as a passport for undesirable persons; that it fails to guarantee sobriety, cleanliness, and order on the part of the wearer; and that it reduces to a formula a very vital human habit which should be the subject of constant experiment and active private enterprise. All such objections are thoroughly un-English. They appeal only to an eccentric few, and may be left out of account with the fantastic objections of men like Ruskin, Tennyson, Carlyle, and Morris to tall hats.

But I submit that what is sauce for the gander is sauce for the goose. Every argument that applies to the regulation of the man's dress applies equally to the regulation of the woman's. Now let me describe what actually happened to me at the Opera. Not only was I in evening dress by compulsion, but I voluntarily added many graces of conduct as to which the management made no stipulation whatever. I was in my seat in time for the first chord of the overture. I did not chatter during the music nor raise my voice when the Opera was too loud for normal conversation. I did not get up and go out when the statue music began. My language was fairly moderate considering the number and nature of the improvements on Mozart volunteered by Signor Caruso, and the respectful ignorance of the dramatic points of the score exhibited by the conductor and the stage manager – if there is such a functionary at Covent Garden. In short, my behaviour was exemplary.

At 9 o'clock (the Opera began at 8) a lady came in and sat down very conspicuously in my line of sight. She remained there until the beginning of the last act. I do not complain of her coming late and going early; on the contrary, I wish she had come later and gone earlier. For this lady, who had very black hair, had stuck over her right ear the pitiable corpse of a large white bird, which looked exactly as if someone had killed it by stamping on its breast, and then nailed it to the lady's temple, which was presumably of sufficient solidity to bear the operation. I am not, I hope, a morbidly squeamish person; but the spectacle sickened me. I presume that if I had presented myself at the doors with a dead snake round my neck, a collection of blackbeetles pinned to my shirtfront, and a grouse in my hair, I should have been refused admission. Why, then, is a woman to be allowed to commit such a public outrage? Had the lady been refused admission, as she should have been, she would have soundly rated the tradesman who imposed the disgusting headdress on her under the false pretence that 'the best people' wear such things, and withdrawn her custom from him; and thus the root of the evil would be struck at; for your fashionable woman generally allows herself to be dressed according to the taste of a person whom she would not let sit down in her presence. I once, in Drury Lane Theatre, sat behind a matinee hat decorated with the two wings of a seagull, artificially reddened at the joints so as to produce an illusion of being freshly plucked from a live bird. But even that lady stopped short of the whole seagull. Both ladies were evidently regarded by their neighbours as ridiculous and vulgar; but that is hardly enough when the offence is one which produces a sensation of a physical sickness in persons of normal humane sensibility.

I suggest to the Covent Garden authorities that, if they feel bound to protect their subscribers against the danger of my shocking them with a blue tie, they are at least equally bound to protect me against the danger of a woman shocking me with a dead bird.

Yours truly,
G. BERNARD SHAW.

Sir Henry Irving died on 13 October 1905 and the *Neue Freie Presse* commissioned Shaw to contribute an obituary article. Shaw stipulated that Siegfried Trebitsch, the Austrian who translated Shaw's plays into German, should translate his article, but the task was given to a hack whose version distorted parts of the original. Shaw knew nothing about this until he saw Stephen Coleridge's letter in *The Times*. Coleridge, a relative of the poet, younger son of the famous judge, the first Lord Coleridge, and a great friend of Ellen Terry's, had encountered Shaw's article, not in the *Neue Freie Presse* but in other German papers which had printed glosses derived from the *Neue Freie Presse*. What offended Coleridge particularly was the statement attributed to Shaw that Irving had solicited his knighthood, – Coleridge refuting 'on the authority of personal knowledge, Mr. Shaw's statement that Irving ever solicited at any time or place for a knighthood.' Although Shaw would allow, when he eventually obtained copies of the original translation, that it was 'fair' on the whole, he absolutely denied having indulged in any such innuendo. Hence the two letters that follow. There were other distortions and all in all, when the article, now translated back into English, featured in the press, Shaw became the most vilified man in London, to such an extent, as he told Trebitsch, that when he appeared at a public meeting, 'an attempt was made to prevent me from speaking.' (See Laurence, *Collected Letters, 1898–1910*, pp. 566–71.)

To compound Shaw's grievance, *Major Barbara,* which opened at the Court Theatre on 28 November 1905, provoked critical and public denunciations for its 'blasphemies,' including a leading article in the *Morning Post* that referred to Shaw's 'slanderous depreciation' of Irving. Shaw sent copies of his original article to all the leading London papers; only the *Morning Post* published it.

～ 1905, October 25 ～

SIR HENRY IRVING'S KNIGHTHOOD.

Sir, – Mr. Stephen Coleridge's hotheadedness is sometimes useful and always amiable; but he has caused a good deal of unnecessary pain this time by informing the public, on my authority, that Sir Henry Irving importuned the Court for a knighthood. Many people, knowing that I am not in the habit of publishing false or inconsiderate statements, and imagining, because I am a playwright, that I must have special sources of information concerning Sir Henry Irving, will conclude that I am right and Mr. Coleridge wrong – all the more readily as Mr. Coleridge's citation of Sir Henry's objection to a knighthood in 1883 can hardly weigh against the unquestioned fact that he accepted one in 1895.

The explanation is the usual simple one. I did not make the innuendos attributed to me. I gave a straightforward account of the emphatic public act by which Sir Henry Irving openly and boldly demanded and obtained for his art the same official recognition (his own phrase) accorded to the art of painting by the custom of knighting the President of the Royal Academy. I have not seen the translation of my article made by *Die Neue*

Freie Presse; but it is inconceivable that even the worst translator could mistake Sir Henry's famous lecture at the Royal Institution for such a crawl up the backstairs of a palace as Mr. Coleridge's unfortunate phrase suggests. There never was an act more publicly done by the head of a profession on its behalf, and never one more honourable to the doer. Mr. Coleridge does well to remind us that, when the title was conceded, no personal use of it was ever made in a playbill; but, as I mentioned that fact in the same spirit in my article, he must not imply that I have forgotten or suppressed it.

As to the allusion to 'romantic millionairesses', I leave Mr. Coleridge to apologize for it in the proper quarter. In writing for the Viennese public, which has one of the most magnificent theatres in Europe provided for it by public endowment through the hands of the Emperor, it is necessary to mention the fact that in England the splendours of the Irving Management of the Lyceum Theatre was made possible only by private subsidy; and that the end of it all was that Irving had to abandon his theatre to a music hall syndicate and work himself to death in provinces when London, which so effusively gives him a stone in Westminster Abbey now, had left him penniless at the age at which eminent men in other professions retire with comfortable fortunes.

If I have offended Mr. Coleridge's sentiment of private regard for his deceased friend at a moment when his feelings are very strongly stirred by that friend's death, I am sorry; but the burial of an eminent man in Westminster Abbey is not a proper occasion for the indulgence of private partialities, whether hostile or friendly. Literature has its public rights as well as acting; and, whilst I have insisted strongly on the enormous social services Irving rendered to his own profession, I am bound to insist with equal emphasis on the fact that he did nothing for mine. I may say so without suspicion of personal animus, because my career as a playwright did not begin until his career as an actor was virtually over. Irving, honestly and accurately described, was a quite sufficiently remarkable and interesting man. The illusory Irving of the obituary notices, the scholar, the Shakespearian, the model in every public and private virtue, the distributor of sovereigns to refreshment-housekeepers, and of £100-notes to starving actors does not interest me in the least. The same things were said about Gladstone and Sir Augustus Harris; the same things will be said about Lord Roberts, Mr. Chamberlain, President Roosevelt, and possibly about Mr. Coleridge and myself, if by some accident we should become popular idols. My business is not to multiply stuff of that kind. The real Irving was an enigma worth studying just because, having hardly one of the qualifications which are claimed for him, he proved, by his extraordinary success, that these qualifications are somehow not the genuine diagnostics of assignees. And, unless I greatly mistook the man, he would much rather be known for the very curious, rare, and distinguished person he really was, than for the blatantly cheap compound of philanthropic bustler on a monument and gorgeous satire in a melodrama which most of his obituarists have made of him.

Yours truly,
G. BERNARD SHAW

Shaw's acute sense of having been grossly misrepresented emerges in this short letter from a 'slandered journalist'.

～ *1905, OCTOBER 27* ～

SIR HENRY IRVING'S KNIGHTHOOD.

Sir, – Mr. Stephen Coleridge translated 'offentlich und unmisverstandlich verlangte' as 'importuned'. A duped Press, a disgusted public, a needlessly wounded circle of private friends, and a slandered journalist are waiting for an apology, not for further selections.

Yours truly,
G. BERNARD SHAW.

Queen Alexandra actively encouraged and supported several charities, some of which did not enjoy the support of government. After a call by the Prime Minister to help the poor, she initiated an appeal for the jobless on 12 November 1905, launching it with a personal donation of £2,000. Charles Booth (1840–1916) was a social reformer whose researches, the first of their kind, included the great *Life and Labour of the People of London* (1903). Beatrice Webb worked with him as an assistant in the 1880s.

Shaw is speaking here as a Fabian, first in criticising the government for failing to take action, then also in commenting on the Queen's charity as 'the last resource of a bankrupt civilization'.

The allusion to 'when the windows of the clubs in Pall Mall were broken' refers to the Trafalgar Square demonstration and riot of 8 February 1886, sometimes referred to as Black Monday, when two rival leftist organisations (London United Workmen's Committee and H.F. Hyndman's Social Democratic Federation) held meetings simultaneously in Trafalgar Square. The meetings occurred without incident, but when the speakers left the square a crowd of 5,000 streamed west along Pall Mall and resumed a fiery meeting in Hyde Park. Due to misinformation, the police believed that there was trouble in The Mall, so they marched away to protect Marlborough House and Buckingham Palace, while a few hundred metres north the mob rushed along Pall Mall and St. James's, smashing the local club windows along the way.

THE QUEEN'S COUP D'ETAT.

Sir, – Like everybody else in London with a spark of social compunction. I am boundlessly delighted with the very womanly dash made by the Queen to do something for the unemployed. She has waited for Parliament to deal with the question, and Parliament has done nothing – has, indeed, with great difficulty been prevented from doing less. She has waited for the Prime Minister to advise, and the Prime Minister avows his utter helplessness. The resources of the Constitution being thus exhausted, she had boldly thrown the Constitution to the winds and taken the matter in hand herself. She has said, in effect, to our wise men. – 'Well, if you cannot get my people work, I will give them bread. Who will come and help me?'

In doing this the Queen has precipitated a crisis that was bound to come sooner or later. The situation is not new. In cities like ancient Rome or modern London competitive commerce always finally creates a proletariat too numerous to be effectually coerced and too clever to be duped by spurious political economy and pious platitudes about the sacredness of law and order. In 1886, when the windows of the clubs in Pall Mall were broken, the classes represented by those clubs immediately paid £49,000 ransom to the Mansion-house fund, most of which went into the hands of the anything-but-hardworking. Trade revived and staved off the emergency for a time; but it is upon us again, and now the question is, are we to accept *Panemet Circenses* as a regular part of our metropolitan organization? We must, if the alternative is to leave the unemployed to choose between starvation and plunder. The Queen will not allow us to starve her people She has forced our hand, and is going to organise *Panem* (the circuses will come later,) with her own hands, unless we find work and wages for the unemployed, who, by the way, will very soon acquire a taste, like their social superiors, for incomes without work.

It is a critical situation, and one that may become dangerous if those who understand it are too courtly or too cowardly to speak out. The Queen's charity is the last resource of a bankrupt civilization. If we can do nothing better we must adopt it, and she is right to force the alternative on us. But can we do nothing better?

For my part I see no difficulty in finding work for the unemployed. Take the places they live in, for instance. There is the urgently necessary work of knocking those places down, turning their putrid debris, and replacing them with decent dwellings in airy and handsome streets. The spots to begin with are already marked by Mr. Charles Booth on the map of London in black. If instead of directing the attention of the unemployed as in 1886 to the possibility of extorting a demoralizing ransom by destroying the houses of other people, we could set them to the eminently desirable and honourable work of destroying their own and building better ones to replace them, the Queen would not need to empty her private purse with the heartbreaking knowledge that her money would save her people's lives at the expense of their characters.

It is true that there is no commercial demand for a new and decent city; but pray for what great social work is there any commercial demand? How long more will it take us to see that great nations work for national profits, and keep the little souls who can understand nothing but commercial profits out of the national councils?

I wish I could persuade the Queen that there is no lack of money, no lack of work, no lack of charity. It is character and statesmanship that we want, and these, alas cannot be created by cheques and subscription lists.

Yours truly,
G. BERNARD SHAW.
10, Adelphi Terrace, W.C.

Stephen Coleridge persisted in his attacks on Shaw, as Shaw's quotations in the following letter indicate. The long-suffering tone and infinite politeness of the letter should not blind one to Shaw's steely inflexibility. Coleridge had been misled by an inaccurate translation of the article in the *Neue Freie Presse*. Shaw's is a crushing reply, even though he leaves 'Mr Coleridge in possession of the field'.

~ *1905, December 8* ~

MR. BERNARD SHAW AND SIR HENRY IRVING.

Sir, – One of the pleasures of controversy with Mr. Stephen Coleridge is that you cannot hurt his feelings. The most crushing confutation seems to afford him the same exultant gratification that ordinary men get from decisive victory. I convict him of unpardonable mistranslation and misrepresentation; he triumphantly quotes the original passage – the damning evidence of his misdemeanour – as irresistible evidence against me. He circulates through the London Press, and consequently through the Press of the whole English-speaking world, an innuendo concerning the late Sir Henry Irving, and gains extensive credit for it by attaching to it the name of a well-known dramatic critic author and critic. I show that the innuendo is not to be found in that critic's utterance; that, on the contrary, the facts are stated by him in such a way as to render the innuendo impossible by even the most careless inference. Mr. Coleridge replies that he 'is glad to be able to afford some protection to the memory of Sir Henry Irving,' and that 'his function in the matter is precisely confined to vindicating his dead friend'. As to the facts of the case, when I refer him to Sir Henry Irving's lecture of February 1, 1895, with the articles written on that lecture by the *London Press* next day, and am immediately confirmed by the *Saturday Review*, by Mr. William Archer, and by every same journalist who recollects an incident as public and undeniable as the falling of the roof of Charing-cross Station the other day, he waves off my 'ridiculous attack' with an assurance that Sir Henry Irving thought he would be misunderstood in 1883 if he had then accepted a hypothetical knighthood suggested by Mr. Coleridge himself, and that he only changed his mind in 1895 because he was afraid of hurting the personal feelings of the late Queen Victoria! What must Mr. Coleridge think of Mr. August Manns, who repeatedly refused knighthood for his inestimable services in the art of music at the Crystal Palace? And finally Mr. Coleridge hopes I will 'not proceed to express to him any penitence for my inaccuracy or regret for my folly'.

Well, on the whole I think I will oblige him on this point. I have already made my apology and expressed my regret in the proper quarter for trying to shield Mr. Coleridge by a suggestion that he had been misled by an inaccurate translation. I now know that it is in the power neither of the German nor the English language to get Mr. Coleridge right on any subject whatsoever. I should perhaps have been kinder to the late Sir Henry Irving if I had known that he suffered for 30 years from a friendship so damaging in its enthusiastic good intention. I have placed my article freely at the disposal of the English Press. It has been published, and can make no more mischief with those who have read it. I can do no more.

I had better add that I do not think that the version of his protest which he sent to Vienna did not contain that phrase about 'importuning the Court for a knighthood,' which has raised the only serious issue between us. I for a moment doubted Mr. Coleridge's good faith; but when he presently sent to the English papers a frank copy of his letter to Vienna I saw that I was face to face with a sacred simplicity, an incalculable force of pure unreason and misunderstanding, which forbade me to meddle further. I believe Mr. Coleridge will go on to the end of his life repeating his version of the affair, and that he will finally, by his indomitable and fact-proof perseverance, convince the world that he has my authority for the statement that Henry Irving meanly begged for himself the title, worthless as a personal honour to a man in his position, which he haughtily and honourably demanded as an official recognition of his profession. If Mr. Coleridge ends by making the slander believed, the fault is not mine; I have done all that lies in my power to make Irving's real attitude understood and appreciated; and now I leave Mr. Coleridge in possession of the field, lest I should cause any unfortunate animals to be vivisected by shaking the confidence of the public in the judgement of their most prominent champion.

Yours truly,
G.Bernard Shaw.
10, Adelphi Terrace. W.C.

Shaw here returns to the debate on flogging in the navy, which had lapsed some months before, because the Irish MP for South Donegal, J.G. Swift MacNeill, (1887–1918), who was also a professor of law, had spoken on the matter in Parliament, supporting a bill to abolish its practice.

Ernest Pretyman was Civil Lord of the Admiralty from 1900 to 1903. Austen Chamberlain, a Liberal-Unionist MP, was Civil Lord of the Admiralty from 1895 to 1900.

One notes (with some amusement) Shaw's suggestion that Parliament introduce a Bill for flogging MPs for the frequent dereliction of their duties.

∼ *1906. February 23* ∼

THE ALLEGED ABOLITION OF FLOGGING IN THE NAVY.

Sir, – I hope the public is not deceived by the apparent concession made to Mr. Swift MacNeill by the Government in the matter of flogging in the Navy. To withdraw the birch and leave the cane is very much as if the wife beaters of the metropolis were to offer to abandon the use of the broomstick and confine themselves in future to the poker. The cane is a much more formidable instrument than the birch; and it hurts just as much when applied by the captain's orders as by any one else's.

The prevarications of the late Government on this subject were sufficiently trying. First there was no flogging in the Navy, because thrashing a boy with a cane or a birch was not flogging; it was only birching or caning. Secondly, there were no boys in the French Navy (where they do without flogging), because lads of 14 are rated as men. But at least Mr. Pretyman did not make a pretence of abolishing corporal punishment and make humanitarian speeches about it under cover of a regulation which will in all probability rather increase than diminish the severity of the flogging, and will do nothing to clear us in the eyes of Europe from the extremely disagreeable associations of a reputation for flogging.

Further, the withdrawal of the birch is only an experiment for one year. The implication is that, if the boys do not become faultless, the abolition of the birch will be considered a failure. That is, we are in the position of a society of burglars who should resolve to try honesty for one year, and then, if their incomes had at all decreased in consequence, to resume the jemmy and the dark lantern.

Mr. Chamberlain's speech is particularly interesting, though it is not clear why he did not make it when his party had the power to act on his views. It reveals the fact that our public schools are prepared to make private compacts with parents stipulating for decent and honourable treatment of their sons. It also makes it clear that it is still possible for a leading English statesman to declare that blackguardism in a criminal justifies blackguardism in British justice.

I trust some of our new members will lose no time in introducing a Bill for flogging members of Parliament for disorderly interruptions, absence from the House during business hours, tedious speeches, and inability to answer questions as to the information contained in the Blue-books with which the nation, at great expense, supplies them. All the arguments brought forward for flogging in schools and on board ship will be available for the support of such a measure. Members will perhaps then be glad to fall back on that sense of human dignity which makes flogging abhorrent to men of honour.

Yours truly,
G. BERNARD SHAW.
10, Adelphi Terrace, W.C.

Sir Edward Grey, 1862–1933 (later Viscount Grey), was at one time (1892–95) Under-Secretary for Foreign Affairs. He appealed in Parliament to an end to the debate on flogging on account of its use in countries under England's control and the questions that may thus be raised in those quarters. The details concerning the incident of the Denshawi floggings are amply noted in the preface to *John Bull's Other Island*. The 'author of the Madrid explosion' was Matteo Morall, an anarchist who had carried out a bomb attack in Spain (in May 1906) against the King of Spain and his bride as they rode in an open carriage, an outrage that received wide coverage at the time.

SIR EDWARD GREY AND THE DENSHAW I FLOGGINGS.

Sir, – Sir Edward Grey's appeal to us all to sit silent and hold our breaths lest we should provoke that formidable power, the fellaheen of Egypt, to rise up and sweep us out of their country is touching, and will undoubtedly have a great effect on constitutionally timid supporters of the Government. But there is no reason why we should not give Sir Edward Grey a piece of our minds as regards his own personal part in the incident which has scared him. Before the sentences of flogging were carried out at Denshawi the whole nation, including the Foreign Secretary, had 24 hours' notice of what was going to take place. There was time for the Minister in whose charge the honour of British humanity and civilization stood, to telegraph our disapproval of barbarous punishments and our repudiation of the spirit in which the tribunal passed its disgraceful, sycophantic, and panic-stricken sentences. Had that been done our troops and their officers would have done justice upon the murderers (whose guilt I assume pending the report) like civilized gentlemen, and not lashed them like vindictive savages. But Sir Edward Grey did not take that view of his trust. He not only did not intervene, but actually asked the House of Commons to accept his statement that the tribunal had been the highest possible. The statement was absurd. A tribunal which passes sentences of flogging is not 'high' at all; we might just as well be assured that the author of the Madrid explosion was the most humane anarchist available, and asked to refrain from criticizing him on that ground. The tribunal put itself out of court by its admittedly lawless sentence; and to ask us to assume, pending further particulars, that the sentence was carried out by highly popular officers of the most refined sensibilities, and with the most scrupulous regard to the feelings of everybody concerned (which is what Sir E. Grey's appeal comes to) shows a want of sense of reality which constitutes a national danger when the patient is at the head of the Foreign Office.

We are all, of course, aware that there are utilitarian reasons for flogging people. There are also utilitarian reasons for the employment of judicial torture, for infanticide, for duelling, for cannibalism, and for bomb throwing. The difference in public life between a civilized nation and a savage one, and in private life between a gentleman and a blackguard, is that civilization and gentility, though fully aware of the convenience and utility of these expedients, rule them out as dishonourable, and face the task of solving political and social problems by higher and nobler methods. We have at present a Government which stops to argue about such things. What some of us want is a Government which never for a moment regards flogging as being any more permissible by a civilized Power than burning alive to which, by the way, all Sir Edward Grey's apologies for the floggings would apply equally if the tribunal had adopted that method of impressing the fellaheen with the greatness of England.

I suggest that Sir Edward Grey should exchange portfolios with the Home Secretary. Flogging is an institution in England; and Sir Edward Grey's insensibility to its dishonour would not shock Europe, which has become accustomed to regard us as a cruel people, much as we ourselves used to regard the Spaniards. But in Egypt the rescue of the fellaheen from the kurbash of the Khedive's floggers was one of the main pretexts for the Franco-English occupation. It is therefore clearly desirable that the Foreign Secretary should be in advance of English ideas on humanitarian questions. Now it happens very conveniently that Mr. Herbert Gladstone is bound by the Gladstonian tradition to be indignantly sensitive to outrages on humanity abroad, whilst remaining disastrously reactionary and obsolete with regard to the industrial administration with which his department is charged at home. On the other hand, Sir Edward Grey, whilst apparently in no way more advanced on humanitarian questions than the Mahdi, is thoroughly aware, when our Factory Code is in question, that we are no longer in the year 1832.

The immediate transference of Sir Edward Grey to the Home Office, and of Mr. Herbert Gladstone to the Foreign Office, would seem, under these circumstances, to be clearly indicated as a desirable instalment of Liberal reform.

Yours truly,

G. BERNARD SHAW.

Shaw developed an interest in phonetics in 1879, perhaps initially as an abstract discipline. When he became a practising playwright and wished to indicate the speech patterns of his characters, pronunciation and rendering by means of conventional orthography became more immediate problems to him. One sees him grappling with this and obliquely making his point about the inexactness of established Roman-based orthography in his play *Captain Brassbound's Conversion*, where a couple of his characters, one being the cockney Rankin, are given lines of such density ('there ynt naow awm in it,' as Rankin says) that not even experienced actors could read them. Spelling reform was in the air at the turn of the nineteenth century; Shaw soon made it a public issue, arguing the case for a phonetic system which would, he believed, be more practical and economical and eliminate class divisions created by pronunciation. *Pygmalion,* together with its preface, was his principal word on the subject, dramatically speaking: the informing theme was the questions of phonetics, and the salute went to the philologist Henry Sweet (1845–1912, mentioned in the following letter), on whom the character of Henry Higgins is based. Shaw had written before to the press on this topic, notably in 1901, when he criticized the British Spelling Reform Association. In this letter to *The Times*, he castigates the proposals, supported by President Theodore Roosevelt and Andrew Carnegie, for spelling reform recommended by the American Simplified Spelling Board. As Shaw says, '... it is not really a simplified spelling; it is a shortened spelling ... And it anxiously disclaims any pretence at being phonetic.' So great was Shaw's commitment to phonetics that he left his residuary estate to the promotion and establishment of a new English phonetic alphabet. The bequest was set aside in a High Court judgment in 1957 on grounds of its unfeasibility. The letter contains a mild criticism of Sir Isaac Pitman (1813–97), who developed the phonetic shorthand system which Shaw learnt and used to speed up his writing.

◇∕ *1906, September 25* ◇∕

THE SIMPLIFIED SPELLING PROPOSALS.

Sir, – It is to be regretted that the scheme of the Simplified Spelling Board, so energetically and wisely forced on our attention by President Ruzevelt (if he will allow me to simplify him to that extent) has been received, not only with the outburst of ignorance and folly which any sensible proposal may nowadays count on, but with a false delicacy which has led genuine phonetics experts to withhold serious technical criticism.

It is bad enough to have men of letters passionately defending such a recent, absurd, and transient aberration as our pseudo-etymological spelling on the ground that it is the spelling of the Bible and Shakespear (a libel gross enough to make Tyndale and Shakespear turn in their graves); but it is far worse to have the defects of the scheme passed over in polite silence by the people who know authoritatively that, though the President does not overrate the enormous importance of spelling reform, his methods cannot be regarded as an advance on those of Artemus Ward and Josh Billings. I tried to express this myself by comparing his action to the reform of the calendar by Mahomed, who divided the year into 12 lunar months, with results on the caravan season arrangements from which Arabian commerce has not recovered to this day. But I find that most of your contemporaries regard Mahomed's arrangement as an excellent one, and accordingly report me as enthusiastically in favour of the Presidential scheme.

Pending some really authoritative comment by Mr. Henry Sweet, whose proposals of 1881 are hardly to the point to-day, or by some expert of his school, let me point out a few obvious shortcomings in the scheme. To begin with, it is not really a simplified spelling; it is a shortened spelling, which is quite a different matter, as a short spelling may leave a foreigner or a child quite as much in the dark as to the sound of the word as a long one. And it anxiously disclaims any pretence to be phonetic. Now it is doubtless wise, when a reform is introduced, to try to persuade the British public that it is not a reform at all; but appearances must be kept up to some extent at least; and the fact is that a board which disclaims phonetic spelling puts itself out of Court. Unphonetic spelling is as impossible a figment as secular education. Unless we adopt a system of Chinese ideographs, and learn by heart a separate arbitrary symbol of every word in the dictionary we must spell phonetically. We may corrupt and confuse our phonetic spelling by etymologic fads, spelling det with a b and foren with an ig, just as we might spell man mapn or mkyan to show that we are descended from apes or monkeys; but we shall not spell man ape nor shall we ever spell cat dog. If we did the only result would be that we should presently spell dogma catma. We cannot get away from phonetic spelling, because spelling is as necessarily and inevitably phonetic as moisture is damp. To say that English and French spelling are not phonetic is absurd; all that it means is that the French and English spell much worse than the Germans and Italians, being relatively conceited arid inhibitive people who take an uppish delight in making knowledge difficult, not to mention their love of excuses for punishing children. English spelling contains thousands of excuses for rebuking children, for beating them, for imprisoning them after school hours, for breaking their spirits with impossible tasks. It is more effective even than teaching a short-sighted child the clock, and then beating it because it cannot tell the time from Big Ben.

But in the long run phonetics have their revenge. When we begin by refusing to spell as we pronounce we end by having to pronounce as we spell. The etymologists, to show the French origin of the word oblige, refused to spell it phonetically; and a generation of superior persons despised those who did not say obleege, and were themselves despised by a still more select circle who said obleezh. But who dares say obleege now, except Joseph Surface on the stage? The history of the word envelope tells the same story. Onvelope and Ann Velope have had their day; we spelt it ennvelope and now we have to pronounce it ennvelope. The American reformers want us to spell catalogue catalog, a word in such common use that its pronunciation has been traditionally maintained in spite of the spelling. But what of epilog and prolog? These two words, which most Englishmen never utter or hear uttered in their lives, and the rest use perhaps once in 20 years, are on those rare occasions mispronounced, nine times out of ten, as epiloag and proloag.

As the working classes become literate and please themselves by dragging into ordinary conversation more and more long words which they have never heard pronounced, they introduce ways of their own of pronouncing them, founded necessarily on the spelling. Programme, a vulgarism which offends the eye as Paris pronounced Paree in English offends the ear, has been in my hearing pronounced so as to rhyme to Damn me. That is how we shall all have to pronounce it some day. I foresee the time when I shall be forced to pronounce semi-conscious as See my Conscious. Then there is the march of preciosity. Already I blush when old habit betrays me into calling clothes cloze. I have heard a tenor pronouncing the l in Handel's Where e'er you walk. If Detford has become Depped Ford in spite of usage, I see no reason to doubt that det will presently become debbed. I am fond of the word ham, meaning a country place larger than a hamlet. I am still allowed to speak of East Ham and West Ham, because the words are written separately; but when I speak of Lewis Ham, Elt Ham, or Peters Ham, I am suspected of a defect in my speech, almost as if I had spoken of Cars Halton (properly rhyming to Walton) instead of Ker Shalltn. The received pronunciations nowadays are Louis Sham, Peter Sham, EL Tham, and so on. And the people who support the bad spelling which is corrupting the language in this fashion pretend to have a special regard for it, and prattle of the Bible and Shakespear! They remind me of a New York Police Commissioner who once arrested a whole theatrical company for performing one of my plays, and explained, on being remonstrated with, that the Sermon on the Mount was good enough for him.

The worst of it is that this want of conscience in spelling has led to anarchy and indifference in the interpretation of spelling. London children are deliberately taught to speak hideously by teachers who speak that way themselves. I have passed a public elementary school and heard a class of children chorusing the alphabet as follows.

I, Ber-ee, Ser- ee, Der-ee, Er-ee, Aff, Jer-ee Iche, Awy, Ji, Ki, Al, Am, An, Ow, Per-ee, Kioo, Aw, Ass, Ter-ee, Yer-eoo, Ver-ee, Dabblyew, Ax, Wa-eey, Zad.' Already the West End and Oxford have acquired more than half this horrible pronunciation, and they will soon acquire it completely. They are lulled into a false security by the fact that the coarsely nasal resonance of the costermonger distinguishes him socially from the Oxford graduate in spite of the identity of the mispronunciation. But the snarl will no doubt conquer Oxford in time. When smart society says 'Ow now' for 'Oh no' and 'dahn tahn' for 'down town' and calls a 'humbug with a gun' a 'hambag with a gan' it is not very far from complete mastery of the language of what it already calls the Mile End Rowd, and will soon call, with native perfection of accent, the Mawl Enn Rowd. Even on the stage young actors are rebuked for speaking as ladies and gentlemen used to speak, and are deliberately taught, not even parvenu English, which is bad enough in all conscience, but positively Hoxton English. The classic beauty of speech by which Mr. Forbes Robertson makes *Hamlet* still fascinating in spite of its intellectual obsolescence will soon be mimicked (let us hope successfully) as an eccentric dialect; and Mr. – (the name of this excellent actor escapes me for the moment) will perhaps die prematurely, worn out by his efforts to conceal his natural propensity to speak like a gentleman and to acquire the common language of the barrow and the motor-car in all its abhorrent smartness.

I insist on this aspect of the case because, whilst we seem incapable of grasping the enormous advantage of making English a universal language both for writing and speech, or of understanding how our spelling obstructs that consummation, most Englishmen and women would almost rather die than be convicted of speaking like costermongers and flower girls. Our governing classes dropped half the continent of North America from sheer carelessness. Sooner than drop an h they would steep Europe in blood. I therefore hit them purposely in their vulnerable point.

For this very reason, however, the reform cannot be effected by a shortened spelling which is indistinguishable from ordinary wrong spelling. If any man writes me a letter in which through is spelt thru and above abuv, I shall at once put him down as an illiterate and inconsequent plebeian, no matter what Board or what potentate sanctions his orthography. Really phonetic spelling is quite unmistakable in this way. No lady or gentleman will ever be persuaded to spell like the late Sir Isaac Pitman, who was a very energetic bookseller and a very bad phonetician; but anybody might spell like Mr. Henry Sweet without compromising himself – indeed with a positive affirmation of having been at Oxford. A practically correct phonetic spelling justifies itself at once to the eye as being the spelling of an educated man, whereas the shortenings and so-called simplifications suggest nothing but blunders. I therefore respectfully advise the President and the Board to take the bull by the horns without wasting further time, and enlarge the alphabet until our consonants and vowels are for all practical purposes separately represented, and defined by rhyming with words in daily use. We shall then get a word notation which may be strange at first (which does not matter), but which will be neither ludicrous nor apparently ignorant (which does matter very much indeed).

One other point is of importance. The new letters must be designed by an artist with a fully developed sense of beauty in writing and printing. There must be no apostrophes or diacritical signs to spoil the appearance of the pages of the new type. It is a mistake to suppose that the Bible teaches us the sacredness of pseudo-etymological spelling; but it does teach us the comeliness of a page on which there are no apostrophes and no inverted commas.

Yours truly,
G. BERNARD SHAW.

The following extremely long, not to say long-winded, letter indicates how strongly Shaw felt about the subject of publishing. There would be more letters on the same theme in 1906 and 1907. The fact that The Times was prepared now to grant him this amount of space is a measure of the stature he had achieved as the pre-eminent playwright of the day and as a man of affairs. The fact that he vigorously supported the Times Book Club, in so doing becoming a major advertisement for the Club, should not be discounted.

Although this is a dead issue today, this letter and the others that followed remain relevant in what they reveal of Shaw as a professional writer. He ran his own business, not ever referring his accounts to an outsider, and kept check on his earnings in a receipt book where amounts (down to the last penny) would be scrupulously recorded. He was also his own publisher, controlling the printing done by R. & R. Clark of Edinburgh as well as the publication and marketing carried out by Constable and Co. of London and other publishers both British and American. If, to some, his pernickety accounting seemed obsessive, it should be remembered that he had travelled a long and impecunious path to relative success. His earnings in the early 1900s, for example, amounted to a pittance. By 1906 his meagre earnings had increased to £1,346 11s 11d, the first time his royalties had risen above three figures. This was no guarantee for the future, however, and Shaw had necessarily to maintain an eagle eye on the sale of his books, hence his support for an enterprise which, as he saw it, would augment these sales. As he said to the Society of Authors: 'As authors, what are we here for except to make the greatest gain as we can from our efforts? . . . Our special object here is to look after the business interests of authors' (quoted in Laurence, ed., *Collected Letters*, 1898–1910, p. 677).

H.G. Wells and Rudyard Kipling were against the project. Moberly Bell (1847–1911) was a British journalist who played an outstanding part in the management of *The Times* (London) during a troubled period.

This and the other letters also reveal a good deal of the topic with such serio-comic observations as 'I read *The Times* because I am a superior person . . .' and 'The majority [of newspaper readers] prefers Dick Swiveller, because his high spirits are amusing, his slovenly colloquialism familiar and intelligible, and his inveterate inaccuracy and illiteracy matters of indifference.' (Dick Swiveller is a character from Charles Dickens's *The Old Curiosity Shop*.) The following month, Shaw would create his own 'Dick Swiveller' in The *Doctor's Dilemma* and grant him ample opportunity to be illiterate and inaccurate.

Publishers and the Public.

Sir, – To my great regret I find myself for the first time in complete and whole-hearted disagreement with the majority of my colleagues on the managing committee of the Society of Authors. Unfortunately, in the face of the panic which has set in, there is no time for us to argue out our differences or to ascertain the opinion of the members of our society (who live mostly out of reach of a general meeting in London) by taking a referendum. There is nothing for it, therefore, but to agree to place our conflicting views before the public for what they are worth.

It is stated in the resolution of the committee that 'the course of business pursued by *The Times* Book Club is in important respects opposed to the interests of authors'. In the official letter, three-quarters of a column long, which follows, none of these important respects are defined. I do not know what they are, though I have repeatedly pressed for the information. On the other hand, there is no lack of instances of injury done to the author in this matter. The publishers do not conceal the fact – indeed they rather glory in it – that having received from a new and important distributing agency called *The Times* Book Club large orders for new books, and having no other relevant business in the world but to sell those books for the author in consideration of his allowing them a share in the profits of his monopoly, they have deliberately refused to execute the orders. For example, they inflicted this injury on Mr. Rudyard Kipling, with the amazing result that Mr. Kipling writes to *The Times* to complain of the conduct, not of the publishers who refused to sell his books, but of the enterprising distributor who gave the order for them. This does not prove that *The Times* Book Club is a delinquent; it proves that Mr. Rudyard Kipling, like most authors, believes everything his publishers tell him. From the business point of view I can see no excuse for these publishers; from the moral point of view they are above suspicion, as the transaction damaged them as much as it did Mr. Kipling. Possibly that is why Mr. Kipling sympathizes with them instead of taking an action for damages against them. If I have done an injustice to Mr. Kipling's publishers in this way of putting the matter I invite them to explain.

I now proceed to my own case. The fact has become public that my publishers did to Miss Marie Corelli what Messrs. Macmillan did to Mr. Kipling. When the leading London circulating library gave them a large order for her new book they refused to execute the order – that is, they boycotted *The Times* Book Club. *The Times* Book Club naturally retaliated by boycotting my publishers. The consequence is that I and all the other authors who have entrusted their books to the same house are boycotted by one of the largest customers in the trade I do not know whether these unfortunate brother authors of mine consider themselves damaged by this or not; I can only speak for myself. I am so convinced that I have been damaged that, unless I can get a clear undertaking that my next forthcoming volume of plays will be sold impartially, without the slightest hesitation or restriction, to all distributors who will pay the trade price for it, I will either create a new and sensible publisher, as Ruskin did under analogous provocation, or make a proposal for its publication to Mr. William Whiteley, or ask *The Times* Book Club to undertake the publication themselves. I may add for the encouragement of the enterprising managers of the Book Club that once they pay me full trade price for my book, they are perfectly welcome to sell it five minutes afterwards at half-price or quarter-price, or even, if they prefer it, to present the copies to the public for nothing for the sake of an advertisement or any other object that may seem to them worth the expenditure. The only feature of the Book Club routine to which I object is the refusal to allow the subscriber, when a new copy has been supplied him, to buy it at once as a second-hand book. He has to send it back to the Club, so that the officials may solemnly consider whether it has been read hard enough to be placed in Class B. I should much prefer to have my own books sold second-hand at once, no matter how new the copy, without any such formality and as cheaply as possible. The more *The Times* pays me for my books and the less it charges my friends for them, the better I shall be pleased.

Now let us get our minds clear on the question of monopoly. There is no doubt that *The Times* has a monopoly of *The Times*, just as Mr. John Murray has a monopoly of John Murray and Messrs. Macmillan and Company have a monopoly of Macmillan's. But if these monopolists ever fall out over a book of mine they will very soon find out who is the real monopolist in that matter. The arch monopolist in the book trade is the author. The moment an author writes a book he has an absolute monopoly of it for 42 years, not only in the British Empire, but in all the countries which have adopted the Berne Convention. His British property creates automatically and simultaneously a dozen colonial and foreign properties for him. It is this startling monopoly that the publisher exploits. If the public want the author's work he can do practically what he likes with both publishers and distributors, finding his limit only in the satiety of the public. It is, of course, perfectly possible for a clever publisher or a clever distributor, with a genius for advertising, and using, if he can compass it, a newspaper as one of his weapons, to create a demand in excess – quite possibly enormous in excess – of the demand created by the author's unaided genius. If we take *The Times* Book Club as the latest example of such a clever and well equipped distributor, it is conceivable that the Book Club may presently be in a position to say to an author, 'Whether you sell 2,000 or 20,000 copies of your next book depends not on you but on us. The 2,000 copies represents your monopoly; the other 18,000 copies represents our organization; and the profits of these we propose to keep, leaving you no better and no worse off pecuniarily than you were before, though much more widely known.' This would be a good bargain for the author; for at the next deal the spread of his reputation would have added to his 2,000, and he could then raise his figure. Besides dealing thus with the author, *The Times*, by superior resources and organization and the clear advantage to the public of dealing with it rather than with competitors who cannot afford the same accommodation, might finally supersede a great many small and unenterprising distributors and reduce publishers of no more than average ability to the condition of literary agents or mere outdoor employees of the Club. It might be able to dictate its own terms to the large proportion of authors who are often impolitely called literary hacks.

But this development cannot be averted merely by screaming at it. And if it could be, the author would be very foolish to avert it. For at present the literary hack is merely an employee of the publisher, worse off than the publisher's clerk, who is at least furnished with an office, a stool, pens, ink, and paper at his employer's expense. How these unfortunate authors are sweated we members of the managing committee of the Authors' Society know better than anybody except the sweaters themselves and the victims of that system. The poorer and less capable the employer the more mercilessly is the employee sweated. And the less reputation the employer has the more impossible it is to touch him by the methods of public agitation. Suppose such an employer, whether he be bookseller or publisher, is swept away by the all-devouring *Times* Book Club, is it likely that his wretched employees will be worse treated by *The Times* than they were by him? On the contrary, *The Times* is richer and can afford to be more generous, is more powerful and can afford to be more magnanimous. Failing either generosity or magnanimity (I notice that my colleague of the Authors' Society declare that 'in its heart' it is deceitful above all things and desperately wicked), it can always be made the object of a vigorous public agitation and compelled to justify itself to public opinion as the present agitation abundantly shows. I wish I could say as much for all the publishers, though I have been fairly fortunate in my publishers.

But all this applies only to the moment during which *The Times* has a monopoly of its new method. That moment cannot last, nor has *The Times*, whilst it lasts, any such monopoly as the author. The author's monopoly is absolute for 42 years. Mr. Kipling or Mr. Wells can charge a thousand guineas a copy for their next book if they please; and neither *The Times* nor the public will be able in that case either to procure a copy on any lower terms or to provide a substitute by their own enterprise. And if *The Times* Book Club refuses to distribute Mr. Kipling's next book, the public will soon find distributing agencies that will. Let us, for the sake of argument, assume the most devastating success for the Book Club at the expense of existing competitors. Let us imagine every bookshop closed and done for.

There are still other libraries – Smith's and Mudie's. How are they to compete with a library backed by a newspaper, and looking for its profits, not to the book department, but to the advertisement department? Very simply, by combining with another newspaper and challenging *The Times* at its own game. What is to prevent Messrs. Mudie from approaching Mr. Franklin Thomasson and combining their library with his paper into a *Tribune* Book Club? What is to prevent Smith and Son co-operating with the great firm of Lloyd and bringing the driving power of the *Daily Chronicle, Lloyd's Weekly*, and the Lloyd paper mills to bear on their big book machine? *The Times* is at no advantage in competing with these papers. Thousands of people who today, in their clubs and newsrooms, have the halfpenny and penny papers side by side with the threepenny Times at their choice on the table never dream of taking up *The Times*, preferring to steep themselves in the romance of the Daily Mail or the strenuous Radical gospel of the Morning Leader. I read *The Times* because I am a superior person to whom leading articles are mere party chatter, and current events at home and abroad serious matters which I wish to hear about from literate and responsible journalists and not from a casual staff of Dick Swivellers. But that places me in a minority. The majority prefers Dick Swiveller, because his high spirits are amusing, his slovenly colloquialism familiar and intelligible, and his inveterate inaccuracy and illiteracy matters of indifference. The circulation of *The Times* is thus limited by its quality. It has a select circulation; and when the other papers and libraries, instead of helplessly abusing it, learn its lesson and adopt its methods, they will easily take from it all but the select library business. The public will have a dozen book clubs to choose from, all kept in order by competition; and the author, unassailable in his monopoly, will be master of the situation, not only to the full extent of his own direct popularity, but to the extent of a lion's share of the addition to his circulation created by the new system. It is said that Mr. H.G. Wells's new book '*Before the Days of the Comet*' has been 'pulled' by *The Times* Book Club because the publishers tried to pull the Club. Now Mr. Wells's book was published as a serial by the *Daily Chronicle* before it came upon the book market. Mr. Wells's book on America was similarly published by the Tribune. By the time these two papers have started their book clubs both of them will be side by side with *The Times* on their knees to Mr. Wells, crushed by his monopoly.

It has been suggested in connexion with the case of Mr. Wells, who is a fearless speculator on forthcoming social changes, that *The Times* will finally submit all manuscripts to the censorship of Mr. Moberly Bell (assumed for the purposes of the argument to be a fiend in human form) and suffer no opinion contrary to his to reach the public through the printing press. Now this touches me nearly, because it happens that Mr. Moberly Bell is in the erroneous and deplorable position of differing from me on the burning public question of municipal trading, of which he takes the same view precisely as that taken by the Publishers' Association of *The Times* Book Club. I have written a book entitled '*The Common Sense of Municipal Trading*' which reduces Mr. Moberly Bell's position to absurdity and the arguments of his friends to unthinkable pulp. Our difference is more than a speculative one; millions of pounds are concerned in it. If Mr. Moberly Bell cannot nor will not pull my book, he cannot nor will not pull any book. As a matter of fact he has not filled the Oxford Street window with copies and with placards drawing attention to them; and this omission may perhaps amount to pulling in Mr. Kipling's sense. Well, I hereby openly taunt, deride, and provoke Mr. Moberly Bell, challenging him to do his worst to stifle my book. If he can prove that I am a penny the worse at the end of the year than I was before the Book Club existed, I will subscribe sixpence to the Industrial Freedom League. I invite any member of the Club to go in and demand a copy of my book and see whether the library assistant will venture to declare before high heaven that there is no such book, or that he has never heard of me, or that 'We don't keep it, madam,' or that no lady would ask for the works of such an author. Mr. Kipling's idea is that Mr. Moberly Bell will gradually ruin all the booksellers, extinguish all the libraries, and buy up all the newspapers in England, until at last there is no other publisher or bookseller in London; and that then I shall be at his mercy. On the contrary, then he will be at mine. For I, and Mr. Kipling, and Mr. Wells, and Mr. Hall Caine, and Miss Corelli, compacted in the Society of Authors, will threaten to open our own shop and manufacture and sell our own books. And when Mr. Moberly Bell asks the public to boycott us for the sake of his beautiful eyes – and for the life of me I cannot see what more he could do – we shall abide the reply of the public with perfect composure.

But, of course, Mr. Moberly Bell can do none of these things. He cannot even run down prices against us, though we can, and probably will, run up prices against him. His enterprise will stimulate demand in every department of literature, from journalism to metaphysics; and that means that it will increase the opportunities and rewards of authorship. So much for all this ridiculous panic about authors crushed and literature gagged by monopoly.

I think I could go on to show, if it were my cue to do so, that those publishers who are real publishers and not mere routine middlemen calling themselves publishers had far better have great organizations of *The Times* type to distribute their books for them than the host of small shopkeepers with whom they could not cope even now if it were not for that other middleman, the wholesale bookseller. But the publishers are my natural enemies; it is not my business to teach them their own business when the knowledge would be instantly used to outwit my fellow authors. They have changed their minds once in this matter; and they will probably change it twice without any help from me.

Meanwhile, I suggest that, if the public can stand any more of the controversy, the disputants should try to bear in mind that copyright is a monopoly, and that no matter how cheaply *The Times* Book Club sells books, it cannot sell them without buying them first. About ten columns of your valuable space would have been saved if your correspondents had borne these facts in mind. If I were the public I should not excite myself too much about the business. After all, what has happened is very simple. There has arisen a development in the book trade which, after making all allowances for those discrepancies between the promise in the advertisement and the performance across the counter (sometimes discoverable even in the enterprises of the Publishers' Association), enables the public to obtain much more for their money than ever it got before. Consequently, those distributors who have not capital, credit, and ability enough to adopt the development find themselves threatened with supersession. In commerce this is the fortune of war; our pity for the ruined stage coach proprietor does not prevent us from travelling by rail; our sympathy with the pinched children of the small draper does not keep us out of Whiteley's, or Shoolbred's, or the Stores. The draper feels particularly bitter because Mr. Whiteley, instead of confining himself to haberdashery, launches into a thousand other departments as well, and often makes his profit by the ancient method of saving on the swings what he loses on the roundabouts. Just so does the bookseller complain that *The Times*, instead of confining itself to book distribution, combines journalism with it, and makes on the advertisements what it loses by distributing books at rates which no small man can compete with. No one can blame the small bookseller and the obsolescent librarian for calling wildly for help. It is not pleasant to be ruined; but in competitive commerce progress is possible only by new methods reducing old ones to bankruptcy by its superiority in economy and popularity. That is what is happening in the present case; and it will continue, the larger organizations driving out the small, to the great advantage of both employees and consumers. Later on, combination among the larger organizations will replace competition, until, finally, the whole industry gets consolidated and co-ordinated to a point at which it can pass altogether out of private hands, if the nation chooses to adopt that solution.

Before concluding it is worth noting that Mr. Hall Caine and myself, who are not in the least frightened, and are somewhat scandalized at the terror of so many of our colleagues, are writers for the theatre as well as for the bookshop. We have not yet forgotten that short-lived agitation against the Theatrical Trust into which several of our newspapers were entrapped not long ago by an American gentleman who was trying very hard to organise a new trust himself. At that time I stood almost alone in advocating the supersession of the one-theatre-one-manager system by whole circuits of theatres controlled by a single wealthy and powerful management. (Why not a *Times* Theatre Trust, by the way? I should welcome it.) We were told then that authors' fees would be brought down; that actors' salaries would be reduced; and that only the most worthless musical comedies would stand a chance of production. That agitation has now perished in the face of the fact that these terrible and unscrupulous syndicate bosses pay higher fees and larger salaries, produce plays of a higher class, and fulfil their contracts more faithfully than the needy provincial speculators they are replacing. It is hardly worth while making the same mistake over again with reference to book distribution.

Yours truly,
G. BERNARD SHAW.

The only question at issue between *The Times* and the Publishers is as to whether the Book Club shall or shall not be allowed to sell second hand net books before they are six months old. *The Times* Book Club maintains its right to sell bona fide second hand books when it likes and at what price it likes. The Publishers try to prohibit this, and to enforce their prohibition by charging higher prices to *The Times* than to other purchasers and by withdrawing their advertisements from *The Times*. (Italicised editorial note by the editor of *The Times*.)

The Fabian Manifesto No. 2 of 1884, written by Shaw, stated that the Fabian Society supported women's suffrage. Shaw never departed from this view and even in 1906 advised women to 'have a revolution – they should shoot, kill, maim, destroy – until they are given the vote.' However, he was often equivocal on the issue, seeing the vote as of little importance in itself – unless backed up by at least 50 per cent representation of women on all government and other decision-making bodies. The letter that follows was prompted by a letter to *The Times* of 30 October 1906 from the distinguished artist craftsman, T.G. Cobden-Sanderson, whose wife, a leading suffragette and a friend of Shaw's wife Charlotte, together with other militant suffragettes (the 'terrible ten'), had been imprisoned for 'civil disobedience' (invading the floor of the House of Commons). Cobden-Sanderson's personal outrage, to say nothing of the outrage perpetrated on his wife, received full support in Shaw's heavily sarcastic yet deeply felt remarks.

Charles Bradlaugh (1833–91) was a republican and social reformer famous for having at one time faced trial over printing a pamphlet on birth control. He successfully defended the charge and thus cleared the way for contraception to be freely advertised.

WOMAN SUFFRAGE.

Sir, – This is a terrible moment in our national life. We are not often thoroughly frightened. When England trembles the world knows that a great peril overshadows our island. It is not the first time that we have faced dangers that have made even our gayest and bravest clench their teeth and hold their breath. We watched the Armada creeping slowly up the Channel. We wiped our brow when chance revealed the treason of Guy Fawkes. We are listening even now for the bugle of the German invader, and scanning the waves we rule for the periscope of the French submarine. But until now we have faced our fate like men, with our Parliament unshaken in our midst, grandly calm as the Roman senators who sat like statues when Brennus and his barbarians charged bloodstained into their hall. When Charles Bradlaugh, the most muscular man in England, dashed into the House of Commons to claim a seat in that august Assembly the police carried him, titanically struggling, down the stairs, deposited him in the yard with a shattered fountain pen, and disdainfully set him free to do his worst. It was but the other day that a desperado arose in the Strangers' Gallery of the House of Commons and burst into disorderly eloquence. Without a moment's hesitation the dauntless attendants hurled themselves upon him, and extracted him from our Legislature. He was not haled before the magistrate; he was not imprisoned; no man deigned to ask securities for his good behaviour; the British lion scorned protection against so puny an antagonist.

But the strongest nerves give way at last. The warriors of Philip were, when all is said, only men. German soldiers, French bluejackets, Guy Fawkes, Bradlaugh, and the stranger in the gallery, bold and dangerous as they were, were no females. The peril to-day wears a darker, deadlier aspect. Ten women, ten petticoated, long-stockinged, corseted females have hurled themselves on the British Houses of Parliament. Desperate measures are necessary. I have a right to speak in this matter, because it was in my play *Man and Superman* that my sex were first warned of woman's terrible strength and man's miserable weakness.

It is a striking confirmation of the correctness of my views that the measures which have always been deemed sufficient to protect the House of Commons against men are not to be trusted against women. Take, for example, the daughters of Richard Cobden, long known to everybody worth knowing in London as among the most charming and interesting women of our day. One of them – one only – and she the slightest and rosiest of the family – did what the herculean Charles Bradlaugh did. To the immortal glory of our Metropolitan Police they did not blench. They carried the lady out even as they carried Bradlaugh. But they did not dare to leave her at large as they left him. They held on to her like grim death until they had her safe under bolt and bar, until they had stripped her to see that she had no weapons concealed, until a temperate diet of bread and cocoa should have abated her perilous forces. She and the rest of the terrible ten.

For the moment we have time to breathe. But has the Government considered the fact that owing to the imperfections of our law these ladies will be at large again before many weeks are passed? I ask, in the name of the public, whether proper precautions have been taken. It is not enough for Mr. Herbert Gladstone, Mr. Haldane, Mr. Asquith, and Sir Henry Campbell-Bannerman to sit there pale and determined, with drawn lips and folded arms, helplessly awaiting a renewal of the assault – an assault the consequences of which no man can foresee. It is their duty without a moment's delay to quadruple the police staff inside the Houses of Parliament. Westminster and Vauxhall bridges should be strongly held by the Guards. If necessary, special constables should be enrolled. I am no coward; but I do not want to see a repetition of the folly that found us unprepared in 1899.

I submit, however, that if these precautions are taken we might, perhaps, venture to let Mrs. Cobden-Sanderson and her friends out. As a taxpayer, I object to having to pay for her bread and cocoa when her husband is, not only ready, but apparently even anxious to provide a more generous diet at home. After all, if Mr. Cobden-Sanderson is not afraid, surely, the rest us may pluck up a little. We owe something to Mr. Cobden-Sanderson, as one of our most distinguished artist craftsmen and as a most munificent contributor in crises where public interests have been at stake. If Mrs. Cobden-Sanderson must remain a prisoner whilst the Home Secretary is too paralysed with terror to make that stroke of the pen for which every person in the three kingdoms is looking to him, why on earth cannot she be imprisoned in her own house? We should still look ridiculous, but at least the lady would not be a martyr. I suppose nobody in the world really wishes to see one of the nicest women in England suffering from the coarsest indignity and the most injurious form of ill-treatment that the law could inflict on a pickpocket. It gives us an air of having lost our tempers and made fools of ourselves, and of being incapable of acting generously now that we have had time to come to our senses. Surely, there can be no two opinions among sane people as to what we ought to do.

Will not the Home Secretary rescue us from a ridiculous, an intolerable, and incidentally a revoltingly spiteful and unmanly situation?

Yours truly,
G. BERNARD SHAW.

On 14 November, H.G. Wells wrote to *The Times* to express his displeasure over the Book Club, claiming that they had misquoted him. He also said that his good friend Shaw was ignoring the fact that some of his books (primarily *Kipps*) were being 'boycotted' to force the price down. Mrs Humphrey Ward (1851–1920) was a famous novelist who also led the anti-suffrage league.

~ *1906 November 17* ~

PUBLISHERS AND THE PUBLIC.

Sir, – My friend Mr. H.G. Wells has given you his opinion of your Book Club management in a very pointed manner. What the public now wants from Mr. Wells is his opinion of the Publisher's Association. He says you are greedy for gain and unscrupulous in method. To Mr. Wells and myself as Socialists that is the general character of competitive private enterprise – nay, more, its compulsory character. But the point at issue at present is not between capitalism and Socialism – not between *The Times* Book Club and a public department of literature with Mr. Wells as its president with a seat in the Cabinet, and Mr. Moberly Bell as its permanent chief of staff (severely lectured all day by the Minister), but between *The Times* Book Club and the Publishers Association.

Now the Socialist or Ruskinian criticism of competitive capitalism may be a very good stick to beat *The Times* with; but every whack of it hits the publishers just as hard as it his *The Times*. It is true that the spread of literature can be effected by *The Times* Book Club only as an incident of profit making. But that is true of Macmillans also. It is true of all science, art, and industry under our competitive system. There is no other way in which either *The Times* or Macmillans, or Mr. Wells, or myself, can undertake the commercial production and distribution of books or anything else. We have, as a nation, rightly or wrongly, adopted money gain as the incentive, and competition as the regulator, of production and distribution; and for Mr. Wells to call *The Times* greedy and unscrupulous is as little to the point as if *The Times* were to call Mr. Wells a monopolist and a thief because he lives partly by copyrights and partly on dividends unearned by his own labour. Such recriminations are not to the point; they are really criticisms of Adam Smith, not of Mr. Wells and Mr. Moberly Bell. It is really not fair to attack the poor defenceless *Times* with Socialistic arguments, because, not being a Socialist paper, it cannot hit back again.

My own concern in the affair is that of an author who sees many of his fellow-authors being duped by an interested trade agitation into supporting a trumped-up moral case against *The Times* in the mistaken interests of the publishers. Englishmen have a natural facility for virtuous indignation; they think it becomes them. They love teaching one another manners and morals. The temptation to lecture *The Times* is great. I like doing it myself when my business interests are not concerned. But I will not have my moral fervour exploited by the publishers in the interests of the booksellers and against the interests of the authors. What does Mr. Wells complain of? That *The Times* bought as small a number of copies of 'Kipps' as it dared. In other words, that *The Times* bought exactly as any bookseller would have bought, except that the number reached by the bookseller on this principle is often zero, whereas the number required by *The Times* Book Club can hardly be less than two figures. I dare say the Club buys as few of my own books as it dares; and I deplore this sordid subjection of first-class literature to mere pecuniary considerations on its part; but for the life of me I cannot see how I should gain by preventing it from buying any at all.

As to the boycott of 'Kipps,' what it comes to is this. *The Times*, having a certain power of pushing a book by advertising – whether in its daily columns or in its library lists does not matter – refuses to push unless it is paid. No doubt this conduct is as mercenary as that of a baker who refuses to give the unemployed loaves unless they pay him, or that of Mr. Wells in refusing to let us read his message as the 'The Future of America' unless we pay him half a guinea. But *The Times* at least offered its services at a price. Messrs. Macmillan did not think them worth the price. Possibly they were right; in Mr. Wells's case, for instance, no special advertisement is needed, and any attempt to suppress his books would recoil on the head of the library which attempted to ignore him. But if this is to called a boycott, then every man who withholds his wares or his services until he gets his price is a boycotter. If Messrs. Macmillan have lost by refusing *The Times* terms, then they made a business mistake in not accepting them. If they did not lose, then they have nothing to complain of. Messrs. Macmillan have often enough refused to publish books unless the author signed agreements far more onerous than the terms *The Times* Book Club have sought to impose on them. Messrs. Macmillan are parties, I presume, to the monstrous draft agreements drawn up by the Publishers' Association for the bondage and spoliation of authors – agreements which have been repeatedly pilloried in the journal of the Society of Authors. But sensible authors do not call that boycotting. They simply refuse to sign the agreements, and they go to less exacting publishers. Mr. Wells must know that Messrs. Macmillan are as keen men of business as any in London, and in their ordinary course render no service to literature or to authors without getting the full value of it. I do not blame them; I should not recommend any author to deal with them if they were sentimentalists trading with moral claptraps instead of men of business minding their business and expecting the author to mind his. Let them by all means refuse *The Times* terms, and let *The Times* refuse their terms according to their respective judgments in the trade battle now waging between them. But, in the name of common sense, let us have no more moral attitudes and attempts to persuade the public that the publishers are a body of high-minded patrons of literature, organizing the book supply *en grands seigneurs* for the benefit of authors, whilst *The Times* represents a gang of vulgar tradesmen employing Yankee methods for the hideous and unheard-of purpose of making money.

As to all this pious horror about throwing new books at scrap prices on the market, pray how many books do we see every year produced by publishers who, too languid to sustain their interest in them, too poor to advertise them, 'remainder' them at a few pence a copy, and leave the author penniless or out of pocket whilst the bookseller sells off the stock with a very fair profit at a large reduction on the published price?

Can folly go further than that of the authors who have nothing to say about this abuse, but who shriek at *The Times* when it, too, remainders at full price?

My friend Mr. Maurice Hewlett is quite right in his discovery that every book sold means a customer lost. The man who buys 'Richard Yea and Nay' enjoys a rare treat; but he is struck off the list of possible purchasers for ever. That is the tragedy of trade. The butcher who sells you a chop knows that it will destroy the hunger upon which his livelihood depends. Possibly the logical way of trading is never to sell anything at all. Many publishers act on it. From this point of view everybody who sells a book inflicts an injury on the author. Having pushed the argument home, I leave it to speak for itself.

I quite agree with Mrs. Humphrey Ward that there is no objection whatever to a time-limit, or, indeed, to any other condition that the owner of a copyright chooses to impose. But I object to a cast-iron time-limit for all books indiscriminately-imposed without consulting the authors. Further, there should be one time-limit for the distributor and another for the publisher. For the publisher I invariably insist on an eternity-limit – that is, I do not allow him to remainder me at any time or on any terms. For the distributor, including *The Times* Book Club, my time-limit is ten seconds. And I strongly advise my fellow authors to follow my practice on both points.

Yours truly,
G. BERNARD SHAW.

*The only question at issue between *The Times* and the Publishers is as to whether the Book Club shall or shall not be allowed to sell second hand net books before they are six months old. *The Times* Book Club maintains its right to sell bona fide second hand books when it likes and at what price it likes. The Publishers try to prohibit this, and to enforce their prohibition by charging higher prices to *The Times* than to other purchasers and by withdrawing their advertisements from *The Times*. (Italicised editorial note by the editor of *The Times*.)

The correspondence on the Book Club grew in intensity. The Society of Authors was set up in 1884 'to protect the rights and further the interests of authors'. Sir Sidney Lee (1859–1926) was a member of the editorial staff of the *Dictionary of National Biography* and himself a noted author and biographer. Bram Stoker was a novelist (*Dracula*) and a secretary to Henry Irving, Morley Roberts a well-known actor, Comyns Carr a dramatist. 'Khaki elections' were any elections influenced by wartime activities.

~ 1907 March 25 ~

THE SOCIETY OF AUTHORS.

Sir, – The discussion has taken such an alarming turn since the meeting of the Society of Authors, that I ask you to allow me to intervene once more. Unless 'An Author of Eighteen Years' Standing' and Mr. Sidney Lee and the Manager of *The Times* Book Club firmly grasp the fact that their opponents in the Society of Authors are not a gang of intriguers in the pay of the publishers, but a body of high-minded and honest gentlemen who on this particular subject have been hypnotized into acute Tempophobia, they will do nothing but mischief. Mr. Sidney Lee must have noticed that most of the authors who spoke against him at the meeting were as mad as hatters on the subject. Take the case of Mr. Bram Stoker. His publisher has assured us that his '*Reminiscences of Sir Henry Irving*' had not done any the worse for his refusal to sell it to *The Times* Book Club, a statement which no sane person could possibly have believed, though it was no doubt made in all the pathetic good faith of monomania on the war path. Mr. Stoker gave away his publisher by avowing that he had suffered; but he declared with tears in his voice that he was proud of his martyrdom, and implied that he would willingly go to the stake with Mr. Heinemann in so good a cause as the destruction of *The Times*. Mr. Morley Roberts, ordinarily a collected and even sceptical observer, poured forth such a hysterical profession of affectionate devotion to his publisher, and indeed to all publishers, as has never before been heard from the lips of an author. Mr. Comyns Carr, his visage glowing with the fanaticism of a Crusader, called on the meeting to remember that a vote for Mr. Sidney Lee meant a vote for *The Times*. Not, please observe, for *The Times* Book Club, but for *The Times*. Not since the khaki elections has there been such a mafficking instinct of destruction in an electorate. *The Times* must be destroyed at all hazards if literature is to be preserved, if life and honour are to be reconciled. Mr. Zangwill, who came down to vote for Mr. Lee, finally yielded to the passion of the moment, and recanted in a series of demented interruptions, calling on the name of Mr. George Meredith, and repudiating with horror the ignoble suggestion that the business of the society is to look after the financial interests of authors, and not to demolish the Bastille in Printing House Square. All pretence that the publishers were acting in our interests was dropped, and even cried shame upon: what carried the day was the passion for suffering like Mr. Stoker's, for devotion like Mr. Morley Roberts's, for sacrifice and self-immolation in the sacred cause of justice, honour, truth, freedom (set forth in the model agreements of the Publishers' Association) as against the coarse commercialism and indelicate advertising habits of *the* (I have forgotten the appropriate adjective, but it was used, I believe, by Cobden) *Times*. Finally our chairman, Sir Henry Bergne, found himself confronted by a body of raging lunatics who, in the proportion of about ten to seven, thirsted for the blood of an amazed minority which grouped itself for defence round Sir Alfred Lyall, Sir Martin Conway, Mr. Sidney Lee, and the vice chairman, looking into one another's eyes to ask whether they were awake or asleep.

I at once called on Sir Henry Bergne to count the meeting. It was, I confess it, the trick of a platform tactician; for I knew that he could not count it. When Vesuvius erupts, you cannot count the cinders. On trying myself to count Mr. Zangwill alone, I reckoned him as six the first time and, by a great effort at concentration, as only three the second. Sir Henry was undoubtedly right to give it up: his decision was substantially correct: the madmen were in a majority. There was no unfair intention in the matter: it was to the interest of the anti-*Times* party to be counted, and of the sane party to leave the result doubtful.

Under these circumstances, what is there to be gained by attempting to form a new society? The only result would be to disable the old one and destroy a stable, solvent, well established, solidly financed, and normally excellent society by two shattered and embittered fragments. Tempophobia will pass like other epidemics. The committee is not always mafficking against *The Times*: by far the greatest part of its activity consists in exposing or defeating in detail the unscrupulousness of the agreements foisted on authors by the members of that very Publishers' Association which it holds up as the disinterested champion of literature against *The Times*, and the first friend and final refuge of the struggling author.

This contradiction is too gross to last. My colleagues on the committee are honourable and scrupulous authors and gentlemen who are quite incapable of acting perfidiously. They have the countenance of authors so eminent and above suspicion of corrupt motives as Mr. Maurice Hewlett, Mr. H.G. Wells, and Mr. Rudyard Kipling. My own attitude is perhaps more irritating than conciliatory; for, do what I can, I fail to conceal my opinion that they are all babes and sucklings in the hands of the men of business who have organised this boycott. But in the long run the facts will be too much for them. There is no doubt now that the boycott is not meant to stop remaindering at low prices, since the publishers do it themselves and let Mudies do it, but simply a movement to ruin one particular establishment, *The Times* Book Club, which is a possible rival in the publishing business, and has introduced methods that compel a lazy elderly publisher to hustle instead of growing fat on high prices and small circulations while the impoverished authors are kept on their knees for advances, advances, advances. The energetic publishers will soon have had enough of this nonsense. In fact even now many of them are in the hue and cry against *The Times* solely because they, too, are slightly off their heads on the subject.

As to the government of the Society of Authors by the shareholders of the company, the members must be very helpless if they cannot get round that. The committee could not ignore any expression of opinion by the members. The members can call a meeting and recommend or censure anything they like. If their resolutions be ignored they can stop paying their subscriptions until they are satisfied. The society is absolutely dependent on the annual subscriptions. To assume that a merely formal capital of £60 can control an annual subscription list of between one and two thousand guineas is childish.

What is wanted is not a new society, but more activity in the old one, and patience until the epidemic is over. We need sane recruits, not angry fugitives. The absurd scene of Wednesday last would not bear repetition: the minority can easily make itself master of the situation without resorting to threats of secession, which is the one certainly disastrous course for all of us. Authors must learn, like other people, to face temporary reverses and turn defeats into victories. After all it is the Book Club that is suffering most from the boycott; and if its supporters in the society had been as active and clamorous during the last six months as its opponents, I should have been able to appeal to my colleagues with some evidence of support from the society instead of having an air, as I sometimes had, of being in a minority of one.

Yours truly,
G. BERNARD SHAW.
10, Adelphi Terrace, W.C.

No headline was given for the following letter but the topic is plain enough: Shaw is responding to his fellow author and associate in the Society of Authors, H.G. Wells, for typifying *The Times* Book Club as 'greedy for gain' and 'unscrupulous in method'. Here, although Shaw's disagreement with Wells was fundamental (and at this time the two had crossed swords in other fundamental ways, notably in the Fabian Society, where Wells had tried to initiate a 'revolution' and been put down by Shaw), his courtesy and humour are unfailing. One notes, as well, his adopting a capitalist stance, if only to point out the absurdity of adopting a socialist stance at hand. Adam Smith (1723–90) was the author of *An Inquiry into the Nature and Causes of the Wealth of Nations* (1776) and 'founder' of capitalism. Maurice Hewlett and Mrs Humphrey Ward were well-known novelists. Vedrenne-Barker produced two plays by Hewlett at the Court Theatre, dramatisations of novels by him.

~ *1907, September 23* ~

BOOKS AND THE PUBLIC.

Sir, The result of the experiment I tried with '*John Bull's Other Island*' ought to convince the most quixotic publisher of the folly of sacrificing himself to save the bookseller from your competition.

From the first I warned the publishers that they were being used by the booksellers and would be left in the lurch by them. When my publishers warned me that if I did not boycott you the booksellers would boycott me, I seized the opportunity to prove that the booksellers would do nothing of the sort. I challenged the boycott; I made my refusal to boycott you as public as possible by printing a special edition for you; and I had the booksellers informed of my intention. My publishers kept honourably to their agreement with the booksellers, and refused to touch your edition, thereby incurring a dead loss solely for the booksellers' sake. It was now the turn of the booksellers to stand by the publishers and refuse to handle a single copy of my work. Instead of which they of course jumped at the demand created by your advertisements, and the result was that, though you were by far my best individual customer, all the booksellers together only sold two copies to your one. This may seem a ridiculously poor result of their efforts, as they represent the whole trade as against your single bookshop; but it beats their own best previous record for similar books of mine. In fact, I should almost have suspected them of helping you to push it if it had been possible to imagine an English bookseller pushing anything, or indeed selling anything, except under strong protest. At all events, there has been no boycott of my book; and the sole sufferers in the transaction are the publishers.

I have made money by your enterprise; the booksellers have made money by it; I trust you yourself have not lost by it; but the publishers, though they have been saved from an absolute loss by selling, with the help of your advertisements, more copies than they usually sell of a new book by me in the same time, have refused to handle your order for 2,500 copies for the sake of the booksellers, only to find when it came to the point that the booksellers refused to boycott me for the sake of the publishers.

After all, the position of the booksellers is plausible enough. They say 'We have not sold any copies to *The Times* Book Club: therefore we have boycotted it. But we have not boycotted Bernard Shaw: why should we? The publishers have not boycotted him: they have published for him; so we are both in exactly the same position.' Which is true; but the upshot of it is that the publisher is to sacrifice his interest in a third of the sale for the sake of the bookseller's beautiful eyes; and the bookseller is to sacrifice nothing at all for the publisher. And the object of the publishers' sacrifice is not attained. *The Times* Book Club gets the books it ordered with its own imprint on them, and has the satisfaction of knowing that its order has not benefited its assailant the publisher. The author also gains by getting for himself the publishers' profit on the transaction. I repeat, the author gains; the Book Club gains; the bookseller gains; and the publisher loses without achieving the end for which he faced the loss.

But this does not prove that the bookseller is a good man of business, though it does prove that he is not so quixotic as the publisher. For – let the authors note – if I had been in the power of the publishers, they would have sacrificed me as well as themselves; the book would have lost the advertisement it got from *The Times* Book Club; and the booksellers would have lost the profit on the sales that advertisement brought them. In the case of another book of mine which is unfortunately completely under the publishers' control that is just what has happened.

The reason which was most often given me for the boycott by the booksellers which was to have taught me a lesson, and the collapse of which has, I hope, taught our publishers a lesson, was that booksellers would not stock a book at the risk of presently seeing the price reduced to a trifle by *The Times* Book Club. I replied that, as to the vast majority of booksellers, it would not matter, as they never stocked books at all, but, when asked for them by resolute customers, first questioned the fact of the book's existence, and then reluctantly undertook to order it and invited the customer – not too hospitably – to call again next Friday week on the chance of the undertaking not having been forgotten. As to the small minority who are really worth considering, I replied that they order books at the risk of the publisher remaindering them, which is greater than the risk of *The Times* Book Club remaindering them, because the temptation to remainder is inverse to the opportunities for selling. So I went on with the experiment. The result is before the public, the Publishers' Association, and the Society of Authors. *The Times* Book Club is still ordering copies from me at full trade price, and its soiled second-hand copies are offered at a reduction of 7d. 3s. 11d. for a second-hand copy of a 4s. 6d. book – a positively extortionate price. If I wanted such a copy I should go to the ordinary second-hand bookseller, who would cut that price without hesitation, unrebuked by the leaders of the conspiracy against the Club. The high price of your Class B copies is not, I hope, supposed to be the result of any restriction imposed by me. I have adhered to my original 'ten seconds time limit'; and *The Times* Book Club is free to buy a million copies from me and sell them next day for a halfpenny apiece, or give them away in Oxford Street if it likes. The publishers are convinced that by doing so it could hugely increase the profits of *The Times* newspaper. I do not see how; but it is welcome to try, as far as I am concerned. I will even supply the million at a considerable discount.

However, it must be understood that the maintenance of the price of '*John Bull's Other Island*' is due solely to the fact that it is worth its price in the market. I could easily have published it at 30s. with the certainty that *The Times* Book Club and the other libraries would have had to buy copies for the use of their subscribers at that price. But the sale of single copies to private purchasers would have been practically negligible; and when I had compelled the libraries to stand and deliver, and the time came for them to clear their shelves, they would have either sold second-hand at the present price or else, if barred by a time limit, sold them for a few pence to a regular second-hand bookseller with a rummage basket and a choice collection of torn sheet music. The present 'book war' began over a life of Lord Randolph Churchill, which was published at a standard library price. This price had to go down with a run when the library harvest was over and the librarians had to clear out by selling to individual customers. My book is nominally one of the usual 8s. novel type; but a publisher would have either made at least five separate books of its three plays and two long prefaces or else have priced it at anything from 12s. net to 30s. Now I am sufficiently acquainted with the distribution of income in this country to know that quantity as well as quality has to be considered by most bookbuyers. An expenditure of 4s. 6d. by the father of a family on a piece of *belles lettres* would be an impossible extravagance if it had to be repeated too often. Books must last a reasonable time as well as boots. I do not regard the buyers of my book as the devotees of an eminent author; I regard them as customers who buy family reading from me, and are very particular as to the number of days my four sixpenn'orth will last them. The success of my experiment, therefore, gives no countenance whatever to the notion that either *The Times* Book Club or the publishers or any one else can find a market for a book at higher than market prices.

It now remains for the united publishers and booksellers to make a signal example of me by boycotting me and all my works. They can do this if they are really in earnest and really united; and the inevitable effect will be first to force me either to place you at their mercy, by joining their boycott, or else to place them at yours by asking you to act both as my publisher and wholesale bookseller, and then to bring into the field a new set of publishers who will throw over the petty bookselling trade as hopeless, and send their travellers to *The Times* Book Club and to the big general distributors like Whiteley, Shoolbred, Gamage, &c., for large orders and no time limits. Even at that I believe the booksellers would thrive better on the mere overflow and backwash of such a system than they do now on their foolish little attempts to restrict a trade which they cannot handle and to stop steamrollers with straws; but I dare say it will take them longer to grasp the new conditions than it has taken me.

Meanwhile, I am perfectly comfortable, and greatly obliged to you.

Yours faithfully,
G. BERNARD SHAW.
Llanbedr, Merioneth.

No more was done at the Book Club for 'John Bull's Other Island' than has been done for hundreds of other books. As in the case of most works expected to arouse exceptional interest, a circular was issued to subscribers reporting its publication and offering to take orders. As regards second-hand sales, copies in Class B were exhibited in the windows and on the counters of the Book Club side by side with new copies, without affecting in any manner the sales of new copies. (Tailnote by *The Times*.)

Shaw next takes up a discussion that had been going on in the columns of *The Times* for some months, begun by Sir Henry Cotton, a retired Indian government official who attacked the practice of polygamy by a certain Hindu sect – in letters to *The Times* on the 1st, 2nd and 3rd of October. Shaw enters the debate to present the 'common sense' view. The letter is indicative of his range of interests and of his ability to present a unified argument that takes in the question of Kulin polygamy, then widens to include eugenics and 'to cap it', 'Clapham.' He would soon write a play on the topic aired here: *Getting Married* (1908). Sir George Birdwood (1834–1917) was Professor and Registrar at Bombay University. Sir Henry Prinsep was an Indian civil servant.

$\sim$ *1907 October 5* $\sim$

KULIN POLYGAMY.

Sir, – Will you allow me, as a subject of the British Empire, to join Sir George Birdwood in his protest against the gross insularity with which the subject of Kulin polygamy has been discussed in your columns since Sir Henry Cotton, by putting his denial of its existence in the form of a defence of Indian morality, assumed that the test of morality is simply conformity to English custom? In this all your correspondents except Sir George have followed him, the only difference being that his intentions were civil, and theirs openly offensive To an Indian that can hardly weigh as a difference at all. If (to illustrate) an Indian paper were to publish a controversy between two Bengalis, one holding up the Archbishop of Canterbury to the execration of all pious Hindus as a Christian, and the other defending him as a man of far too high character to be tainted with the Christian superstition, the Archbishop would hardly feel much more obliged to his defender than to his assailant.

If the Empire is to be held together by anything better than armed force – and we have neither energy nor money enough to spare from our own affairs for that – we shall have to make up our minds to bring the institutions and social experiments of our fellow-subjects to a very much higher test than their conformity to the customs of Clapham. It is true that mere toleration for its own sake is out of the question: we are not going to tolerate suttee or human sacrifice on any terms from anybody, if we can help it. We are far too tolerant as it is, if not of other people's abominations and superstitions, at all events of our own, which are numerous and detestable enough in all conscience. But before we begin to hurl such epithets as 'revolting' and 'abhorrent' at any customs of our Indian fellow-subjects, we had better consider carefully why we are shocked by them. Very few of us are trained to distinguish between the shock of unfamiliarity and genuine ethical shock. Kulin polygamy is unfamiliar: therefore it shocks us, and causes gentlemen of ordinary good breeding to use abusive and intemperate language in your columns. Under these circumstances, I, having ascertained that my opinion in this matter is representative enough to be of some importance, am emboldened to say that the institution of Kulin polygamy, as described by your correspondents, does not seem to me on the face of it an unreasonable one. Let me compare it with our own marriage customs. We are told first that the Bengalis do not marry out of their caste. To them, therefore, the promiscuity which we profess must be 'revolting' and 'abhorrent'; but we have the ready and obvious defence that our promiscuity is only professed and not real, as our Deputy-Lieutenant class and our commercial traveller class, for instance, do not intermarry. Further, the Bengalis hold that it is part of the general purpose of things that women should bear children, and that childlessness is a misfortune and even a disgrace. It will not be disputed, I think, that this, under the surface, is as much an occidental as an oriental view. Again, the Bengalis attach great importance to their children being well-bred. So do we. On all these points the only difference between India and England is that England holds her beliefs more loosely, less religiously, less thoughtfully, and is less disposed to let them stand in the way of pecuniary gain and social position.

How then do the parents of an English family, of the class corresponding to the Indian Brahman class, secure well-bred grand-children for themselves and also for their nation? They use their social opportunities to put their daughters promiscuously in the way of young men of their own caste, in the hope that a marriage with someone or other will be the result. Frequently it is not the result: the daughter becomes an old maid, one of the wasted mothers of a nation, which, as Mr. Sidney Webb and Professor Karl Pearson have warned us, is perishing for want of well-bred children. Even when chance is favourable, and the daughter finds a husband, she often refuses to become a mother because her religious and social training has taught her to regard motherhood as a department of original sin, and to glory, not in the possession of children, but of a husband; so that the childless woman with a husband despises the mother who has no husband.

What does the Bengali father do under the same circumstances according to Sir Henry Prinsep? He selects a picked man – a Brahman – representing the highest degree of culture and character in his class; and he pays him £700 to enable his daughter to become the mother of a well-bred child.

Now this may strike the parochial Englishman as unusual or, as he would put it, 'revolting', 'abhorrent', and so forth; but it is certainly not unreasonable and not inhuman. Far from being obviously calculated to degrade the race, it is, on the face of it, aimed at improving it. Sir George Birdwood has just told us in your columns that the Kulin 'happen, for the most part, to be of fine physique'. Sir George has no doubt also noticed that the products of our system happen, for the most part, not to be of fine physique. Is it quite clear that this is mere happening? Is it not rather what one would expect under the circumstances? And is the practice of taking deliberate steps to produce and reproduce men of fine physique really revolting and abhorrent to our British conscience as distinguished from our British prejudice?

Let us, however, do justice to our system, indefensible as it is in many respects. It secures what most men want: that is, a sharing out of the women among the men so that every Jack shall have his Jill, and the able men and attractive women shall not accumulate partners and leave mediocrity unprovided. If this were the end of public policy in the matter, and if the race might safely take its chance of degeneracy provided monogamy, even on the hardest conditions, were maintained, there would be nothing more to be said. But as the whole Imperial problem before us is fundamentally nothing else than to produce more capable political units than our present system breeds – in short, to breed the Superman – this is not a time to rail at experiments made by people who are not under the harrow of our prejudices, or to persist in calling the customs founded on those prejudices by question begging names such as purity, chastity, propriety, and so forth, and to speak of a Brahman who is the father of a hundred children as a libertine with a hundred wives Any man of thirty may have a hundred children without having a wife at all and still be positively ascetic in his temperance compared with an average respectable and faithful British husband of the same age. And if the hundred children 'happen, for the most part, to be of fine physique', the nation will be more powerful and prosperous in the next generation than if these hundred children were replaced by a hundred others of indifferent physique, each having a different father, promiscuously picked up in a Clapham drawing-room.

A system which limits the fertility of its men of fine physique to the child-bearing capacity of one woman, and wastes the lives of thousands of first-rate maiden ladies in barrenness because they like to own their own houses and manage their own affairs without being saddled with a second-rate or tenth-rate man, must not take its own merits for granted. It may be the right system; it may be bound up with all that is best in our national life and fortunate in our national history; it may be all that our stupidest people unanimously claim for it. But then again it may not. The evidence on the other side is weighty; and the population question is pressing hard on us. The case must be argued, not assumed; and the final verdict will be that of history and not of our modern suburban villas with no nurseries.

Yours truly,
G. BERNARD SHAW.
10, Adelphi Terrace, W.C.

A Mr Harold Cox, a former member of the Fabian Society, had pointed out in a letter on 19 October that, at a recent lecture, reported in *The Times*, Shaw and Sidney Webb had quoted figures about London rents that were widely divergent. Shaw puts him right.

~ *1907, October 21* ~

SOCIALIST 'FACTS'.

Sir, – I am surprised that an old Socialist like Mr. Harold Cox should fail to recognize the familiar figures of 16 millions and 40 millions given by myself and Mr Sidney Webb last Thursday as the rent of London. Both figures, as I was careful to explain, are some years out of date and, consequently, a good deal under the mark; but there is no discrepancy between them. The 16 millions are that part of the 40 which may be called 'prairie value'. The 40 includes the value added in the quinquennial valuations for buildings. I spent much rhetoric in making this distinction clear to my audience, and if the reporters (who would probably like to tax the whole 40 millions to save their rates) suppressed the distinction, that is neither Mr. Webb's fault nor mine.

Yours truly,
G. BERNARD SHAW.
10, Adelphi Terrace, London, W.C.

A circular letter threatening death to vivisectors was printed by *The Times* as part of an article. Stephen Coleridge, one of the leaders of the anti-vivisection society, wrote a letter on 25 January denying any connection with this circular letter. A number of letters then appeared in *The Times*, some of them quite heated, both for and against vivisection. Some anti-vivisectors in their protest had asked that humans be substituted for animals in experiments; one at least had mooted that it might be appropriate to 'make earnest prayer that the Almighty will promptly remove all holders of licences to experiment on living animals'.

Shaw was a practising vegetarian almost his whole life and abhorred vivisection. He also believed in certain forms of healing which today are known under the umbrella heading of 'alternative medicine', and consulted their practitioners on occasion; but he did not openly encourage 'quackery'. If it is true to say that he appeared to enjoy a brush with the so-called orthodox medical authorities, we should – remember that he numbered among his friends several members of the profession, some quite eminent in their field. What he attacked was the 'closed shop' mentality: 'every profession is a conspiracy', he once piercingly observed. It is also pertinent to recall his famous remark to an enquirer who asked, 'Mr. Shaw, have we lost faith?' 'No, madam,' he replied, 'we have only transferred it from God to the General Medical Council.'

Of course, today, the wheel has turned again, and people could be said to be transferring their faith to alternative methods of healing as resistance grows towards the drug companies, with their enormous profits and narrow interests.

꧁ *1909, January 26* ꧂

ANTI-VIVISECTIONIST FANATICISM.

Sir, Surely the protests of the Anti-Vivisection Society in this matter are very unnecessary.

The genuine vivisectionists would be the last people in the world to protest against an experiment so interesting, so important, and so thoroughly scientific in method. It is true that it may cost one or two of them their lives; but what is a life or two when weighed in the balance against the extension of scientific knowledge, and the enormous national economy which will result if the experiment should happily succeed in proving that our vast military and naval expenditure is entirely unnecessary, and that the destruction of our country's enemies may in future be cheaply and comfortably conducted at home upon our knees? The suggestion by Mr. Sidney Trist, that instead of praying for the deaths of the vivisectors we should pray for their regeneration would break down in practice owing to the extreme difficulty of deciding whether the vivisector had been actually regenerated or not, whereas there can be no manner of doubt as to whether he is dead or alive. I confess I do not see how the vivisectors can object without a complete surrender of their position. The attitude taken by their champions is obviously purely sentimental.

Yours truly,
G. BERNARD SHAW.
10, Adelphi Terrace, London, W.C.

In January 1909 Keir Hardie (1856–1915), then leader of the Labour Party, delivered an address in which he stated that the increase in national income had not been shared with the working classes. W.H. Mallock, a member of the Anti-Socialist League, was the author of a number of papers attacking Socialism. He accused Hardie in a letter to *The Times* on 3 February of being ignorant of economics, because the increase in national income had been brought about by the initiative of employers and inventors. Shaw here comments on the exchange of correspondence, in so doing demonstrating his grasp of economics and his vision of socialism – and, not incidentally, his view of the 'gentleman' and the 'cad'. Sir Leo Chiozza-Money (1870–1944), an authority on finance, became a junior minister in Lloyd George's government. On 1 February he had replied to Mallock and quoted figures that supported Hardie.

~ *1909, February 5* ~

MR MALLOCK IDEALS.

Sir, – Mr. Mallock's controversy with Mr. Chiozza-Money over the figure of Mr. Keir Hardie may very well be left to the embarrassed silence in which good-natured people sit when a person of some distinction volunteers an absurd blunder as a contribution to a subject which he has not mastered. The notion that the people who are now spending in week-end hotels, in motor-cars, in Switzerland, the Riviera, and Algiers the remarkable increase in unearned income noted by Mr. Keir Hardie have ever invented anything, ever directed anything, ever even selected their own investments without the aid of a stockbroker or solicitor, ever as much as seen the industries from which their incomes are derived, betrays not only the most rustic ignorance of economic theory, but a practical ignorance of society so incredible in a writer of Mr. Mallock's position that I find it exceedingly difficult to persuade my fellow Socialists that he really believes what he teaches. They regard me as a cynic when I tell them that even the cleverest man will believe anything he wishes to believe, in spite of all the facts and all the text-books in the world.

However, that is not the point that moves me to utterance on this occasion. If Mr. Mallock does not know the difference between the rents of land and capital and the 'rent of ability' – if he is so ignorant of ordinary business and patent law as not to know that the cleverest inventor cannot possibly extract a farthing more from his invention than his stupidest competitor when it has been communized 14 years after its registration – he must not expect the Socialists to educate him. My quarrel with him is deeper than the technics of distribution. Mr. Mallock is preaching an ideal; and I want every gentleman in England to repudiate that ideal, whether he be Socialist, Individualist, Liberal, Free-Fooder, Tariff Reformer, or Home Ruler.

The ideal is, not that the greatest among you shall be servants of the rest, but that, whenever one of us discovers a means of increasing wealth and happiness steps should be taken to restrict the increase to the discoverer alone, leaving the rest of the community as poor as if the discovery had never been made. If Mr. Mallock does not mean this, he means nothing. If he does mean it, what does his University say to him? What does the Church say to him? What does every officer in the Army and Navy say to him? What does every civil servant say to him – every statesmen, every member of the humblest local authority, every professional man, every country gentleman, every man of honour, gentle or simple, who asks no more than a sufficient and dignified subsistence in return for the best service he is capable of giving to his country and to the world? This is not a question of the difference between the Socialist and the anti-Socialist; it is a question of the difference between the gentleman and the cad. Lord Lansdowne is not a Socialist, and Lord Charles Beresford is not Socialist; but Lord Lansdowne has not asked for the hundreds of millions which he saved Europe by making our treaty with Japan; and Lord Charles Beresford, if the German fleet attacked ours, would not refuse to conduct our naval defence unless the country were to be given to him as prize money when he had saved it. It is true that we have tradesmen – some of them in business on a very large scale both here and in America – impudent enough and base enough to demand for themselves every farthing that their business ability adds to the wealth of their country. If these canaille were surgeons with a monopoly of a capital operation, they would refuse to save a patient's life until they had extorted his entire fortune and a fee. If they were judges, they would sneer at a judge's modest £5,000 a year, and demand the total insurance value of the protection they afforded to society. If they were lifeboat coxswains or firemen, they would bargain for the kit of a drowning sailor or the nighty of a child in a burning house before they would throw a lifebuoy or mount a ladder. They are justly despised by men of Mr. Mallock's profession and education; and when Mr. Mallock challenges the right of our workmen to a share in the increase product of industry by asking whether their labour 'has become more productive in respect of the labourer's own exclusive operations,' he not only lays himself open to the obvious counter-question as to whether the 'exclusive operations' of our employers could produce anything more than the exclusive operations of our labourers, but, what is far more serious, he seems to be lending the credit of his reputation, his education, and the high social and intellectual prestige of his class to the most abandoned sort of blackguardism that is still outside the criminal law.

It is fortunate for us that few of our tradesmen are so vile or so silly as the commercial theory by which theorists attempt to justify them. The man who has 'made' £20,000 a year for himself knows very well that his success does not afford the smallest presumption that his services have been more important to society than those of a police constable with 24s. a week. He does not dream of posing as the superior of the captain of a ship with his modest income of three figures. Mr. Carnegie 'divides' up his surplus millions, and makes wildly Socialistic proposals, never for a moment suggesting that he is 50 times as clever as Mr. Mallock because he is 50 times as rich. I am not supposed to be an exceptionally modest man, but I did not advance the fact that I have made more money by a single play than Shakespeare did by all his plays put together as a simple proof that I am enormously superior to Shakespeare as a playwright. Our millionaires unload – awkwardly and unwisely sometimes, it is true, but still they unload – and do not talk nonsense about being 650 times as clever or as sober or as industrious as a dock-labourer because they have 650 times his income. The man who pretends that the distribution of income in this country reflects the distribution of ability or character is an ignoramus. The man who says that it could by any possible political device be made to do so is an unpractical visionary. But the man who says that it ought to do so is something worse than an ignoramus and more disastrous than a visionary: he is, in the profoundest Scriptural sense of the word, a fool.

In conclusion, may I confess that nothing is so terrifying to the Socialist to-day as the folly of his opponents. There is nothing to keep the inevitable advance steady, to force the rank and file to keep their best men forward. A paper called the Anti-Socialist is brought out with a flourish of trumpets. I open it, and find *merde de société* and a caricature, of myself by a French artist, who depicts me in a French frock-coat, a 'Grand Old Man' collar, and the countenance of Henri Rochefort. A Belgian navvy is labelled 'Ramsay Macdonald'; an American knockabout from the café chantant is carefully marked 'Keir Hardie'. Is it worth while to spend so much money to provide our Socialist debaters with footballs? If the Socialists did not know the difficulties of Socialism better than their opponents, and were not therefore far sterner Tories than the tariff reformers and far sounder

Liberals than the free-traders; if all decent men were not nine-tenths Socialists to begin with, whether they know it or not; if there were any possibility of controversy as to the fundamental proposition of Socialism that whoever does not by the work of his price repay the debt of his nurture and education, support himself in his working days, and provide for his retirement, inflicts on society precisely the same injury as a thief, then indeed the prospect would be black for civilization. As it is, I will continue to back the red flag against the black one; and with that I leave the Anti-Socialist League to sweep up the fragments of Mr. Mallock and produce their next champion.

Yours truly,
G. BERNARD SHAW.

Shaw, together with others, had long envisioned a National Theatre (whether Shakespearean or not) and campaigned tirelessly for it. (His one-act play *The Dark Lady of the Sonnets* (1910) was written to further the aims – of the campaign.) The success of the Vedrenne-Barker seasons at the Court Theatre convinced him that a National Theatre was not only attainable but a spiritual necessity: one notes the rhetorical force with which he emphasises this belief. Charles Frohman (1860–1915) was an American impresario who, encouraged by James Barrie (1860–1937), initiated a season of 'advanced' plays in repertory at the Duke of York's Theatre in London. The enterprise soon folded and Shaw's contribution, *Misalliance* (1910), was a box-office and critical failure. (Sir) Arthur Wing Pinero (1855–1934), Barrie, Granville Barker and John Galsworthy (1867–1933) were prominent playwrights who contributed plays to the Frohman enterprise. The Bancrofts, Squire (1841–1926) and his wife Marie Wilton (1839–1921), were highly regarded nineteenth-century actors and innovative and influential theatre managers. 'Tom' Robertson (1829–71) was a progressive nineteenth-century playwright.

~ *1909, May 10* ~

THE NATIONAL SHAKESPEARE THEATRE AND THE NEW REPERTORY THEATRE.

Sir, – The anarchist that is latent in every Englishman seems to have been roused by recent announcements to a hope that the new repertory theatres of Mr. Charles Frohman and of Mr. Herbert Trench may fulfil the objects of the National Shakespear Theatre and thereby relieve our consciences of the obligation, and our pockets of the drain, of subscribing to it. I have even been told that the fact that such ardent supporters of the National Theatre as Mr. J.M. Barrie, Mr. Granville Barker, Mr. Galsworthy, and myself have undertaken to cooperate with Mr. Frohman implies that we have abandoned the National Theatre and are converted to a belief in the sufficiency of private commercial enterprise.

It is hardly possible to repudiate this misconception too vehemently. Those who have fallen into it forget that the National Shakespeare Theatre is not yet built. Of the half million needed for its construction and endowment not more than one-sixth has yet been actually subscribed; and though there is now no reasonable doubt that the rest will follow, the most sanguine estimate of the date of the opening performance does not bring it within four years of the present moment. Now I presume nobody supposes that Mr. Barrie, Mr. Granville Barker, Mr. Galsworthy, and myself propose to go to sleep for that period. We flatter ourselves that by our former activity at the Court Theatre and elsewhere, we helped to make the National Theatre scheme credible and practicable by trying how near we could get to it in an ordinary privately owned theatre. We proved that most of the alleged impossibilities were by no means impossible. We proved that there was a real demand for uncommercial art in the theatre, a real sense of its enormous national importance, and plenty of material available. But it would never do to drop this work for four or five years. It must be carried on without a break until the National Theatre opens its doors. There is a gap of at least four or five years to be filled by private enterprise; and as this is precisely what Mr. Charles Frohman and Mr. Trench promise to do for us, we naturally welcome them and are ready to throw into their enterprises all the work that the National Theatre cannot yet offer us a stage for.

These interim schemes are not commercial speculations. Mr. Trench's does not pretend to be; but there is a prevalent impression that Mr. Charles Frohman is a hardheaded American man of business who would not look at anything that is not likely to pay. If Mr. Frohman were really that sort of man, I should not waste five minutes on his project. He is the most wildly romantic and adventurous person of my acquaintance. As Charles XII. became a famous soldier through his passion for putting himself in the way of being killed, so Mr. Charles Frohman has become a famous manager through his passion for putting himself in the way of being ruined. The repertory theatre will be one of his extravagances; and this is probably its attraction for him. It cannot under any circumstances be a commercial scheme. This statement requires a word of explanation, because it is known that the Court Theatre did for some years support its managers and paid its way on lines not unlike those laid down for the new schemes. But commercial soundness does not merely mean avoidance of bankruptcy. If the profits of repertory are much smaller and the work involved much harder than the profits and work of ordinary long run management, then a repertory theatre is not what Mr. Frohman calls a commercial proposition, even though it yield enough for plain living and high thinking. Mr. Frohman will run his repertory theatre as Messrs. Vedrenne and Barker ran theirs, with a constant sense that the profits can be largely increased and the work decreased at any moment by simply announcing that the most popular play in the repertory will be played night after night until its attraction is exhausted.

Besides, if the truth is to be told, Messrs. Vedrenne and Barker's success at the Court Theatre can be explained away, though perhaps the explanation might come more gracefully from some one else than myself. Just as the success of an earlier management at the same theatre depended on a single author, Mr. Pinero, and the success of the Bancrofts at the old Prince of Wales's Theatre depended on a single author, Robertson, so the success of the Vedrenne-Barker management also depended on a single author. Not that he was the only author who paid his way; a few notable successes were secured and reputations made by others, but there is no getting over the deplorable fact that the *Trojan Women of Euripides* in Professor Murray's translation (or rather resurrection), quite a wonder of beauty and grandeur, was performed eight times, whilst my hackneyed comedy *You Never Can Tell* was performed 149 times, a result flattering to me as an author but quite disgusting to me as a citizen.

Later on, when the experiment was pushed to its limits by transferring the enterprise to the central West End theatres, including the Savoy, the Queen's, and the Haymarket, it was found impossible to proceed with the repertory policy without an endowment; and though the actual loss would have seemed the merest fleabite to Mr. Frohman, the accounts were not closed without imposing on Mr. Barker a pecuniary sacrifice out of all proportion to his means and very effectually convincing the other parties concerned that they had spent as much money and work on the cause of dramatic art as could be reasonably expected from them in one lifetime.

But the profit to the public, to the theatre as an institution, to the culture of London has been worth, at the most modest estimate, five times the deficit; and if London had any corporate conscience or the nation any honesty in the matter of artistic services, the County Council and Mr. Lloyd George would dispute for precedence in making a grant to Mr. Vedrenne, Mr. Barker, and myself to repay us at least our out of Pocket expenses. As they are not likely to do anything of the sort, we ask the public to pay the debt by subscribing to the National Shakespear Theatre. When I contemplate the really ghastly waste of private and public money by millionaires and even thousandaires who in the name of charity and education pauperize their country by thoughtless almsgiving and demoralize it by indiscriminate book distribution, I ask myself what crimes these people have committed that they confine their conscience money so timidly to institutions that are recommended by the clergy. Why will they build an uncommercial cathedral to accommodate 50 churchgoers when 500,000 playgoers are left without an uncommercial theatre? The theatre is literally making the minds of our urban populations to day. It is a huge factory of sentiment, of character, of points of honour, of conceptions of conduct, of everything that finally determines the destiny of a nation. And yet it is openly said that the theatre is only a place of amusement. It is nothing of the kind; a theatre is a place of culture, a place where people learn how to think, act, and feel: more important than all the schools in Christendom. A healthy Englishman amuses himself in the field and in the society of his friends; the theatre can offer nothing in the way of amusement to compete with these except vice; and at that it can easily be beaten by places that are not theatres. Would any sane man call the National Gallery or the British Museum a place of amusement? It is true that these institutions are commercial failures, just as Westminster Abbey is a commercial failure. And I sincerely hope that the National Theatre will be an equally conspicuous and equally priceless commercial failure. It is with that view, in fact, that we are asking for an endowment of half a million for it. Who speaks first?

Yours truly,
G. BERNARD SHAW.
10, Adelphi Terrace, W.C.

The movement against dramatic censorship – as exercised in the person of the Examiner of Plays, a retired bank manager, G. A. Redford – had been gathering momentum since the turn of the century, particularly among *avant garde* playwrights, who felt themselves under threat by the Examiner's extreme conservatism, pointing to the works of Ibsen, Maeterlinck, Brieux, Housman and Shaw (*Mrs Warren's Profession*) – not to mention Sophocles's *Oedipus Tyrannus* – as having suffered at his hands. In 1906 another 'advanced' play, *The Breaking Point* by Edward Garnett, was refused a licence, to which Garnett responded with an angry broadside, 'A Letter to the Censor,' that revealed how high-handed and arbitrary Redford's actions had been. A year later, in 1907, Granville Barker's *Waste* was also banned. This was more fuel to the fire. Shaw was at the forefront of those who condemned the veto, peppering the press with sarcastic comments about the Examiner and extolling *Waste* as a triumph of modern dramaturgy. The issue became a general talking point, particularly after a letter of protest, signed by seventy-one playwrights (followed by a similar letter signed by seventy-two prominent public figures) was placed in *The Times* in October 1907 and February 1908. The abolition of the censorship was in the air and *The Times*, reading the mood aright, published two long articles (27 December 1907 and 2 January 1908) on the history and application of dramatic censorship. A deputation of playwrights (Shaw was not one of them) met the Home Secretary, Gladstone, in February 1908 to voice their grievance. Nothing came of this. The following month, Robert Vernon Harcourt introduced in the House of Commons a Bill designed to put an end to the censorship, following this up with repeated 'Questions' in the House. Prime Minister Asquith duly appointed a Joint Select Committee to look into the matter. (Harcourt was a friend of Shaw's and a one-time playwright whose *A Question of Age* had been produced by Vedrenne-Barker at the Court Theatre: it failed.) Shaw campaigned ceaselessly to gather support for the anti-censorship movement, while on the other side the anti-abolition lobby mustered its not negligible forces. The Joint Select Committee met from July to October 1909, gathering evidence from a wide spectrum of witnesses, and issued its report in November. It did not recommend significant changes to existing practice.

Shaw gave evidence but was met with a rebuff at his first session when his offer to present his monograph on the subject, written for the enlightenment of the Committee, was rejected. (He incorporated it later as 'The Rejected Statement' in his preface to *The Shewing-Up of Blanco Posnet.*) He also at this time submitted two plays to the Examiner, *Blanco Posnet* and *Press Cuttings,* both of which were refused a licence, *Blanco Posnet* for being 'blasphemous' and 'obscene,' *Press Cuttings* for representing prominent public personalities on stage.

This is the background to the ten letters on the dramatic censorship that follow.

〜

The 'public statement' to which Shaw refers appeared in several papers, not all of which, *The Times* included, published it in full; the 'prohibition of one of my plays' refers to *The Shewing-Up of Blanco Posnet.* Shaw makes a good deal of the 'Royal Connection' here, and continued to do so in muted form in subsequent letters, even after the noted jurist, Sir Harry Poland, had written to – *The Times* on June 3 and 5 correcting Shaw's attribution of the Examiner's authority to the King. (As Shaw should have known, and in spite of what he says here and in subsequent letters, this authority was vested in Parliament in terms of Walpole's Licensing Act of 1737, and Parliament had appointed the Lord Chamberlain (who appointed an Examiner of Plays) to do the job because it had been his traditional function to control stage presentations. Subsequent modifications of the Act, in 1843 for example, would confirm this delegation of authority.)

Shaw's comparison of Granville Barker's banned play *Waste* and Bernard Fagan's *The Earth* touches on another grievance: that essentially licentious plays were often given licences, while a 'sternly conventional' play like *Waste* was suppressed. His remark that 'suffering in silence does not agree with my temperament' may be noted. This would be fully borne out in the correspondence that ensued.

Dramatic Censorship.

Sir, Mr. Harcourt's question in the House of Commons, and the Premier's very gratifying answer thereto, will, I hope, help to clear up a much misunderstood constitutional position. I have just had occasion to make a public statement concerning the prohibition of one of my own plays.

It was necessary for me to be scrupulously correct in defining the authority with which I was in conflict. As that authority happened to be the King, several journalists proceeded to lecture me severely evidently believing that I had committed a gross solecism by mentioning the King instead of mentioning the Minister representing the Government and responsible to the House of Commons. They also expressed a sense of wounded chivalry at the spectacle of a defenceless monarch attacked by an all powerful and merciless playwright. A certain importance was given to all this nonsense by the fact that *The Times*, though its traditions place it beyond all suspicion of being a respecter of persons in public questions, showed some doubt as to the constitutional position by omitting all references to it from my statements.

I therefore wish to point out that when we speak of Mr. Redford as the Censor, and the Lord Chamberlain's function as a censorship, we are taking a liberty with these gentlemen which can only be excused by its convenience for purposes of discussion. To hold them responsible for the control of the theatres is really as great a solecism as it would be to hold the King responsible for the Budget. They act simply as officers of the King's Household. It happens that in the days of Shakespear and his predecessors players could escape being classed as rogues and vagabonds only by procuring permission to attach themselves to the household of some nobleman or of the reigning monarch. Thus a tradition grew up that this was the natural English way to keep actors and theatres and authors in order; and the only effect of legislation has been to attach all the theatres and all the actors and all the authors to the King's Household, to be controlled by him absolutely like the rest of his houses and servants. The officials appointed to carry out this control are not responsible to Parliament. No really direct question as to their proceedings can be asked in Parliament. Mr. Harcourt was muzzled until he hit on the expedient of asking a question about foreign censorships. A vote to reduce their salaries could only take the form of a proposal to cut down the King's retinue. An attempt on the part of any playwright to treat a dispute over the licensing of a play as a matter between himself and the Lord Chamberlain would be as incorrect as an attempt to treat a dinner invitation as a matter between the guest and the butler.

The position is, of course, obsolete and unworkable; but it is not unreal, as I know to my heavy cost. If a cotton manufacturer or an ironmaster had been injured in his business, both as to money and reputation, as I have been by it, legislation would have been promised within twenty-four hours to remedy the matter They tell me that the King cannot defend himself. I do not know that he has any cause to; what I do know is that I cannot defend myself. When a soap manufacturer is accused of giving short measure he is able to bring his accuser before a jury and recover damages that are not only adequate but exemplary. When a precisely analogous injury is done to me, I have no remedy except to state my grievance; and because this grievance happens to lie technically against the King I am told that it would be in better taste for me to suffer in silence. I can only reply that suffering in silence does not agree with my temperament.

I now wish to call attention to a very remarkable example of the way in which every attempt made by the Lord Chamberlain to exercise the functions of Censor recoils on the King's Household in a cloud of discredit and suspicion. At this moment the play which is attracting most attention in London as an essay in serious drama is *The Earth*, by Mr. Bernard Fagan, at Miss Lena Ashwell's Kingsway Theatre. Last night I was one of an eager crowd of people who witnessed this play. I found that its subject is the subject of Mr. Granville Barker's prohibited play *Waste*. It is the story of a Cabinet Minister who, on the eve of crowning his Parliamentary career by the introduction of a great Bill, is discovered to have been engaged in an intrigue with a married woman, So far the resemblance to Mr. Granville Barker's forbidden theme is complete; it even goes so far in detail that the injured husband is an Irish country gentleman. As far as the morality or immorality of the situation goes, the two plays are identical. But there are differences. In Mr. Barker's play the guilty lady is presented as a person of light and unworthy character, and the retribution that overtakes the Cabinet Minister is his utter political ruin, followed by suicide. In Mr. Fagan's play the lady is successfully thrown on the sympathy and admiration of the audience as a noblehearted and devoted woman; the adulterous Minister recovers his position and brings in his Bill triumphantly without a stain on his character; and the man who has effected the exposure is forced to deny his own words (which are perfectly true), and is held up to contempt and execration as a scotched viper who has attempted to poison with his venom an exquisite and poetic human relationship. This highly unconventional version has been licensed without a word of demur, whilst Mr. Granville Barker's sternly conventional one has been suppressed; and as the suppression is widely advertised and the play remains buried, the public is left to infer that Mr. Granville Barker has committed the disgraceful act of writing an improper play.

But this is not all. If the case were merely one of a severely ethical play being suppressed whilst a romantic one was licensed, it would not be worth mentioning, as these occurrences are so common as to have become almost a matter of course. But in this case the anomaly is so glaring that it is impossible not to seek for some explanation; and unfortunately that explanation is only too easily found. Mr. Bernard Fagan's play is something more than a love story with a very unconventional moral. It is a furious attack on the halfpenny daily newspaper, made strongly personal by presenting, as the villain of the piece, the owner of several such newspapers. Now if a play with a moral so conventional that the Archbishop of Canterbury might father it without discredit is prohibited, and precisely the same story with the moral turned in the opposite direction, and adultery left triumphant at the fall of the curtain, is licensed by the same official, is it possible to avoid the suspicion that these permissions and prohibitions, avowedly based on the conventions of religion and morality, are really based on private prejudices and political partialities which should have no place whatever in the Censorship of the stage? Here, at all events, is a straight case. Whoever prohibited *Waste* and licensed *The Earth*, was evidently some one who may have loved morality much, but who certainly hated the halfpenny Press more. And we are all forced by the existing ridiculous state of affairs to assume technically that this prejudiced person is no other than the King. If that is not enough to convince all the authorities concerned, Royal, Ministerial, journalistic, and common, that the situation is altogether intolerable, nothing is.

Yours truly,
G. BERNARD SHAW.
10, Adelphi Terrace, W.C.

Shaw responds below to Sir Harry Poland's letter of 'correction' regarding the Examiner's authority. Shaw had to have the last word and, of course, hammer the central theme of his campaign, which was that the Examiner stood outside the due process of law and could with impunity 'destroy . . . another man's moral reputation and ruin him financially'.

~ *1909, June 4* ~

DRAMATIC CENSORDHIP.

Sir, Sir Harry Poland's opinion that the Lord Chamberlain is a private and irresponsible monopolist to whom Parliament, in a fit of insanity, gave despotic powers over the theatre, including the levy of taxes, is, I hope, as sound as might be expected from so eminent a lawyer.

Will he now add to my obligation to him by telling me how a certain Mr. George Alexander Redford, who describes himself as 'the King's Reader of Plays', levies a play tax of two guineas (or one guinea for a one-act play), and carries on his operations at St. James's Palace, can be prevented from compromising the Crown in this manner, and from causing the public to believe that his conviction that I am a blackguard and a blasphemer is the King's conviction?

May I also take it that my private opinion of the Lord Chamberlain's qualifications for his theatrical function is not, as I have hitherto supposed, a horrifying extremity of high treason and *lèse majesté*, but simply the natural impression that his proceedings would leave on any intelligent citizen?

Yours truly,
G. BERNARD SHAW.

~ *1909, June 7* ~

DRAMATIC CENSORSHIP.

Sir, – I owe Mr Redford an apology for having said that he described himself as King's Reader of Plays. On consulting the documents in my possession I find that he describes himself as 'Examiner of Plays', 'Examiner of all Theatrical Entertainments', 'Examiner of Plays, &c.', and 'Examiner of Stage Plays'.

In '*Whitaker's Almanack*' he is not to be found under the heading Civil Service. He is in the King's Household as Examiner of Plays, in the same list with, for example, Pages of the Presence. Am I to understand from his letter that he is not the King's Examiner of Plays, and that the Pages of the Presence are not the King's Pages, but Pages Positive, owing allegiance to nobody? Suppose I say that Mr. Redford has nothing to do with the King, what will Mr. Redford say and what will the King say? Take away from Mr. Redford the authority and dignity of the King, and what becomes of his pretension to sit in judgment on Shelley, on Ibsen, on Tolstoy, and on Brieux, or even on me? If he is not the King's Examiner of Plays, then who is he? What is he? Why should anybody pay special attention to his opinion on any question of morals, religion, philosophy, or politics in dramatic literature? Without his place of King's Examiner of Plays, he would, if he pretended to greater authority in these matters than the acknowledged masters of them, escape being known as the most presumptuous of nobodies only by not being known at all. As it is, he is one of the most important men in England, because the King has placed him in that position and maintains him in it.

To Sir Harry Poland I protest that I know all about that Act of 1843. But it does not constitute Mr. Redford Examiner of Plays to the Cabinet. Whose Examiner of Plays is he? His salary is paid under the Civil List Act of 1901. Does Sir Harry Poland regard that Act and the Succession Act 12 and 13 William III. as proving that Mr. Asquith won the Derby? That is not at all a bigger jump in logic than Sir Harry's to the conclusion that the Act of 1843 makes Lord Althorp independent of the King and responsible to Parliament.

Let us get back to common sense and hard fact, Mr. Redford is the King's Examiner of Plays just as much as the Dean of Windsor is the King's Chaplain, Sir Frederick Treves the King's Surgeon, or Sir Arthur Davidson the King's Equerry; and he would be the last man living to even seem to repudiate that honour except in the throes of a devoted attempt to shield his Sovereign from the public suspicion of the wisdom of his decision concerning poor Blanco Posnet. Parliament can control him only in the sense that Parliament can starve the King out by repealing the Civil List Act, which I understand it is not willing to do for the sake of getting Blanco licensed. The real control over Mr. Redford is the control of the King, because the King can dismiss him at pleasure, which no one else can. The Act of 1843 gave powers to the Lord Chamberlain solely because the Lord Chamberlain was responsible to the King. I repeat that had the Lord Chamberlain been a private, uncontrolled, irresponsible person, the Act would have been an act of lunacy. As long as the present arrangement lasts, Mr. Redford is the King's Examiner of Plays; and the King is responsible to public opinion for his selection, his maintenance in his post, and consequently for his decisions.

I must add, however, that Mr. Redford is virtually irremovable, even by the King, as long as he remains a well-conducted, solvent, reputable gentleman, because the task which so signally beats him would beat anybody. He fulfils it no worse than much more pretentious authorities. If two of the great Churches of Christendom have made themselves laughing-stocks by the mischievous absurdity of their censorships of literature, it is not likely that an official wiser than they can be obtained for Mr. Redford's modest emoluments. Put in Mr. Redford's place the Archbishop of Canterbury and the Lord Chief Justice; and they would, let us hope, be the first to admit that when an Ibsen or a Tolstoy sees that there are certain things that the world needs to be told, it is not for them to pretend either that they know better or that they dare share the responsibility by saying officially, It is good. And they would also be the first to see that if they tried to evade this dilemma by hiding behind a set of official rules, any rascal could get round those rules, and every writer of genuine inspiration would come into direct conflict with them; so that, finally, all the most serious plays would be prohibited and all the most licentious ones officially licensed – which is just what happens at present. If the power of suppressing plays before they are produced is to be given to any one, it may as well be given to Mr. Redford as to another; for his successor will be in as ridiculous a position as he the moment he pretends to be a greater authority on public morals than some author who has gained the ear of Europe.

The only conveniently workable solution is to control theatres as hotels are controlled, by licences renewable from year to year by a public representative authority, and revocable on proved misconduct by a public vote of that authority. Mr. Harcourt's Bill shows much more thorough knowledge of the subject than any other measure yet formulated. But, whatever solution be adopted, one point is vital. Hang the author by due process of law for writing his play the day after it is produced if you like; but let no mere mortal man have arbitrary power to prevent another man's play from ever seeing the light, and incidentally to destroy that other man's moral reputation and ruin him financially without disclosing the evidence or facing public examination. The author and the manager have more at stake than any censor can possibly have, and it is they who must bear the main responsibility of the decision in any case, censor or no censor. I cannot see why this guarantee cannot be accepted in theatrical as it is in all other business.

Yours truly,
G. BERNARD SHAW.
10, Adelphi Terrace, W.C.

Shaw wrote *The Shewing-Up of Blanco Posnet* for Herbert Beerbohm Tree (1853–1917, knighted 1909), the celebrated actor-manager, for a series of 'After Noon Theatre' productions, the proceeds from which went to charity – hence Shaw's opening remarks together with his clinching comment that 'It only remains for the King to make me a duke to complete the situation.'

However, his focus in the following letter is on *Press Cuttings*, also refused a licence, because of its alleged representation of Balfour ('Basquith') and Kitchener ('Mitchener'). Barrie's representation of Shaw on stage was in a skit entitled Punch; J.B. Fagan had represented him in a benefit matinee skit entitled *Shakespear v. Shaw;* and Granville Barker had been made up to look like Shaw when playing Tanner in the first production (at the Court Theatre) of *Man and Superman.*

Shaw wrote *Press Cuttings* for the London Society for Women's Suffrage. Public staging having been disallowed, the Society hastily formed a spurious but legal 'private' Dramatic Guild, which could then stage the play, doing so at the Court Theatre in July 1909. (See Shaw's letter of 14 July below for his account of the difficulties he and the London Society for Women's Suffrage had to overcome before *Press Cuttings* could be performed.) Later that year, to circumvent the

Examiner's veto, Shaw changed 'Balsquith' and 'Mitchener' to 'Johnson' and 'Bones' – the names of the Christie Minstrels.

Reed, Sambourne, Partridge and Lucy were well-known magazine and newspaper caricaturists (today's 'cartoonists').

~ 1909, June 26 ~

THE CENSOR'S REVENGE.

Sir, – A few weeks ago one of the most popular of London actors and managers was found guilty by the Lord Chamberlain of attempted blasphemy, and mulcted and suppressed accordingly. Today the King makes that manager a knight. But the Lord Chamberlain, now that Sir Harry Poland has shown that the Act of 1843 makes him independent of the King, has not taken the rebuke lying down. An hour after I read in *The Times* of Sir Herbert Beerbohm Tree's triumph the counterblow fell on me (the accomplice in Sir Herbert's blasphemy) in the shape of the Lord Chamberlain's refusal to licence my sketch entitled Press Cuttings, and announced by the Women's Suffrage Society for performance at the Court Theatre on July 9 and 12. It only remains for the King to make me a duke to complete the situation.

This time my alleged offence is not blasphemy, but, in Mr. Redford's own words, 'personalities, expressed or understood.' Now as to personalities understood I can say nothing, for the Lord Chamberlain's understanding is a thing totally beyond comprehension or even conjecture. But I can assure the public that I have been careful not to express a single personality that has not done duty again and again without offence in the pages of Punch.

Also attention is officially called to the rule 'No representation of living persons to be permitted on the stage'. This wholesale prohibition of holding the mirror up to nature does not, of course, mean what it says. On what it is understood by the Lord Chamberlain to mean I have to observe, first, that I have myself been 'represented on the stage,' with the Lord Chamberlain's full approval, in a little fantasy by no less well-known an author than my friend Mr. J.M. Barrie, and that on another occasion my appearance was so exactly imitated that a near relative of my own was deceived by the resemblance. After this it is hardly worth stating that unless a grotesquely imaginary Prime Minister under the well-worn *Punch* name of Balsquith, and a wildly impossible Teutophobe general whom I christened Mitchener in order to clear him of all possible suspicion of being a caricature of Lord Roberts, are to be considered as representations of living persons in any more serious sense than the topical people in our

Christmas pantomimes, I feel so little guilty that I cannot bring myself to believe that the reason given for destroying the value of several weeks of my work is the real reason.

The Women's Suffrage Society will, however, not suffer. Two entirely private performances of the little play, with nobody present except the London Press and perhaps a thousand people or so, will enable the society to discharge the obligations it has incurred. But these performances, though private, will not be privileged. If any of the 'living persons' on whose behalf the Lord Chamberlain has intervened find themselves damaged, they have their legal remedy against me, just as they have it against Sir Henry Lucy, Mr. Reed, Mr. Bernard Partridge, Mr. Linley Sambourne, or any other political satirist. I sincerely hope there will be no more occasion for them to do so than there was for me to take an action against Mr. Barrie.

Yours truly,
G. BERNARD SHAW.
10, Adelphi Terrace, London, W.C.

The following rhetorically charged letter is Shaw's response to the actor-manager George Alexander's defence of dramatic censorship in his letters to *The Times* on 26 and 29 June. Gilbert and Sullivan's *The Mikado* was temporarily banned, but not by Redford, when a Japanese delegation visited London. The advice to the West End Society of Theatre Managers to 'put its house in order' reiterates Shaw's criticism of theatre management in his 'Rejected Statement.' The 'standard English work approved of for private reading by the Primate' is of course the Bible.

~ *1909, June 30* ~

The Censorship of Plays.

Sir, – May I ask Mr. George Alexander to enlarge a little on the subject of the Censorship?

Why does he regard dramatic art as unfit to deal with serious questions, which are all political questions? Why does he believe that a Court official, none of whose duties involve any higher qualifications than those of the acting manager of a box-office, is a better judge of the propriety of a play than Sir Herbert Beerbohm Tree, Sir Arthur Pinero, or the British public? Why does he believe in the Spanish theory of the inquisition rather than in the English theory of liberty? Who told him that 'the police have no right to interfere in our theatres'; and why does he 'sincerely hope that they may never be given such a right'? Are we to understand that there is anything wrong going on in the theatre? Who told him that 'under the present system a play, once licensed, can be performed without any interference by the authorities in any part of Great Britain'? Has he ever heard of a piece called *The Mikado*, not to mention others which, after being licensed, have been subsequently withdrawn under pressure from the Lord Chamberlain? Who told him that 'under the present system the licences of the theatre are safe'? In what sense can a licence which is at the mercy of a single virtually irresponsible official be said to be safe?

Does his statement that his relations with the Lord Chamberlain's department have always been of the most harmonious character mean anything more than that he has never personally assaulted, or been assaulted by, any of the members of that department; that he subscribed to give a service of silver plate to a former holder of the office, who accepted the – shall I call it a perquisite? – without a blush; and that he perforce confines himself at the St. James's Theatre to the production of plays which are suited to Mr. Redford's capacity? Why does he make his entirely justifiable objection to censorship by the local authorities, which would at least be subject to the control of a representative body responsible to the public, a reason for supporting an infinitely more odious censorship which is responsible to no one, and which classes him with the disorderly footmen and waiting-maids of a bygone period?

Pending an answer to these unanswerable questions, may I appeal to the Society of West End Theatre Managers to set its house in order and make up its mind what safeguards it will need when the present censorship succumbs, if not to my arguments and to those of practically the whole body of dramatic authors, but to the even more destructive arguments of its defenders? For if the managers have nothing more to say than that, to their infinite shame, they are satisfied with their present comfortable slavery, no account will be taken of them when they are freed in spite of themselves: and they may find, just as they fear, that the finger of the new licensing authority may be thicker than the Lord Chamberlain's loins (I hasten to assure Mr. Redford that this is not one of my improprieties, but a quotation from a standard English work approved of for private reading by the Primate). Surely Mr. Alexander has by this time sufficient experience of municipal work to be able to formulate conditions which would prevent the power of licensing theatres from year to year being used to prevent the production of particular plays, or to place the manager of a theatre at any disadvantage with the manager of a bank, whilst yet providing him with a licence which would protect him much more effectually against the common informer than the now hopelessly discredited licence of the Lord Chamberlain. It would at the same time make the manager feel continuously responsible to public opinion for the honourable conduct of his theatre, instead of being, as he is at present, able to procure for two guineas, and compliance with a few transparent hypocrisies, a licence for practically anything that the lowest class of playgoer will stand.

Yours truly,
G. BERNARD SHAW.
10, Adelphi Terrace, London, W.C.

This next letter, about the private performance of *Press Cuttings*, is self-explanatory. James Anning was the theatre manager, and J.H. Leigh the lessee of the Court Theatre. One notes Shaw's comment about the critics, whose feeling about his plays had been and would long remain one of Shaw's major obstacles as a playwright, notwithstanding the public success he had achieved at the Court Theatre, in America, Germany and, increasingly, elsewhere. *An Englishman's Home* was a play by Daphne Du Maurier (1907–89) first performed in 1909. J.M. Barrie's 1906 play *Josephine* was a three-act revue that questioned social divisions.

~ 1909, July 14 ~

MR. BERNARD SHAW'S PLAY AND THE CENSOR.

Sir, – Mr. James Anning's letter in your issue of today, evidently written under pressure from the Examiner of Plays, positively unhinges my mind and bereaves me of breath. I dare not say what I think of it, lest my language should make it impossible to print my letter. I will try to state the facts baldly.

Mr. Redford received the play with his fee in the usual course. He returned it, stating that it contained 'personalities, expressed or understood', and that it violated the rule of his department that living persons are not to be represented on the stage. Thereupon began all the trouble, expense, and loss that the withholding of a licence entails. The money paid for seats had to be returned; a proposal from one of the most popular actor-managers in London for the inclusion of the play in his programme fell through; the Civic and Dramatic Guild had to be created *ad hoc*; and I had to ask Mr. Leigh, the lessee of the Court Theatre, to incur the very serious risk of offending the Lord Chamberlain by allowing the Guild to give a technically private performance, which he did with a public spirit and personal generosity which I am glad to have this opportunity of acknowledging. Meanwhile I wrote to Mr. Anning, who was managing the theatre for Mr. Leigh, that as Mr. Redford had not specified the personalities he objected to, and as it was quite impossible for me, in view of Mr. Barrie's Josephine and other pieces, to guess where he drew the line between the allowable and the inadmissible, his refusal had better be faced as final. This letter was communicated to Mr. Redford. He thereupon gave the usual official intimation that his department does not condescend to any intercourse with authors, and invited Mr. Anning to call on him. Mr. Anning did so. This was Mr. Redford's opportunity to point out the passages he objected to, and enable the sketch to be publicly performed if he wished to do so. He knew that he had nothing to fear in the shape of an obstinate refusal on my part to meet his views; for I had just made a very extensive alteration in another play (Blanco Posnet) to please him, and made it in vain. Instead of proposing any alterations, Mr. Redford put forth all his powers of intimidation with such effect that Mr. Anning went straight to the Civic and Dramatic Guild to beg them to give up the performance; and it was only when reassured by legal advice that he felt justified in proceeding even with Mr. Leigh's consent.

The sequel is before the public. The performance took place; and although almost all the critics – to their shame be it said – support the principle of the censorship; and though, furthermore, as the Press notices of my last licensed play show, the feeling of the critics against my plays has reached detestation point, yet not one paper has been able to discover or even conjecture why Mr. Redford refused to license *Press Cuttings*. The German Press, however, has no doubt on the subject, as a reference to the *Berliner Tageblatt* of the 8th instant shows. It concludes that St. James's Palace is suffering from anti-German war scare, and that the banning of my sketch, coupled with the recent refusal to allow *An Englishman's Home* to be burlesqued, was part of the war scare policy. Here again you have what I have so often pointed out: Mr. Redford compromising the Lord Chamberlain, and the Lord Chamberlain compromising a really important personage who knows nothing of the Examiner's vagaries.

If Mr. Redford has changed his mind about Press Cuttings, he has only to send along the licence. His fee has been paid, and all formalities complied with on our side. He cannot undo the trouble he has caused; and he probably will not repair the breach he has made in my unfortunate income; but he can at least prevent the mischief going any further. In the meantime his subtle distinction between refusing to license a play and abstaining from licensing it will not impress the public as important. A refusal, accompanied by an issue of the licence, would not have hurt my feelings in the least. The withholding of the licence is the practical part of the grievance.

Yours truly,
G. BERNARD SHAW.

Shaw refers to his 'letter of the 13th (published on the 14th). The 'twenty-one pieces of silver' – an obvious biblical echo – was the one guinea required by the Examiner for licensing a one-act play. It was two guineas for a two-act or longer play.

∼ 1909, July 16 ∼

MR. BERNARD SHAW'S PLAY AND THE CENSOR.

Sir, – The statement in my letter of the 13th that 'Mr. Redford's fee has been paid' requires an additional piece of information which did not reach me until to-day. It seems that Mr. Redford, apparently in a fit of remorse, has returned the twenty-one pieces of silver.

Yours truly,
G. BERNARD SHAW.

When the Joint Select Committee rejected Shaw's proffered statement, Shaw wrote to the Chairman of the Committee, H. L. Samuel, to express his 'grievance' – 'always a valuable property in an agitation like this.' He would, he told Samuel, 'fly to the last refuge of the oppressed: a letter to *The Times*' (letter of 31 July 1909, in Laurence, ed. *Collected Letters*, 1898-1910, pp. 853-4). This is the letter.

John Hare (1844–1921, knighted in 1907) was a noted actor-manager; Clement Scott (1841–1904) was the fiercely conservative theatre critic for the *Daily Telegraph*.

∼ 1909, August 2 ∼

THE SELECT COMMITTEE ON THE CENSORSHIP.

Sir, – In the excellent report of the proceedings of the Select Committee in your issue of to-day there is a passage which states that I asked the committee to place a 'booklet' or 'pamphlet' on their notes. I was guilty of no such absurdity, though the new departure in procedure made by the committee was so startling that your reporter may very well be excused for concluding that I had committed some irregularity. The facts, which I trouble you with only because they are of public importance, are these.

The precedents for the committee's procedure are to be found in the report of the committee of 1892. As it was obviously inconvenient and indeed impossible to elicit the general case for or against the censorship by the method of question and answer, the witnesses before that committee were allowed to plead their case by reading carefully-prepared statements on which they were afterwards questioned. Thus Sir Henry Irving, Sir John Hare, and Mr. Clement Scott were enable to place such statements on the notes, and have them permanently recorded in the report of the committee. Mr. Scott's statement of the case for 'free trade in amusements' is specially notable for its florid rhetoric and literary character. All three were in favour of the censorship.

Relying on this precedent, I carefully prepared a similar statement of the case against the censorship – a statement that cost me several hundred pounds' worth of solid professional work. For the convenience of the committee I had it privately printed in the most legible type and the hand-iest form at my own expense. It was marked confidential, and treated by me in the strictest order as confidential. I was informed when I attended to give evidence that the committee had decided to follow precedent. In due course when I was called I cited the precedents, and formally proffered my statement, only modifying the Irving precedent in so far as I suggested that instead of my reading that statement to the committee it should, to save time, be taken as read, since the chairman and members had been provided with copies for two days beforehand. To my amazement I had no sooner made the suggestion than the chairman cleared the room, and the committee went into secret conclave to discuss the matter. As the room had already been cleared once in order to consider a play licensed by Mr. Redford which was too scandalous to be discussed otherwise than in camera, there was a good deal of speculation as to what was the matter. One agitated pressman asked me, 'Have you attacked the King?' When we were readmitted, the chairman informed me without explanation that my statement could not be received and placed on the notes. Since it is not, I understand, admitted that this was a departure from precedent, it is clear that the precedent followed is not that of admitting statements impartially, but of receiving statements in favour of the censorship only. I take it therefore, that the committee will permit all witnesses in favour of the censorship to state their case before they are questioned, but that those who are, like myself, opposed to the censorship, will not be allowed to state their case at all, except in so far as they can interpolate disconnected scraps of it into their answers to questions. In short, we are to be treated as we should have been if we had been indicted for high treason in the 17th century.

I make no further comment. I only wish to clear myself from the accusation of having made an irregular and ridiculous application, and to make public the fact that the committee, whilst apparently discriminating in favour of the censorship, has not offered any explanation. I daresay there may be an explanation; but it certainly cannot be founded on any breach of order or precedent on my part. Further, in view of the suspicion of my friend the pressman, I send a copy of my statement so that you may convince yourself that there is no foundation for the suspicion that it contained any of those improprieties which Mr. Redford has taught the public to suspect even in my most innocent utterances.

May I trespass on your space for a few lines further about a private matter? My statement in its present form, printed for the convenience of the 12 members of the committee, will presently be worth about five guineas as a curiosity. The members of the committee have such a lively appreciation of this fact that most of them promptly lost their copies and applied to me for fresh ones. I gave them the copies I had reserved for the Press after the acceptance (as I expected) of my statement. But now they want a third set; and here I really must strike. The secret conclave and the mysterious censoring of the document has intensified curiosity at Westminster to such an extent that it is no longer a question of supplying 12 committee members with spare copies each, but supplying 670 members of the House of Commons, 615 peers, peeresses innumerable, and several thousand common persons in London generally. I am sorry; but I cannot afford it. My printer's bill, incurred for the sake of an ungrateful country and a thankless committee, is quite heavy enough as it is. Pay for the printing of another copy I simply will not.

Yours truly,
G. BERNARD SHAW.
10, Adelphi Terrace, W.C.

What follows is Shaw's version of his second, and final, appearance before the Select Committee. The official transcript of the proceedings indicates a 'touch of comedy' in his reference to Lord Gorell (a noted judge) as an 'advantaged public man' as against Shaw's position as a 'disadvantaged' playwright. Shaw, having been handed back most of the copies of his statement from the members of the Committee and in spite of the 'snub' they had inflicted on him, summons up his customary good humour.

∼ *1909, August 6* ∼

THE DRAMATIC CENSORSHIP.

MR. SHAW AND THE COMMITTEE.

Sir, – I have great pleasure in adding to my letter of the 2nd inst. that the Select Committee yesterday made the *amende honorable* on the private point – not, alas! on the public one – in the matter of my statement. On entering the committee room I found the members in a condition of distress of conscience which I really had no intention of inflicting. One honourable and gallant member frankly handed me back his two copies (to which I may now say he was more than welcome) *coram populo*; and the secretary gave me a many of the rest as he had been able to collect, amounting to at least one for each of the other members present. The restitution is, therefore, formally complete and honours are easy.

As to my release from further examination, the secrecy in which it was decided makes it impossible for me to guess whether I am to take it as an act of consideration for the very great pressure on my time, or as a repetition of the snub of Friday last. On public grounds I am sorry for the touch of comedy with which my appearance before the Committee ended; but its members will, I am sure, do me the earnest efforts to place this very important public question before them with the most entire respect for their dignity and consideration for their convenience, and received for my pains a very pointed and deliberate rebuff – which I hope all who were present will admit I took with good humour – did I permit myself the harmless amusement of trying whether a Select Committee of the two Houses could keep its temper under trying circumstances as well as a playwright. I prefer to believe that the committee was equal to the occasion; and if any member who cares to have a copy of my statement is really left unproved with one, I shall be delighted to supply the deficiency privately.

G.B.S.

Below is Shaw's account of the further adventures of *Blanco Posnet* when it was accepted for staging at the Abbey Theatre, Dublin. The confrontation between the two directors, Lady Augusta Gregory (1853–1932) and W. B. Yeats (1865–1939), and the 'Castle' during the Lord Lieutenant's absence, was considerably fiercer than Shaw's rendering allows. In the event the Lord Lieutenant returned to Dublin in time to countermand the banning and the play, when produced, was a great success.

Annie Horniman, to whom Shaw then submitted the play (only, once again, to be rebuffed by Redford), was a Fabian and friend of Shaw's. She assisted Shaw in 1894 by helping to finance the London production of *Arms and the Man*. (She also built the Abbey Theatre in Dublin in 1904 and later made it over to the Company.) At this time she owned and ran her own repertory theatre company in Manchester.

The rest of the letter has Shaw pursuing his anti-censorship campaign; it also provides an amusing take-off of some members of the Select Committee – the Lords Newton, Plymouth, Gorell and Ribblesdale. Harcourt, also on the Committee, tried in his cross-questioning of Shaw to get the anti-censorship view across, but to no avail. The Bishop of Southwark, singled out in Shaw's commentary, did in fact give evidence of an extraordinary open-minded kind. George Edwardes (1852–1915) was a theatre manager, one among many who gave evidence. Clyde Fitch (1865–1909), author of *The Woman in the Case*, was an extremely popular playwright.

'BLANCO POSNET' AND THE CENSORSHIP.

Sir, – It will add to the signal service which *The Times* has rendered to the English theatre in the present crisis if you will allow me to complete, through your columns, the story of *Blanco Posnet* and the Censorship.

It is within public recollection how this play was announced for production at His Majesty's Theatre; how the performance was prohibited by the Lord Chamberlain on the ground that the play was blasphemous; and how the manager was immediately knighted by the King. On this strong hint, the play was taken to Ireland, where the Lord Chamberlain has no jurisdiction, and there announced for production. The Viceroy was absent at the time, and by some unexplained means certain subordinate Castle officials were induced to commit the extraordinary solecism of threatening, apparently on behalf of the English Lord Chamberlain, that the patent of the theatre would be withdrawn if the play were produced. What happened to the guilty officials I do not know, but the return of the Lord Lieutenant was soon followed by the successful and orderly production of the play. The patent was not withdrawn, and the author was tactfully and courteously made to feel, on the personal point, that the Irish Court in no way associated itself with either the opinions or the manners of the English Censorship.

The defeat of the Censorship was as complete as anything human can be. Dublin playgoers are as morbidly sensitive to any attack on religion as London playgoers are morbidly indifferent to it. Everything that could be done to raise prejudice and create suspicion had been done. Even Sir Herbert Tree's jest at the Censor's expense – 'He will never stand vice being called immoral' – was misquoted and misrepresented as a condemnation of the play; and his straightforward and loyal reply to the direct question as to whether the play would shock religious feeling – 'It will heighten religious feeling' – was carefully suppressed. The audience included persons who went with the express purpose of protesting against the supposed blasphemy. The result is now an old story. There was no protest; there was an almost sensational success; and the literary and clerical support given in the Press and pulpit was overwhelming. I was especially helped by the rector of Westport's articles in the *Manchester Guardian* and the *Spectator* on the religious side of the play, and by the sermons of the rector of Ayot St. Lawrence and the Rev. J. M. Lloyd Thomas, of High Pavement Chapel, Birmingham.

The next step was to give the Censorship an opportunity of repairing its mistake. The play was sent in again for licence by Miss Horniman, with a view to production at her Repertory Theatre in Manchester. As usual, the first response was a refusal (quite amiably expressed by Mr. Redford) to reconsider a play already rejected. But Mr. Redford was reminded that he had assured the Select Committee that rejected plays could be reconsidered at any time; and the question was whether 'could be' meant 'would be', as it certainly had not meant in the past. Mr. Redford at once acknowledged the obligation by submitting the play to the Lord Chamberlain. I should add that it was pointed out that the author had rewritten an important passage after it had been tested in rehearsal. It was open to the Censorship to treat this change as a concession, and to save its face and its soul at the same time.

What the Censorship has actually done exceeds the utmost hopes of those who, like myself, have devoted themselves to its destruction. It has licensed the play, and endorsed on the licence specific orders that all its redeeming passages shall be omitted in representation. I may have my insolent prostitute, my blood-thirsty, profane backwoodsmen, my atmosphere of coarseness, of savagery, of mockery, and all the foul darkness which I devised to make the light visible; but the light must be left out. I may wallow in filth, ferocity, and sensuality, provided I do not hint that there is any force in Nature higher and stronger than these. I may belong to the school of the late Clyde Fitch, whose Woman in the Case, now being performed nightly at the Garrick Theatre, should be seen by everybody who wishes to know what the Censorship is forcing, by artificial selection, on our stage and on our most innocently charming and delicate actresses; but if I aspire to be in the great tradition of literature, and to earn my bread by my pen otherwise than as a pandar earns it, I must quit the theatre.

It is necessary to emphasise this situation very strongly, because all through the sittings of the Select Committee, and the discussions it has provoked, it has been assumed and expressly alleged that Mr. Granville Barkers's *Waste* and my own *Mrs. Warren's Profession* have not been licensed. But the truth is much worse than this. They have been licensed. The licence for *Mrs. Warren's Profession* is in my desk. I myself performed a part in the licensed version of *Waste*. The reason the plays are not performed is not that the Lord Chamberlain prohibits them, but that he insists on that assimilation to *The Woman in the Case* by the omission of their lesson. When moralists of the school of Lord Newton and Mr. George Edwardes point with horror at this or that passage in *Waste* which the Lord Chamberlain was 'quite right not to pass,' they are almost invariably pointing to something that the Lord Chamberlain actually has passed. These moralists, who habitually libel the Restoration drama by comparing it unfavourably to modern licensed plays which would have shocked Charles II and Nell Gwyn into Puritanism and which present stories that Pepys would hardly have dared confide to the secrecy of his diary, are ignorant of the fact that the Censorship is not a dam across the steam of the higher literature. It is a filter which, like some other commercial filters, lets all the pathogenic germs through and holds up only the purifying elements which would make them harmless or positively healthy.

It may be asked why I am giving this significant piece of evidence about *Blanco Posnet* to the Select Committee through *The Times*, instead of in the official way across its own table. The reason is that Lord Plymouth, more from constitutional bashfulness than from devotion to the principle (formulated by Dickens) of How Not To Do It, ruled at an early meeting of the Committee over which he presided in Mr. Samuel's absence that the discussion of particular plays is outside the scope of the Committee's reference. This was the result of the first attempt to discuss (with closed doors) one of the Lord Chamberlain's approved selections. This ruling excludes the particular case of Blanco Posnet. It is true that the ruling has been repeatedly violated. None the less, it has been used again and again to harass Mr. Robert Harcourt in his conduct of the case against the Censorship, and might have all but silenced him had he not been clever enough to outwit his opponents, and forensically gifted enough to be able to handle his case brilliantly even at an exasperating disadvantage. Thanks to *The Times*, I am not compelled to accept such disadvantages; and I prefer to give my evidence in the larger arena it provides.

Besides, to be quite frank, several members of the Committee, including all the peers except Lord Ribblesdale (who really can enjoy an intellectual point for its own sake), suffer from a vulgar complaint which, on the analogy of 'stage fright', I may call 'Shaw' fright. They will take from others what they will not take from me. I should perhaps also except Lord Gorell; but Lord Gorell is as yet so unaccustomed to the rough-and-tumble of Parliamentary life, and still carries about him so much of the cloistered innocence and carefully sheltered dignity of the Bench, that the democratic tone of the proceedings visibly impresses him as a monstrous contempt of Court. He terrifies me; I know that he wants to send me to Holloway. Nevertheless, with my suppressed brief in his pocket, he has been to me a most efficient junior, following up my points as to the precise effect of licensing by local authorities very intelligently. Again, the Committee would not allow me to demonstrate that the creation of an appeal from the Censorship would have the effect of leaving it all its power whilst relieving it of all its responsibility. But the Speaker of the House of Commons put that point much more vehemently than I should have done. As to what is supposed to be my great heresy – to wit, my passionate denial that morality is sacred, and my indissimulable contempt for the merely moral man, meaning the creature who, for good or evil, does what everybody else does for no better reason that that everybody else does it – the Committee suppressed my 'proof' sooner than stand it from me; but when the Bishop of Southwark told them, as any honest and able Churchman must have told them, that morality needs a good deal of overhauling, they took it like lambs, though Mr. Harcourt could not resist the profane temptation of asking the amazed Bishop whether he was a disciple of mine. Nothing, therefore, has been lost by the panic which I most innocently and unintentionally spread, except the enormously important historical point.

After all, the solid argument against censorship is that it has been tried again and again, and yet again, to select the good and reject the bad, in politics, in literature, in art, and in religion, on exactly the ground taken by its present supporters; and at every trial it has done exactly what it is doing now in the English theatre, selecting the bad and rejecting the good, and becoming an abomination to every one who is dealing with facts and not with imaginary Superman censors and imaginary purified plays. Why were no questions asked of the representative of the Roman Catholic Church on this point? Why was he not asked for a list of the books on the Index? He was allowed to explain what a censorship is meant to do. We all know what censorships are meant to do, and we should all be in favour of our Censorship if it did it. The serious point is that it does not do it, and in the nature of things never can do it. Who cares whether the Speaker believes that we ought to have the protection of a much more stern censorship? And who does not care, with deep concern, for the fact testified to by him that, though protected by a censorship, he hesitates to take his daughter to the theatre? If the nation still clings madly to the ideal censor clamoured for by so many witnesses – the man of the world, the man of culture, of brains, of public experience, of sympathy with literature and art, of some knowledge of the French and German drama – why not make me Censor? I throw off my natural modesty so far as to challenge Mr. George Edwardes to name any living real (not ideal) person with, on the whole, a better equipment. At all events, if there is a better man, name him. Let us get rid of fantastic abstractions – of that outworn dream, the omniscient, omnipresent, benevolent despot. Let us hear, not *what* the Censor is to be, but who he is to be.

The Select Committee, having finished with the witnesses, will now, I presume, visit all the London theatres and music-halls, as well as a representative selection of the provincial ones. Otherwise its report will not be worth twopence, and the dramatic authors will be obliged to supersede it by writing the report themselves, unofficially. I do not suggest that the present Committee is capable of trifling with a most vital subject, as the Committee of 1892 did, but I do say, very emphatically, that if Lord Newton's reiterated opinion that the authors are making a ridiculous fuss about nothing prevails with the Committee, the dramatic authors will make a fuss about Lord Newton which will make him for the moment almost as famous as his illustrious namesake, Sir Isaac.

Yours truly,
G. BERNARD SHAW.
Parknasilla.

The Suffragette Movement was gathering in intensity as women became increasingly determined to win the right to vote. The lobbying of MPs and peaceful public demonstrations were proving ineffectual, so more militant tactics were adopted. These led to their arrest (which they resisted) and imprisonment, where they pursued their campaign by refusing to eat. The Home Secretary, Herbert Gladstone, then authorised various draconian measures, including forcible feeding.

Shaw is here speaking for himself (the sarcasm is characteristic), while at the same time appearing to speak on behalf of the Fabian Society, which had adopted a resolution condemning the practice.

Lady Constance Lytton (1869–1923), a prominent Suffragette, was one such who went on hunger strike. The quotation in the penultimate paragraph is from John Dryden's *Absalom and Achitophel*. Sardanapalus, last king of Nineveh, was renowned for his luxurious lifestyle.

～ *1909, November 25* ～

THE HOME SECRETARY AND FORCIBLE FEEDING.

Sir – The Fabian Society may congratulate itself on the success with which it has drawn the Home Secretary on the above subject. The letter of Mr. Troup implies some doubt as to whether the resolution so pathetically complained of was actually passed by so responsible a body. As one of those who were present and voted for it I can assure Mr. – Gladstone that it is only too true. It was carried by a large majority; and it was voted for by persons of conflicting opinions on the ground that it was so exactly accurate in every phrase that it became a matter of conscience not to vote in the negative.

It seems, however, to have been misunderstood by the Home Office. Mr. Gladstone is apparently under the impression that the members of the Fabian Society desired to reproach him for not forcibly feeding Lady Constance Lytton. On the contrary, they regarded it as quite a redeeming feature in his campaign; and the resolution expressly urged him to take the same decent and sensible view of all other cases. And though Mr. Gladstone, through Mr. Troup, would seem to protest that he feels no repugnance to the forcible feeding of a woman of Lady Constance's rank, and, in fact, assures us that nothing but the strongest medical remonstrance's restrained him, I prefer to think that the right hon. gentleman is doing himself some injustice in the matter, or else that he has been misled by the statements which he has received and repeated as to the extremely enjoyable nature of a meal administered by the methods practised on Mrs. Leigh and other prisoners.

It may be that Mr. Gladstone is right on this point. I will therefore, undertake to procure the co-operation of the Fabian Society in providing for Mr. Gladstone a banquet which Sardanapalus would have regarded as an exceptional treat. The rarest wines and delicacies shall be provided absolutely regardless of expense. The only condition we shall make is that Mr. Herbert Gladstone shall partake through the nose; and that a cinematographic machine shall be at work all the time registering for the public satisfaction the waterings of his mouth, the smackings of his lips, and the other unmistakable symptoms of luxurious delight with which he will finally convince us all of the truth of his repeated assurances to us that the forcibly fed Suffragist is enjoying an indulgence rather than suffering martyrdom.

I must not conclude this letter without an expression of my sincere concern for the unexpected revelation of the dangerous state of Lady Constance Lytton's health. It only shows how little we can trust to appearances. But yesterday we regarded Lady Constance as one of the most energetic members of a family noted for its genius, its public spirit, its good looks, and its enviable health and longevity. Today we learn that all this was a mere mask for the last feeble pulsings of a shattered heart which cannot be much longer expected to *o'er inform the tenement of clay*.

But I will harrow Mr. Gladstone's feelings no more. Africa stretches out her arms to him. and we should all be sorry to see his parting from his native land embittered by reflections on the condition of the noble lady whose health he has so sympathetically spared. Let him go in peace to the land of the Congo. His talent for taking a pleasant view of extremely unpleasant facts will find opportunities there which even the Suffragists cannot provide in our more fastidious civilization.

Yours truly,

G. BERNARD SHAW.

10, Adelphi Terrace, W.C.

Edward VII died on 6 May and there was a call for general mourning. On 27 January 1901, on the occasion of Queen Victoria's death, Shaw had written to the editor of the Morning Leader deploring 'the rapture of mourning in which the nation is enjoying . . . its favourite festival – a funeral,' calling for 'vigorous remonstrance' (quoted in Laurence, ed. *Collected Letters*, 1898–1910, p. 216). But the editor refused to publish the letter. Here one sees a different, if not changed, Shaw. If he deplores the sumptuary requirement for its expense and impracticality and cannot resist expressing his abhorrence of the 'morbid attitude towards death,' he also respects the Royal Family's 'keen personal grief'.

This was effectively the end of the Edwardian era, during which Shaw had risen in stature to an internationally renowned figure. Many of the issues covered in the previous letters can be more thoroughly understood by reading Leon Hugo's *Edwardian Shaw: The Writer and His Age* (New York: St. Martin's Press, and London: Macmillan Press, 1999).

∼ *1910, May 12* ∼

GENERAL MOURNING: AN OVERLOOKED HARDSHIP.

Sir – So much solicitude has been shown in the highest quarters to prevent any suffering among the working classes from the general mourning that I am emboldened to put in a plea on behalf of the class which, if not the poorest in the kingdom, perhaps suffers most from pecuniary anxiety. Take the case of a man with a professional or business income of a few hundreds a year, with three daughters at the nearest high school. The school is compelled to go into mourning. The dresses provided for the season have to be discarded, and new black dresses have to be bought. To a Court official it may be inconceivable that so trifling an expense could be a hardship to any one. By those who know what life on a small income is to people who have to keep up a social position above that of the working class it will be more justly appreciated as a calamity. The remedy is to drop the vague expression 'decent mourning,' and to define the wearing of a violet ribbon as the appropriate mourning for Royalty. This would be correct, inexpensive, and pretty. Why our schools should be deliberately made hideous with black because an honourable public career has come to its natural close in all peace, fulfilment, and cheerful memory is not apparent to any healthy-minded person.

I hope also that it will be understood that people who, like myself, abhor mourning, and have never worn it for their own nearest relatives, making it, indeed, a point of honour to discourage what we regard as a morbid attitude towards death, are as susceptible as any of the mourning wearers to the sympathy which goes out quite naturally and spontaneously to those to whom the late King's death brings too intimate a loss to be felt for the moment otherwise than as a keen personal grief.

Yours truly,
G. BERNARD SHAW.

Just prior to the following letter there had been a Budget Statement in *The Times* that touched upon the super-tax. There had also been a rash of letters for and against the Suffragette movement that was in full swing.

The 'Edwardian Age' lingered on after Edward's death and would only wither and die after the outbreak of the First World War in 1914. By now (1910) Shaw had made himself into one of the most eminent of Edwardians and would in the few remaining years of the era consolidate his position as the most celebrated, the most discussed (and frequently vilified) personality of the age. He was internationally recognised as the outstanding dramatist of the day, with a long string of plays to his credit, to which, as the months went by, he would add several one-act plays – among others *The Dark Lady of the Sonnets* (1910) and *Overruled* (1912) – and in 1911, 1912 and 1913 three full-length plays, *Fanny's First Play* – his first box office success – *Androcles and the Lion* and *Pygmalion*, the last two first performed in Germany to evade the usual put-down of the London press. In addition, Shaw's contributions to newspapers other than *The Times*, to magazines and journals in the form of letters, articles, statements and self-drafted interviews, ran into the hundreds, while his work for the Fabian Society and Socialism generally continued unabated, even after he had resigned from the Executive Committee of the Society in 1911.

The correspondence given here, between Shaw and the Special Commissioners of Income Tax in the person of N.F.W. Fisher (later Sir Norman Fisher, 1879–1948), was possibly instigated by a long letter on the subject by an unknown correspondent on the 14 May, and covers the legalities surrounding the application of the super-tax, Shaw's position as a husband *vis-à-vis* his wife's income, and the Suffragette stand on the matter. Shaw's letters are remarkable for their lucidity and the engaging yet forceful way in which he presents his arguments. David Lloyd George (1863–1945), who introduced the super-tax, was Chancellor of the Exchequer from 1908 to 1915. Winston Churchill (1874–1965) succeeded Gladstone as Home Secretary in 1910 when Gladstone was 'banished' to South Africa – as Shaw had it in his letter of 25 November 1909 – as the first Governor-General of the newly formed Union.

For other utterances on the super-tax and related issues, see 'Sorrows of the Supertaxed' (19 December 1916) and 'Taxation of Capital' (15 January 1917) below.

THE HUSBAND, THE SUPERTAX, AND THE SUFFRAGISTS.

Sir, – The following correspondence on a matter of public interest has passed between me and the Special Commissioners of Income Tax. The matter on which it arose was the official demand, made for the first time this year, for a return of my income from all sources for the purpose of supertaxation. In former years such a return was only required in cases where exemption or abatement was claimed: –

Office of the Special Commissioners of Income Tax.
49 Wellington Street, Strand, W.C.

Sir, – In pursuance of the provisions of the Finance (1909-10) Act, you are hereby required by the Special Commissioners, whether you are or are not liable to supertax, to make a return of your total income from all sources in the form on page 3 hereof, and to forward the same, duly signed, by you, to this office within 28 days from this date. Your attention is called to the sections relating to the supertax printed on the fourth page hereof, and especially to section 66(2), which enacts that the basis of your return shall be the statutory income of the previous year, that is to say, your income 'estimated in the same manner as the total income from all sources is estimated for the purposes of exemptions or abatements under the Income Tax Acts' – subject to certain specified additional deductions.

Directions as to the manner in which the third page of this form is to be filled in are given on page 2; and some explanatory notes have been added at the foot of that page.

If you desire further information on any point I shall be glad to furnish it on application.

I am, Sir, your obedient servant,
N.F.W. FISHER, Clerk to Special Commissioners.

Dear Sir, – In reply to your letter dated May 4, which concludes with an invitation to apply to you for further information, I beg to submit the following points to you:

I. In the third explanatory note I am directed to make a return for supertaxation, of what is called my gross income, meaning, apparently, my gross dividends without deduction of Income-tax. Let me put an extreme case to you. A large number of Socialists, representing a political force which is growing with remarkable rapidity in all the countries of Europe, advocate a tax of 20s. in the pound on incomes derived from rent and interest. The supertax is avowedly an advance in this direction. Let us suppose for the sake of illustration that Mr. Lloyd George next year introduces an income-tax of 20s. in the pound on unearned incomes. Am I to understand that in that case not only will incomes derived from rent and interest be entirely confiscated, but that the recipients of such incomes, though left entirely destitute, will be called on to pay a supertax on the income they have not received? No doubt this extreme event is not likely to occur; but you will see that long before the point of 20s. in the pound is reached a rate of taxation may be imposed which will raise this question in a very serious form. My contention is that the Special Commissioners must sooner or later adopt in their practice the principle that a man cannot be taxed on income that he has not actually received. Even under Schedule D, it is already a hardship that we should be taxed on our gross incomes; but in that case, we at least enjoy the possession of the income for a year or a fraction of a year. In the case of rent and interest, the gross amount never reaches us at all; and you have only to conceive the taxation getting to a certain figure to foresee a situation in which you will be taxing a poor man on the scale of a rich man, and finally taxing a destitute man on the assumption that he is enjoying £20,000 a year.

2. Direction (e, page 2, reads as follows: – 'The income of a married woman living with her husband is deemed by the Income Tax Acts to be his income, and full particulars thereof must be included in any statement of income rendered by him for the purpose of supertax.' Now I have absolutely no means of ascertaining my wife's income except by asking her for the information. Her property is a separate property. She keeps a separate banking account at a separate bank. Her solicitor is not my solicitor. I can make a guess at her means from her style of living, exactly as the Surveyor of Income Tax does when he makes a shot at an assessment in the absence of exact information; but beyond that I have no more knowledge of her income than I have of yours. I have therefore asked her to give me statement. She refuses, on principle. As far as I know, I have no legal means of compelling her to make any such disclosure; and if I had, it does not follow that I am bound to incur law costs to obtain information which is required not by myself but by the State. Clearly, however, it is in the power of the Commissioners to compel my wife to make a full disclosure of her income for the purposes of taxation: but equally clearly they must not communicate that disclosure to me or to any other person. It seems to me under these circumstances that all I can do for you is to tell you who my wife is and leave it to you to ascertain her income and make me pay the tax on it. Even this you cannot do without a violation of secrecy, as it will be possible for me by a simple calculation to ascertain my wife's income from your demand. I need not dwell on the further obvious objection that as my wife enjoys a fixed income

derived from property, whereas a large part of my own is a fluctuating income derived from the precarious profession of play-writing, my income may in any year be much smaller than my wife's, in which case I shall have to pay on a much larger income than I enjoy, without, as far as I know, having any legal power of recovering from my wife the amount I have paid on her income.

I shall be very glad to hear from you on both these points. The second is perhaps the more important, because you can compel me, whilst the rate of taxation remains as low as it is at present, to pay on my gross instead of my net income if you can obtain the support of the law for that unreasonable course; but by no possible process, legal or illegal, can you extract from me information which I do not possess, and to which I have no means of access.

Yours faithfully,
G. BERNARD SHAW
10 Adelphi Terrace, W.C. May 5th.

N.F.W. Fisher, Esq., 49,
Wellington Street, Strand, WC.

Sir, – In reply to your letter of the 5th inst. I am directed by the Special Commissioners to inform you that the Income Tax Acts determine, with certain specified exceptions, the basis of computation of income for the purpose of the supertax.

Under these Acts the 'total income' of a taxpayer is the amount of the income before the liability to income-tax has been settled. Moreover, the income of a married woman living with her husband Is deemed to be the husband's income, and he is made accountable to the Revenue for the liability arising in respect of that income.While the Special Commissioners are happy to furnish any information as to the basis on which returns should be made, their functions do not extend so far as to admit of their advising as to the means to be adopted in a particular case to enable the taxpayer to acquire the information necessary to put him in a position to make the return required by the Acts.

I am, Sir, your obedient servant,
N.F.W. Fisher, Esq., 49, May 27th.

G. Bernard Shaw, Esq.

Dear Sir, – Your letter 5452 S.T., dated the 27th May, for which I thank you, does not meet my second point.

You say 'the income of a married woman living with her husband is deemed to be her husband's income, and he is made accountable to the Revenue for the liability arising in respect of that income'. To which I reply, 'By all means, I am quite willing to have my wife's income deemed to be my income, and to pay the tax on it; but you have gone beyond this: you have required me to ascertain the amount of my wife's income, which I have no means of doing.'

The Income Tax Acts give you power to obtain from my wife a return of her income. Do they give me that power? If so, can you refer me to the particular clause?

Observe that I claim neither exemption nor abatement, and am ready to pay when you assess me.

Yours faithfully,
G. BERNARD SHAW.

This last letter led to a personal interview, in which I was able to satisfy the Commissioners that the difficulty was in no sense a personal one, and that we were both up against two obstacles – first, an oversight in the Income Tax Acts; and, second, the suffragist movement. Beyond that the solution of the problem has not advanced. To elucidate the matter I may explain that what some of your readers may consider my gross ignorance of my own domestic affairs is quite genuine, and probably not uncommon within the sphere of supertaxation. I can guess what my wife's income is within, say, £1,500; but that is no use for the purposes of an income-tax return. Now the women who are leading the suffragist movement at present not only very strongly resent the clauses in the Income Tax Acts by which the income of a married woman living with her husband is regarded as his income (a resentment which, on quite other grounds, he usually heartily shares), but they object to any compulsory disclosure to a husband of a wife's income unless it involves a reciprocal disclosure to her of his income. There are obvious grounds for this; for example, there are cases in which a man, either from parsimony or because he is spending a good deal of money on his relatives, or on a clandestine establishment, or on sport, or in other ways which he conceals from his wife, supplies her with much less money than she might reasonably demand if she knew the real extent of his resources. Even in the supertaxed class there exists the equivalent of the working man who earns 34s or 38s. a week, but tells his wife that he gets only 25s. Therefore, many of these ladies are of opinion that women should refuse, on principle, to disclose their incomes to their husbands. It. is not clear at present that any legal power exists to compel them to make the disclosure even to the State (it seems that I was wrong in my assumption on this point); but they do not, as far as I know, object to make such a disclosure, though here again they would object to the State communicating it to their husbands.

Now comes the question of what is to happen to husbands in my predicament. Let us suppose that the interpretation of the law can be strained to the point of inducing the Courts to enjoin me to make the required disclosure. I am unable to obey the injunction, because no man can tell what he does not know. I go to my wife and tell her that I shall be put in prison if she does not tell me her income. She replies that many women have gone to prison for the cause, and that it is time that the men should take their turn. Am I to languish in gaol, to the delight of the whole suffragist movement, because I cannot perform impossibilities? Take the obvious alternative. Suppose the Courts enjoin my wife to disclose her exact income to me. She refuses. She is sent to prison. She promptly resorts to the hunger strike. Mr. Lloyd George and Mr. Winston Churchill have then either to forcibly feed her, and be banished to South Africa as their unfortunate colleague the Viscount Gladstone was banished by Lady Constance Lytton, or else surrender at discretion.

I submit that neither of these alternatives can be regarded as a short cut out of the difficulty. On the contrary, the stoutest statesman night well blench before entering on the second, which is the more reasonable of the two. I suggest that Mr. Lloyd George had better cut the Gordian knot by hurrying through a short Act making married couples independent of one another in their liability of supertaxation. I need not occupy your space with details of adjustment that are obvious the moment the nature of the difficulty is grasped.

This would also be an opportunity of doing away with the absurdity of taxing gross instead of net income. I need not say that I do not raise this difficulty as a device for avoiding taxation. It does not matter to the Chancellor of the Exchequer whether the rule is to tax on net or gross, as he can get the same revenue in either case by simply altering the rate. But as long as the taxation is on the gross it will mean that the propertied classes in this country will be taxed, not only on their own incomes, but on the entire revenue derived by the State from taxing them; that is to say, on a considerable part of the State's income. This is indirect taxation masquerading as direct taxation. It may end in an income-tax of several shillings in the pound, figuring in the Budget as an income-tax of 1s. 6d. or so.

Finally, may I say that though, as a Socialist, I have nothing to urge against the Marxian policy of 'expropriating the expropriators', I do wish that when the people of this country make up their minds to Socialist measures they would elect Socialist Governments to carry them out? If the Cabinet had consisted of members of the Fabian Society it would not have made this mess of the supertax. I suggest that the Government should, as an item of pressingly needed Parliamentary reform, institute 50 Parliamentary aldermen, sitting in the House of Commons with rights of speech, but without votes. They might be elected on the Hare system of making the entire country a single constituency. Under such circumstances serious political students of the type of John Stuart Mill, or Mr. Sidney Webb, or, shall I say, myself, might possibly obtain that access to Parliament which we can hardly hope for at present, as no single constituency contains a sufficient number of politically-educated voters to return us. As we should have no votes, our revolutionary views could do no harm; and our acquaintance with the elementary principles of politics would enable us to show the House of Commons how to discover difficulties otherwise than by breaking other people's shins against them.

Yours truly,
G. BERNARD SHAW.
10, Adelphi Terrace, W.C.

The Times published two articles purporting to be reviews of the French actor Edmond Got's (1822–1901) Diaries on 21 March 1910 – 'Got and the New Dramaturgy' – and on 20 June 1910 – 'Leaving Aristotle Out.' They were unsigned but seem to have been written by A.B. Walkley, the formidable theatre critic of *The Times*, and they were heavily critical of the 'new dramaturgy' which in February-March of that year was represented in productions of Shaw's *Misalliance* and Granville-Barker's *The Madras House*, both of which failed at the box office. Shaw ignored the first article but Granville-Barker impatiently commented that he wished the critics would 'leave Aristotle out' – hence the title of the second article in which Walkley insisted that he would not 'leave Aristotle out.' Shaw's response in the following letter throws light on his methods as a playwright, specifically on his rigorous application of the classical – the Aristotelian – unities to his work. Here again one sees him inveighing against London theatre critics for their 'vituperation' of his plays. Francisque Sarcey (1827–99) was the well-known dramatic critic and champion of Eugene Scribe's 'well-made plays' and Victorien Sardou's 'thesis plays'.

The Rosherville Ecclesiastical Gardens in Gravesend were a popular attraction for Londoners. They consisted of pleasure gardens and theatres that put on popular performances.

'LEAVING ARISTOTLE OUT'.

Sir, – The writer of the article under the above heading challenges me so repeatedly and pointedly that it would be discourteous to pass his article over without a word of explanation. Let me briefly offer him the following assurances.

1. I am no party to Mr. Granville Barker's demand for the omission of Aristotle. I take the greatest pains to secure 'unity of impression, continuity, and cumulative force of interest'; and it is noteworthy that such mastery as I have been able to achieve has led me finally to the Greek form of drama, in which the unities of time and place are strictly observed. And whenever I find a critic complaining that my plays are no plays because my scenes do not jump from Jerusalem to Madagascar, and my playbills are not filled with such aids to the spectator as 'Six weeks elapse between Acts I and II and two years between Acts II and III,' I conclude that the critic has learnt his business from Sarcey, and not from Aristotle.

2. I entirely agree that 'right views, sound opinions' are more desirable than 'original views'. At the same time, I regard a writer who is convinced that his views are right and sound as a very dangerous kind of lunatic. He is to be found in every asylum; and his delusion is that he is the Pope, or even a higher authority than the Pope. Original views, in the sense – the only possible sense – of being sincere, unaffected, unborrowed views, are at least humanly attainable. This point has been admirably demonstrated by no less able a critic than Mr. A.B. Walkley, to whose collected articles I would refer the author of your weekly notes on the theatre.

3. I most solemnly protest that I have never 'told my critics how they ought to criticize my next play'. I have told them repeatedly how they actually would criticize it; that is, by falling victim to 'the psychology of the crowd' (Mr. Walkley will explain), and helplessly repeating a ridiculous litany first invented by the least competent and least literate among them, and having no relation either to the facts of the theatre or the science of criticism. And on every such occasion they have fulfilled my prophecy to the letter.

4. I am quite aware that my phrase 'the vituperation of the Press' would be neither accurate nor grateful if the Press consisted of *The Times*, which is apparently the only paper your contributor reads. Unfortunately *The Times* is in this matter, as in others, an exceptional paper. Let me state one fact which speaks for itself. From Germany I have for years past received repeated and urgent requests to allow my plays to be produced in the first instance in Berlin, on the ground that

the announcements of their unutterable tedium and disastrous failure which invariably follow their production in London makes it necessary to hold them back in Berlin until the verdict is forgotten. Your contributor is misled by that 'handsome tribute from criticism' which consists in praising my old plays in order to throw into greater relief the infamy of my new ones. Thus *Misalliance* was unworthy of the author of *Getting Married; Getting Married* had none of the brilliance of *The Doctor's Dilemma; The Doctor's Dilemma* was a pitiful falling-off from Major Barbara; and nobody could sit out *Major Barbara* without asking why the author did not give us another masterpiece like *John Bull's Other Island* – poor *John Bull*, which first established the tradition that my plays are not plays, but mere talk!

Substitute for these titles *The Marriage of Ann Leete, The Voysey Inheritance, Waste* and *The Madras House*, and the story applies equally to Mr. Granville Barker. To say that 'these reservations turn the whole praise sour for us' is quite true. They do. When I am told that it is a pity that a man who only last year was so honest as I, should have become a thief, a liar, a blackguard, an incendiary, and a murderer, and I lose some thousands of pounds and a great deal of credit in consequence, it is perhaps ungrateful in me to overlook the compliment to my previous good character. It may even show an appetite for 'indiscriminate and fulsome praise.' But I cannot help it; I am built in that hypersensitive way. When I am held up to the world as a 'go-as-you-please dramatist' I don't know exactly what is meant, and neither would Aristotle; but for the life of me I cannot feel as if I were receiving 'a handsome tribute from criticism'. I actually prefer the downright vituperation.

5. I greatly regret that your contributor should have succeeded in dashing the faith Mr. Walkley once had in my work. Mr. Walkley's very handsome tributes in *Le Temps* were the beginning of my literary vogue in France. Even when he seized the opportunity of a recent public dinner to make a quite unprovoked attack on the projected National Theatre, and to assure the public that he had allowed his obscurer fellow critics to convert him to the vulgar view of the work at which Mr. Barker and I are toiling – a view which I confess I cannot distinguish from the Rosherville view of a Beethoven symphony – I held my peace. I shall continue to hold it, because my personal and private feelings are entirely friendly to him. But it is my steady and impenitent purpose to 'permit myself', whenever, like Mrs. Gamp, I feel so disposed, to do with his unworthy colleagues what Heine reproached Lessing for doing – namely, not only to cut off their heads, but to hold them up on the scaffold, to show the public that there is nothing in them.

Yours truly
G. BERNARD SHAW.

A new Copyright Bill was being introduced in Parliament and there had been several letters both for and against it. A long letter (*The Times*, 2 May) by a J. Drummond Robertson, who was concerned as to how the new bill would affect what was then known as the mechanical music industry, stirred Shaw into contributing to the debate with an argument that, though characteristically paradoxical, comes out strongly in favour of the invariably unacknowledged and uncompensated composer. (See below, 'Composers and their Property', 2 December 1929.)

~ 1911, May 4 ~

THE COPYRIGHT BILL
COMPOSERS AND COMPENSATION.

Sir, – The letter of Mr. J. Drummond Robertson is unanswerable, not because it is convincing, but because its audacity paralyses all the nervous centres which make controversy possible. Our comfort is that, if it is brought forward and pushed to its logical conclusion in a speech in the House of Commons, that Assembly, if it has any conscience and any logic, will be stupefied beyond all power of passing the Copyright Bill or anything else for the remainder of the Session.

Let me attempt to deal with his point sanely. Every extension of property necessarily involves an exaction of payment for something that was formerly derelict. If you enclose a common you deprive poor men of a supply of free mushrooms and goose pasture. On the other hand, if you abolish rights of property you destroy values for which large sums may have been paid. For instance, the abolition of the slave trade deprived the slaves of their commercial value, and thereby left many of them much worse off, besides turning a large part of the capital of their proprietors into waste paper. Accordingly, it is customary on such occasions for the losers to claim compensation, and, when they have sufficient political power, to get it.

The Copyright Bill threatens the phonographic industry with a change of this nature. It so happened that when International Copyright began the mechanical reproduction of music was carried on mainly by makers of musical- boxes and street-organs. The musical-box manufacturers were mostly Swiss toy-makers, unable to afford any such increase in cost of production as a composer's novelty would have involved. They were privileged by custom to steal their tunes; and the whole business was regarded as negligible. Consequently, when Switzerland took the lead in establishing International Copyright by giving hospitality to the Berne

Convention, the exemption of the musical-box manufacturers from the obligation to comply with the Copyright Laws was passed politely as a matter of course, like a vote of thanks. Since then the invention of the phonograph and the perfecting of the pianola have changed the whole situation. Every musical household that can afford it now has a pianola; and both musical and unmusical households often have phonographs of one kind or another. That is to say, they spend considerable sums every years on rolls and records which would formerly have been spent on sheet music.

Mr. J. Drummond Robertson tries to make a distinction between rolls and records and sheet music, but without success. Like many another ingenious controversialist, he has proved too much.

However, that is not the point. Rightly or wrongly, a large amount of capital has been invested in the pianola and gramophone industries on the assumption that the musical material could be stolen with impunity. Now comes an Act of Parliament declaring that the impunity shall cease, and that violation of copyright is a crime punishable by fine and imprisonment, not to mention civil damages. The manufacturers demand compensation for their lost impunity, and I think they ought to get it. No man is to blame for calculating his enterprises according to the law or no law of the land. If housebreaking were a tolerated occupation – as it is to some extent an admired one – and it were proposed to introduce a law making it felony, I should support the claim of our burglars to be compensated for the scrapping of their jemmies, chisels, drills, and oxy-hydrogen jets, and also for the loss of an occupation which demands for its successful pursuit many virtues and accomplishments, both valuable to the community and difficult of acquirement.

So far, I take it, Mr. Drummond Robertson and I are in agreement. But, it seems, I get on more questionable ground when I declare that, in the hypothetical case of the burglars, I should certainly not levy the compensation on the already burgled. When we set our slaves free we compensated the slave-owners, but we did not ask the slaves to pay the compensation. In disestablishing the Irish Church we did not make the Irish clergy pay the commutation; on the contrary, we invited them to receive it so liberally that there was throughout Protestant Ireland an extraordinary revival of piety, in which all sorts and conditions of persons, previously unconscious of any ecclesiastical vocation, rushed into the Church.

The moral, I hope, is obvious. Compensate your pianola and gramophone manufacturers by all means. Compensate them handsomely. But in the name of common sense do not make the unfortunate composers, who have already been robbed, pay the compensation. They did not ask the manufacturers to invest their money in phonographs and pianolas. For several years past they have had to look on helplessly at enormous profits being made out of the music they have composed. The better the music, the worse they have been paid for it. It is appalling to read the life of so great a composer as Richard Wagner and to realize that he had produced several of the greatest works of art the world possesses, and was far past middle-age before he was free from the most humiliating pecuniary anxieties. And now, if you please, the manufacturers, who have made more money out of Wagner's music than he ever spent in his whole life, and who never paid him a farthing, want his heirs to compensate them for the loss of their power to steal his music with impunity. The proposal is so monstrous that a simple statement of it ought to dispose of it without further words. The community sinned, and the community should atone. The musicians suffered, and if there is to be any compensation they should share it.

Of course the official retort is ready for us poor artists. The Copyright Bill places us in a much better position than we were before. But the mechanical record people will not let the Government pass it unless they are compensated. The Government cannot and will not find money to compensate them, as it ought to compensate them, at the expense of the community. Sooner than attempt that, it will drop the Bill. An injustice has to be done either to us artists or to the manufacturers. We, being artists, are poor and politically insignificant. They, being industrialists, are rich and can bully Governments. I suppose we must go to the wall, but I do not see why we should do so without politely informing the public and the Government that we thoroughly understand what is happening to us, and that we submit to injustice because we cannot help ourselves, and not in the least because we are imposed on by the special pleading of Mr. Drummond Robertson and those whom he represents.

Yours truly,
G. BERNARD SHAW.

The introduction of a National Insurance Bill by Lloyd George was causing controversy on both sides of the House. The Birkbeck Bank collapsed at the same time with liabilities of £11,000,000, causing hardship to many – particularly, in Shaw's eyes, to sections of the middle class.

THE BIRKBECK SUSPENSION AND THE INSURANCE BILL.

Sir – An institution which has for 60 years been of incalculable service to that section of our middle class which has to content itself with bank balances beneath the notice of rich men's bankers is, through no apparent fault of its own, compelled to close its doors because it is short of £400,000, or somewhere between £6,000 and £7,000 per year for its term of service. Will any one who has imagination and business faculty enough to understand what banking means and what it saves, and how it helps men to be really thrifty, deny that it would have paid us as a nation to subsidize the Birkbeck to four times this sum annually had such help been necessary? Now that the help is necessary – now that 112,000 people, who, if they had had their houses shaken down by an earthquake, would have been rescued by the public as a matter of course, are thrown into the most distressing anxiety and threatened with a calamity that will spread far beyond the direct sufferers – why should the Chancellor of the Exchequer hesitate to come to their assistance, and not only enable the Birkbeck to reopen its doors and resume its altogether beneficent and nationally profitable activity, but if necessary to give it hopes of such an annual grant-in-aid as will save it from retreating, like the other banks, into the service of the comparatively rich only?

Just consider the situation. Here we are on the eve of the Parliamentary Committee stage of a National Insurance Bill. It is in some respects so monstrous a Bill that its passage into law as it stands is unthinkable. It is a Bill to enforce saving on people who already cannot afford to feed themselves properly (that is, a Bill to make suicide and child-murder compulsory), and to enforce it, moreover, by an official machinery which would make even the millennium a nuisance. But it contains certain provisions which have won approval from all parties It proposes to pay a handsome subsidy to those bodies which, like the friendly societies, have by voluntary effort organised thrift and orderly business habits among the working classes, justly recognizing that they render social services and effect social economics for which they can make no charge and which can therefore figure directly in no commercial balance-sheet. Now the Birkbeck has done for the less fortunate section of the middle class exactly what the friendly societies and trade unions (which can be brought within the scope of the Bill by a simple amendment) are doing for the working class.

Excepting only the hopeless residuum which represents the wreckage of our industrial system, there is no class in which the struggle for existence is so wearing and incessant as in the class that banked at the Birkbeck. Are they, because they are totally unrepresented in Parliament, to be abandoned to a calamity which will do several millions' worth of mischief, when the yield of about half a farthing on the income-tax would avert it?

Yours truly,
G. BERNARD SHAW.

Shaw's next letter provides additional comment on the Insurance Bill, stimulated by a public address given by Lloyd George, as reported in *The Times*. This response is a long, well argued article on the lines of the Fabian tracts Shaw had been producing for over twenty years. He did not include this article-letter among his Collected Works, perhaps because of the ephemerality of the issue. The Syndicalists were a group that advocated direct action to abolish the Capitalist system. George Lansbury (1859–1940) was the MP for Bow and Bromley who was credited with converting Keir Hardie to Christianity and later became editor of the *Daily Herald*. F.E. Smith (1872–1930, later Earl of Birkenhead) was a Conservative MP and well-known Victorian diarist.

∽ 1911, October 24 ∽

National Insurance and Political Tactics.

Mr Shaw's Protest.

Sir, – Up to October 14, when Mr. Lloyd George delivered an address on the National Insurance Bill at Whitefield's Tabernacle, there was still some hope of persuading him to withdraw his contributory clauses (made in German), and replace them by a sound and considerate scheme based, not on German mistakes, but on German experience of those mistakes, and also – if that were not too much to ask – taking some account of English facts and English investigations of a very complicated and difficult subject. These hopes are now extinguished. Mr. Lloyd George is not going to redraft his Bill, not going to reconsider his Bill, not going to delay his Bill by one hour. He is convinced that after recent electioneering experience of the results of opposing Old-Age Pensions, the Opposition will not dare oppose his Bill or raise the party issue on it. And he is quite certain that if once it gets through, the overwhelming effect of its benefits on the working classes will at the next General Election carry his party to victory with an irresistible rush, no matter what foreign or domestic question may arise in the meantime to divert attention from it.

If Mr. Lloyd George's colleagues are as satisfied with his forecast as their curiously reserved acquiescence seems to imply, there is a sensational disappointment in store for them. Had the Bill been drafted for Mr. Lloyd

George by Mr. F.E. Smith himself with the express object of stirring up at the next General Election a hornets' nest against which no Government could stand, it is this Bill of Mr. Lloyd George's. His guarantee of a Liberal victory at the polls if the Bill is passed is worth just as much as his guarantee that under the Bill every worker attacked with consumption will be cured in four months in his sanatoria.

In saying this I lay myself open to an obvious retort. Mr. Lloyd George will say, 'Who are you, pray? If the Labour members, who are the accredited representatives of the working classes in Parliament, support the Bill – If the Opposition itself admits that it cannot oppose the Bill, am I to concern myself because one grotesquely unrepresentative individual imagines he knows better than the Labour Party, the Cabinet, the majority of both parties in the House of Commons, and, generally, of all the rest of the world?' To that question the reader of this letter can give his own answer when he has read to the end of it.

The Secret of the Labour Party's Assent.

It is nothing to Mr. Lloyd George's point that the Labour Party accepts the Bill *faute de mieux*. To obtain such reluctant support, all any statesman has to do is to produce a Bill that is better than nothing. And things are so bad that even this Bill is better than nothing, it is not disputed that it will improve the position of friendly societies and trade unions, and that it will secure to many poor people benefits which, pitiful as they are, seem enormous in contrast with their present destitution. The fact that an attempt will be made to do this at the cost of a permanent degradation of the working class standard of subsistence is, as I shall presently show, not a real factor in the case, because the attempt will not succeed, though the insurance will remain And so, mischievous as the methods of the Bill are, its benefits are too valuable to throw away on the chance of Mr. Lloyd George being any wiser three months hence The Labour members must vote for the Bill. But I wonder will the Labour members tell Mr. Lloyd George and the public what the consequence will be. Lest they should not, let me tell him, as follows.

I am not a Labour leader. But I have been a Socialist agitator for nearly 30 years; and my services as a public speaker are still in demand in the Labour movement. If I were a Labour member in Parliament I should vote for the Bill. But if Mr. Lloyd George inferred that my vote pledged me to use my influence to persuade the working classes to submit to the reduction of wages proposed by the Bill, he would make a stupendous mistake. What I should do as a Labour member is just what I shall do as a public speaker that is, urge the workers to prepare for a determined struggle in defence of their living wage by accumulating strike funds, recruiting the unions, and rallying enthusiasm for the coming fight over the first attempt to reduce the week's wage by 4d. or 6d. Many of your readers will think this very wicked of me; but I assure them that if I gave any other advice I should not only fail as completely as the trade union leaders failed when they tried to prevent the railwayman from striking but I should be dismissed from the confidence of the workers as one who had sold them and their living wage to the Government by which word Government most of them would mean the King, Mr. Balfour, Mr. Asquith, Mr. Chamberlain, Lord Rosebery, Mr. Winston Churchill, General Roberts, the Archbishop of Canterbury, Mr. Carnegie, Sir Herbert Tree, General Sir Robert Baden Powell, and the House of Lords in general; for it is a wild mistake to suppose that the inhabitants of this country, in any class, understand the Constitution accurately, or discriminate nicely between one party and another. Now as I happen to be independent of working class confidence both as to money and fame, such a repudiance would not hurt anything but my feelings. But to a Labour leader or Labour member it would mean extinction and ruin.

The Syndicalist Peril.

Further, the most dangerous rivals of the Parliamentary Labour Party in France and England just now are the Syndicalists, whose doctrine – unfortunately a very plausible one – is that Labour inside Parliament is nobbled and outwitted and bought off, whilst Labour outside Parliament, militant and threatening, is a force that Parliament dreads and obeys. And its weapon is the general strike, which absurd as it is in logic, can nevertheless be put in practice quite far enough to do a great deal of mischief. If the Labour members show the least sign of taking the side of Mr. Lloyd George when his onslaught on the living wage begins with the first week's operation of his scheme, they will give an impulse to Syndicalism and strike a blow at their own position which will lame them for a generation. Does Mr. Lloyd George think they are going to do this for the sake of his *beaux yeux*?

The Labour leaders know well that no Bill that Mr. Lloyd George or any-other statesman can introduce can compel a man who is worth 17s. 6d. a week in the labour market to accept 17s. 2d. on any pretext whatever. For more than a century British trade unionists have kept their eyes and ears tightly shut against all the speeches and arguments and figures of economists and politicians, and have instinctively urged the workers to insist on a living wage, and to fight desperately against every attempt to reduce it. And experience has shown that they were right and that the economists and politicians were wrong. There is not a member of the Labour Party nor a trade union leader throughout the country who, even if he were disposed to, would dare pledge himself to Mr. Lloyd George to ask his constituents to submit to the reduction threatened by this Bill. As the Labour Party is nothing if not independent, it cannot pledge itself to support the Liberal Party even on matters in which both parties are in sympathy. How can it do so in this matter, in which Mr. Lloyd George is going to make a wholesale attack on the manifestly insufficient subsistence of the poor to save the visibly overflowing pockets of the rich?

The Supremacy of the Living Wage in Labour Politics.

However, I grant that Mr. Lloyd George should be frankly dealt with. The Labour members have no right to leave him under the impression that their acceptance of the Bill means that they will help him to collect the premiums by reducing wages. They are bound in honour to give their votes in open protest, and to warn the Government that when the time comes when the inevitable strikes in defence of the living wage break out in all directions, embittered as they will be by the rise in the cost of living which has already driven even respectable middle class people to join bread riots on the Continent – they will throw all their weight on the side of the strikers; denounce the Government without stint for having disregarded all the warnings of Mr. Lansbury; and take advantage of the crisis to capture for labour many constituencies which are now too inveterately Liberal to be detached from their old allegiance except by a sensational crises in the Labour movement.

Such is likely to be the reality of that transport of affectionate gratitude from the Labour Party and the working classes to which Mr. Lloyd George is looking forward, and to which he has taught his colleagues to look forward, at the next General Election.

The Middle Class Struggle for Life.

Now let us see whether the poorer middle class, the class of small employers, strong in Nonconformity and implacable on the subject of the Church in Wales, will be any more grateful to him than the workers. The answer can be anticipated by any one who foresees that it is just this poor and worried class which will at first have to pay not only its own contribution but the workers' as well. For the workers will succeed in their resistance to the reduction of wages. If the poorest employers could induce their men to accept 17s. 2d. instead of 17s. 6d. they would not wait for the Insurance Bill to make the reduction. They can no more get their labour cheaper by an Insurance Act than the workers could get a higher wage by an Act compelling millionaires' wives to insure their diamonds against burglary. Such employers are always nibbling at wages because their customers are always nibbling at prices. The notion that there is a margin of 4d. a week for them to play with at Mr. Lloyd George's command is a delusion. What will happen is that, after a more or less acute struggle, the employer will have to pay the same wages as before, or possibly more if the labour market has risen, or if the shock of the Bill nerves the workers to a more determined exaction of the last farthing of their market value.

Now, to the salaried manager of a joint stock company this may not matter. The shareholders will have so much less dividend; that is all. To the able employer of large resources, with time to turn in, it will at least not be ruinous: he can adapt himself to the increased cost of labour in various ways, one of them being to obtain a reduction of rent by threatening to move into cheaper premises or by executing his threat. But the small employer, living from hand to mouth often paying his skilled workmen more than he has left for himself, rack rented and forced by competition to cut his prices down to the lowest bearable point, will be ground into the dust by the Bill. With no reserves, no time to talisman, and a burden of rates to carry out of all proportion to his means, he will find himself compelled, possibly after a strike that will 'bleed him to the white,' to pay both the employer's contribution and the worker's contribution.

The more men you employ, the worse you are to be treated.

All this is bad enough; but worse remains behind. The employer will be taxed by this Bill not only oppressively, but most iniquitously. It is clear that an employer's taxable capacity depends on his net income. Now, the notion that the net income of an employer varies according to the number of persons he employs may seem plausible in circles where men are judged by the length of their retinue of domestic servants; but to any one acquainted with practical business it is a cruel absurdity. A house agent with one clerk and an office boy may be making a larger income than his next-door neighbour with tea shop assistants or a yard full of wagoners. If the House of Commons declines to take any interest in these petty ratepayers, let us take an example from the fine arts. The greatest sculptor in the world is paid at present for a portrait in marble exactly half what is paid to the most fashionable painter in London for a portrait in oils; yet the painter employs no labour except his own, whilst the sculptor has to keep a builder's yard and staff for the handling of his marble, Compare the wages bill paid every week by an architect and by a builder, by a farmer and by a greengrocer, by a dentist and by a restaurant keeper. Then compare their net incomes, and conceive, if you can, any sane statesman proposing to tax them on their wages bills and not on their incomes. Already it is a sufficiently bitter grievance that local rates are levied on premises and not on incomes; so that the palmists and astrologers get off for the merest fraction of what the carriage builders and haberdashers must pay; but to pile on to this injustice, which is at least a foreseen one, a new and worse one which no employer foresaw when he made his contracts with his landlord, or borrowed his capital, and this at a time when the burden on the ratepayer has become all but unbearable, is to show a want of sense of the realities of practical business life, and of the desperate condition of the poorer section of the middle class, which makes one despair of the House of Commons.

If there were no alternative available or if the alternative involved the devising of a new and elaborate scheme of taxation, Mr. Lloyd George would have the excuse of practical emergency. But the facts are just the other way. The machinery for taxing net income is there under his hand in working order, with 60 years' practice behind it, and with all the latest supertax improvements in full swing. And yet he deliberately sets up a new, costly, endlessly inquisitorial, extremely troublesome, grindingly oppressive, and monstrously inequitable scheme for no other purpose than to produce a childish illusion that national insurance is not Socialism, but only an extension of the operations of the ordinary commercial insurance societies.

The temper of the employers, especially the small Nonconformist ones, at the next General Election may now be imagined by even the most sanguine Liberal. The only Liberal consolation is that so many of these employers will have been evicted for non-payment of rent, that few will be on the register when the moment for revenge comes. Their own consolation will be the head of the Welsh Church on a charger.

The Contributory Bait.

And now what about the rich propertied members of Parliament who Mr. Lloyd George has conciliated at the expense of his humanity and common sense by promising them that the cost of the Bill shall be extorted from the working classes and employers, and not raised by income-tax and supertax from themselves? He will have duped them as completely as he will have duped himself. After the enormous loss caused by strikes against the reduction of wages, resulting in diminished dividends and unpaid rents, the workers will succeed, after all, in shifting the premiums on to the employers; and these, being part of the working class, will in their turn shift it on to their landlords and shareholders. It would be far better, far cheaper, far wiser tactically for our rentiers to pay at once gracefully instead of paying in the not very long run morosely, and standing the loss of a labour war into the bargain. And let it not be forgotten by petty employers that their part of the inevitable shifting of the burden will be far harder and slower than the workers' part. The workers can strike and settle the matter in a few weeks. But strikes of middle class men of business are unknown. No landlord will reduce the rent of a shop until the bankruptcy of his tenant and the lying idle of the shop on his hands for at least six months convince him that the conditions have changed and that he is asking too much. In the meantime the bankrupt is ruined.

If not Socialism, What?

But at all events the anti-Socialist Liberals can now say, 'Our Mr. Lloyd George has purged himself of all suspicion of Socialism.' Granted; but may one now ask, as Mr. Lloyd George is not a Socialist, what he is? When he put on the supertax, there was a clear alternative. If he was not a Socialist he was simply organizing the plunder which usually follows political conquest by a newly enfranchised class. But now even this Intelligible and to some extent time-honoured position does not fit him. For he has now put a supertax on the poor, and reduced the limit of income-tax exemption from £160 a year to 23 guineas. Having supertaxed the man with £5,001 a year at the rate of twopence in the pound, he now supertaxes the man with £46 a year at the rate of 4d. in the pound. He admits that the lad with nine shillings a week cannot afford the luxury of insurance, but maintains that the lad's father with a wife and several children to keep on 17s. 6d. a week, can afford it. How are we to class Mr. Lloyd George?

For my part I class him as a sentimental amateur. I wish our Governments would either let Socialism alone or else, since this is now impossible, get it done by somebody who understands the business and is not ashamed of it. I wish the Liberals would read the history of their own party, and learn how it came into existence to put a stop to attempts at paternal government by well meaning Tories who did not in the least know how to do it, and invariably left matters worse than they found them when they tried to make them better by amateur legislation. I wish our Bishops would realize that thrift means thriving, and that thriving means spending before it means saving. And I wish the Cabinet could be compelled to live and support their families on 17s. 6d. a week for a whole Session and then debate a motion by Mr. Balfour to give them 17s. 2d. in future. It would be quite merrie England even then; but it would at least not be quite so absurd as the England this silly Insurance Bill has revealed to us.

Yours faithfully,
G. BERNARD SHAW.

A *Times* article entitled '*Drama of Discussion*' had commented that public debates seemed to be drawing larger audiences than plays and misquoted Shaw to support the claim, stating that 'Mr. Bernard Shaw says that the new kind of play should be no play but a discussion and should contain as little drama as possible.' It is this error that Shaw takes up and corrects in the following letter. Gilbert Keith Chesterton (1874–1936) was the well-known author and critic. His and Shaw's series of debates on public issues, which began in 1911 and continued formally and informally until 1927, were extremely popular. One critic described Shaw and Chesterton as the 'debaters of the century'. The aeroplane that comes down and smashes a greenhouse refers to an incident in *Misalliance*.

'THE DRAMA OF DISCUSSION'.

Sir, – Your article on this subject in Monday's issue is disabled by an odd mistake. It assumes that I described the human race as having outgrown the drama and reached a phase in which it cares only for platform discussion. The improbability of any sane mortal putting forward such a proposition is enormous. In my case it is not only improbable, but impossible. It is quite true that pure platform discussion is extremely popular. For example, Mr. Gilbert Chesterton is to debate with me at the Memorial Hall on the 30th of this month, and though not a single advertisement has been issued, every seat in the hall has been sold for some time past and asked for five times over since: a phenomenon which I may safely challenge the most profusely-advertised theatrical performance to equal if it can. We have therefore already arrived at the point of finding a good debate more attractive than nine out of ten plays.

But what I actually said was that every individual playgoer passes through three phases. First, the phase of childish illusion, in which the Fairy Queen seems really a Fairy Queen, and the policeman in the harlequinade a real policeman. Second, the phase in which the play is known to be a play and the persons on the stage to be actors, but in which all the old theatrical situations seem fresh and thrilling and the principal actors fascinating and lovable. Third, the phase in which the old situations have become the dreariest of platitudes, and in which the once admired and beloved actor or actress (now a little older) is, on the whole, less attractive than the domestic fireside or the club smoking-room. Now the English people, being mostly in the third phase, does not go to the theatre, though it does go to discussions when it gets the chance. The theatre at present lives on the young, the ignorant, and the fanciers of divorce cases. The bulk of the nation occupies itself with business, politics, religion, and open-air sport, with a dash of music and pictures, and leaves the theatre aside as the most expensive and worst ventilated way to boredom and influenza.

My contention is that, if you are to tempt the adult, married, sensible Englishman from his comfortable house (and if you cannot you will have no real national drama), you must give him plays in which life is presented, not as a string of imitations of incidents from the sensation columns of the daily papers, with actors pretending to fight duels and actresses pretending to have their feelings hurt, and both pretending to kiss one another in transports of simulated passion, but as an enormously interesting mass of problems of conduct which every member of the audience has or may have to solve for himself or herself. In order to raise such problems 'things must happen,' as your article very properly insists. Also, they must happen to credibly human beings. I may have omitted to mention these two conditions in my address. I omitted many things: for example, I did not remind the audience that there are milestones on the Dover road. I was vain enough to think that any one who had ever been inside a London theatre would give me credit for knowing the rudiments of my own business and being incapable of such a contradiction in terms as that 'a play should be no play, but a discussion.' Let me ask now as to this cry of 'things must happen,' What things? When a brick falls on a man's head, is that something happening? When a doubt falls into his soul as to whether he may not be wrong on a point on which he has hitherto felt confidently right, is that something happening?

Well, people over 30 will not go to the theatre to see an imitation brick weighing half an ounce fall on an imitation scalp made of strong pasteboard. They will go to the theatre to see doubts attack the soul. And unless the actor is skilful enough to convey the conflict in his soul by making faces at the audience (which would seem to be the ideal of the critics who object so strongly to 'talk' in a play) I am afraid the doubts must be discussed, even if the result be that 'drama of discussion' practised by Euripides, Aristophanes, Molière, Shakespeare, Goethe, Ibsen, Tolstoy: in short, which is the invariable symptom of the highest dramatic genius.

But even on the plane of childish make-believe it is ungrateful to reproach me for lack of physical action. Why, in one of my plays an aeroplane comes down and smashes a greenhouse. What more can you possibly want?

Yours truly,
G. BERNARD SHAW.

A letter by Sir Herbert Beerbohm Tree about the censorship of the stage appeared in *The Times* of 15 February 1912, commenting on a previous letter of the 14th-. He was writing, he said, on behalf of the theatre, warning that though he was in favour of the fullest religious and social freedom for the stage, he was apprehensive that the removal of the censorship could lead to chaos. Those involved should take care. He said that he was speaking on behalf of the 'silent majority of theatre goers' and expressed the view that although he was in favour of the fullest freedom for the stage, he thought that censorship should be retained and strengthened as a defence against falling morals under the cloak of art that might influence the young. Shaw and Tree had been 'pilloried as blasphemers' when the then Examiner of Plays, Redford, banned *The Shewing-Up of Blanco Posnet*, written for Tree. Eden Phillpotts (1862–1960) was the well-known novelist and occasional playwright. His *The Secret Woman* had been refused a license by Charles Brookfield, the new Examiner and author of successful (and smutty) plays, hence Shaw's sarcastic remark about 'Many strait-laced persons' and 'children in arms'. *Orphée aux Enfers* (1858) refers to Jacques Offenbach's operetta; *The School for Scandal* (1777) is a play by

Richard Brinsley Sheridan, where the character Sir Peter hides in a closet when surprised during a tryst. The closet scene refers to *Hamlet* III.4.

~ *1912, February 16* ~

THE DRAMATIC CENSORSHIP.

Mr. Bernard Shaw and Sir Herbert Tree.

Sir, – I am sure that my friend Sir Herbert Tree will allow me, for the sake of the days when we stood side by side in the pillory as blasphemers by command of the Lord Chamberlain, to ask him whether he will support a proposal to extend the Censorship to actors. It is notorious that an actor can make the most innocent play or the most harmless speech indecent by gesture, stage business, or by mere grimace. Is there any possible object-ion, once the principle of censorship is granted, to the rehearsals at His Majesty's Theatre being attended by Mr. Brookfield, whose orders to Sir Herbert Tree as to how his lines are to be delivered, and what strokes of stage business he may or may not be allowed to introduce, shall be final?

Then as to Sir Herbert's view that the theatre is 'primarily for the young.' May I ask how young? Sir Herbert's notion of appropriate fare for the young includes *Orphée aux Enfers*, the Screen Scene from *The School for Scandal*, and the Closet Scene from *Hamlet*. Is not this a rather mature diet for those who are too young to be allowed to witness Mr. Eden Phillpott's *Secret Woman*? Surely it is dangerous to attempt to impose age-limits. Many strait-laced persons have suggested that even Mr. Brookfield's plays should not be witnessed by children in arms.

Yours truly,
G. BERNARD SHAW.

One of the weapons the Suffragettes used when arrested and imprisoned was to go on hunger strike. Prison officials, instructed by the Home Office, force-fed them. Shaw regarded this with abhorrence, as a barbarous measure unbefitting a civilised society. The following two letters are concerned with the humanitarian aspects of the law's handling and treatment of the Suffragettes. Emmeline Pankhurst (1857–1928) was founder and leader of the Suffragette Movement; the funeral Shaw refers to was that of Suffragette Emily Davison who, to highlight her cause, had died by throwing herself under the King's horse at the Derby, one of the premier events of the horse-racing calendar. The Dickinson Bill, allowing limited franchise to women, had been introduced because it was more acceptable to the Liberals, but failed by 175 votes.

MRS. PANKHURST'S TREATMENT.

MR. BERNARD SHAW ON GOVERNMENT METHODS.

Sir – I am quite confident that when I say that the moment chosen for the arrest of Mrs. Pankhurst on Saturday last made the proceeding a revolting one I am giving expression to the feelings of a large body of your readers. There was no necessity to rearrest her until after the funeral. Any official or Minister realizing the situation would, if he had a spark of decent feeling, have taken care to order a postponement. As no such order was given, we must conclude that the Government does not yet realize the situation.

May I call attention to two new considerations? The first is that it is now clear that the plan of the Home Office is, first to relieve the worst tension of public opinion by turning Mrs. Pankhurst out of prison, and then, by rigidly imprisoning her in the house in which she has taken refuge, produce all the effects of the closest confinement whilst escaping the responsibility which would attach to those effects if they occurred in prison. It is alleged that Mrs. Pankhurst's condition is very serious. It is quite clear that it cannot be very favourable, as Mrs. Pankhurst is not made of iron. Suppose Mrs. Pankhurst dies! Will the Government, merely because it has contrived that she shall die out of Holloway, still cry 'Don't care', as it did by arresting Mrs. Pankhurst before Miss Davison's funeral instead of after it?

The second point is the newly declared attitude of the Prime Minister. In the debate on the Dickinson Bill Mr. Asquith for the first time opposed the franchise for women explicitly on the ground that woman is not the female of the human species, but a distinct and inferior species, naturally disqualified from voting as a rabbit is disqualified from voting. This is a very common opinion. Mahomed's efforts to discredit it 14 centuries ago were lost on many Arabs as completely as on Mr. Asquith. But it makes the position extremely uncomfortable. A man may object to the proposed extension of the suffrage for many reasons. He may hold that the whole business of popular election is a delusion, and that votes for women is only its reduction to absurdity. He may object to it as upsetting a convenient division of labour between the sexes. He may object to it because he dislikes change, or is interested in businesses or practices which women would use political power to suppress. But it is one thing to follow a Prime Minister who advances all, or some, or any of these reasons for standing in the way of votes for women. It is quite another to follow a Prime Minister who places one's mother on the footing of a rabbit. Many men would vote for anything rather than be suspected of the rabbit theory. It makes it difficult to vote for the Liberal Party and then look the women of one's household in the face.

The situation, then, is that if Mrs. Pankhurst dies public opinion will consider that the Government, for which Mr. Asquith is in effect finally responsible, will have executed her. Mr. Asquith will not be moved by that; in his opinion it will matter just as much as killing a rabbit. I cannot convince him that he is mistaken, but I can assure him that a very large section of the public will not agree with him.

I suggest that the authorities, having had to let Mrs. Pankhurst out of prison, should now let her alone. There was something to be said for not letting her out; there is nothing to be said for pursuing her, now she is out, with a game of cat-and-mouse that will produce on public feeling all the effect of vindictive assassination if she, like Miss Davison, should seal her testimony with her blood.

Yours truly,
G. BERNARD SHAW.

Popular novelist Algernon Gissing (1860–1937), brother of the more famous author George, responded to Shaw's letter of 19 June with a long letter to *The Times* on 23 June, objecting to and heavily criticising Shaw's sympathetic attitude to the Suffragettes and stressing the criminality of their actions. Emily Davison, he insisted, could not be considered a martyr. Shaw did not use the word in his letter to *The Times*, but may well have done so elsewhere. Gissing wrote to *The Times* again on 27 June, refusing to accept Shaw's challenge and insisting that there was no necessity for women to have the vote. The women Shaw mentions in this letter were Suffragettes.

∼ *1913, June 25* ∼

MARTYRDOM AND WOMAN SUFFRAGE.

Sir – Your correspondent Mr. Algernon Gissing must, I think, be aware that the consecrated English phrase for the final sacrifice of a martyr is 'sealing one's testimony with one's blood'. That Miss Davison was a martyr is a fact, and must be recognized as a fact as much by those who object to her views as by those who agree with them. No intelligent Republican who knows the historical facts denies that Charles I. was a martyr. No similarly qualified Roman Catholic denies that Ridley and Latimer were martyrs. I am myself so lukewarm about martyrdom that one of the oftenest quoted passages in my works is to the effect that martyrdom is the only way in which people can become famous without ability; but I know the difference between a martyrdom and a fatal accident. Therefore, when Mr.

Gissing demurs to my calling Miss Davison a martyr I infer that as the quality of a martyr is a human quality, and that as Miss Davison, being a woman, was to him not human, he finds something grotesque and exaggerated and fussy in my application of the consecrated phrase to her act, much as if I had said of the giraffe which killed itself the other day that it had sealed its testimony with its blood. But Mr. Gissing must allow for the fact that his view and Mr. Asquith's is not my view. If I were writing of Miss Davison's dead body I should not describe it as a carcase. I regarded Miss Davison as a human being like myself and like Mr. Gissing. He will perhaps take the comparison as an insult. I cannot help that: natural history has no respect for personal susceptibilities.

And now, as Mr. Gissing has been pedagogue enough to lecture me, may I ask him a question? Suppose a Government of women, coming to the conclusion that he, being male, was not human, refused him the vote, excluded him from Parliament and from the juries by whom persons of his sex had to be tried, turned him out of Court on occasions when questions most intimately affecting his sex were at issue, wrote up on the walls of the churches that a woman's property included her ox and her ass and her husband and everything that was hers, and absolutely refused to be moved from this position by any appeal to reason or feeling, merely pointing out superciliously from time to time that Mr. Gissing's letters showed an unbalanced mind, and that some of the best men had never had votes, had avoided serving on juries, and had been proud and glad to wheel perambulators instead of unsexing themselves by pushing into women's professions. What would Mr. Gissing do? I really want to know. We all want to know. I am quite sure that if he can suggest any alternative to militancy the militants will be the first to bless him; for it cannot be very pleasant to be imprisoned and forcibly fed or brought to death's door by starvation, or to be kicked to death by racehorses.

Meanwhile Miss Kenney and three of her friends, having said in the dock that they would not serve their sentences and would force the Government to release them, have kept their word. It was the Government's latest chance of showing your quite logical correspondent Mrs. Grosvenor that they could rise to her appeal and prove what stern stuff they were made of by letting Miss Kenney starve to death. But when it came to the point they crumpled, and Miss Kenney won.

What is going to happen now? Is the Home Office going to picket Miss Kenney's doorstep and persecute her illegally out of mere spite at having been beaten by her? That will not save the credit of the law. The proper way to surrender to Mrs. Pankhurst and Miss Kenney is to give them the vote. It is silly to go on shrieking 'No surrender!' The surrender has taken place, and its ungraciousness cannot disguise its nature. The women who want the vote say in effect that we must either kill them or give it to them. In spite of lawyers' logic our consciences will not let us kill them. Then in the name of common sense let us give them the vote and have done with it. The women who do not want it need not go to the polls. They will no doubt feel their interests safe in the hands of Mr. Algernon Gissing.

Yours truly,

G. BERNARD SHAW.

A group of clergy had protested at a sketch performed at the Palace Theatre that led to its banning by the Lord Chamberlain. This prompted a letter in *The Times* of 8 November 1913 from the Bishop of Kensington on 'The Lord Chamberlain and Music Halls'. His objection was that the sketch had apparently been altered after licensing and he wanted such actions to be made illegal. He further criticised the London County Council for being slack. The following letter by Shaw, in reaction to the Bishop's views and criticism, plays on certain key words with the ease and fluency of a master of language, thus exposing the Bishop's absolute judgments for the hollow things they are. Gaby Deslys was a well-known actress who had made her name in silent movies.

~ *1913, November 8* ~

MR. SHAW ON MORALS.

A REPLY TO THE BISHOP OF KENSINGTON

MUSIC HALLS AND CHURCHES

Sir, – May I, as a working playwright, ask the Bishop of Kensington to state his fundamental position clearly? So far, he has begged the question he is dealing with: that is, he has assumed that there can be no possible difference of opinion among good citizens concerning it. He has used the word 'suggestive' without any apparent sense of the fact that the common thoughtless use of it by vulgar people has made it intolerably offensive. And he uses the word 'objectionable' as if there were a general agreement as to what is objectionable and what is not, in spite of the fact that the very entertainment to which he himself objected had proved highly attractive to large numbers of people whose taste is entitled to the same consideration as his own.

On the face of it the Bishop of Kensington is demanding that the plays that he happens to like shall be tolerated and those which he happens not to like shall be banned. He is assuming that what he approves of is right, and what he disapproves of, wrong. Now, I have not seen the particular play which he so much dislikes; but suppose I go to see it tonight, and write a letter to you tomorrow to say that I approve of it, what will the Bishop have to say? He will have either to admit that his epithet of objectionable means simply disliked by the Bishop of Kensington, or he will have to declare boldly that he and I stand in the relation of God and the Devil. And, however his courtesy and his modesty may recoil from this extremity, when it is stated in plain English, I think he has got there without noticing it. At all events, he is clearly proceeding on the assumption that his conscience is more enlightened than that of the people who go to the Palace Theatre and enjoy what they see there. If the Bishop may shut up the Palace Theatre on this assumption, then the Nonconformist patrons of the Palace Theatre (and it has many of them) may shut up the Church of England by turning the assumption inside out. The sword of persecution always has two edges.

By 'suggestive' the Bishop means suggestive of sexual emotion. Now a Bishop who goes into a theatre and declares that the performance there must not suggest sexual emotion is in the position of a playwright going into a church and declaring that the services there must not suggest religious emotion. The suggestion, gratification, and education of sexual emotion is one of the main uses and glories of the theatre. It shares that function with all the fine arts. The sculpture courts of the Victoria and Albert Museum in the Bishop's diocese are crowded with naked figures of extraordinary beauty, placed there expressly that they may associate the appeal of the body with such beauty, refinement, and expression of the higher human qualities that our young people, contemplating them, will find baser objects of desire repulsive. In the National Gallery body and soul are impartially catered for: men have worshipped Venuses and fallen in love with Virgins. There is a voluptuous side to religious ecstasy; and a religious side to voluptuous ecstasy; and the notion that one is less sacred than the other is the opportunity of the psychiatrist who seeks to discredit the saints by showing that the passion which exalted them was in its abuse capable also of degrading sinners. The so called Song of Solomon, which we now know to be an erotic poem, was mistaken by the translators of the 17th century for a canticle of Christ to His Church, and is to this day so labelled in our Bibles.

Now let us turn to the results of cutting off young people – not to mention old ones – from voluptuous art. We have families who bring up their children in the belief that an undraped statue is an abomination; that a girl or a youth who looks at a picture by Paul Veronese is corrupted for ever; that the theatre in which *Tristan and Isolde* or *Romeo and Juliet* is performed is the gate of hell; and that the contemplation of a figure attractively dressed or revealing more of its outline than a Chinaman's dress does is an act of the most profligate indecency. Of Chinese sex morality I must not write in the pages of *The Times*. Of the English and Scottish sex morality that is produced by this starvation and blasphemous vilification of vital emotions I will say only this: that it is so morbid and abominable, so hatefully obsessed by the things that tempt it, so merciless in its persecution of all the divine grace which grows in the soil of our sex instincts when they are not deliberately perverted and poisoned, that if it could be imposed, as some people would impose it if they could, on the whole community for a single generation, the Bishop, even at the risk of martyrdom, would reopen the Palace Theatre with his Episcopal benediction, and implore the lady to whose performances he now objects to return to the stage even at the sacrifice of the last rag of her clothing.

I venture to suggest that when the Bishop heard that there was an objectionable (to him) entertainment at the Palace Theatre, the simple and natural course for him was not to have gone there. That is how sensible people act. And the result is that if a manager offers a widely objectionable entertainment to the public he very soon finds out his mistake and withdraws it. It is my own custom as a playwright to make my plays 'suggestive' of religious emotion. This makes them extremely objectionable to irreligious people. But they have the remedy in their own hands. They stay away. The Bishop will be glad to hear that there are not many of them: but it is a significant fact that they frequently express a wish that the Censor would suppress religious plays, and that he occasionally complies. In short, the Bishop and his friends are not alone in proposing their own tastes and convictions as the measure of what is permissible in the theatre. But if such individual and sectarian standards were tolerated we should have no plays at all, for there never yet was a play that did not offend somebody's taste.

I must remind the Bishop that if the taste for voluptuous entertainment is sometimes morbid, the taste for religious edification is open to precisely the same objection. If I had a neurotic daughter I would much rather risk taking her to the Palace Theatre than to a revival meeting. Nobody has yet counted the homes and characters wrecked by intemperance in religious emotion. When we begin to keep such statistics the chapel may find its attitude of moral superiority to the theatre, and even to the public-house, hard to maintain, and may learn a little needed charity. We all need to be reminded of the need for temperance and toleration in religious emotion and in political emotion, as well as in sexual emotion. But the Bishop must not conclude that I want to close up all places of worship: on the contrary, I preach in them. I do not even clamour for the suppression of political party meetings, though nothing more foolish and demoralizing exists in England today. I live and let live. As long as I am not compelled to attend revival meetings, or party meetings, or theatres at which the sexual emotions are ignored or reviled. I am prepared to tolerate them on reciprocal terms; for though I am unable to conceive any good coming to any human being as a set-off to their hysteria, their rancorous bigotry, and their dullness and falsehood, I know that those who like them are equally unable to conceive any good coming of the sort of assemblies I frequent;

so I mind my own business and obey the old precept – 'He that is unrighteous, let him do unrighteousness still; and he that is filthy let him be made filthy still; and he that is righteous let him do righteousness still; and he that is holy let him be made holy still.' For none of us can feel quite sure in which category the final judgement may place us; and in the meantime Miss Gaby Deslys is as much entitled to the benefit of the doubt as the Bishop of Kensington.

Yours truly,
G. BERNARD SHAW.

The Bishop replied at length on 10 November 1913 and Shaw responded with the following letter. (Sir) Henry Irving also wrote on 11 November, calling Shaw to task for making misleading comments and defending the Bishop's stance. Alfred Butt (1878–1962) was the managing director of several London Theatres. Lord Sandhurst was a former governor of Bombay and a committed Christian.

~ *1913, November 15* ~

PUBLIC MORALS

MR. SHAW'S REJOINER.

Sir, – I note the Bishop of Kensington's explanation that in his recent agitation against the Palace Theatre he has been concerned not with public morals but solely with a technical infraction of the Lord Chamberlain's regulations. In that case I have nothing more to say, partly because the management of the Palace Theatre strenuously and indignantly denies that the infraction has occurred, partly because Lord Sandhurst is quite well able to take care of himself, but mainly because this astonishing episcopal reply to an earnest demand for a statement of principle sends me reeling into a dumb despair of making any Englishman understand what political principle means or even persuading him that such a thing exists.

It is useless for me to repeat what I said in my former communication. If the Bishop was unable to grapple with it yesterday, there is no reason to expect that he will be able to do so tomorrow. But lest I should seem to fail in patience, I will comment on one or two points of his letter. I am very glad he has pointed out that the Lord Chamberlain has no real control over performances, and that the guarantee of decency which the Censor's licence is supposed to carry is illusory. I have pointed that out so often that I cannot but feel encouraged when a Bishop repeats it. I am glad that he agrees with me also that the power of influencing people for good is inextricably linked with the power to influence them for evil. But if this is so, why does the Bishop still imagine that he can suppress and destroy the power for evil without also suppressing and destroying the power for good? An evil sermon – and there are many more evil sermons than evil plays – may do frightful harm; but is the Bishop ready to put on the chains he would fasten on the playwright, and agree that no sermon shall be preached unless it is first read and licensed by the Lord Chamberlain? No doubt it is easier to go to sleep than to watch and pray; that is why everyone is in favour of securing purity and virtue and decorum by paying an official to look after them. But the result is that your official, who is equally indisposed to watch and pray, takes the simple course of forbidding everything that is not customary; and, as nothing is customary except vulgarity, the result is that he kills the thing he was employed to purify and leaves the nation to get what amusement they can out of its putrefaction. Our souls are to have no adventures because adventures are dangerous. Carry that an obvious step farther and Bishop of Kensington will be gagged because he might at any moment utter false doctrines. He will be handcuffed because he might smite me with his pastoral staff. The dog-muzzling order will be extended to the muzzling of all priests and prophets and politicians. The coward in all of us will seek security at any price.

But this does not touch the present issue. I repeat that there is no consensus of opinion as to what is objectionable and what is desirable in theatrical entertainments. Mr. Butt's audiences are as big as the Bishop's congregations, and they pay him more than they pay the Bishop. If the Bishop may say to these people, 'You shall not go to the Palace Theatre, or, if you go you shall not see what you like there, because I do not consider it good for you,' then these people may say to the Bishop, 'You shall not preach the doctrine of the Atonement; for in our opinion it destroys all sense of moral responsibility.'

I need not again elaborate the point; but I will point out something that the Bishop may not have thought of in this connexion. Not only is art, or religion, a power for evil as well as for good; but the self-same exhibition or sermon that effects one man's salvation may effect another man's damnation. The placing of the Bible in the hands of the laity by the Protestant Catholics produced great results; but it also produced all the horrors that were predicted by the Roman Catholics as their reason for withholding it, from an epidemic of witch-burning to the political excesses of the Anabaptists and Puritans, and the sour misery of 16th century Scotland. The case against the freedom of the Palace Theatre is as dust in the balance compared with the case against the freedom of the Bible Society. Is the Bishop, having attacked the Palace Theatre, going to attack the Bible Society *a fortiori*? Of course not, because he can see the overwhelming argument in favour of scriptural freedom which he is unable to see in the case of the theatre, because the theatre is the Church's most formidable rival in forming the minds and guiding the souls of the people. Well, he must compete with fair weapons, not with the bludgeons of official tyranny. He cannot dissect out the evil of the theatre and strike at that alone. One man seeing a beautiful actress will feel that she has made all common debaucheries impossible to him; another, seeing the same actress in the same part, will plunge straight into those debaucheries because he has seen her body without being able to see her soul. Destroy the actress and you rob the first man of his salvation with saving the second from the first woman he meets on the street.

It is reported that the Bishop of London, preaching on Sunday in the church of St. Mary Magdalen, Paddington, dealt with this subject. Far be it from me to accuse any man of the fantastic things our reporters put into all our mouths; but I can believe that he proposed 'a vigorous campaign for a clean, pure life.' If by this he means, as I may with offence assume that he does, life according to the highest conception his lights can show him, then he is on the right tack, though, if his conceptions are at all lofty, he will get more kicks than halfpence for his pains. As long as he sticks to the propagation of noble impulses and aspirations he cannot go far wrong. But if once he turns aside from that honourable work to the cheap and rancorous course of persecuting the people who do not share his tastes under pretext of weeding out evil, he will become a public nuisance. He is reported to have declared that, 'It has been said that no Christian Church has any right to criticize any play in London.' It may be that there exists some abysmal fool who said this. If so, he was hardly worth the Bishop of London's notice. The Christian Church ought to criticize every play in London; and it is on that right and duty of criticism, and not on the unfortunate Lord Chamberlain, that the Christian Church ought to rely, and, indeed, would rely without my prompting if it were really a Christian Church.

Finally, may I thank the Bishop of Kensington for alleging as a reason for persecuting the Palace Theatre (for he does not, after all, combat my demonstration that his action was persecution) that I should probably disapprove of the entertainment myself? As to that, I can only say that, if the Bishop sets out to suppress all the institutions of which I disapprove, he will soon have not one single supporter, not even

Yours truly
G. BERNARD SHAW.

Over a year would pass before Shaw wrote to *The Times* again. In the meantime, in 1914, *Pygmalion* opened at His Majesty's Theatre starring Beerbohm Tree and Mrs Patrick Campbell. Eliza Doolittle's famous 'Not bloody likely' was seen by some as 'scandalous', but not so scandalous as to prevent the play from being a great success. The run ended in July after 118 performances because Tree wanted to go on holiday. It would have ended a few weeks later when, in early August, the First World War ('The Great War') broke out. As a result, serious theatre fell away and Shaw,- ceased being an active playwright.

Instead, he turned his attention to the immediate issue – the war – and in the weeks following the outbreak of hostilities penned a long essay, *Common Sense about the War*, in which he castigated the 'Junkers' of both sides for fomenting war. This essay, when published in *The New Statesman* in November 1914, immediately earned him the denunciation of all shades of political opinion- and of many erstwhile friends and colleagues – he was expelled from the Dramatists' Club – while libraries and bookshops removed his books from their shelves. Practically the entire country, overflowing with patriotic fervour and in no mood to be lectured on the 'insanity' of what had been allowed to happen, repudiated him. Much of the press applied a selective censorship to his utterances and even *The Times* in these years suppressed him as one of its principal correspondents.

It is a little surprising, therefore, that Shaw was allowed to express opinions in its pages soon after publication of *Common Sense about the War*. However, it is clear that he is unambiguously against German militarism and pro-British, and the issue is uncontroversial – the question of launching a propaganda campaign in Italy, neutral at the outset of the war, against German propaganda. The following letter was prompted by a Richard Bagot, who wrote to *The Times* on 14 December 1914 proposing that a leaflet to counter German propaganda be distributed in Italy.

∽ *1914, December 16* ∽

PROPAGANDA IN ITALY.

Sir, – Mr. Richard Bagot's proposal to distribute in Italy half a million (why only half a million?) pamphlets setting forth the official reasons why Great Britain is at war with Germany is evidently worth considering; but I venture to suggest that what we want to disseminate in Italy and on neutral ground elsewhere are not the official reasons why we are at war with Germany, but the real reasons why the neutral nations should support our side in that war with their sympathy if not with their active intervention later on. I say 'our side' advisedly; for it is obvious that the neutral nations are concerned with the case for supporting France and Russia quite as much as with the case for supporting us. Indeed, what we want to impress on them is not so much any national case as the world's case for destroying the military prestige of the Prussian system, which means destroying the system itself, as it has no other asset.

Besides, we have at least two official cases, each addressed to a section of our own people, and only one of them at all interesting to foreigners. The first, addressed to our governing classes, who mostly uphold the old and famous diplomacy which has won so many victories for Britain since it was begun by William of Orange two centuries ago, presents us as a warlike and powerful nation undertaking the championship of the world against the Prussian system, and, by superior strategy, securing not only the choice of the moment most unfavourable to the enemy for giving battle, but massing against him the greatest odds possible in the European situation. Now this case, put by Mr. Balfour, Mr. Churchill, and in your own columns, is the case that will appeal to the numerous and influential people in all neutral countries who back the winner or have reason to dread his disfavour.

The second official case is addressed to the English electorate, largely composed of persons who have (very naturally) a horror of war and no grasp of foreign policy, with, as far as the supporters of the present Government are concerned, a tradition that non-intervention is the correct thing. What these very worthy people want is excuses for the war, and assurances that we are an unsuspicious, peaceful, unprepared, shopkeeping sort of people, unexpectedly forced to defend ourselves against an act of brutal aggression by a foreign Power addicted to the worship of Odin and his prophet, the Nietzschean Anti-Christ. Now this may catch the votes of the Free Churches effectively enough at the next election; but it is of no use for foreign consumptions. In fact, it is highly mischievous; for those who believe it conclude that Germany is stronger, braver, and craftier than we; and those who do not believe it are irritated at what seems to them a clumsy attempt to practise on their credulity. If anyone doubts this, I advise him to read the articles by which the Germans are trying to influence American opinion in their favour. They are written by Germans to please Germans, and by courtiers to please 'their noble Kaiser'. The writers are simple enough to think that what will please the Germans and the Kaiser will please the Americans. They are so completely mistaken that, if the German subsidies fail to keep up their Press campaign, it will be well worth our while to come to the rescue with a liberal contribution of secret service money.

But are we ourselves less likely to make this mistake than the Germans-? Is there not a serious danger that if we issue the half million leaflets demanded by Mr. Bagot they will prove extremely gratifying and convincing to us here at home, whilst leaving their Italian readers either cold or irritated, if not hostile? I should no doubt be accused of paradox were to say that the less likely a pamphlet on the war is to please an Englishman, the more likely it is to influence an Italian in our direction; but I will say without hesitation that if nine-tenths of the stuff that the British public passionately demanded from its Press during the first six weeks of the war could be reprinted and spread broadcast through the neutral nations, we should, presently, have to face a world in arms.

It is not enough for Mr. Bagot to demand 'a pamphlet printed in Italian.' Who is to write the pamphlet? and what is the pamphlet to say? I suggest that it should be written, not by some gentleman at the Foreign Office, but by an Italian with a sincere love of his country (not necessarily of ours), and a conviction that an Austro-Prussian hegemony would be worse for Italy than the nearest approach to a hegemony a Franco-Russian combination could achieve. He should, as to the causes of the war, say just exactly nothing. To the commercial and governing classes of Italy he should urge that events have proved (see the Yellow Book) that we hold the balance of power as between the Alliance and the Entente, and that since we have thrown our practically inexhaustible resources so effectively, and in point of time so judiciously, against Prussia, Italy has only to await the result in a friendly attitude to find herself placed in a far stronger position as to Austria and Turkey (plus Germany) than she occupied before the war. To ask her to join us would be a blunder; she must settle that for herself without obviously interested advice. And to the Italian masses, with their loathing of Potsdam discipline, he should appeal against the Kaiser as the apostle of a system which destroys human happiness and popular liberty without even justifying itself as better for fighting purposes than the voluntary system of England or the comparatively easy-going Republicanism of France. Such a document, appealing on the one hand to the glory of aristocratic patriotic tradition, and on the other to democratic indignation, hope, and enthusiasm, would do no harm and might do us' considerable service.

If we cannot produce it, we had better leave Press propaganda to the Germans, because they are not doing it well. Their system does not encourage the sort of writer who does such work well. They deal in excuses, denials, recriminations, and statements which they believe solely because they want to believe them. That is all very well for home consumption; we do a good deal of it ourselves for that market; but as an export line it helps the enemy. Still, if we can produce the right thing, there is no reason why Mr. Bagot should not have his pamphlets until our success in the field becomes decisive, which is the best propaganda of all.

Yours truly,
G. BERNARD SHAW.

Two full years were to pass before *The Times* re-opened its pages to Shaw. By now in 1916, Shaw had been proved right in his 1914 prophecy about the incalculable waste and devastation the war would bring, and he was being gradually re-admitted to the fold. He was even invited by the War Office to visit the Western Front, which he did in early 1917. His re-emergence into the full glare of public notice was now only a matter of time.

The issue in the following letters boils down to another protest at the tax burden on the rich. Shaw's not infrequent warnings throughout his life on taxation and the way it worked against individual and national interests earned him a fair measure of sneering deprecation. But he was consistent in his argument and a true Fabian in pointing to the inherent absurdity of the system and to the difference between occasional windfalls (such as came the way of artists, among whom he included himself) and inherited wealth: unearned income such as regularly and consistently came the way of landowners and other beneficiaries of the capitalist system. Dr. (later Sir) James Paget (1814–99) was one of the founders of the science of pathology. The Fortuny lighting installation was the brainchild of Mariano Fortuny (1871–1949), Spanish inventor of the cyclorama dome, a stage lighting device that created effects such as a bright sky or faint dusk. Bonar Law (1858–1923) was conservative PM from October 1922 to May 1923.

～ 1916, December 28 ～

SORROWS OF THE SUPERTAXED.

INCOME AND WINDFALL.

THE INVENTOR'S REWARD.

Sir, – We are close to the day when the only class which has to bear its war burden not only without sympathy but amid general exultation in its sufferings – that is, the payers of supertax – will again have to stand and deliver. In their desolation they will envy even the conscientious objector, who is consoled in his prison by the knowledge that his name is inscribed at least on the pacifist roll of honour.

Nevertheless, though nobody has ever sympathized with the goose that laid the golden eggs, it is now widely recognized that it was bad policy to kill him. And, though it would be hopeless to plead the cause of those who are rich enough to have to pay more than a third of their incomes under our supertax and income-tax graduation, I hope I may be allowed to state the case of those who will be compelled next month to pay more than twice their actual income under the form of paying 20 or 30 per cent of it.

As matters stand incomes of more than £2,500 are taxed £5. in the pound. Incomes exceeding £3,000 pay supertax in addition, the rate for every pound over 10,000 being 3s. 6d. On an income of £21,000 this taxation will be £7,954 3s. 4d. Jolly lucky to get off so easily, most of us will exclaim. It ought to be double. It ought to be £20,000. A thousand a year is enough for anybody to live on in war time.

But wait a moment. If the £21,000 is really an income – that is, if the taxpayer has a permanent £21,000 a year – no doubt he gets off lightly enough from the point of view of the vast majority of British citizens, to whom £1,000 a year is a fortune. But suppose the £21,000 is only a windfall that has come in war time to a man of moderate means who can never hope for another such stroke of luck, and who has hastened patriotically and prudently to invest it in Four-and-a-Half Per Cent War Loan! His income is not £21,000 a year: it is £945. He is not a millionaire, not even a thousandaire. If he has a family on his hands, and has to keep up the status of a man of business or a professional man, he can at best live in a semi-detached villa at Baling, or possibly in a small detached house in Hampstead Garden Suburb. He travels third class. He has to pay war prices for everything; and, in addition to income-tax and supertax, he must pay rates and all sorts of indirect taxes, from stamps on receipts and theatre tickets to legacy duty.

Next door to him is a gentleman who has also an income of £945 from Investments, which he has enjoyed all his life. The Commissioners of Inland Revenue come to this next-door neighbour with a demand for £165 7s. 6d., not an easy sum to spare from such an income. But to our man of the windfall, who has exactly the same income, they present a demand for £2,104 35. 4d., to be repeated next year and the year following – that is, twice and a quarter his actual income for three years in succession. Forty-five shillings in the pound for three years! How is he to pay it? Only by selling out, thus surrendering nearly a third of his capital. This leaves him between £600 and £700 a year at the permanent 4.5% rate, whilst his neighbour retains his £945 simply because he has enjoyed it for many years. To put it another way, he is taxed on his capital, whilst his neighbour is taxed on his income. Now it is possible without unreason to argue that our taxation on incomes derived from investments is too light.

It is even possible to argue, with an appearance of reason, that capital should be taxed, because few people – few professed economists even – know what capital is; most of us foolishly imagine that we could all take our shares simultaneously into the market without finding them drop to zero with a crash. But no sane person can defend the equity of taxing one citizen on his income and taxing his next door neighbour on his capital when both have precisely the same means.

It may be said that windfalls are in the nature of miracles: they occur too seldom to be legislated for. But this is not the case. They are a part of our system; and in certain cases they are legislated for. For example, that of an inventor. Most inventions have as their object the economizing of labour and the suppression of waste. The vested interests in waste – always enormous under our system – may baffle him until war produces a pressure to which these interests have to yield. Take the case of an inventor enabled by the war to sell a long-neglected invention for £21,000. Well, the law very properly allows him to treat this windfall as capital and taxes him only on the income it yields. But it does this righteous thing for an absurd reason. A department committee once solemnly decided that invention was not a profession; that the earnings of an inventor are therefore not income derived from the exercise of a profession; and that an inventor is accordingly not liable under schedule D. The committee was wrong, of course; the professional inventor is as hard a fact as the professional dentist; but they blundered into justice and reason; so we need not quarrel with the usage they established.

But take the parallel case of an inventor of books or plays. He too often struggles all his life against 'toil, envy, want, the patron (now a publisher), and the gaol (on judgment summons)'. But he is sometimes rescued by windfall. At last a book or a play of his makes a great success. He sells the copyright or stage right for £21,000; a stroke not wholly impossible in these days of international copyright. He knows how little chance there is of its ever occurring again. He pays his debts, invests the balance, and hopes to be treated like the mechanical inventor: that is, taxed on his income and not on his windfall of capital. But no. That departmental committee decided that authorship is a profession, and that all the gains of an author must be classed as income derived from the exercise of a profession. The wretched author's £21,000 is therefore taxed as income under schedule D, and he has to sell out nearly a third of it to pay. But, if you please, when the publisher who has paid the £21,000 to him asks to be allowed to debit it in his income-tax-return, he is told that he must count it as capital invested in his business.

I give this particular instance because I am an author, and can speak feelingly as one part hit by the anomaly. But it only illustrates a much wider case The lucky dramatic actor earning three or four hundred a week for three months and perhaps nothing at all for the ensuing two years (or ten) is but one among many of those whose income for any given year is no index to his real resources Speculative businesses are a necessary feature of our economic system Even armament manufacturers, who are so curiously denounced in war time because they are at last justifying their existence, must feel pretty strongly that their profits would be estimated more fairly on a 30 than on a three-year average.

But I plead specially for the professional man, because he has not the manufacturer's refuge of keeping his excess profits out of the category of income by investing them in a business in the shape of new plant, and claiming allowances for depreciation, reserve, and so forth. The great doctor who, like Paget pays for a few years of laborious success with three quarters of a lifetime of poverty, and whose brief golden moment comes unluckily in time of war, cannot buy £5,000 worth of improved stethoscopes and gold watches with centre seconds to keep down his taxable balance. A famous barrister's history is that of the famous doctor; and the legatee whose windfall is the reward of a lifetime of humble service is equally cut off from the industrialist's power of capitalizing the windfall before it can emerge as income. Shakespeare, who, after writing plays of such excellence that one of them did not get performed for 300 years (I witnessed its reputed first performance myself), retired to Field Place on the strength of a few pot boilers. If he were alive to-day he would rebuild the Globe Theatre and fill its stage with a superfluity of hydraulic lifts and bridges, and a Fortuny lighting installation, to rescue the profits of *As You Like It* from the clutches of the Commissioners of Inland Revenue.

I leave it to the economists to devise a remedy. It may be that all professional men should share the inventor's privilege, though I must warn those who favour that solution that modern scientific industrial management will soon compel us to class the really skilled manufacturer as a professional. It may be that the three-year average, which is now accepted for taxation purposes as the actual income should be a 10 or 20 or 30, or past-life average. It may be that we should tax, not income, but expenditure, exempting all sums that are invested instead of spent; and this, which seems to me on the whole the best plan, as it directly encourages the accumulation of capital at the expense of the extravagance which is now so revolting, would be easily practicable if income-tax returns were made as complete as supertax returns, so that the Surveyor of Taxes could immediately spot the selling-out of an investment, and tax its proceeds if they were not re-invested. But whatever plan be adopted I hope it will be adopted soon; for I am not one of those who are always convinced in autumn that the war will be over next spring, and in spring that it will be over next autumn; and whilst we wait, many poor professional men are having all their hope of providing for their old age and their dependents by the harvest of a lifetime of obscure toil destroyed by being taxed as millionaires when their income does not run into four figures, much less seven.

If Mr. Bonar Law will look to this matter in his first Budget, perhaps he will also do away with the absurdity of taxing on gross instead of on net income. This was possible at the old low tax rates, and is possible even still. But it has been suggested in the House of Lords that the tax may go up to 15s. in the pound. If this means that we are to receive every pound of our dividends less 10s. income tax, and that then we shall have to pay an additional 5s. in the pound supertax on the gross, we shall be supertaxed 10s. in the pound on our real income. But if the income-tax is to be 15s. in the pound and the supertax 7s. 6d. on the gross, we shall have to pay the Chancellor of the Exchequer our entire income, plus half-a-crown in the pound, which would be amusing, but not financially sound. Supertax is only a steeper graduation of income- tax; and now that the fancy name induced us to swallow it, it is not clear that there is anything but confusion to be gained by retaining the double category.

Yours truly
G. BERNARD SHAW.

The previous letter stimulated several challenges from 'experts', although A.J. Marriott, a fellow Fabian, wrote in support of Shaw's contentions in *The Times* of 9 January 1917 on Income and Capital. Below Shaw goes into greater detail. Robert Owen (1771–1858) was a social reformer with many advanced ideas on profit and working practices. Joseph Fels (1854-1914) was an American soap manufacturer who tried to promote the idea of a single tax.

~ *1917, January 15* ~

TAXATION OF CAPITAL.

Sir, – In my former communication I mentioned that the notion of taxing capital generally, though illusory, was reasonable compared to the existing practice of taking two citizens with precisely the same income, and exacting from one a bearable percentage of that income whilst compelling the other to pay the whole of it twice over. This remark seems to have conveyed to some of your correspondents, including even my new disciple Mr. Marriott that I regard a levy on capital as absolutely reasonable. I do not even regard it as possible. Mr Marriott is quite right in his contention that it would disappear by depreciation in the process. But there is something more fundamental in that phenomenon than mere depreciation; and since there seems to be some danger that an attempt at it may be made, either directly or in the guise of what is called taxation of values (land values for example), I had better try to make the situation even clearer than Mr. Marriott has left it.

There is one thing that the most energetic Government of practical business men cannot do even if its omission means defeat in the field; and that is, take from a citizen within the space of a financial year what he does not possess and cannot procure because it does not exist and cannot within that period be produced. I take that to be self-evident.

Now let me ask, What is a millionaire capitalist? Many people think he is a man with a million pounds in his pocket: He is not. He is only a man with £50,000 a year. Tax his million at the current rate of 5s. in the pound income-tax plus 35. 6d. supertax, and the collector will demand from him more than eight times his entire income for the year – three hundred thousand odd pounds. He will simply reply, 'I haven't got it.'

But the practical man of business will stand no nonsense of that kind. He will say, 'You haven't got it; but you can get it. All you have to do is to instruct your stockbroker to sell your income of £50,000 a year, and he will get you a million for it before you can say Jack Robinson.'

Fantastic as the operation seems, it is not impossible under certain conditions. The first is that the millionaire's investments have been so widely distributed that he can sell out without throwing upon the market a huge block of shares in any one concern: a condition that would checkmate most of our industrial millionaires. The second is that all the other millionaires and investors generally are going on just as usual, buying and selling neither more nor less than the average. But this is just what would not happen as the result of a general tax on capital. All the other capitalists would be selling out at the same moment to pay the collector; and the consequence would be not merely depreciation, but zero, a total disappearance of the capital values owing to the fact that all the capitalists would be trying simultaneously to sell to one another, not the existing produce on which they were living for the year, but the as yet non-existent produce of next year and many succeeding years as well. Now, even in a world which lives, as our does, mostly from hand to mouth, it may be possible, as an isolated transaction, to sell £50,000 worth of the wheat or coal or hardware of 1920 to a very rich man, because he can afford to wait for it. But you cannot put your hand on the entire harvest and output of that year in 1917–18 for immediate consumption at the front. Yet that is exactly what a tax on capital would attempt. It is flatly impossible. Within certain rather narrow limits you can defer consumption by tightening your belt. You cannot anticipate consumption on any terms. The wheat must be grown and the bread baked before you can eat it and fight on it. At most you can borrow spare wheat from the current harvest of the neutrals. You cannot borrow wheat that is not yet sown or grown from anybody.

What we call a capitalist is simply a person for whom we have agreed to earmark, year after year, a certain share of our national income in consideration of his having deferred consumption of part of his income at some past period when we needed the spare money for starting elaborately equipped industries. For a while his contribution is represented by machines and steel rails and so forth; but they soon wear out, and have to be renewed out of the income of the concern; all that is left of his advance being his claim on that income. The fact that now and then he can sell his claim to X for as much as, or perhaps more than, it cost him, and that X may, as an isolated case under a pressure peculiar to himself, sell it to Y, and Y to Z, and Z to A, and so on, until it has become the subject of a hundred fresh individual investments, does not multiply it by a hundred nor alter the fact that it remains a claim on the future and not, except as to the current year, a body of immediately consumable goods. In other words, you must tax income because there is nothing but income to tax. The depreciation foreseen by Mr. Marriott would be the outward and visible sign of the discovery that, 'Where there is nothing the King loses his rights.'

The point is one of pressing importance, because the war has driven us into a phase of collectivist activity which we have confided to a great extent to experienced men of individualist business. Now it happens that collectivism has always been one of the hobbies of experienced men of business who have made large fortunes. From Robert Owen to Joseph Fels, a long string of them might be named. A great deal was expected from their practical good sense and knowledge of men and affairs; but the truth is that in collectivism they were all incorrigible Utopian failures, with the single exception of William Morris, who was a poet forced unto business by the inadequacy of the people who had devoted their lives to it. We already see how the practical man of business, having experience of the fact that an economy can be effected in a counting-house by cutting down the office boy's joy rides, infers that a public economy can be effected by hampering the locomotion of the whole nation at a moment when facilitation of transport both for men and goods has reached a value that would probably justify us in doubling the number of trains and abolishing fares. This pseudo-practicality is precisely of the kind that may lead its possessors to conclude that because an isolated individual or firm can 'realize his capital' and spend it in shooting, a whole nation can do the same.

Let us suppose that Sir Douglas Haig comes to Mr. Lloyd George, or General Hindenburg to Herr Bethmann Hollweg, with the assurance that with unlimited munitions and men he can win the war. And let us add the further terrifying supposition that the statesman answers the soldier as a practical man of business as follows. – 'First, you will understand, we must win: that goes before everything. Now, as to our resources, let me see. The national income before the war was estimated at £2,000,000,000. How much capital does that represent? I will take it at 5 per cent., because, though many of my friends get much more than that, still, as a cautious practical man of business, I will put it at that moderate figure. I therefore, being pledged, always as a practical man looking facts in the face, to the last shilling of our money and the last drop of our blood, at my disposal £40,000,000,000 ready capital under the hand of the Chancellor of the Exchequer. And I daresay I can borrow a lot more if the worst comes to the worst. You can lay your plans accordingly. Are you satisfied?' The soldier points out that owing to the prodigious impulse given to production by the war the national income must have at least doubled since 1914, and that the capital now available must therefore be nearer a hundred thousand millions than thirty thousand, The statesman congratulates him on his practical knowledge of business, and admits that this is so. The soldier proceeds to plan his spring offensive on the presumption that he has a hundred thousand millions ready money to play with. In the middle of May, he surrenders at discretion; and all the practical statesmen are torn to pieces by an infuriated patriotic mob in Palace Yard.

Let nobody think that this is a joke. It is a quite possible mistake; and if it is to be made at all, I hope it will be made by the Imperial Chancellor, and not by our Prime Minister.

Yours truly,
G. BERNARD SHAW.

The Armistice was still a year in the future, the war still in full deadly spate, but by now, as the following letter indicates, victory was assured and the nation could turn its attention to more peaceful matters.

This letter was Shaw's contribution to a correspondence in which three eminent playwrights, the other two being Sir Arthur Wing Pinero and Henry Arthur Jones, explained their methods of work.

Shaw was generally reticent about the 'how and why' of his playwriting technique, preferring usually to cite 'inspiration' as the mainspring of his art. This letter is no exception. What one has instead is perhaps no less revealing in that it shows how totally a man of the theatre he was, dedicated to serving the exigencies of the medium.

There was at this time a controversy surrounding the texts of Shakespeare's plays. Shaw has a brief, somewhat incidental, say on this here. He would have a good deal more to say on the subject in ensuing correspondence.

∿ *1917, October 25* ∿

PLAYWRIGHTS' TEXTS.

Sir, – I cannot give you a general answer covering all the plays. When I began I could not get my plays acted in this country at all. I therefore proposed to publish them as books. Heinemann, whom I consulted, told me that plays were not read in this country; those which were published sold in batches according to the number of characters in the play; one copy per character and one for the prompter, showing that they were purchased for the rehearsing of amateur performances and for no other purposes. He allowed me to see an actual ledger account to satisfy me on the point.
I contended that the business was in a vicious circle: that plays were issued in unreadable acting versions, with revolting stage directions like telegrams with all the definite articles left out, and peppered with technical prompter's terms that insulted the human imagination: for example

SIKES – Take that, damn you (strikes her with bludgeon).

NANCY – Oh, God forgive you, Bill (staggers – business with eyes – dies).

SIKES – Now to escape the police (takes hat from table R.C. brushes it with elbow, grinding teeth: crosses L.C. up; sees ghost; shrieks; back to R.C. and exit R.U.E.)

I asked whether anyone could read *Oliver Twist* if Dickens had written it in this way; and I made a resolution, which is still unbroken, that no play of mine, however full its stage directions, should ever mention the stage or use any technical term that could remind the reader of the theatre or destroy the imaginative illusion. Grant Richards, who was then starting in business, published two volumes of plays written in this manner; and their success practically re-established the public habit of reading plays, though I am sorry to say that my system of stage direction is so little understood that even burlesques of it often include references to 'the centre of the stage', and such specifications as 'to the right of the stage, a small table', &c., &c. naturally, what my parodists overlooked is not noticed by authors generally; and though I am followed purely as a fashion, the point of my fashion is missed, and telegram English and references to the theatrical mechanism still survive, and still make people prefer novels to plays as instruments to produce illusion.

This by the way. What you are concerned with is the fact that whereas my earlier plays were printed first and acted afterwards, my later ones were 'produced' by me, and acted, years before they were collected into volumes, to be finally revised for press in the light of my practical stage experience of them, and prefaced by essays to which they had no more relation (if so much) than a text has to a sermon.

Let me illustrate the consequences by an example. My *Caesar and Cleopatra* was written and published before it was acted. It was, except for the old copyrighting farce which has no importance and is now abolished by the last Copyright Act, first produced in Berlin. During the rehearsals it was discovered that I had forgotten to remove one of the characters, Apollodorus the Sicilian (the hero of the carpet incident) from the stage in the third act. I had accordingly to write in a speech or two to dismiss him; and this speech of course appears in the later editions and is not in the earlier ones. Later on, when Forbes Robertson, for whom the part of Caesar was written, was at last able to take it up, he said one day at rehearsal that the scene with Septimius in the second act, which is one of the great acting points in the play, required a little more explanation and additional preparatory ferment to enable him to make the most of it; and I immediately wrote in about a dozen speeches to get it right for him. An edition printed from Forbes Robertson's prompt copy would contain those speeches, which I regret to say I have been too lazy to have inserted in my own editions.

But there is a further complication. The great length of *Caesar* and *Cleopatra* led to several expedients to shorten it. I first cut out the third act; but the fascination of this episode of fun for the actors, and its success in Berlin, produced a rebellion against the author; and it had to be restored. To make room for it I struck out the first scenes of the first and fourth acts, and replaced them by a prologue to be spoken by the god Ra. But the difficulty was that this tremendous exordium required another Forbes Robertson to deliver it; and the English stage produces only one at a time. But several ambitious actors tackled it, and established this version for a time on the stage. Now suppose some XX century Heminge and Condell print in folio a version of the play from the authentic prompt copies used by our Burbage, the original Caesar; and take my editions as the equivalent of the Shakesperian quartos. The quartos will have scenes omitted in the folio; and the folio will have an entirely different opening and several passages omitted from the quartos. The quartos will have scenes omitted in the folio; and the folio will have an entirely different opening and several passages omitted from the quartos. *The Literary Supplement* of that day will be able to keep a correspondence going for months about the discrepancies.

Man and Superman has also had its vicissitudes. If its texts had to be put together from prompt books and scene plots, the materials would be, first, a three-act comedy, and second, a piece of an indescribable genre entitled 'A Dream of Don Juan in Hell', the connexion between them being discovered by the documents of later performances in which this Dream, with an additional scene to explain its introduction, was performed as the third act of the comedy.

From *John Bull's Other Island* to *Pygmalion*, the prompt copies and the printed editions should be identical because the plays passed through the furnace of production by the author before they were passed for press; but they are not quite so. I made revisions, of no great extent, but of importance (as such things go) in many of them. And further changes are possible. The rehearsals of future revivals may suggest changes to me. An actor at a loss for his line may improvise one happy enough to be annexed by an author who has always taken his goods where he found them and been thankful. The passage that was just right for one actress may be just wrong for another, and may be modified accordingly. The changes need not be improvements: they may be adaptations to inevitable circumstances. The more skilful an author is, the more apt he is to adapt his work to the conditions instead of quarrelling with them.

You must consider also that an author may make a change and neglect to make the contingent changes it involves. Shakespeare's *Julius Caesar* is played to this day with alternative scenes containing the revelation of Portia's death retained altogether.

Probably Shakespeare never dreamt that any producer would be unobservant enough to see that the Brutus–Cassius quarrel scene, evidently written in later to strengthen the end of the play, involved the omission of the earlier version; but he may have forgotten all about it. In *Fanny's First Play* the third act was written as two acts with an interval of a month between; but I hate these violations of the very valuable unity of time; and finally I ran the two acts together as they now stand. But, if you please, I never took the trouble to make the contingent alterations; and the act now presents the phenomenon called 'double-time' like *A Midsummer Night's Dream*, which is both a night and a week, my act being both an afternoon and a month.

The long and the short of it is that any play that has passed through the hands of the author in several successive theatrical productions and literary editions may present wide variations, all equally authentic, and that the alterations, if their order of date can be established, are not necessarily intended as refinements and improvements (except in the literary versions) but may be adaptations to theatrical circumstances more or less favourable. And, I repeat, it is not the ablest author who stands most obstinately by his original text, and can produce his effect only in one way: on the contrary the able author has to check a tendency in himself to play about with his work and perform *tours de force* of mere adroitness at the risk sometimes of overlooking serious damage to his original inspiration.

You may of course use this letter as you please. Excuse its haste, it is only a rough and ready memorandum to assist you.

Yours sincerely,
G. BERNARD SHAW.

Shaw's re-emergence in the latter stages of the war and into the uneasy peace that settled over a devastated Europe after the Armistice of 11 November 1918 ensured that he became paradoxically 'greater' than he had been before the war. As Stanley Weintraub has put it: 'By war's end he was not that persecuted but proud figure, a major prophet whom his own people refused to honour, but a confirmed oracle, a prophet who had survived into his own time' (*The Portable Bernard Shaw*, Penguin, 1977, p. 18).

Now well into his sixties, Shaw had not lost his commanding voice, and he would continue to use it to point to the egregious errors of his contemporaries and to urge social and personal redemption through the rigorous application of common sense, which he believed lay in Fabian Socialism and the tenets on which it was based. Nor had he lost his creative energy: many significant works lay ahead, among them his greatest play, *Saint Joan*, first performed in 1923.

The war over, he focused on ideas that might be instrumental, as he says in the following letter, in preventing another war. However, a report in *The Times* (a special article on 3 February 1919) from its American correspondent misinterpreted and criticised a series of articles he had written in support of President Woodrow Wilson's plan for a League of Nations. These articles, syndicated among the 'Hearst Newspapers', appeared first in *New York American* between January and March 1919. Not long afterwards, as reported in *The Times*, a question was raised in Parliament about the need for British propaganda to counteract such reports and how to justify the cost. The book Shaw refers to was his *Peace Conference Hints*, published in March 1919.

∽ *1919, February 6* ∾

ANTI-ENGLISH PROPAGANDA IN AMERICA.

Sir, – A communication from your New York Correspondent, dated the 3rd inst., and published in your issue of the 4th, describes a series of articles by me, now appearing in the Hearst newspapers in America, as 'weapons' used to foment ill-feeling between the two countries.' The context may well have led your readers to conclude that my articles dealt with a dispute concerning war restrictions on the ports, of which I know nothing.

I need not occupy your space with an account of the real gist of my articles. They are now in the press here and will appear in book form in the course of the next week or so, when you will have an opportunity of reviewing them. But in the meantime it is undesirable that a series of articles written expressly to support President Wilson in his struggle for the League of Nations in the common interest of Britain and the United States should be attacked in your columns as anti-English propaganda. In writing them it has been necessary for me to paraphrase from your columns the authoritative account of the military and diplomatic operations of this country given by Lord Haldane the Monday after the election. Now there are many people who have such a blind horror of war that the mere statement that a fleet has been munitioned, an expeditionary force prepared, an alliance made, and a strategy studied, seems to them an accusation of intent to murder, and a state of suicidal improvidence and helplessness in a Europe bristling with bayonets the only virtuous one. Your Correspondent is evidently such a simpleton (I am not using the word in its offensive sense), otherwise he would not have described my explanation of how much England was prepared for the war as a demonstration of 'how much England was *to blame* for the war.' My readers have no such nonsense to fear from me.

The real urgency of the situation as between England and America is no mere squabble about port restrictions. The Secretary of the United States

Navy declares unequivocally (the question having been raised by the admirals) that unless there is a League of Nations to alter the present relations between the Powers, the United States will build an invincible fleet. And it is obvious enough that in making this declaration he is only yielding to the necessity that obliges us to say that in that case there will be two invincible fleets. How, in the face of such stern necessities and of the dreadful catastrophe they have just led to, is it possible to find little people still nagging at one another as to who was 'to blame for the war'? My business, like that of your Correspondent and every one who has any sense of the value of civilization, is to prevent the next one.

Yours truly,
G. BERNARD SHAW.

This next group of three letters on Shakespeare were published in the *Times Literary Supplement*. The correspondence on the question of a standard text of Shakespeare's plays was initiated in *The Times* by historian and clergyman F. Simpson (1883–1974), Fellow of Trinity College, and the eminent Shakespearian actor and director William Poel (1852–1934). A. W. Pollard (1859–1944), who also contributed to the discussion, was a highly regarded Tudor scholar and the author of, among other works, *Shakespeare's Fight with the Pirates* (1917). They are included because of the link with earlier letters on Shakespeare.

After Pollard added his comments, Shaw decided to join in the debate. Shaw had strong views on how Shakespeare's plays should be introduced, and at times his views appeared contradictory. Some felt that this was because Shaw disliked the fact that certain audiences would put up with any interpretation of Shakespeare's plays through snobbery or just plain ignorance. His own knowledge of the stage and Shakespeare's texts, in addition to his experience as a critic, gave him a distinct advantage.

The belief that Shaw thought himself 'better than Shakespeare' took root in the 1890s when, as theatre critic for the *Saturday Review*, he declared that there was 'no eminent writer . . . whom I despise so entirely when I measure my mind against [Shakespear's]'. It would, he said, be a relief to dig him up and throw stones at him. This was calculated to provoke outrage; it was also calculated exaggeration containing a three-pronged attack: on Irving for his mutilated productions of Shakespeare's plays; on 'bardolators' and their unquestioning veneration of the 'Bard'; and on Shakespeare's thinking, which was, Shaw asserted, four hundred years behind *The Times*, in particular behind such modern masters as Wagner, Ibsen and, of course, Shaw himself. He would later, in his preface to *Three Plays for Puritans*, pose the question 'Better than Shakespear?' (most readers missed the question mark) and declare that he was no more than a minor apostle of a more modern and relevant system of human conduct than Shakespeare could offer. On another occasion, in a moment of rare modesty, Shaw rated himself among the top ten English playwrights.

Though ever prepared to acknowledge Shakespeare's verbal mastery, he had certain blind spots regarding his predecessor's enduring 'philosophy of humanity' and the way it was incorporated in the densely textured lines. All the same, his criticism was based on as thorough a knowledge of Shakespeare's texts as any scholar could muster. As an experienced playwright and director, to whom the 'reality' of the play became manifest only in performance, he could bring unique authority to his comments, as he does in the three letters that follow. Here, while dwelling on the question of a phonetic (or a musical) notation of dramatic texts, he argues the case of the practicalities underlying an immemorial theatrical tradition.

The 'clever young writer' Shaw mentions was Noel Coward, who sent Shaw the draft of his first play. Shaw told him to go off and be himself, not pastiche Shaw. 'Shakespear' was Shaw's idiosyncratic spelling of the name. Rowe, Johnson, Pope, Malone, the Cowden Clarkes, 'Q' (Arthur Quiller Couch) and Dover Wilson were contemporary or former editors of Shakespeare's plays. 'Baconian cipher hunting' refers to Francis Bacon (1561–1626), held by some to have been the author of Shakespeare's plays. The Quartos and the (First) Folio were versions of Shakespeare's plays published in his lifetime (the Quartos) or after his death (the First Folio of 1623); John Heming (1556–1630) and Henry Condell (d. 1627) were the joint editors of the First Folio. Barry Sullivan, Forbes Robertson and David Garrick were eminent actors of their day. Shaw's friend the British composer Edward Elgar (1857–1934) composed the tone poem Falstaff. Ben Jonson (1572–1637) and Philip Massinger (1583–1640) were Elizabethan–Jacobean dramatists.

~ *1921, March 17* ~

SHAKESPEARE: A STANDARD TEXT.

Sir, – May I, as a publishing playwright, point out to Mr. William Poel (who knows it already) that it is at present impossible to write or print a play fully or exactly in ordinary script or type? And it never will be possible until we establish in popular use a fixed and complete notation, such as musicians possess. No such notation exists in a shape intelligible to the general reader. Therefore the first flat fact to be faced is that the printers of the Shakespear Folio and the Quartos could not indicate how the Elizabethan actor spoke his lines, whether they were trying to do so or not. No doubt, when the Elizabethan punctuation of plays is more than usually crazy, as where, for instance, an unaccountable colon appears where there should be no stop at all, it may not be a mere misprint: the compositor may have set up some mark made in his copy by somebody in the theatre for some purpose. It does not follow that it was a stop written by Shakespear for publication. If we found one of Shakespear's handkerchiefs with a knot on it, we might reasonably conjecture that he had knotted it to remind him of something he was afraid of forgetting; but what sane producer of *Othello* would tie a knot in Desdemona's fatal handkerchief on the ground that all Elizabethan handkerchiefs were worn knotted? All actors and all producers and all prompters make marks on their parts and copies to indicate emphasis, strokes of stage business, signals, calls, and the like; but except in the matter of underscoring words, which is common practice, they each make different marks according to private codes of their own. Dots, strokes, crosses, angles indicating the position of the arms, crude footprints mapping the position of the feet, make memoranda perfectly intelligible to the actor who scrawls them, and inscrutable to anyone else. Every producer who knows his business, and does not merely fudge along at rehearsal from entry to entry by trial and error, sprinkles his copy of the play with a home-made shorthand which nobody but he can decipher. Even the prompter, whose copy should serve for his successors as well as himself, distractedly blackleads it until it is often difficult to make out the text, and impossible to understand the directions.

Now imagine manuscript copies treated in this way and then handed to a printer to set up, or to a scrivener to make fair copy for the printer. How is the scrivener to tell whether these dots and dashes and scriggles and crosses and clockhands and queries and notes of admiration are meant for stops or not? It is easy to say that he can use his common sense; but neither scriveners nor compositors are highly educated enough to understand everything they copy or set up: setting up Shakespear must often be very like setting up Einstein or Homer in the original. Thus what looks like a colon, and is set up as such in the Quarto, may mean 'emphasise the next (or previous) word', or 'pause significantly', or 'don't forget to pronounce the h', or merely the Elizabethan equivalent to 'curtain warning' or 'check your floats and take your ambers out of your number bone batten'. To cherish it as Shakespear's punctuation, or pretend to greater authenticity for it than for the colons of Rowe or Dr. Johnson or Pope or Malone or the Cowden Clarkes or Q, or any modern editor is next door to Baconian cipher hunting.

Let me recapitulate the process by which the plays got into print. First, Shakespear wrote a play. It may be presumed that he punctuated it; but this is by no means certain. I have on my desk a typed play by a clever young writer whose dialogue is very vivacious, and is that of an educated man accustomed to converse with educated people. It bristles with mad hyphens *à tort et à travers*; but there is not a stop in it from beginning to end except the full stops at the ends of the speeches; and I suspect that these were put in by the typist.

Oscar Wilde sent the MS. of *An Ideal Husband* to the Haymarket Theatre without taking the trouble to note the entrances and exits of the persons on the stage. There is no degree of carelessness that is not credible to men who know that they will be present to explain matters when serious work begins. But let us assume that Shakespear punctuated his script. From it the scrivener copied out the parts for the actors, and made a legible prompt copy. That the scrivener respected Shakespear's stops and 'followed copy' exactly is against even modern experience; and in the XVI–XVII fin de siècle, when scriveners were proud of their clergy and tenacious of their technical authority, the scrivener would punctuate as he thought Shakespear (whom he would despise as an amateur) ought to have punctuated, and not as he did or did not punctuate. The copies so produced were then marked at rehearsal in all sorts of ways by all sorts of people for all sorts of theatrical purposes. Thus marked, they were fair-copied again by a scrivener – possibly the same, possibly another – for the printer. Now, as all authors know, the printer who does not consider that punctuation is his special business, and that authors know nothing about it (they mostly know very little), has not yet been born. Besides, the printer of that period would have the tradition that his page should look well, and that the letterpress should not be disfigured, as in modern books, by wide spaces between sentences and words and letters, or by awkward-looking stops. And so we get two opinionated scriveners, a whole company of actors and stage officials, and a tradition-ridden compositor, between Shakespear's holograph and the printed page. Such a process applied to an imperfect and inexact notation, as to the use of which authors and even grammarians are so little agreed that it cannot be used in legal documents, leaves the punctuation of the Quartos and the Folio practically void of authority. Even if it could be proved that Shakespear corrected the proofs of the best Quarto texts, I should still defy any modern editor to follow them stop for stop without publicly washing his hands of all responsibility for them.

This does not mean that there is not a case, and a very strong case, for making facsimiles of the earliest printed texts. A glance through any of the facsimiles already published will discover points at which changes made by modern editors are changes for the worse. But when the utmost has been said that can be said for the reading of the Quartos and the Folio, no middle course is open to a modern editor between a photographic reproduction and a text doctored precisely as the conventional editions have been doctored. If the editor be Mr. Granville Barker, so much the better: he will test the questionable passages on the stage, and retain readings that a mere man of letters would tamper with. If the editor be Mr. William Poel, he will print the text in the way that best suggests his divination of its proper delivery. He will run the words together in rapid passages, and bring out keywords in ways undreamt of by Heming and Condell. Such editions would be much more valuable and interesting than superfluous repetitions of existing editions made in the study; but they would not be a whit more 'standard' or authentic.

Besides, they would introduce more controversial new readings than any merely literary editor dare venture. For example, take the following ranting and redundant utterances of Macbeth:

Hang out your banners on the outer walls.
The cry is still they come.

Barry Sullivan cured both the rant and the redundancy very simply. He entered at the back of the stage throwing an order over his shoulder to his subalterns, and then came down to the footlights to discuss the military situation. Thus we got the reading:

Hang out your banners. On the outer walls the cry is still they come.

This, tested on the stage as Mr. Granville Barker would test it, is a convincing improvement. But the authority for it is not the text as it has come down to us, but Barry Sullivan's conjecture submitted to Mr. Barker's test. And Barry Sullivan went further than that. Instead of saying, as Hamlet, 'I am but mad north-north-west: when the wind is southerly I know a hawk from a handsaw,' he said, 'I know a hawk from a heron. Pshaw!' This may read strainedly; but Mr. Barker's stage test would favor its adoption. Such readings, however, would compel Mr. Barker to interpolate scores of stage directions for which there would be no authority but his own artistic instinct.

As to Mr. Poel, there is no living enthusiast more firmly convinced than he that knows the mind of Shakespear; and this conviction has nerved him to do yeoman's service to his master. It would serve him equally to feats that Dr. Johnson would have funked. The liberties he would take with the text to square it with his own original and vivid conception of character, theatrical technique, and Elizabethan political history and social structure would rouse a fury of controversy. On that very account a Poel Shakespear should be published, even if it were to consist of only a few specimen plays; and a Granville Barker Shakespear should rival it. But neither edition could be called a standard edition except by the courtesy which allows every theatre to call itself the Theatre Royal. And the question which of the two famous Shakespearian producers were the more unscrupulous would never be settled.

Now may I be allowed a suggestion of my own? Why not try to make a record of our language as it is spoken to-day on the stage classically? We have in Forbes Robertson an actor whose speech is unchallengeable in every English-speaking land, not only in Oxford and the West End of London, but in countries where the dialect of Oxford and West End is received with shouts of derisive laughter. It does not matter how Forbes Robertson pronounces this or that vowel: his speech will carry any Englishman anywhere. It is unquestionably proper for a king, for a chief justice, for an archbishop, or for a private gentleman; having acquired it, no one has anything more to learn to qualify himself as a speaker for the most dignified employment. Well, why not begin with an edition of *Hamlet* in which this Robertsonian speech shall be recorded by phonetic spelling? I am aware that this cannot be done completely except by using Bell's Visible Speech, which nobody but Mr. Graham Bell and perhaps a few others can read; but by eking out the ordinary alphabet with a few letters turned upside down, and coming to a clearly stated understanding as to the meaning of those which remain right side up, it is quite possible to make a very useful record, supplemented by the existing phonographic records of which Sir Johnston can specify the defects exactly. Such a phonetic edition of *Hamlet* could be fairly described as a standard Hamlet, valid for its day. The Academic Committee of the Royal Society of Literature could justify its existence by undertaking this work.

As to the text, by all means let Mr. Poel's points, and Mr. Granville Barker's points, be considered in editing it. Both gentlemen might very well be co-opted to the editing committee. But I implore Mr. Poel to dismiss from his mind the notion that there are two punctuations: a grammatical and an oral. The two are the same. Dr. Johnson's punctuation of Shakespear's plays, far better on the whole than that of the Quartos or the Folio, is highly suggestive of the stage delivery of Garrick's day. The authorized version of the Bible, punctuated by preachers for preachers, is as oral as it is grammatical. What people call grammatical or literary punctuation is simply unskilled punctuation: the work of writers who pepper a page with commas, and disfigure it with dashes, leaving the printer to supply the semicolons, which he does with a conviction that it is wrong to have two in the same sentence, and that colons are of the nature of sacred music. My own punctuation, which is as definite as the multiplication table, is founded on the best Bible usage (the Bible is not consistently stopped throughout) and on the distinctions I find it necessary and possible to make; and it is both grammatical and oral.

But I must repeat that the notation at my disposal cannot convey the play as it should really exist: that is, in its oral delivery. I have to write melodies without bars, without indications of pitch, pace, or timbre, and without modulation, leaving the actor or producer to divine the proper treatment of what is essentially word-music. I turn over a score by Richard Strauss, and envy him his bar divisions, his assurance that his trombone passages will not be played on the triangle, his power of giving directions without making his music unreadable. What would we not give for a copy of Lear marked by Shakespear 'somewhat broader', 'always quieter and quieter', 'amiably', or, less translatably, 'mit grossem Schwung und

Begeisterung', 'mit Steigerung', much less Meyerbeer's 'con esplosione,' or Verdi's fffff and ppppp, or contando or parlando, or any of the things that I say at rehearsal, and that in my absence must be left to the intuitions of some kindred spirit?

It will be seen now, I hope, that this discussion about the punctuation of the Shakespear Quartos raises the much more serious question of making the great invention of reading and writing really effective and educational. It is at present a wretched makeshift. Children are taught to read at great expense; and they cannot open their mouths without proving that the sound of their noble native speech has never been conveyed to them. They see on paper the words of their poets, and repeat them in the voices of their slums. Men whose noses were rubbed ruthlessly into books and copybooks every day for nine year at elementary schools are unemployable as butlers or West End shop assistants because they cannot form a grammatical sentence nor utter a sound that is admissible in cultivated society. Others, cultivated in country houses, and educated at Eton and Oxford, have their speech represented by Oxford's greatest phonetic experts as follows:

Tell mii not in menfi nambez
Laif iz bat an emti driim
Fo dhe sowl is ded dhet slambez
Aend thingz as not whot dhei sijm.

To turn this into a coster's cockney, all that is necessary is to change 'tell' into 't'yoll', 'laif' into 'lawf', 'as' into 'aw', and 'dhei' into 'dhy'. Ask Forbes Robertson to declaim the verse, and you will hear something quite different from either: to wit, the English language in the only form that has a right to call itself standard. But this English will be dead presently, unless we take the trouble and cultivate the artistic conscience to provide it with a notation. At most, I suppose, we shall continue to dispute whether 'labour' or 'labor' is the correct spelling, in crude ignorance of the fact that both inaccuracies are merely confessions of our inability to write the obscure vowel that is the commonest sound in our language. As to enabling me to hand down my plays as Sir Edward Elgar can hand down HIS Falstaff, I see no chance of that in literature. Perhaps the phonograph may be able to do something for me before I die: otherwise, like Shakespear, I shall take the secret of their performance to the grave with me, and with it almost all their artistic value, leaving posterity (if it troubles itself about them) to gnaw the cold bones of their intellectual skeletons.

Yours truly,
G. BERNARD SHAW.

On 24 March 1921, Pollard wrote again to the *Times Literary Supplement* and challenged the remarks made by Shaw, who answered him in the following letter.

∽ *1921, March 31* ∽

SHAKESPEARE: A STANDARD TEXT.

Sir: – Professsor Pollard challenges me. Well, if it comes to that, I challenge him. I challenge him to prove (1) that Shakespear knew how to write, and did not dictate his inspirations to the theatre scrivener; (2) that Shakespear ever used a comb before he became bald, or that Queen Elizabeth ever used hairpins; (3) that any mortar or scantling was used in the construction of the Globe Theatre; (4) that the lady at whose house Burbage found Shakespear on a famous occasion was ever baptized: and finally (not to go on like this for ever) that my own plays have not been studied and stage managed in the theatre from my own original manuscripts and subsequently set up by the printer from them. He cannot do it.

A still better game than challenging is asking questions. I ask Professor Pollard has he ever seen Shakespear's handwriting; and would he like to study the part of Hamlet from it if he were an actor and the first night were only a fortnight off? I ask him has he ever written a play; and, if so, would anything induce him to sit down and copy out all the parts separately for the actors with his own hand when he could get somebody else to do it more legibly and tidily for the fiftieth part of the value of his own time?

In this, as in every other historical question, we must, in the absence of evidence, proceed upon normal assumptions, positive as well as negative. I contend that Professor Pollard can escape my positive assumptions only by advancing negative assumptions which are manifestly outrageous. There must have been somebody in the theatre whose business it was to keep the theatre library of prompt copies, and whose perquisite it was to copy out the parts and make fair copy for the prompter. In the same way, if there was a band, there must have been a music librarian (by tradition the drummer), who kept the band parts, and whose perquisite it was to copy them. To ask me to prove these things is like asking me to prove that Henry the Eighth had a bootmaker. To deny them is virtually to deny that there were any plays or any theatre at all, just as to deny the bootmaker is virtually to deny the boots. Surely Professor Pollard has had enough of the sort of controversy that, beginning with a demand for proof that Shakespear ever existed, has led to the crazy fictions known as 'the man Shakespear', 'Shaxper of Stratford' (both illiterate imbeciles acting as 'ghost' to Bacon), proceeding to Shakespear the illegitimate son of Queen

Elizabeth, and so on to no Shakespeare at all, but to every Elizabethan peer who could knock a sonnet together. All that nonsense followed inevitably from the first suspension of common sense as something too vulgar to be applicable to an immortal. 'Others abide our question: thou art free' was said of Shakespear, not of his commentators, though they have mostly assumed that privilege.

Having now dutifully kept up the readableness of the correspondence by this exhibition spar with the Professor, let me get to business and say, though he is satisfied (having given more attention to the subject and put more work into it than I have) that 'there is a substantial body of evidence that many of the first editions of Shakespear's plays were, as a fact, set up from prompt copies', there is no evidence at all that these copies were made by Shakespear. In fact, if they were prompt copies, meaning copies made for use at rehearsal, or made in the theatre in the same way and by the same official as if they were for use at rehearsal, they certainly were not made by Shakespear. And what other copies could they have been? Heming and Condell would naturally have had copies made for the printer in this way, and would not have used the copies actually wanted on the stage. There is just one barely credible alternative; and that is that Heming and Condell may have given the printer the original manuscript in Shakespear's handwriting from which the first prompt copies were made, and which Shakespear may have used himself at rehearsal as the author's copy. In the case of some of the quartos, Shakespear may have given the printer his own copy: in the case of others, the prompter, bribed by the pirate, may have given the original MS. to save himself the trouble of copying it. These are pitiably thin conjectures; but they are not utterly incredible; and if Professor Pollard can substantiate them he may claim a little more authority for the printed texts than they can be allowed on the far more probable case as stated by me. But in any case the position as I have put it remains unshaken. There is no intermediate possibility between facsimiles of the folio and quartos and an edition edited as all the editions from Rowe's to Quiller Couch's have been edited.

Yours truly,
G. BERNARD SHAW.

Conscious no doubt of his position as a Tudor scholar, Pollard tried to retrieve his reputation by implying that Shaw was making assumptions and again replied at some length, with Shaw responding below. J. Dover Wilson (1881–1969) was the renowned Shakespearian scholar.

SHAKESPEARE: A STANDARD TEXT.

Sir, – I gather from Professor Pollard's letter that I somehow managed in my last communication to assume that the theatres in which Shakespear's plays were first produced were equipped with revolving stages, hydraulic bridges, electric lights, Fortuny horizons, telephones, typewriters, and cinema lanterns. This was an unfortunate aberration on my part; for I protest I was perfectly sober when I wrote the letter, and meant to assume nothing beyond the barest necessities of the simplest theatrical establishment in the spacious times of great Elizabeth. I am sorry I did not make myself clear.

This time I hope it may emerge from the obscurity of my style that if Shakespear had wasted his time making legible copies of the parts in *A Midsummer Night's Dream* when he could have set himself free to write *The Merchant of Venice* by hiring some poor devil of a scrivener to make the copies for a few groats per folio, he would never have been able to buy the best house in the main street of his native town. Is that clear?

Ben Jonson complained that Shakespear could not be induced to read over his own plays when he had written them. Professor Pollard thinks that he sat down and laboriously fair-copied them word for word for the actors. Or can it be that Professor Pollard thinks that all that is necessary for the production of a play is one copy, from which a dozen actors learn their parts simultaneously? Here be 'normal assumptions' indeed.

I take Professor Pollard's word for it that it was Massinger's autograph of *Believe As You List* that was submitted for licence to the Master of the Revels. Of course it was. Surely the Professor does not believe that managers spend money on a play, whether for copying or dressing or scene painting or what not, until they know whether they are going to be allowed to perform it or not. The original manuscript must have been the one sent up for licence whenever the author could write legibly enough. It was not until the licence had been obtained that the rehearsals began, and with them the need for copies. It is possible that the original may have been used at rehearsal by the author or prompter or stage manager. If it was, it would get scrawled with such flowers of dramatic poesy as 'whistle Boy', just as I explained so laboriously in my first letter. So what on earth is Professor Pollard nagging me about? Did I offer to say a word to the gentleman?

Finally, I assure Mr. Dover Wilson that I have no doubt that the Cambridge University Press will follow the punctuation of the Folios and Quartos as closely as possible. Why shouldn't it? But how closely will that be without consigning the editor to an asylum for hopeless illiterates? Will the C.U.P. edition be virtually a facsimile of the Elizabethan printed texts or will it not? If so, I told Mr. Dover Wilson so. If not, the editor will have to use his judgment just as Dr. Johnson did. I told Mr. Dover Wilson he would.

Is this correspondence about a standard text of Shakespear or is it about me? If the former, I suggest that future contributors should have the self-denial not to contradict me when they do not disagree with me.

G.- BERNARD SHAW.

The following letter was a collective appeal, instigated by Shaw, for a complete English translation of the works of Count Leo Tolstoy (1828–1910), to be undertaken as a matter of some urgency. Aylmer Maude, a fellow Fabian, *The Times* editor, wrote: 'Among the signatories to Mr. Shaw's letter are: Rev. Dr. Cyril Alington, William Archer, Maurice Baring, Arnold Bennett, A. Clutton-Brock, Dr. W.L. Courtney, Sir Arthur Conan Doyle, J.L. Garvin, Sir Anthony Hope Hawkins, Sir Oliver Lodge, H. W. Massingham, Dr. Gilbert Murray, G.H. Roberts, Sir Paul Vinogradoff, A.B. Walkley, H.G. Wells, Mr. J.H. Whitley and C. Hagberg Wright.'

Thomas Hardy also wrote: 'Although I have no first-hand knowledge of the details mentioned in Mr. Bernard Shaw's letter on translations of Tolstoy, I agree with the opinion that a good rendering of his works into English – so far as that is possible – should be made practicable by the concentration of effort on one production; and I believe that Mr. Aylmer Maude's competence for the task is special and trustworthy.'

～ 1922, April 29 ～

TOLSTOY'S WORKS.

MR SHAW'S APPEAL.

Sir, – We desire to call public attention, especially in circles interested in literature and in general cultural questions, to the lack of a complete edition of the works of Leo Tolstoy in the English language. Unfortunately, the means adopted by Tolstoy to secure the widest possible circulation for his books had just the opposite effect.

He invited all publishers in all countries to take the fullest advantage of the absence of international copyright between Russia and other countries by publishing his writings in such translations as they could procure without any reference to his moral or legal rights. In the case of any less famous author this step would have prevented his works being translated at all, as it is practically impossible to engage modern capital in publishing or any other enterprise without property rights. In Tolstoy's case it led to the appearance of a great number of translations, including some very incompetent ones, of a few of his books which were considered specially interesting as stories, or were capable of being turned to account for propaganda. These few books have consequently become more or less well known; but the profits of their publication have been so divided that they have in no instance been able to carry a complete edition on their backs.

Accordingly, no complete edition has yet appeared; and the one projected for the Tolstoy Centenary of 1928 by the Oxford University Press, translated by Aylmer Maude, whose competence and acceptance by Tolstoy himself are unquestionable, may prove commercially impossible unless the public, by spontaneously giving it the privileges of a copyright edition, both by subscribing for complete sets and specifying this edition in their purchases of separate volumes, makes up for the absence of legal rights and for the miscarriage of Tolstoy's public-spirited intention in the matter.

The Oxford Press translation will be complete and unique, and certain to remain so, as it is not now possible for any new English writer to bring to a translation of Tolstoy's works the personal knowledge of the author, and the peculiar experience of Russian life and of the Tolstoy an social experiments that followed the first publication of his writings, enjoyed by Mr. Aylmer Maude and his wife and collaborator, who is a native of Russia. We feel that its failure to appear would be a grave loss to our national literary equipment, and we earnestly hope that the opportunity of completing the nineteenth-century bookshelf, both of our public and private libraries, by a complete edition of his works in English will not be missed.

Yours truly,
G. BERNARD SHAW.
10, Adelphi Terrace, W.C.2.

Mr. Oliver Brett responded to the foregoing appeal in a letter to *The Times* of 4 March 1922 to point out that Constance Garnett, the wife of the writer Edward Garnett, had produced good translations of Tolstoy's work. Dan Laurence has noted in *Collected Letters, 1874–1897* that she was elected to the Fabian Executive in May 1894 and that, according to her son, Shaw had once been in love with her. Aylmer Maude would eventually publish *The Life of Tolstoy* (2 vols, Oxford: 1929–30). Although Tolstoy respected Shaw's achievements, he did not appreciate Shaw's humorous attitude toward God.

Garnett's translations of Tolstoy and other Russian writers are now thought to be 'prudish' (hence perhaps Shaw's compliment on her 'delicate talent'), but their general competence was undeniable. William Archer (1856–1924), a leading theatre critic and one of Shaw's great friends, had translated Ibsen's plays; William Ashton Ellis (1852–1919) had translated Wagner's writings.

~ *1922 May 8* ~

TOLSTOY'S WORKS.

MR. AYLMER MAUDE'S CLAIM.

TO THE EDITOR OF *THE TIMES.*

Sir, – In reply to Mr. Oliver Brett's letter, may I say that when I signed the appeal which appeared in your columns on April 29, Mrs. Garnett's work was certainly not forgotten by me? Her claim was the first question I raised when the appeal was suggested.

But Mr. Brett himself explains the difficulty we are in when he says the 'Mrs. Garnett has already provided the reading public with perfect translations of the two greatest of Tolstoy's novels.' If Tolstoy's works consisted of great novels there would be no need to bother: such works are sure to get themselves translated everywhere. But one '*Candide*' does not make a Voltaire, nor one '*Anna Karenina*' a Tolstoy. What is now in question is a mass of doctrinal work which has no attraction for novel readers and admirers of Tolstoy as an artist. No publisher will touch it except as a necessary part of a complete collected edition of the works of Tolstoy. No translator will touch it except as a fanatic with a hobby. Heaven forbid that Mrs. Garnett should waste an hour on it, as long as there is a chapter of Russian artistic fiction untranslated.

As far as we have been able to ascertain, no publisher except Oxford University Press contemplates a complete edition in English; and no accredited translator except Mr. Aylmer Maude is prepared to drudge through such an edition to the bitter end. Other publishers and other translators have picked the plums out of the pudding; but that only increases the difficulty of procuring what the plum epicures would call the stodge, though to omit it is to keep us ignorant of a body of doctrine which is leavening popular thought in the world to an extent that makes it very necessary that we should know about it, whether we agree with it or not. In any case, Tolstoy's commanding position as a writer makes a complete edition of his works an indispensable item in modern culture equipment.

Experience shows that such jobs are one-man jobs. Without Mr. William Archer we should have had a few translations of Ibsen's most striking works, and perhaps a few dozen of '*Peer Gynt.*' But we should not have had the Heinemann complete Archer-Ibsen edition which is one of our national possessions. Without the late William Ashton Ellis we should have had some scattered translations of the 'Essay on Conducting' and 'The Art Work of the Future'; but we should not have the complete prose works of Richard Wagner in English. When we look round for the one man who stands in the same devoted relation to Tolstoy as Archer to Ibsen or Aston Ellis to Wagner, we can find no one but Aylmer Maude. It seems our only chance of getting a complete Tolstoy in English. That is why we signed the appeal. If we were wrong – if there is another publisher and another translator ready, let them speak: we shall be only too glad to hear of them. But, personally, I hope the unfortunate translator will not be my old friend Mrs. Garnett, as there is plenty of more remunerative and more congenial Russian literature to employ her delicate talent, which I never heard anyone question.

Yours &c
G. BERNARD SHAW.
Stratford-on-Avon

The occasion for the letter that follows was a touring holiday of Wales and Ireland that Shaw and Charlotte undertook in the summer of 1923, not long after the end of the Irish Civil War. While in Ireland Shaw fell on a rock and injured his back. The letter, quite possibly the only 'travel brochure' Shaw ever penned, was written before his injury and reflects his optimistic view of the future of the country, in spite of the Coercion Act passed by the Government. Perhaps he hoped his rosy-hued depiction of Ireland would strengthen his claim to be included in the discussions then pending on Ireland's future. He was rather markedly excluded. It was to be Shaw's last visit to the land of his birth.

'Poincaresque France' refers to the period of economic uncertainty that came about in France of the 1920's when France was experimenting with the *franc-poincaré*, based upon the ideas of mathematician Jules Poincaré, in an attempt at parity with the dollar. The 'bottomless mark chute' refers to the collapse of the German currency, and 'Anglophobe Fascists' to the newly formed Fascist movement in Italy and its violent dislike of things English.

HOLIDAYS IN IRELAND

Sir, – Several persons have complimented me on my courage in venturing into the South of Ireland for my summer holiday. These people feel safer in the friendly atmosphere of Poincaresque France, or in the land of the bottomless mark chute, where merchants chain up their typewriters with Krupp chains overnight, only to miss them, chains and all, in the morning. They are not afraid even of being dosed with castor-oil in Italy by Anglophobe Fascists. But they dare not set foot in Ireland. I admit that there is some excuse for them. The Irish Government has just passed a Coercion Act which would make Trotsky gasp, and which makes the history of Dublin Castle under English rule seem like freedom broadening down from precedent to precedent. It contains a flogging clause, directed specially against robbery under arms, of such savagery that foreigners may well be led to believe that no man's property or person is safe.

The truth is that Cork and Kerry are much safer, in respect of both person and property, than the Administrative County of London. A year ago no owner of a bicycle in Ireland risked riding it out of call of a barrack, as it was sure to be stolen 'under arms'; and even the cheapest motor-cars were hidden more carefully than illicit stills. Today not only Fords but Vauxhall 38s and Crossley 25s career over the mountain roads as carelessly as over the Surrey hills. The tourist's heart is in his mouth when he first crosses a repaired bridge on a 30 cwt. car, for the repairs are extremely unconvincing to the eye; but after crossing two or three in safety he thinks no more of them. Since I arrived I have wandered every night over the mountains, either alone or with a harmless companion or two, without molestation or incivility. Naturally there is plenty of room in the hotels; and the quality of the potatos, the butter, and the milk is such as to make one feel that one can never eat the English substitutes again. In short, there is not the smallest reason why Glengarriff and Parknasilla should not be crowded this year with refugees from the turbulent sister island and the revolutionary Continent, as well as by connoisseurs in extra-ordinarily beautiful scenery and in air which makes breathing a luxury. However, the dock strike must be reckoned with. The passengers must unload the ship and must therefore leave Saratoga trunks behind. It is hard on the dockers to have to look on idly whilst potential employers whose rate of pay varies from twelve to thirty shillings an hour handle their own luggage and evidently enjoy it for once in a way as a holiday lark; but it need not hinder the passenger traffic from Paddingon to Cork via Fishguard.

Perhaps I should explain that though the Coercion Act empowers every superintendent of police or army captain to seize any man's property, even to his clothes, leaving nothing on him but the onus of proving that he ever possessed them or had any right to possess them, this power (in force for one year only) is not exercised at the expense of the errant Englishman, and exists only because the loot from plundered houses has to be redistributed by rough-and-ready methods for which the permanent law is too slow and contentious. Ireland is at present in a reaction of quiet, with the hands of its Government reinforced by extraordinary temporary measures, and is therefore at this moment probably the safest country in the world for visitors

Yours truly,
G. BERNARD SHAW.

Although Shaw all but ceased being an active playwright during the war, he continued to keep the pot boiling with playlets and sketches intended for the music halls. He also worked at the play that would finally take shape as *Heartbreak House*. Shaw's bitter epitaph on the generation that allowed the drift into the cataclysm of the Great War-was first produced in New York in 1920 (125 performances), then, for a brief run, at the Court Theatre in London in 1921, where it was, as usual, panned by the critics.

His next major play was Back to Methuselah, his self-proclaimed 'world classic or . . . nothing,' A dramatised rendering in five plays of his ideas on Creative Evolution and its corollary the Life Force, it was first produced in New York in 1922 (fifty-six performances) and then in 1924 at the Court Theatre where, yet again, the critics complained long and loud.

The theatre critic for *The Times*, A.B. Walkley, was one who complained and criticised. Shaw's lampooning of two leading politicians (Lloyd George and Asquith) in the second play, 'The Gospel of the Brothers Barnabas', was held to be in bad taste. In the letter that follows Shaw defends himself against both Marsh's and Walkley's criticism and, for good measure, on the question of the pronunciation of 'isolate' as rendered by one of his leading ladies, Eileen Beldon. Silas Wegg is a character in Dickens's *Our Mutual Friend*.

'BACK TO METHUSELAH'
PERSONALITIES AND POLITICS.
MR. SHAW TO HIS CRITICS

Sir, I am very reluctant to make any comment on the expressions of irritation which my play at the Court Theatre must inevitably provoke from the short-lived, but Mr. Edward Marsh, whose sensibilities I have every personal reason for respecting, must not accuse me of 'pouring scorn on a politician who actually allowed his own son to be killed in the war'. In what sense did any man 'allow' his son to be killed in the war? Would any man have allowed such a thing if he could have prevented it? Many men, who were more or less responsible for the war, had that responsibility brought home to them by the loss of a well-beloved son; but they will hardly, I think, regard that as a fact to be suppressed as shameful, or deny the son his right to his record and his share in the moral of the greatest tragedy of his time. Does Mr. Marsh really believe that his delicacy is greater and more consoling than mine when he dismisses the son with the remark that 'somebody must be killed in a war', and treats his fate as a mere personal episode in which a father 'allows his own child to sacrifice himself', and is to be contrasted with 'one who saves his family at the expense of others'? In the framework of my play such phrases would be heartless nonsense; the case is bigger and deeper than that.

As to 'pouring scorn' on anyone, what I have done is to exhibit our Parliamentary politics in contrast with politics *sub specie aeternitatis*. If under this test they shrink to a ridiculous smallness and reveal a disastrous inadequacy, that is not a reason why the exposure should be spared; it is a most urgent reason for submitting them to it ruthlessly. And as the dramatic method requires that the politics should be expounded by politicians, and the test can be valid only if the politicians are recognizably true to historic fact, the politicians must to some extent share the fate of the politics. This inevitable effect may scandalize critics who, being innocent of political life, imagine that statesmen approach elections with their minds wholly preoccupied with abstract principles, oblivious of the existence of such persons as voters, and most undemocratically indifferent to their likes and dislikes. Such critics imagine that in representing two ex-Premiers, on the eve of a General Election, as keenly alive to such considerations, and only too bitterly aware of our electoral ignorance, folly, and gullibility, I am representing them as unprincipled scoundrels; but I can hardly be expected to defer to a judgment so ludicrously uninstructed. My play, as far as it goes outside the public history of public men, contains not a word against the private honour of any living person; and if I do not share the delicacy as to equally public and politically active women which restrained Silas Wegg from going into details concerning the Decline and Fall of the Roman Empire, I can only say that my blue pencil is at the service of any lady who can find a single reference to herself which is not within the privilege of the friendliest good humour.

I have been accused in your columns of 'shouting scandal from the housetops'. Is it scandal to say of one statesman that he is happily married? or of another, who has an almost embarrassingly clever and famous wife, and two daughters whose achievements in politics and literature threaten to eclipse his own, that he is in this fortunate condition? Surely my apology is due to these ladies for having given them minor and even mute parts in a drama in which they actually played much more important ones, and not to your critic, who grudges them any mention at all. It is true that in stage fiction many marriages are scandalous, and most of them triangular. The critic's mind becomes at last like the dyer's hand: the wedding ring suggests nothing to him but the Divorce Court. But my plays are not theatrical plays in that sense; and I hope an honest woman may be mentioned in them without a stain on her character.

Finally, as Miss Eileen Beldon has been accused by your critic of mispronouncing the word 'isolate' (perhaps he rhymes it, as many do, to 'why so late'), may I ask him how he pronounces it himself? I once asked Thomas Hardy how he pronounced The Dynasts. He replied that he called it The Dinnasts, but that so many people knew no better than to call it The Die-nasts that he was getting shy about it, and preferred not to mention it at all. I appeal to your critic not to make Miss Beldon shy, and, after consulting the pronouncing dictionaries, to send her a suitable apology.

Yours truly,
G. BERNARD SHAW.

The following letter, in response to Walkley's comment in *The Times* of 26 February, continues the correspondence on, principally, the pronunciation of 'isolate'. One notes Shaw's insistence on the use of 'issolate' for platform and stage use, invoking the 'intelligent ear' as his criterion. Nevertheless, he was losing the battle and received pronunciation today is 'eye-se-late'. The 'scandal' Shaw mentions refers to comments made by Walkley. Shaw had stated that a certain statesman was happily married but then went on to remark that 'he has a reputation as a profligate' and 'his name is coupled with celebrated beauties'. Gilbert Murray (1866–1957), a great friend of Shaw's, was a noted classical scholar; his translations of three of Euripides's plays were produced by Vedrenne–Barker at the Court Theatre in 1904–07.

'BACK TO METHUSELAH'

Sir, – Your critic's bluff is so magnificent that it would be unchivalrous to call it were not Miss Beldon's orthoepic honour engaged. He dares refer me to Murray, knowing well that Murray gives issolate as a received pronunciation, though he has the bad taste to prefer eye-solate. Webster gives isolate, Ogilvie gives issolate, the invaluable Chambers, compared to whom and to the others Murray is the merest upstart, gives issolate and izzolate, and the monumental Anglo-German Muret-Saunders gives issolate also. Is a lady with these masses of authorities at her back to be told that she mispronounces, and, when she is vindicated, to be propitiated by an assurance that she is young and charming, and that I have taken advantage of her innocence? Your critic now owes two apologies instead of one.

For the information of your readers, let me say that ice-olate is a vulgar pronunciation, which has forced its way into acceptance by general use so effectually that nobody can pretend that it is incorrect or objectionable in private conversation. But for platform and stage use, and in poetry, the ambiguity and ugliness of the long 'i' make it impossible for any speaker with an intelligent ear. On the stage, therefore, the received pronunciation is the old standard one of issolate; and your critic must reserve his I-so-late for the intimacies of the tea-table.

I have no further quarrel with your critic about the scandal. He has produced a specimen of which he has made the worst by audaciously omitting the clause that places its harmlessness beyond all question. But even as debowdlerised, I can safely say that if there is nothing more terrible behind his protest against 'scandal shouted on the housetops,' I forgive him for it, and leave it to the judgment of your readers, who have, I feel sure, received it with a unanimous cry of 'Is that all?'

Your critic should not listen to my very mild chaff through a microphone, and put cotton-wool in his ears when Methuselah is shouting his loudest.

Yours truly,
G. BERNARD SHAW.

The foregoing correspondence on the critical reaction to *Back to Methuselah* predates by a few weeks the London premiere of *Saint Joan*, which had already had a triumphant run in New York (23 December 1923, with 214 performances). The play opened (26 March 1924) to widespread plaudits in London, although some critics were ambivalent about it (Walkley being one). It amounted to a Shavian apotheosis, as one critic has said, and even the Nobel Prize committee could no longer look away. Shaw was awarded the prize for literature in 1925 and, while accepting the prize, turned down the money, saying that he no longer needed it and requested instead that it be used to fund an Anglo-Swedish Literary Foundation. (The Swede Hugo Vallentin had been his faithful translator for many years; this was possibly one of Shaw's considerations.)

In 1923, Shaw had freely adapted his German translator Trebitsch's melodrama *Frau Gittas Sühne*, titling it *Jitta's Atonement* and turning it into near farce.

Shaw then took a five-year 'holiday' from play-writing, turning his attention to the composition of his treatise *The Intelligent Woman's Guide to Capitalism and Socialism* (1928), which, ten years later, he augmented with short sections on Sovietism and Fascism. This monumental work was scarcely completed when he wrote his next play, *The Apple Cart*, a 'political extravaganza', first performed in 1929.

Not surprisingly, in view of the time and creative energy poured into these projects, Shaw's letters to *The Times* had become comparatively infrequent. Neither perhaps were there any issues that merited attention through *The Times* – until his old adversary smallpox returned in 1925. The controversy was sparked by a Mr Hesketh, who was querying the efficacy of vaccination in combating the new outbreak. There had been a series of lectures on the topic by a Fleet Surgeon, W.E. Home, to sailors of the Fleet to convince them to take up the vaccination. The Fleet Surgeon then wrote to *The Times* on 4 May to answer the criticisms of Mr Hesketh, which prompted Shaw to comment, now with more than a hint of impatience, on what he still saw as the inflated claims of vaccinators. His arguments are much the same as those of twenty years before, not least in their reiteration of the need for better housing and sanitation. 'Captain Marryat' (Frederick Marryat, 1792–1848) followed a career in the Navy before becoming a pre-eminent novelist of the sea. Shaw's reference (and Home's allusion) is probably to Marryat's first novel, *Frank Midway* (1829).

~ 1925, May 12 ~

THE MARCH OF THE SMALLPOX.

EFFICACY OF VACCINATION.

Sir, – Dr. W.E. Home, Fleet Surgeon, states that the wrecking of women's complexions and appearance through smallpox was 'almost universal' in the 18th century. This amazing assertion is supported by a quotation from one of Captain Marryat's novels in 1829, after 30 years of vaccination. It is perhaps appropriate that our Fleet surgeons should study Marryat rather than Jenner; but Marryat was merely echoing Jenner, who made exactly the same remark before vaccination was introduced, and attributed the alleged phenomenon to inoculation, which is now a criminal practice.

Dr. Home's lectures to bluejackets appear to have reflected the teaching of our newspapers on vaccination very faithfully. He exhibited terrifying pictures of cases of confluent smallpox, but omitted the pictures (now in extensive circulation) of cases of that equally hideous and more deadly disease, generalized vaccinia. He 'told of the scourge smallpox was before vaccination came in 1800, and how it lessened thereafter', but said nothing of cholera, typhus, and the other scourges, which had practically disappeared during that period, whilst smallpox marched to its climax in the appalling epidemic of 1871, which gave vaccination, then ruthlessly compulsory, its death blow. He contrasted arm to arm vaccination with vaccination by 'good and safe' calf lymph, but omitted to explain in what sense undefined pathogenic matter scraped from an ulcer on a calf infected with vaccinal syphilis can be good and safe for any other purpose than that of infecting anyone inoculated with it with the calf's disease. As the doctor had to go off to China without waiting to see what happened to the 120 victims of the operation, possibly the 'week or fortnight of slight illness' prescribed for them may have been the worst that ensued. But I remember an experiment made by the Metropolitan Asylums Board, in which the men working on a certain job during an epidemic were induced to submit to revaccination, not by lectures and pictures of confluent smallpox, but by a bribe of 5s. per man. The resultant 'slight illnesses' included some that were much worse than any ordinary case of smallpox. The medical report was never published.

I have two reasons for inflicting these commonplaces of the vaccination controversy once more on your readers. The first is that the Press and the administrative departments seem to be relapsing into that infatuated ignorance of the strength of the popular and scientific opposition to vaccination which received such a shock when the compulsory clauses had to be repealed by a scared House of Commons in 1898. If the departments and the Press persist in ignoring and suppressing the case against vaccination until there is another explosion, the result may possibly be that vaccination will be made a crime, as inoculation (equally well accredited) has been.

My second reason is that, although smallpox is now a comparatively negligible disease – so much so that in the little outbreaks which seem so trumpery to those of us who remember 1871 and 1881, we sometimes find no deaths, and the whole affair dismissed by old hands as chicken-pox – yet the shortage of houses has produced so much overcrowding that there is a serious danger that Nature may strike again, and strike hard, as she does always when she is too long defied. It is an established fact that adequate housing and sanitation can avert the blow. It is an equally established fact that revaccination cannot. Anything that leads us to rely on vaccination and neglect housing and sanitation is therefore most mischievously inopportune at the present time. But for these considerations nothing would have induced me to take up my pen again in argument with a profession which has surrendered itself to a fixed idea. I fear it is now too late for it to put its house in order; but when the laity – the consumers and victims – take it in hand, as they presently must, at least it will not be able to plead that nobody warned it of the wrath to come.

Yours truly,
G. BERNARD SHAW.

The renowned sculptor Jacob Epstein (1880–1959) had been commissioned to design a memorial in Hyde Park, London, to the naturalist and writer W.H. Hudson (1841–1922). He produced a *bas relief* entitled 'Rima' which depicted a naked female surrounded by birds. Like much of Epstein's work in its time, it aroused controversy and protestors daubed it with green paint. 'Rima' survived this desecration and is still in its bird sanctuary in Hyde Park. Several letters appeared in *The Times* during May and June of that year. Epstein would later (1934) produce a bust of Shaw, which Shaw and particularly his wife Charlotte did not like. Shaw's letter is characteristic: tongue-in-cheek while containing the usual quota of serious comment. Actress Fay Compton (1894–1978) had appeared in many of J. M. Barrie's plays and several Shakespearian productions. Actress Gladys Cooper (1888–1971) had been highly acclaimed for her portrayal of Mrs Higgins in *My Fair Lady.*

~ *1925, June 17* ~

MR. EPSTEIN'S PANEL.

Sir, – On visiting the Bird Sanctuary on Saturday I found my way by an eloquently trampled path to a crowded railing, where I was confronted with a very remarkable sample – I use the word advisedly – of the great art of monumental wall sculpture which we rather feebly call *bas relief.* It was unquestionably the real thing, with all the power of stone and all the illusion of strenuous passion, and even movement, that live design can give. But it was a sample, and a ridiculously small one. It reminded me of a Quaker cloth merchant in my native Dublin, famous for the imperturbability of his temper. A young English officer, after making him take down every roll in his shop, at last selected a cloth, and gravely said he would take a halfpennyworth of it. The unmoved Quaker cut out a piece the exact size of the halfpenny, wrapped it neatly in paper, and handed it respectfully to his customer.

It is evident that the Hudson memorialists, having collected what they could, were compelled to go to Mr. Epstein and say, 'Please, sir, mother England wants four yards of your best monumental wall sculpture to put up in the Park for one of her famous sons.' And Mr. Epstein solemnly delivered the four yards, which bear about the same proportion to what was needed as the Quaker's halfpennyworth of cloth to a suit of clothes. That is what comes of ordering a monument when you have only money enough to pay for a Christmas card. We get a monument to our national meanness in matters of high art. If it had been Wembley now! Next time, if we cannot afford to give Mr. Epstein *carte blanche*, we had better get the job done in the Euston Road in a thoroughly commercial manner.

I have a great deal of sympathy with the people who hate Mr. Epstein's sample. Some of them feel the reproach and the inadequacy for which they innocently blame Mr. Epstein. Some of them do not like monumental wall sculpture, and are in the grievous position of people who want a fox-trot and have a Beethoven symphony thrust into their ears. Why should not these people, who have a perfect right to their own tastes, have a monument and a bird sanctuary all to themselves? There is plenty of room in the Park for both. It need not cost much. There is a process called photo-sculpture with an establishment in the West End, by which very pretty relief's can be made by the camera. If Miss Fay Compton or Miss Gladys Cooper would pose as Rima, with a stuffed pigeon on each wrist, the artist who touches up the photo-sculpture could throw in a few swallows, a robin, and a holly branch; and the result would be exactly what is wanted by the honest folk whose sense of beauty is outraged and mocked by Mr. Epstein's powerful proceedings. Why not please everybody when it is so easy?

G. BERNARD SHAW.

The next two letters were occasioned by the General Medical Council's striking off the register of a retired 87-year-old medical practitioner, F.W. Axham, for the alleged offence of 'covering', a practice which Shaw explains in his letter of 12 November 1925. The first of these letters, that of 23 October, is notable for his encouragement of osteopathy (then known as 'bone setting') a highly controversial and officially unsanctioned practice in the medical profession. Shaw wrote more than once in support of it. Both letters are notable for their demonstration of Shaw's readiness to fly to the support of victims of medical malpractice, not least that exercised by the General Medical Council's 'trade unionism'. Herbert Barker (1877–1946), a practising osteopath, was eventually knighted for his services to medicine, notwithstanding the refusal of the GMC to sanction his work.

GENERAL MEDICAL COUNCIL

THE CASE OF DR. AXHAM.

Sir, The difficulty about Dr. Axham does not seem to be understood. Dr. Axham did his clear duty as a member of a profession devoted to the relief of human suffering by every means within the competence of a physician, and to the encouragement and aid of every extension of those means. The public has benefited by his action and owes him its protection. Yet it has allowed him to be stigmatized for his services as guilty of infamous professional conduct and struck off the register. The striking-off will not hurt him nowadays, when unregistered practitioners are at a heavy premium because they have mastered the modern techniques of which registration guarantees ignorance; but at 87 he is past practising, and the stigma is deeply felt and justly resented by him.

Meanwhile, Sir Herbert Barker, whom he was one of the first to recognize as a great manipulative surgeon, has been knighted in public recognition of his eminence at the instance of four famous surgeons, who petitioned the Prime Minister on the subject. The G.M.C. holds that they were guilty of infamous professional conduct, in which they were abetted by the King; but it does not act on its view, because the King and his advisers are not so helpless as Dr. Axham was. Only by continuing the victimization of Dr. Axham can it make its opinion quite clear, and intimidate every registered practitioner who would like to follow his admirable example.

Obviously it is useless to appeal to the G.M.C. But what about the really responsible bodies who are supposed to represent the nation in the matter – the Privy Council and the universities and the Government? It is they who, in gross neglect of their duty, and in spite of the plain provisions in the Act for public and scientific representation, have thrown the control of the profession, including powers which no political ruler in the civilized world now enjoys or would dream of claiming, into the hands of practising doctors, with the inevitable result that the Council has become a trade union of the worst type – namely the type in which the entry to the trade and the right to remain in it are at the mercy of the union. Not only is the type the worst, but in this particular instance it is at the crude stage of preoccupation with professional earnings and sullen defiance of public opinion, which produced the Manchester and Sheffield outrages in working class trade unionism in the last century. Within the last month or two a distinguished doctor has written to the Press declaring naively that the first duty of the G.M.C. is to protect the livelihood of the registered practitioners. He would be quite right if the G.M.C. were a trade union *de jure* as well as *de facto*; but as it is, on the contrary, a constitutional authority, its first duty is to protect the public and secure to it the advantages of all the latest developments in medicine and surgery. It has become in effect a trade union solely through the carelessness or superstition of the controlling bodies representing us poor laymen who are so vitally interested as patients, as well as disinterested science.

It seems hopeless, however, to make people understand this. My own efforts to call attention to it result only in what I must call editorial imbecilities to the effect that I have 'a down on doctors', and that every quack would have to be registered if Sir Herbert Barker were registered, which is about as sensible as saying that because Brahms was made a Doctor of Music without doing the curricular exercises in counterpoint the universities are logically bound to confer degrees on all our street piano men. As a matter of fact, few persons can have had more or better doctor friends than I; indeed, that is why my utterances have been so well informed; but they may not speak for themselves, whereas I, being free to open my mouth without being ruined and stigmatized as infamous, can act occasionally as the mouthpiece of a gagged profession. Leaving that aside, I have my own interests and grievances as a citizen. My wife suffered from a laming traumatic dislocation for eight years. Thanks to the obsolete training maintained by the G.M.C., the registered surgeons were unable to correct it. They did not pretend to: the final verdict was. 'You must go to Barker.' But the G.M.C. said: 'If you go to that blackleg, you shall howl for it, as we will ruin any man who dares administer an anaesthetic.' And, in fact, the operation, which was completely successful, was performed without an anaesthetic, though I hasten to add that this was an effect of my wife's curiosity rather than of any serious difficulty in circumventing the trade union.

Later on, in an accident, I displaced one of my own bones rather badly; and again, though nothing could exceed the kindness of the registered medical gentlemen on the spot, they were unable to replace it for want of a perfectly well-known technique which every qualified surgeon should have at his fingers' ends. It took me ten days to get to Birmingham, where an American D.O. (doctor of osteopathy), also classed as a blackleg by the G.M.C., set me right after 75 minutes' skilled manipulation. Had the process been an unbearably painful one, which it fortunately was not, any anaesthetist saving me the pain would have done so under penalty of being rattened (as the term went in Sheffield) to the extent of being deprived of his livelihood.

No wonder I am overwhelmed with requests from the medical societies in all the medical schools in London to lecture to them on the situation. But I have nothing more to say than I have already said often and clearly enough; and I simply dare not use the language that the ablest leaders of the profession pour out on it. All I assert is that if the constitutional authorities will only do their duty by getting rid of the practitioners from the G.M.C. (save as assessors in case of need), and replace them with representatives of the public and of disinterested hygienic science, Dr. Axham will be reinstated almost automatically, and the conquest of Harley Street by the unregistered, now in active progress, may be checked. For there is really nothing that the unregistered practitioners do that cannot be done by registered ones if only they are apprenticed to the techniques of today instead of to those of a century ago.

Yours truly,
G. BERNARD SHAW.

In this next letter there is reference to Christian Science healing (based upon the teachings of Mary Baker Eddy) and to Kellgren Massage that deals with referred pain. The mention of Peculiarism is a Shaw joke. Dr. Graham Little (1867–1950) was a dermatologist and Sir Bryan Donkin (1835–1912) had been a noted psychologist and phrenologist.

~ *1925, November 12* ~

DOCTORS AND THE PUBLIC.

THE OFFENCE OF COVERING

Sir, – Dr. Axham has not been 'covering', nor was it for covering that he was struck off the register. I happen to know what covering means: my uncle was a doctor. Real covering, which is not uncommon, and, in the cases which have come under my observation or to my knowledge, has been practised with impunity and with hardly a pretence of concealment, arises in the following way:

A registered doctor – usually a country doctor – finds that he is getting more patients than he can attend to. Obviously he should take another registered doctor into partnership But this means inviting a rival on to his ground, and sharing fees with him. It is better business to engage an unregistered assistant, who will work as an employee at a modest salary, and who can never capture the practice and set up for himself. It is not difficult to find such assistants. There are always men in the market with a taste for doctoring, who, through poverty, age, or lack of the necessary sort of application and memory, are unable to pass examinations. Some of them, by superior clinical instinct and dexterity, are better doctors than their registered employers, and are preferred by the patients. Employment of such unregistered assistants is 'covering.' I have never heard it defended in principle, and I should be surprised if I heard Dr. Axham or Sir Herbert Barker defend it either in practice or principle. Covering is always the maintenance under false colours of an unregistered practitioner by a registered one, and cannot in its own nature be the converse. If Dr. Axham, being a registered practitioner, and being called in as such to perform a surgical operation, had handed over the patient to 'one Herbert Atkinson Barker', unregistered, but assumed by the patient on the strength of his connexion with Dr. Axham to be registered, then Dr. Axham would have been guilty of covering.

What actually happened was just the opposite. A patient with a dislocated knee, finding, after many expensive experiments, that neither Dr. Axham nor any other available registered surgeon could set it right, and that one Herbert Atkinson Barker, unregistered, and not pretending to be registered, had become famous by his success in such cases, naturally called in the said Herbert to cure him, as he had a perfect right to do without molestation or intimidation from the G.M.C. or anyone else. He asked would it hurt? On learning that it would, he called in Dr. Axham to anaesthetize him, which again he had a perfect right to do. Dr. Axham, having convinced himself that the operation, though neither he nor any of his registered colleagues could perform it, was a surgical one in the technical sense, and that Herbert Atkinson Barker had mastered it, was under the most sacred professional obligation to give the desired relief. There was no covering whatever in the transaction.

To make this clear, let us suppose that the victim of a railway collision lies pinned down beneath the wreckage in such a way that he can be released only by a skilled breakdown gang using compressed air drills, oxyacetylene jets, cranes, and so forth, and that its operations are so unbearably painful that it is doubtful whether the victim can survive them. Let us suppose further that Dr. Graham Little and Sir Bryan Donkin are present, rendering what aid they can. The distracted wife of the victim asks Dr. Graham Little to anaesthetize him. Dr. Graham Little is sympathetic, but regrets that, as the members of the breakdown gang are not on the medical register, he would be guilty of covering, and would be struck off the register for infamous professional conduct, if he relieved the sufferer in any way. If, however, his registered friend Sir Bryan Donkin will be good enough to undertake the salvage operations, he will be happy to act. Sir Bryan Donkin says that he would be only too delighted to be of use, but that, as he does not know how to handle compression drills and oxyacetylene jets, the first effect of his interference would probably be to disembowel the patient and burn his head off. In these circumstances both gentlemen are very sorry, but nothing can be done, as it is evident that if eminent registered doctors were allowed to 'cover' railway mechanics wholly ignorant of anatomy the nation must presently perish.

I must apologize to Dr. Graham Little and Sir Bryan Donkin for this monstrous supposition. I have not the slightest doubt that when it came to the point they would act precisely as Dr. Axham acted. Perhaps they will forgive me in consideration of my having cleared up their minds on the subject of covering.

I am quite opposed to real covering, and wish the G.M.C. would stop it. Take a typical case. A patient, suffering from the very distressing pain called neuritis, calls in a registered doctor. It is clearly a case for some sort of manipulation rather than for the bottle. Possibly massage, the doctor thinks. As he knows nothing about massage, his duty is to call in a skilled Kellgren masseur. If he did, the masseur would at once tell him that massage is contra-indicated in such cases and would only aggravate the illness and give intense pain. But as, if the doctor called in a Kellgren masseur (who has to put in two years of finger training before he is considered manually qualified) he would share the fate of Dr. Axham, he hands the patient over to a nurse who has spent a few hard earned guineas on 12 lessons in massage from the local apothecary, with results that may be imagined. This procedure is tolerated by the G.M.C.; yet, if it is not covering, what is covering? The official answer is, apparently, any offence against the trade union. Offence's against the patients are not only winked at, but in some of the worst instances practically imposed on the practitioner by forbidding him to call in competent assistance. Incompetent assistance is privileged.

May I say that I do not hold any brief for osteopathy, or Kellgren massage, or naturopathy or homeopathy, or Christian Science, or herbalism, or peculiarism, or for the few gifted individuals who, like Sir Herbert Barker, have developed and cultivated, by a course of intensive self training which could not be imposed on any student, a personal technique which is practically incommunicable, and which they therefore do not pretend to teach to all comers any more than I pretend to teach all comers to write plays. My brief is for the public, the patient, the consumer, the victim who pays the piper in purse and person without being allowed to call the tune. My case is that the G.M.C. has been suffered to become a trade union of the most anti-social type, whereas it was meant to be, and if the constituent authorities will only do their plain duty can become, a public body protecting us against medical trade unionism (which is quite permissible in its proper place and under proper control by the community) as well as giving us a trustworthy guarantee that a practitioner who can produce its credentials has had a certain minimum of instruction and training, kept carefully up to date by representatives interested in scientific hygiene and not in the spread of lucrative hypochondria.

Instead of this, the G.M.C. deliberately and openly addresses itself to the anti-social task of preventing the public from calling in any unregistered practitioner who is in competition with those on the register, whilst at the same time allowing the qualification for that register to remain in many respects not merely useless and out of date, but positively poisonous and murderous.

I have plenty of medical support for this view; but it will not appear in your columns, because a doctor cannot join in a Press campaign over his own name and address except at the risk of being struck off the register for 'advertising'. If a doctor wishes to add to his income by writing critical articles in the lay Press, as some of our most eminent Churchmen do, he has to remove his name from the register and renounce clinical practice to secure freedom of utterance. I am not defending medical advertisement, registered or unregistered; I am simply explaining why any appeal for the reform of the General Medical Council must be conducted by laymen without avowed medical support. The situation is intolerable, and the remedy obvious.

G. BERNARD SHAW.

Shaw and Charlotte maintained their London home at 10 Adelphi Terrace, now demolished, which overlooked the Thames at Waterloo Bridge, from 1899 to 1927, when they moved to 4 Whitehall Court, overlooking the Charing Cross Bridge. The London Society was founded in 1912 with the aim of improving and protecting architectural development in London.

Waterloo Bridge is a concrete structure originally designed by John Rennie (1761–1821) modified and built for pedestrian and carriage traffic between 1820 and 1830. The splendid Charing Cross Bridge was preceded by the Hungerford suspension bridge for pedestrians in the mid-nineteenth century; the railway bridge followed later. Steel structures, they were built by the famous railway engineer Isambard Kingdom Brunel (1806–59). Richard 'Dickie' Doyle (1824–83) was a notable Victorian illustrator.

~ 1928, May 3 ~

THAMES BRIDGES.

Sir, – The letter addressed to you by the London Society is really more than I can endure in silence. For 30 years I lived with Waterloo Bridge under my study windows; and my hatred of its incurable ugliness and fundamental wrongness increased during all that time. I now live with Charing Cross Bridge under my study windows; and every glance I give at it convinces me more completely that it is a model of what a river bridge should be.

Waterloo Bridge, originally designed as a string of nine canal bridges end to end, is a causeway with holes in it, blocking the view of the river hopelessly, and all but blocking its navigation, which is no doubt its recommendation to people who have no eye for a great river, and so little sense of art that they can write or read themselves into believing that Rennie was one of the great architects of the world. Charing Cross Bridge is a roadway through the air, supported by pillars which do not hide the river, and which reduce the obstruction of the waterway to a negligible minimum. And that, precisely, is what a Thames bridge should be.

All that is needed for Waterloo Bridge is a sufficiency of dynamite, followed by a law making it a capital offence to make perforated causeways across the Thames.

The enthusiasts who are clamouring for its preservation can then find a new subject in those quaint Dicky Doyle fantasies, straight from the title page of, and painted with all the gay English colours of the Queen of Diamonds, which have sprung up by our dull roadsides to supply us with petrol. The cry for painting them dark green and dirty citrine as a prelude to abolishing them and substituting untidy piles of cans will prove a congenial occupation for our amateur art lecturers.

G. BERNARD SHAW.

Stratford Upon Avon.

Shaw modestly omits to mention that his visit to Malvern was to inaugurate the Malvern Theatre Festival with the first English premiere of *The Apple Cart*. This annual festival, established by Barry Jackson (1879–1961), founder and director of the Birmingham Repertory Theatre, focused on Shaw's plays and throughout the 1930s almost all of his plays of that period, plus revivals of earlier plays, were staged at Malvern. Shaw would therefore have an annual opportunity to witness the ravages wrought on the hills by 'Breakages, Limited', the designation he bestowed on unbridled capitalism in *The Apple Cart* and here singled out as 'the men of business who are literally selling their country'. The letter is characteristic of Shaw's letters to *The Times* in the way he turns a local occurrence into a national issue. The area, covering some 3000 acres, is now a national park, designated as a conservation area. The Levellers were extreme radical Dissenters of the seventeenth century and even Oliver Cromwell (1599–1658), himself a Dissenter, was obliged to suppress them. 'Dynamitards' refers to people or organisations that use dynamite to further political ends. 'In summer time on Bredon' was a popular drawing room song. The Clerkenwell incident alludes to the attempt by two Fenians to blow up London's Clerkenwell Prison (demolished in 1890) to draw attention to Home Rule in Ireland.

An ardent walker and lover of the countryside, Shaw can well be considered an early environmentalist.

The Malvern Hills.

Destruction by Quarrying.

Mr. G.B. Shaw's Appeal.

Sir, – As an occasional visitor to Malvern, I am more forcibly struck by the disappearance of the hills than the permanent residents, who hardly miss in the evening the few score of tons that have been blasted away since the morning. After an absence of some years I was startled last August by the ravages of the men of business who are literally selling their country. The approach to Malvern from the great plain of the Severn, with the hills displayed on the western horizon, has always had a peculiar charm. It has now a peculiar horror. Visitors from Worcester, coming through Malvern Wells, used to see the unspoilt northern hills with an undescribable pleasure. They now see it hideously disfigured by three gigantic scoops, reaching so nearly to the top of the ridge that they bring home with a shock the appalling conviction that before very long the scoops will go right through, leaving between them a couple of enormous jagged teeth of hill, which will presently be blasted away in their turn, changing the Malvern hills into the Malvern flats. Let the visitor then proceed to Great Malvern and investigate the scoops at close quarters. He may have fled from one of our cities to escape the shattering din of the pneumatic drill as it 'takes up' our streets. But in our cities the drill is soon silent: it finishes its job and leaves the street relaid and improved for long enough to be forgotten by the only temporarily maddened residents. In Malvern now the hosts of pneumatic drills never stop while there is daylight for their wielders to work by. Day in and day out, year in and year out, they grind and shriek and destroy. The only respite is when everybody runs away to avoid the dynamite explosions which bring down the hills wholesale.

From this inferno the visitor retreats to the south hills, upon which operations have yet hardly begun. There he can still find streets and hotels which are quieter than Manchester at midday. But when he settles in and takes his first drive to the British Camp by old Malvern Court, he finds a big bite taken out of the hills on his way. If he avoids this by taking the higher Wyche Road, he finds the drills and the dynamite at work there too, changing the Wyche into a waste and a wilderness To escape them, he goes through the Wyche to the glorious west side of the hills; yet here, too, he finds Commerce, like Faith, removing mountains, and incidentally removing natural beauty, and all that natural beauty means to us all.

Commerce will not stop at the Malvern hills. When they are levelled to make roads to a place whither nobody will any longer desire to travel, there are the Ankerdines in sight to the west and Bredon to the east. When the drills get to work on them our sentimental sopranos will no longer be able to move their bearers with 'In summer time on Bredon'. After Bredon the Cotswolds, from Evesham to Glastonbury Tor, will resound with the explosions in which they, too, will disappear. England is delivered over to such a sect of Levellers as Cromwell never had to face. The Irishmen who blew up Clerkenwell prison to turn Gladstone's attention to Rome Rule were pursued by the police as Dynamitards; but what were they compared to those modern Dynamitards, whom the police positively have to protect?

What can be done in this matter depends on what we desire. If we want to get rid of the Malvern hills, then we can achieve that very easily by doing nothing. If, however, we set any store by the hills, the sooner the Government makes them a National Park the better. Obviously, if we are to have national parks, the hills will be among the first on the list. What I hope will not be done is to agitate for a new Act of Parliament to preserve the hills. Three such Acts have already been passed; and nobody who is familiar with legislation to protect public interests against private commerce will be surprised to learn that the public would be in a much better position to-day if the Acts had never been passed. Under pretence, of defining and asserting public rights they limit them. Under pretence of restraining the encroachers they recognize them; secure immunities for them after short periods of years; first make it possible for them to obtain compensation for being stopped in their depredations, and then make such compensation compulsory on a scale which puts them in the position of freehold proprietors; and generally do all that such Acts can to facilitate and protect the operations their preambles eloquently denounce. But they stop short of abrogating the rights of common and estover: that is, the rights to pasture and timber for certain necessary purposes, which the commoners legally enjoy. And they set up an indirectly elected local authority, the Conservators, to maintain these rights and preserve the amenities of the hills for the public at large.

The Conservators take the line of least resistance, which is always the line of no resistance at all. Neither the bodies which elected them nor any national authority has taken stops to make them act. If the local authorities attempted to make Malvern live on its capital, the public auditor would soon bring them to their senses; but nobody seems to object to Malvern living on its own entrails. The local gentry plant trees to shut out the view of the gashes in the hills; but they have never applied to the Courts for orders to compel the Dynamitards and Levellers to refrain from destroying the pasturage and timber, and to restore what they have already destroyed by filling up the ghastly chasms they have made. One longs for a few blast furnaces, which are comparatively quiet, very picturesque at night, and make hills instead of removing them.

To-morrow the Conservators will meet and do nothing but gossip. The day after to-morrow the Dynamitards will assemble for a fresh big deal in the plunder of Nature. Let us hope that both assemblies will have their attention called to the publicity given to their business by *The Times*. There is nothing like a searchlight for making people careful.

I am, &c.,

G. BERNARD SHAW.

That Shaw was not afraid to castigate his 'own people' – the Labour Party was in power and the MP behind the proposed legislation, a Mr. Adamson, was a member of that party – is clear from the following letter. As a playwright, fully aware of the possibility of exploitation of his work, Shaw rigorously protected his copyright and performance rights and did not hesitate to institute legal action when 'piracy' came to his notice, although to be sure many unlicensed performances took place. Composers were possibly even easier to exploit than playwrights and other creative artists.

A long series of letters had appeared both in support of and seeking to influence a new Bill that was being debated in Parliament on copyright and how it would affect musicians. Shaw, always defensive of his own copyrights, supported this right in all artistic ventures. He was very conscious of the fact that creative people needed to be protected from exploitation.

~ *1929, December 2* ~

COMPOSERS AND THEIR PROPERTY.

THE NEW COPYRIGHT BILL

MR. G.B. SHAW'S COMMENTS.

Sir, – May I beg the Government, which has allowed this more than usually insane Musical Copyright Bill to pass its Second Reading, to drop it into the dustbin before it is too late? It has arisen in this way.

As it is considered desirable that composers of music should be able to live by the exercise of their talent, they have been given the right for a limited number of years to prevent any person from multiplying copies of their works or performing them in public without the composer's consent, thus enabling him to attach to that consent the best price he can get for it. He has absolutely no other means of livelihood as a composer.

Now it is extremely hard to make people understand that they have no more right to perform the work of a composer without contributing to his support than to pick his pocket. They annex his property without permission or payment by singing his songs at concerts, especially at the friendly smoking concerts and the like got up by the Labour organizations from which Parliament is now recruited. When they have broken the law they are appalled to find some person, not perhaps the composer, but some petty trafficker in copyrights, who has bought the composer's rights for a trifle, turning up and demanding a fee which is limited only by the ability of the offender to pay. There is a wave of sympathy with the popular singer and of indignation against the copyright proprietor. He is classed as an infamous blackmailer; and all the incipient Labour M.P.s in the society resolve that if ever they reach the House of Commons they will make an end of what seems to them a monstrous abuse.

I take it that this is the explanation of the fact that Mr. Adamson has brought in a Bill to enable any person, on payment of twopence to the proprietor of the copyright of any musical composition, to perform it as often as he likes.

The naivety of this solution of the 'blackmail' difficulty takes away one's breath; but that it should have passed its Second Reading is explicable only on the quite probable hypothesis that the great majority of the members of the present House of Commons are amateur vocalists who have at one time or another been caught out in the act of stealing a performing right. The Bill destroys the composer's right to exact a real price for his licence to perform; but, as a climax of absurdity, it expressly confers on him the power which he already possesses to commit suicide by refusing to allow his work to be performed at all. If he is driven by famine to relent and grasp at the twopence, which, after all, is an important sum to a starving man, 'he shall not,' says the Bill, 'be entitled to demand any payment other than a fee not exceeding twopence per published copy payable by any person who demands a copy, upon the purchase or supply of each published copy'. What the last nine words mean I do not profess to understand, but there can be no doubt as to the well-thought-out lucidity of 'not exceeding'. Sir Edward Elgar may not charge more than twopence for a perpetual licence to perform Gerontius; but he may accept a penny. And yet Mr. Adamson is pledged, like all his Labour colleagues, to put down sweating.

I had intended to make a great rhetorical effort to arouse the public conscience through your columns against this Bill; but I find I cannot. I am defeated by the enormity of its silliness. I can only warn Sir Edward to raise the price of the vocal score of Gerontius to a hundred guineas, and that of the orchestral score to a thousand, and to have them both printed on specially perishable paper in ink guaranteed to fade out completely in six weeks. I may also hint that as Master of the King's Musick he may possibly have an opportunity of suggesting that the Royal Veto may fitly come into play when the House of Commons has obviously taken leave of its senses.

Yours truly,
G. BERNARD SHAW.

Shaw always reacted strongly to censorship, as several of the letters in this collection attest to. His main criticism was that the reasons for censoring a book or play were often illogical (even though with the best intentions) and could easily destroy someone's livelihood. In this next letter, he turns his attention to film censorship. Politician Edward Shortt (1862–1935) created night patrols of police on bicycles to counteract a rise in crime; he later became Chief Censor.

~ *1930, February 17* ~

MR. SHAW ON FILM CENSORSHIP.

'EFFICIENT FOR EVIL'

REASONS FOR REFUSING A LICENCE.

Sir, – May I call attention to the latest example of the manner in which our censorships, with the best intentions, safeguard the very evils they are supposed to prevent?

A lady has made it her business to help homeless and penniless people who spend their nights in the streets and make the Embankment a general address for misery. She has found that many of the men have tramped up to London in the belief, not exactly that its streets are paved with gold, but that there is plenty of employment to be had here at higher wages than in the provinces. She also finds that young women come up in answer to advertisements in helpless ignorance of the existence, much less the address, of the Travellers' Aid and other Societies for the protection of women and children from White Slave agents.

The lady has taken a very sensible step, the only effective one within her means. She has had typical nightly scenes on the Embankment filmed and set in the framework of a simple story showing a miner leaving his family to better them by seeking work in London, and presently finding himself on the Embankment desiring nothing more than to get back to his home and his old job in the country. The film also shows a girl decoyed to London by a White Slaver's advertisement. She is fortunate enough, after being drugged and carried on board a ship bound for the Continent, to escape before anything worse has happened to her, and to be directed to the proper quarter for protection and advice.

Obviously the exhibition of such a film throughout the country would be extremely unwelcome to the White Slavers, and would check the flow of unwanted men to London. To the stupefaction of the lady and her charitable colleagues the film was refused a licence. They came to me and put the case before me. As I knew by what I had seen of licensed films that it was quite possible to exploit night scenes and incidents of the White

~ 196 ~

Slave traffic in an objectionable way I asked to see the film. I was at once invited to a private exhibition, only to find that even this could not be given without permission. Finally, however, I saw it where the Censor's writ did not run; and I can testify that there is not an incident or suggestion in it that could not be exhibited in a Sunday school, the pictures being as innocent in their execution as in their intention.

I asked what reason the examiners who do the work of censorship had given for their decision. I was told that they had relented so far as to license the story of the miner 'for adults', which seemed to me madder, if possible, than its total prohibition. But they would not license the story of the girl on any terms, their reason being that they thought domestic servants were badly wanted in London, and that the film might discourage girls from coming to help London out of that difficulty. How girls could be discouraged from travelling by an advertisement of the means by which they could do so in safety was not explained.

As I never make a public grievance of a matter that can be quietly remedied by a reasonable representation to the responsible authority, I persuaded the owners of the film to say nothing until I had written privately to Mr. Edward Shortt, who lately succeeded the late T.B. O'Connor as Film Censor. As he had survived a term of office as Irish Secretary, and had acted as Home Secretary subsequently, I had no doubt that his experience and good sense would at once convince him that his examiners had blundered, and that he would set matters right without any public fuss. His reply is that he has now seen the film, and agrees with the judgment of the examiners, not for the reasons given by them, but because it Is a rule of his department to allow no reference to the White Slave traffic or to drugs. I could hardly believe my eyes as I read this amazing statement of policy. The most lavish and costly displays of the allurements held out by White Slavers to young women, and by them to their patrons, are licensed without demur, and thereby effectually protected and sanctioned. Licensed scenes of what is politely called exhibitionism have become cinema specialities: one which I cannot describe in your columns was shown recently in a first-rate West End picture-house. But when a film is made to show girls the risk they run of being kidnapped by White Slavers, and to make known to them the address of a society which exists to make such kidnapping impossible, the Censor suppresses it. It is as if the railway companies were to exclude the staff of the Travellers' Aid Society from their arrival platforms whilst giving every facility to the White Slave agents on the very acceptable condition that the real nature of their business must not be disclosed.

I know, of course, that as the series of considered moral judgments for which the public look to the Film Censor are absurdly impracticable, his business reduces itself to the enforcement of a few rules of thumb through which any unscrupulous person can drive a coach and six, though they are intolerably obstructive and injurious to conscientious authors; but this particular rule seems to me beyond all bearing except by those who have pecuniary interests in the White Slave and drug traffics. It convinces me, as one who frequents picture-houses, and knows the lengths to which they go in the direction which the censorship exists solely to bar, that it is quite useless for good and terribly efficient for evil.

As Mr. Shortt cannot be questioned in Parliament, which has no control of him or his emoluments, and as my private appeal to him has been in vain am obliged to resort to the Press through its most influential organ.

The title of the film is *The Night Patrol*; and the lady's name is Miss Baxter.

Yours truly,
G.- BERNARD SHAW.
1. Robert Street, Adelphi,
W.C.2.

Shaw is among several famous signatories to the following letter:

∾ *1930, December 11* ∾

The Slaughter of Animals.

More Humane Methods.

'A Reform Long Overdue.'

Sir, – In making this appeal to our fellow countrymen we are actuated not alone by humanitarian considerations, but by a desire to see the logical progress of scientific development taking place in regard to animal slaughter as well as in the other activities of our national life.

The process of slaughtering animals for human food has remained almost static up to the beginning of the present century. But, happily, in the past 30 years movements have been taking place to enable this process to be more in keeping with the results of scientific investigation and knowledge.

We have now arrived at a stage when we, as a nation, can be convinced that a radical change in this process is both possible and, indeed, essential. The poleaxe and the knife have had their day, and the unnecessary suffering caused thereby can now be ended. By patient experiment, by meticulous investigation, and by actual practice among the most expert scientists, as well as practical butchers, it has been established that the mechanical killer, which produces unconsciousness before slaughter, can now securely take the place of the methods of barbarism in actual slaughter which for centuries have existed.

There is none of us who, when an operation on ourselves or our relatives is contemplated, does not insist on an anaesthetic before the application of the knife. We ask that a similar care is taken in regard to the animals on whom so many of us depend for our daily food and sustenance.

On December 12 a Bill for the humane and scientific slaughter of animals, introduced by Colonel Moore, M.P., is to be submitted for second reading. It is a Bill designed to enforce that all animals killed for human food shall be spared the unnecessary cruelty and suffering which the poleaxe and the knife have hitherto rendered inevitable. A practically similar measure is already law in Scotland, and with supremely satisfactory results. We call with confidence on our legislators as well as the general public to give all the support necessary to ensure that this Bill becomes an Act of Parliament. By so doing they will establish a reform long overdue, and remove a stigma from the good name of Britain.

We are yours, &c.,

H..AUSTIN.	C.T. CRAMP.	J. MARTIN-HARVEY.	SYDENHAM.
CHARNWOOD.	DANESPORT.	WINIFRED PORTLAND.	J.E.C. WELLDON.
CLAREIDON.	WILLIAN IBOR.	**G. BERNARD SHAW.**	FRANCES E. WARWICK.

In a *Times* article, Shaw, then not long returned from a visit to Russia, was quoted as saying. 'I have been preaching Socialism all my political life, and here at last is a country which has established Socialism, definitely made Socialism the basis of its whole political system.'

C.R.V. Coutts then wrote to *The Times* pointing out that Socialism was a vague term and could mean a great many different things. He then quoted from Shaw's *The Intelligent Woman's Guide to Socialism and Capitalism* and what he understood Shaw to mean by it. ("The first and last commandment of Socialism is 'Thou shalt not have a greater or less income than thy neighbour'") and then went on to quote from a recent report based on Soviet sources stating differences of income as official policy in Russia. Of course, not even Shaw was able to countenance the fact that it might be possible to introduce a maximum wealth and minimum wealth that would allow for the shortcomings that Mr Coutts could see in the equal income theory. *The Inevitability of Gradualness* is a theory of socialism propounded by the Fabians.

MR. SHAW ON THE SOVIET.

FABIANISM IN ACTION.

Sir – Mr. Coutts must not be in too great a hurry for absolute equality of individual dividend in the distribution of the national income in Russia. Though, as I have demonstrated (apparently unanswerably), we must come to this at last if we are to have permanently stable civilizations instead of ephemeral ones, as at present, we certainly cannot do it without making up our minds as to the figure at which we can afford to stabilize. Russia can hardly be expected to stabilize at the figure represented by the share of an unskilled labourer to-day. She has never for a moment since the revolution pretended or attempted to do so. A professional section – including practical professors of political science like Lenin and Stalin, diplomatists like Litvinoff and Sokolnikoff, generals like Trotsky, educational and artistic culturists like Lutraharsky, with the rank and file of professional routineers, and the organisers of industry and agriculture – would be impossible at such a level; and, boundless as British credulity seems to be as to nonsensical impossibilities resulting from Russian Communism, nobody can suppose that these eminent men cost their country as little as unskilled labourers. I should guess, roughly, that they cost at least as much as the salary of a British back-bench member of Parliament, plus their official expenses. To be equally comfortable personally and socially in England would cost about ten times that modest sum.

Put it, however, at £400 a year. Russia's business for the moment is to stabilize at that figure, and to 'liquidate' (in Russia liquidation means extermination) the unskilled labourer as fast as she can afford to, substituting for him a comparatively skilled worker capable of using delicate machinery and educated to the point of understanding the Russian political system and intelligently professing the religion which form the constitution of modern Russia. Lenin postulated this much as indispensable to a Communist State. To achieve it, a professional standard of life and, consequently, a professional share of the national income will be needed. But the process will take time; and, meanwhile, it is economically impossible to pay unskilled labour much more than enough to keep it alive, whilst its quality is being improved; and it is imperatively necessary to attract foreign skilled labour and professional direction by adequate pecuniary inducements, Equality of income will be reached by levelling up, not by levelling down. And at no point can the process produce the monstrous absurdities of distribution inherent in our private property system.

May I take this opportunity of repeating in print my spoken warnings that Communist Russia must be taken seriously? Most of our comments so far have been beneath the level of ghost stories. Russian Communism is neither Anarchism nor Syndicalism, both of which are called, and even call themselves, Communism in England. It is Fabian Socialism. Lenin, who studied the histories of trade unionism and co-operation by Lord and Lady Passfield, ci-devant Sidney and Beatrice Webb, would, if our Spiritualists could ascertain his wishes as to a suitable motto for his cenotaph, choose *The Inevitability of Gradualness*. This obvious fact now provokes a peal of both Russian and British laughter; but the reason is not that it is true (truth is always amusing when accurately stated), but that political power in Russia was transferred from Capitalism to Communism by a sudden and sanguinary political catastrophe, whereas the Fabians, knowing that such catastrophes cannot be made to order, have had to confine themselves to British constitutional possibilities. But if we have a violent Socialist revolution in England, however complete the slaughter and expropriation may be, gradualness will be as inevitable the day after as the day before; and this the nature of things has forced on Russia, though Trotsky laughs at me for being a Fabian, just as Engels used to. Lenin had to shoot the Anarchists and Syndicalists quite as assiduously as Trotsky, with the help of 30,000 officers from the Tsar's Army, shot the White counter-revolutionists. The U.S.S.R. is really a Union of Fabian Republics; and the sooner we realize that as such it has the support of our most serious political students, and might even (if so disposed) claim these islands as its ideological and scientific fatherland, the sooner we shall cease incurring the present enormous contempt of its able statesmen for our intelligence by speaking and writing as if it were a transient orgy of drunken buccaneers. Russia is what we call a great country, making a great experiment to which we ourselves have led up through many empirical but steadily converging paths. She is led by men of impressive ability and unprecedented freedom of thought, operating a system from which the disastrous frictions of our continual conflict of private interests, and the paralysing delays of our Parliamentary engines of opposition and obstruction, have been ruthlessly eliminated. If we intrigue against them, as they all very naturally suspect us of doing, in an attitude of moral and intellectual superiority, we shall add dangerously to the series of very unpleasant surprises they have already given us. Even those to whom Russia is the enemy had better not underrate her. Russia has not only political and economic strength; she has also religious strength. The Russians have a creed in which they believe; and it is a catholic creed. The Russian is not trained to regard himself as a Russian: he is a member of the international proletariat, which includes the British proletariat. The Russian carpenter, mason, or ploughman has no hostility to the British carpenter, mason, or ploughman, and will not fight him as such. But if the British capitalist says to the Russian Communist 'For one or both of us the hour is come,' he will find himself confronted with a ruthless, disciplined, and well-armed fanatic; and the famous Marxian law of historical development will be on the side of the fanatic.

At this, too, the Russians laugh as heartily as they do at being called Fabians. They have got rid of religion, they tell us, pointing to churches which are as empty as our London City churches, though those who will may worship in them, as I have seen for myself. To call them religious, and the Third International a Catholic Church, seems to them a Shavian joke, as it may seem to some of our Catholics a Shavian blasphemy.

I refer to both sides to the saying of Father Keegan in *John Bull's Other Island*: 'Every jest is in earnest in the womb of Time.'

Yours truly,
G. BERNARD SHAW.
Great Malvern.

There followed further correspondence from other contributors, which then led to Shaw's rejoinder of August 20 below. St John Hornby was the owner of Ashendene Press and a renowned specialist printer who produced the work of Dante using woodcuts and original techniques. Shaw's great friend Lady Nancy Astor (1879–1964) was the first woman to take up a seat in Parliament. She accompanied Shaw on his trip to Russia.

~ *1931, August 20* ~

THE SOVIET SYSTEM.

MR. BERNARD SHAW'S REJOINER.

Sir, I am divided between a grateful reluctance to abuse your generosity in the matter of space and the courtesy which owes some reply to your correspondents Professor Ernest Barker and Mr. St. John Hornby. I will be as brief as possible.

For Professor Barker I can do nothing. He says, in effect, that he cannot be happy or feel free unless he has more money – or is it less? – than other people. Until he states exactly how much more or less will satisfy him, and why he should be considered more or less than other people, the discussion is in the air and could only waste your space.

Mr. St. John Hornby endorses an alleged general preference of adventure to the dullness of a drab uniformity, and maintains that it makes in the end for a higher, and in every sense better, standard of life. It may be so;

but it does not make for civilization. Perhaps Mr. Hornby would be higher, and in every sense better, as a Pirate King than as the famous artist-printer he is; but he would be hanged in England and get at least three years' imprisonment in Russia all the same. The dullness of a drab uniformity of honesty, security, employment, sanitation, and established expectation of behaviour is the price he must pay for the peaceful prosecution of such bloodless adventures as the Ashendene Press Dante.

As to Democracy in the sense of responsible government in the interests of the governed, and not in those of any class or individual, that is what we all now profess to aim at. As a method of securing it we rely on a routine of adult suffrage and party electioneering. The Russians rely on a system called the Dictatorship of the Proletariat, by which the proletariat is much more effectively dictated to for its own good than under our system. It is a voting system; but the only way to obtain a vote is to show an unselfish interest in public affairs and a competent knowledge of the Communist constitution. It is found as a matter of experience that any group of associated workers – in a factory or on a collective farm, for example – will naturally secrete one or two exceptional individuals with these qualifications, easily recognizable by their voluntarily adding public work to their industrial or agricultural tasks, and by their writings or uttered sentiments When they have given their proofs they are called technically a cell (in the physiological sense) and are accreted by the Communist Party and devoted entirely to public work with no other hold on their new position than their power of making themselves indispensable by their efficiency. They finally constitute the whole Communist Party and elect the committees, with their chairmen and secretaries, by which the government of Russia is carried on. Part of their work is to persuade and educate the workers to form factory and farm committees for criticism and complaint, and to give them such powers of control as they are capable of exercising, so that the Government may always know where and when the shoe pinches. The trade unions have quite a large say in the appointment of managers and general ordering of the industries which immediately concern them.

That is Russia's solution of the democratic problem so far. Obviously it does solve it far more effectually than our system. It excludes from official authority and from the franchise the ignorant, the incompetent, the indifferent, the corrupt, and the pugnacious and politically incapable masses who, though they revel in a party fight or any other sort of fight, can make no intelligent use of their votes, and are the dupes of every interest that can afford the cost of gulling them. Responsibility to such innocents is no responsibility at all. The threat of it kept the oligarchic statesmen of the nineteenth century in order; but the execution of the threat has proved its worthlessness; and now politicians who spend Monday in making promises, Tuesday in breaking them, and Wednesday in being found out are re-elected by enthusiastic majorities on Saturday.

Responsibility to the Communist Party is real responsibility: its members know their business and cannot be humbugged. They are all under skilled criticism, and have not to waste their time and means 'nursing' constituencies. Failures and recreants can be promptly scrapped. Party opposition for the sake of opposition is punished as sabotage; and attempts to paralyse the Government by 'constitutional safeguards' against tyrannies that have long lost their powers are not tolerated. Pious fictions like 'the people's will' or 'public opinion' are not admitted as excuses for *fainéant* statesmen. Liberty does not mean liberty to idle and spunge. The political machinery is built for immediate positive use; and it is powerful enough to break people who stick ramrods into it. In short, it is much more democratic than Parliament and party.

Nevertheless to an average member of Parliament it seems the negation of Democracy, because he or she would not be organically secreted as a governing cell but, on the contrary, convulsively excreted into private trade kulak farming under a suspended sentence of 'liquidation' which might be executed at any moment. To such Unsocialists the Russian system is the Reign of Terror which keeps Mr. Churchill awake of nights. But the nation does not consist of average M.P.s; and their terrors do not trouble it. When Lady Astor asked a worker on a communal farm why he had returned from capitalist America to Communist Russia, he replied that he returned because he wanted freedom of speech. 'But', said Lady Astor, 'surely you are not free to advocate Capitalism here?' 'Certainly not,' he replied, 'but then I don't want to advocate Capitalism: I want to denounce it.' No earnest Government tolerates sedition, but the sedition of the Capitalist west is the constitutionalism of the Communist east and vice versa.

Democratic freedom of speech means the freedom of normal people to say what they want to say and not suffer from compulsory hypocrisy. Who can pretend that our employees have much of this freedom? Freedom to speak one's mind at the cost of getting the sack is hardly worth dying for. Only when Communism is conceived, as by Mr. Churchill, to be a tyranny which all its subjects would denounce if they dared, does it seem reasonable to believe that the Russians must be gagged to prevent them from clamouring to be reduced to the condition of the inhabitants of this highly perplexed island.

Yours truly,
G. BERNARD SHAW.
Great Malvern.

Late in Edward Elgar's life, Shaw persuaded the BBC to commission the composer's Third Symphony (uncompleted). Elgar dedicated his 'Severn Suite' to Shaw. Sir John Reith (1889–1971) was the first Director General of the BBC. The Reith Lectures were established in his honour.

Sir Edward Elgar's New Symphony.

Sir, – I have occasionally remarked that the only entirely creditable incident in English history is the sending of £100 to Beethoven on his deathbed by the London Philharmonic Society; and it is the only one that historians never mention.

Thanks to Sir John Reith it is no longer unique. His action in commissioning a new symphony from Sir Edward Elgar, the first English composer to produce symphonies ranking with those of Beethoven, is a triumph for the B.B.C.

But is it not a pity that Sir Edward has had to wait so long for the advent of a public administrator capable of rising to the situation? The forth-coming symphony will be his third: it should be his ninth. It is true that we have loaded him with honours. I use the word loaded advisedly, as the honours have the effect of enabling us to exact much gratuitous work from him. He has given us a 'Land of Hope and Glory'; and we have handed him back the glory and kept all the hope for ourselves. I suggest that we make a note not to wait until our next great composer is 70 before guaranteeing his bread and butter while he is scoring his Eroica.

Yours truly,
G. BERNARD SHAW.

In replying to a press comment on BBC pronunciation and defending the decisions of the advisory committee, Shaw also took the opportunity to further elaborate his ideas on phonetics. The next three letters stimulated a flurry of correspondence.

1934, January 2

B.B.C. Pronunciation

Mr. Bernard Shaw explains.

The Committee's Canons.

Sir, – As chairman of the committee which in the discharge of its frightful responsibility for advising the B.B.C. on the subject of spoken English has incurred your censure as it has incurred everyone else's, may I mention a few circumstances which will help towards the formation of a reasonable judgment of our proceedings?

1. All the members of the committee speak presently: that is, they are all eligible, as far as their speech is concerned, for the judicial bench, the cathedral pulpit, or the throne.
2. No two of them pronounce the same word in the English language alike.
3. They are quite frequently obliged to decide unanimously in favour of a pronunciation which they would rather die than use themselves in their private lives.
4. As they work with all the leading dictionaries before them they are free from the illusion that these works are either unanimous or up-to-date in a world of rapidly changing usage.
5. They are sufficiently familiar with the works of Chaucer to feel sincerely sorry that the lovely quadrisyllable Christemasse, the trisyllable neighebore, and the disyllable freendes should have decayed into krissmus, naybr, and frens. We should like to vary the hackneyed set of rhymes to forever by the Shakespearian persever, and we would all, if we dared, slay any actress who, as Cleopatra, would dare degrade a noble line by calling her country's high pyramides pirramids. But if we recommended these pronunciations to the announcers they would, in the unusual event of their paying any attention to our notions, gravely mislead the millions of listeners who take them as models of current speech usage.
6. We are not a cockney committee. We are quite aware that Conduit Street is known in the West End as Cundit Street. Elsewhere such a pronunciation is as unintelligible as it is incorrect. We have to dictate a pronunciation that cannot be mistaken, and abide the resultant cockney raillery as best we can.
7. Wireless and the telephone have created a necessity for a fully and clearly articulated spoken English quite different from the lazy vernacular that is called modd'ninglish. We have to get rid not only of imperfect pronunciations but of ambiguous ones. Ambiguity is largely caused by our English habit of attacking the first syllable and sacrificing the second, with the result that many words beginning with prefixes such as ex or dis sound too much alike. This usage claims to be correct; but common sense and euphony are often against it; and it is questionable whether in such cases it is general enough to be accepted as authentic usage. Superior persons stress the first syllable in dissputable, labratory, ecksmplary, desspicable, &c.; and we, being superior persons, talk like that; but as many ordinary and quite respectable people say disputable, laborratory, exemmplary, and despickable, we are by no means bound to come down on the side of the pretentious pronunciation if the popular alternative is less likely to be confused with other words by the new human species called listeners-in.

We have to consider sonority also. The short i is much less effective than the long one; and the disturbance I created in the United States last April by broadcasting privvacy instead of pryvacy was justified. Issolate is a highly superior pronunciation; and wind (rhyming to tinned) is considered more elegant in some quarters than wynd; so that we get the common blunders of trist (rhyming to fist) for tryst and Rozzalind for Rosalynde; but we recommend the long i to the announcers for the sake of sonority.

Some common pronunciations have to be rejected as unbearably ugly. An announcer who pronounced decadent and sonorous as dekkadent and sonnerus would provoke Providence to strike him dumb.

The worst obstacle to our popularity as a committee is the general English conviction that to correct a man's pronunciation is to imply that he is no gentleman. Let me explain therefore that we do not correct anyone's pronunciation unless it is positively criminal. When we recommend an announcer to pronounce disputable with the stress on the second syllable we are neither inciting him to an ungentlemanly action nor insinuating that those who put the stress on the first ought to be ashamed of themselves. We are simply expressing our decision that for the purposes and under the circumstances of the new art of broadcasting the second syllable stress is the more effective.

Yours truly,
G. BERNARD SHAW, Chairman.

There was then a flurry of letters to *The Times* by self-proclaimed exponents of correct pronunciation, both in support of, or antagonistic to, the idea of standards being set by the BBC.

~ *1934, January 25* ~

B.B.C. ENGLISH

MR. BERNARD SHAW'S REJOINER.

Sir, – The correspondence on the subject of B.B.C. pronunciation has proved very amply that the pronunciation of the English language is not the simple matter, perfectly agreed among gentlemen, that most of your correspondents supposed.

Last Monday two broadcasters discoursed on literature and economics. They used the words combated and inextricable respectively. I, who am just as good an authority on pronunciation as either of them, usually say cumbited and ineckstricably. They, being just as good authorities as I said combatted (rhyming to fatted) and inixtrickably. Clearly neither they nor I can claim usage on our side. As cumbited is easily mistaken when atmospherics are raging for comforted I think I shall say cumbatted when next I broadcast, unless indeed I shirk the word I am no longer quite sure about. As to the other, go as you please. There are thousands of words which have no usage because they are not very often used. Thoughtless speakers always bounce at the first syllable and stress it: others have an instinct for the characteristic syllable. Sometimes the first syllable happens fortunately to be the characteristic one: only children say ludickrus instead of loodicrous. But what about exemplary?

My grandfather, an educated country gentleman, occasionally swore by the virtue of his oath. He said 'Be the varchew o'me oath!' He called lip salve sawve. The actors of his time called lute lewt and flute flewt: and their be and me for by and my lasted well into my own day. I can even remember when obleege was heard from old people as well as varchew; but the spelling beat that, as it always does in the long run except when the word like would or could, is in continual use. Pronunciations are always obsolescing and changing. If the B.B.C. had existed a hundred years ago it would have been reviled for recommending vertew and oblyge instead of varchew and obleege. To-day it has to deal with America, which would have pronounce it necessarily neseserrily, rhyming to merrily.

Then there is the trouble about accents. In choosing an announcer regard must be had to the psychological effect of his accent. An Oxford accent is considered by many graduates of that University to be the perfection of correct English; but unfortunately over large and densely populated districts of Great Britain it irritates some listeners to the point of switching off, and infuriates others so much that they smash their wireless sets because they cannot smash the Oxonian. The best English to-day is literally the King's English. Like his Royal grandmother before him King George is the best speaker in his realm; and his broadcasts are astonishingly effective in creating loyalty. If he delivered a single broadcast in an Oxford accent his people would rise up that very day and proclaim a republic.

How little the situation is appreciated is shown by the ridiculous extent to which this correspondence has been occupied with the trivial case of Conduit Street. The name of that street is either grossly misspelt or grossly mispronounced: I do not know which. I have no doubt that if one of the new streets made by the London University and the British Museum be appropriately named Pundit Street it will be solemnly labelled Ponduit Street. What most of those who are supersensitive on the subject seem to mean is that if the name of a street is mispronounced by the inhabitants that name shall always be so mispronounced in every possible context. Let me remind them that Conduit Street is not the only street in London. There is in the City an ancient thoroughfare labelled Ave Maria Lane. The more cultivated of its denizens call it Aivmeryer Lane, the less fastidious Hivemerawyer Line. Are we of the B.B.C. Committee expected to instruct the announcers to say: 'Miss Jenny Lind will now sing a group of songs beginning with Schubert's Aivmeryer'? Are we to beg the songstress to adapt that pronunciation as best she can to Schubert's notes?

These are the questions that go over such bumptious novices as my friend Mr. Edward Marsh like a steam-roller. They have long since left me as I remain at present, in extreme humility,

G. BERNARD SHAW.

Sir Charles Mallet wrote on 26 January to ask Shaw to define the Oxford accent.

As in previous letters, Henry Sweet is again brought forward as the master of philology, and Shaw was ready to accept the difficulty of creating a standard. One presumes that he would have fought hard against the trend in today's global society, where pronunciation of the English language has been dramatically affected by relaxation of standards on radio, TV soap operas and the Internet.

~ *1934, January 30* ~

THE OXFORD ACCENT.

MR. BERNARD SHAW'S DEFINITION.

Sir, – I am asked to define the Oxford accent. I cannot do scientific precision because, as all writers of dialogue know to their sorrow, English speech has no exact notation: we have to make shift with an alphabet which is about a dozen letters short of our crudest requirements, and a ridiculous pseudo-etymological spelling which is the most serious obstacle to the conquest of the whole world by the English language.

However, it is possible to suggest the Oxford accent sufficiently. The late Henry Sweet, the greatest English phonetician of his time, clung to Oxford University all his life with undying hatred, raging against it because it would not place the study of the sounds of our living tongue before the prosodic pedantries of two dead foreign languages, but still, as a much disparaged official Reader of Phonetics, teaching the Oxford accent as standard English. Here is his notation of Longfellow's 'Psalm of Life':

tel mii not, in mawnful nambez
laif iz bat an emti driim
faw dhe soul iz ded dhat slambez
end thingz aa not whot dhei sijm

And again:-

aat iz long en taim is fluiting
end aue haats dhou staut an breiv
stil laik mafled dramz aa biiting
fyuunerel maatshiz tuu dhe greiv.

This not quite a literal transcript because Sweet indicated the vowel aw by a c turned upside down and the obscure vowel which is so common in English speech by an e similarly inverted; but it indicates the Oxford accent plainly enough to those who have heard it.

It is, please note, laboriously affected by many who have never been at Oxford as it is contemptuously avoided by some of the ablest authentic Oxonians. The irritating effect with which the B.B.C. has to reckon must be taken as an unexplained fact. I can offer only a conjecture that the objection is not to its being a dialect of southern English, but to its sounding like a class affectation superimposed on it and robbing it of its full virility.

These matters must be discussed without temper. It is painful to most Englishmen to discover that every deviation from their own pronunciation is not necessarily a vulgar solecism; but they need not thirst for my blood when I call their attention to it. One of your more choleric correspondents, whom I protest I have never injured, asks whether I mean that every Englishman has a right to pronounce as he pleases. Undoubtedly he has : this is a free country in that respect; but if he does not choose to pronounce in a generally intelligible manner he must not aspire to the coveted eminence of a B.B.C. announcer. Even as a private individual he may suffer considerable inconvenience.

Yours truly,
G. BERNARD SHAW.

The articles and letters that appeared when serious issues were being debated showed the substantial influence upon government thinking that was unique to *The Times* in its heyday, and its leading contributors (notably Shaw) were fully aware of this.

As an example, there had been considerable discussion in *The Times* over Italy's incursion into Abyssinia and the shortcomings of the League of Nations in dealing with the crisis. Shaw's practical viewpoint was not exactly popular and today might be considered a trifle racist. The Locarno treaties were drawn up by International

Agreement in Switzerland in 1925 and were concerned with guaranteeing boundaries. They were later to be ignored by Adolf Hitler. The Kellogg–Briand pact was an agreement between 15 nations condemning war. Putumayo and the Congo are references to the atrocities committed by the Germans against Herrero tribesmen.

~ 1935, Octobre 22 ~

OBLIGATIONS OF THE COVENANT.

Sir, – May I, as a civilized man and, incidentally, a taxpayer, call attention to an aspect of the Abyssinian question which is being overlooked in the present warlike excitement?

To make any part of the globe available for human habitation and social development at any higher level than that of the birds and beasts, the first material necessity is a well engineered and policed main road, with water supplies from artificial wells, and refuelling stations. When the natives are ferocious it is unpleasantly necessary to convince them that the constructive powers of the road makers are accompanied by destructive powers which make the police irresistible. England has done this work all over the world, and thereby created the British Empire and founded the United States of America. Spain did it in South America, Holland in the East Indies, and all the Powers in Africa. Long before these things happened ancient Rome made a fortified wall from Newcastle to Carlisle, and made roads as far from Rome as that in all directions.

All this colonization has been done by what we call unilateral action, resulting quite commonly in the expropriation, enslavement, and even extermination of the uncivilized. It is therefore clearly desirable that it should be done in future by concerted action, which means practically by the League of Nations and its International Labour Office. Unfortunately the League is not yet equipped for such work; and the diplomacy of Europe and Japan since the League was founded shows that its constituent Powers are not yet fully grasped the idea of the League. They have on every serious occasion ignored it, or sidetracked it , or tried to supersede its Covenant by Locarno agreements, Kellogg pacts, secret alliances, and the rest of the old diplomatic routine exactly as if it did not exist. As to the International Labour Office, it is never mentioned, and it may be doubted whether the Foreign Office and the Chanceries of the Powers have ever heard of it. Meanwhile, therefore, colonization must go on as before, except that when, as in the present Italian case, the colonizing Power is a member of the League, it can be called to account by the H.O. if it permits such atrocities as those of Putumayo and the Congo, or if it carries the necessary intimidation of savage adversaries to the point of extermination.

~ 211 ~

Italy is making roads through Abyssinia with the avowed intention of colonizing it. The Danakils are doing their utmost to stop the process by killing the road makers and their guards. The League of Nations is being strongly urged by our Foreign Office, represented by Mr. Eden, to assist the Danakils in killing the Italians with the object of stopping the road making and forcing Italy to retire discomfited, leaving the primitive tribesmen triumphant over European civilization. Viewed in its simplicity this situation suggests that either the Foreign Office is stark mad or else so blinded by imperialist jealousy as to be willing to wreck Europe rather than allow any other Power to extend its empire by a single foot of roadway, even when the extension has been contemplated for years in arrangements to which our Foreign Office was a party.

As between the Danakil warrior and the Italian engineer I, as a possible traveller or trader in those regions, am on the side of the engineers. Any policy which results in the taxes I pay being spent on beleaguering and starving the engineer arid encouraging, feeding, and arming the warrior seems to me to be an attack on our civilization which must eventually damage this precariously situated island more than Italy, which I do not wish to damage.

I object also, now that the attempt to secure unanimity at Geneva has failed, to my money being spent in bribing the minority to agree. I see no prospect whatever of France's agreeing to go to war with Italy for our sakes if we can provoke her to fire on us by unnecessary naval demonstrations in the Mediterranean. I do not want the Italians to fire on us. Old as I am I am not yet so pitiably imbecile as to believe that the modern habit of calling torpedoes, mines, blockades, sieges, battles, and bombs 'sanctions' alters their nature so completely that a vote for sanctions is a vote for peace. Things have now been brought to a pass at which a vote for sanctions is a vote for a combined attack on Italy by France and England. It would be far more sensible and humane to drop the Geneva Council down the crater of Vesuvius. I trust there is common sense enough left in England to squash the first alternative and render the second unnecessary.

Yours truly,
G. BERNARD SHAW.

The Abysinnian problem dragged on, and following an editorial in *The Times* concerning ideas to settle the question there was a speech in Parliament by Anthony Eden, who later resigned over his government's appeasement policy towards Benito Mussolini. Shaw would not be denied further input on this subject and these points of view supported his earlier letter. Samuel Hoare (1880–1959), Secretary of State for Foreign Affairs, had arranged a deal with the French premier Pierre Laval to appease Mussolini in the hope of solving the Abysinnian problem. He was forced to resign.

INTERNATIONAL PLEDGES.

Sir, – The Eden speech, with its alarming Parliamentary cadences, seems to me to call for the following observations:

The business of the League of Nations is to police the world and put an end to the existing international anarchy.

At present we have on the shores of the Red Sea a roadless, lawless region inhabited, so far as it is inhabited at all, by pugnacious braves who kill each other for prestige and attach the same prestige to the killing of one European as to three of themselves.

It is not possible for a modern civilized State to tolerate this sort of thing on its frontier. If the League of Nations cannot or will not undertake to replace it by civilized conditions, then its next door neighbour must tackle the job single-handed. That is how the British Empire has grown from a group of trading settlements to its present- dimensions. To call such an advance of civilization an act of aggression on the same footing as an unprovoked bombardment of Venice by the R.A.F., or of Portsmouth by the Italian Fleet, is a most dangerous abuse of language and confusion of thought.

Collective security is only a talking point. What the League stands for is collective civilization. If in the inevitable conflict between civilized mankind and Danakil mankind the League should organise a deadly intervention on the side of the Danakil, it would reduce itself to the most revolting absurdity.

What we call the application of oil sanctions would be just such an intervention. The French, with their instinct for civilization, naturally recoil from it. So do all of us who possess that instinct. The decisive sanction is clamoured for by the groups which are for war at any price with Mussolini – the pacifists because he has drawn the sword, the Liberals because he has made short work of laisser-faire guaranteed by the British Parliamentary system, the Imperialists because they are afraid he will get at the Suez Canal, the Communist's because he has produced Fascism as a counter to Communism, the Labour Party because he has taken the organization of the proletariat out of the hands of the trade unions, and a considerable body of men-in-the-street because he has bullied and frightened them or because, confident that any Englishmen can lick any three Italians, they object to the swanking of a sanguinary foreigner.

Now it is just such motives that the League exists to disarm and defeat. Yet their combined weight shattered the Hoare proposals and dislodged the Minister.

The position now is that we must either stab Italy in the back while she is at grips with the Danakil or else let them fight it out. In the latter case, if Italy wins, well and good, no thanks to us or to the League. But if the Danakils prove unconquerable within a reasonable time or at a reasonable expense, must we not rally the League to the rescue of Italy and civilization, and thereafter civilize the shores of the Red Sea on European and not on exclusively Italian terms?

Yours truly,
G. BERNARD SHAW.

There had been several heated debates in Parliament, in The *Times* leader articles and in the letters columns about whether there was actually a need for a National Theatre. Shaw can be considered one of the early pioneers for this venture (from as early as 1900 when he discussed his ideas with Granville Barker and Archer) and it was his view that it might have to be 'imposed' upon the nation if they were unable to see the advantages for themselves.

~ 1937, September 13 ~

SUBSIDIZING THE THEATRE.
THE MITIGATION OF 'BARBARISM'
MR. SHAW'S VIEW.

Sir, – Your Critic's comments on the National Theatre project are quite sound from his point of view; and I can applaud without reserve his references to myself.

But his opposition is only a fragment of the logical extension of a general scheme for the demolition of the Victoria and Albert Museum at the other side of the road, of the Natural History Museum a little farther down, of the Imperial Institute, of the British Museum, of the National, Tate, and Wallace Galleries, and the occupation of their sites by piles of residential flats and shops, with the conversion of the almost disused City churches into garages and cinemas.

There is a great deal to be said for such a transformation. The British nation does unquestionably want flats and cinemas and garages, and is willing to pay for them. It is equally unquestionable that it does not want a national theatre, though no doubt if one were opened freely a few people could always be depended on to stroll in as they do into the National Gallery. The committee of the Shakespear Memorial National Theatre project long ago exhausted every possible device for coaxing British money to add to the £70,000 put down by a Hamburg financier, and to the comparatively trifling bequests from people who wanted to erect in

Portland Crescent a monument to Shakespear comparable to the imposing Walter Scott memorial in Edinburgh. The response was so negligible that a statement that the British public will not subscribe a brass farthing for a national theatre is accurate enough for all practical purposes. The Government would not give a site. The Duke of Westminster was more public spirited; but the sites at his disposal were not eligible. There seemed to be nothing for it but to allow the Hamburg donation to accumulate for 50 years at compound interest before imposing on a nation partly barbarous and largely convinced that the fine arts except organ music are forms of debauchery, and the theatre door one of the gates of hell, a cultural institution which it either did not want or actively abhorred.

There is nothing surprising nor new in this situation. It is a simple historical fact that cultural institutions have to be imposed on the masses of rulers or private patrons enlightened enough to know that such institutions are neither luxuries nor mere amusements but necessities of civilized life. If the famous scientific academics of Europe had been left to perish stillborn on the ground that the vogue of the differential calculus could safely be left to the operation of commercial demand and supply, Europe would be much more barbarous than it is, impossible as this seems at the present unhappy moment.

I am not suggesting that a scientific academy can, to the order of a Frederick or a Catherine, create a Newton or a Leibniz. A national theatre will not be able to create a Shakespear or a – well, leave it at that. But it can keep him alive just as a National Gallery can keep Van Eyck alive. Molière lives at the Théâtre Français and Shakespear at the great memorial theatre in Stratford: both are as dead commercially as Ibsen. Above all, it can give public prestige and status to the drama as a cultural institution. I am that disreputable thing, a playwright, just as Henry Irving was that disreputable thing, an actor, until he forced the Government to make his art respectable by adding his name to the roll of knights bachelor. As nothing very dreadful happened in consequence the playwrights were elevated to the new standing of the actors: Pinero was knighted and Barrie became a baronet. Later on even I might have had a title for the asking; but that was not what I wanted: these honours are too personal to affect the status of drama as an instrument of national culture. For that we must have a visible national monument, as imposing as our architects can make it, in a fitting situation; and the State must support it even if its finest performances be attended by only one dreaming boy or girl in the gallery, let in for nothing. I have not forgotten how often I was alone in the Dublin National Gallery when I was a dreaming boy.

The South Kensington site is an ideal one: absolutely the best imaginable. The people who are clamouring for another theatre in the slums of Leicester Square or Seven Dials obviously have a morbid taste in sites. Such places will presently be demolished.

I am not greatly concerned as to what will happen inside the theatre. It will presumably have a complete cinema equipment as well as an up-to-date or even futuristic stage, so as to be ready for all conceivable developments; but these will be of little avail without good actors, directors, and playwrights. Of these last the dead ones are still available if the live ones prefer the easier job of writing novels. The national theatre cannot guarantee any extraordinary excellence in its personal staff: it must get the best it can for what it can afford to pay. But it need not pay the gigantic salaries which so often result in painfully small and precarious incomes.. The experience of our commercial theatres and of the royal and municipal theatres all over the Continent proves that the certainty of a year's engagement, to say nothing of the prospect of a pension, will secure the services of first-rate talent on quite moderate terms.

Finally may I ask your Critic to make further inquiries as to the 'great body of professional opinion that is opposed to' the national theatre project. Were he old enough to have stood with me and my colleagues in the breach to defend our fund against the frantic raids made upon it by the professional when its gold first glittered in the stage sunshine he would not think the grapes quite so sour

I am, &c.
BERNARD SHAW.
Sidmouth.

The Bishop of Durham and others were protesting at political moves to recognise Italian sovereignty over Abyssinia, the British government having previously condemned the action together with fifty other states.

Emperor Haile Selassie had been given refuge in Britain. King Emmanuel III of Italy, an ineffective ruler in a country where Mussolini held the real power, was expecting to be recognised as the new emperor of Abyssinia.

~ *1938 February 5* ~

ITALIANS IN ABYSSINIA.

Sir, – I think the Bishop of Durham and his co-signatories might have put in a word for the unfortunate monarch who has taken refuge on our shores. If we are to treat Haile Selassie as Louis XIV treated James II our hospitality should be at least as princely in respect of his personal needs.

I suggest that the Italian Government should content itself with the harmless and amusing reprisal of refusing to acknowledge King George as Emperor of India.

Yours truly,
G. BERNARD SHAW.
4, Whitehall Court (130), SW.1.

The BBC. changes its news hour.

~ *1938, July 7* ~

NEWS AT TEN

Sir, – This island is inhabited by 46 millions of people. Its breadwinners rise at 6 or earlier to begin their daily share of the nation's work. Therefore they have to be in bed at 10 to make room for their eight hours' sleep The present rulers of the B.B.C., presumably belonging to the insignificant fraction of the population which gets up at 11 and goes to bed at half-past 3 or thereabouts, have altered the hour of broadcasting the third news from 9 o'clock to 10.

Would it not be well, now that Sir John Reith has gone, to replace him by someone who knows at least a little about the lives of the common people whose 10 shillingses keep the B.B.C. going?

Yours &c,
G. BERNARD SHAW.
4, Whitehall Court (130), S.W. 1.

This letter centres around correspondence in *The Times* over a proposal of the then London County Council to institute a new local tax on the capital value of land. It gave Shaw a chance to show his mastery of economic theory. Sir Raymond Unwin (1863–1940) was an architect and town planner who designed the first garden city in Yorkshire.

TAXATION OF LAND.

CAPITAL VALUE

Sir, – Sir Raymond Unwin, perhaps our most experienced authority on the subject, has left nothing to be said of the dangers of treating land as if it had no value except its lucrativeness to an out-and-out exploiter for cash. It's amenity value and its hygienic value do not come into that calculation; and if all the squares and open spaces in London were crammed to the last inch with skyscrapers and giant factories the huge increase in rateable value would be cited as a magnificent addition to our metropolitan prosperity.

But there is another point which is in still greater danger of being overlooked. What are called capital values, site values of land being the fundamental instance, are not taxable, for the conclusive reason that they do not exist. It is true that landlords every day sell land for the estimated cash value of its next 15 or 20 years' harvests. But by no magic can the harvest of 1958 be brought into existence in 1938; and any attempt to tax it by a Chancellor of the Exchequer or the Finance Committee of London County Council would fail because where there is nothing the King loses his rights. What really happens at these sales is that some person who has saved as much cash out of past harvests as the piece of land in question promises to produce in the next 20 years wishes to exchange that for the income he could secure as proprietor of the land. There is some other person who holds the land and wishes to exchange it for ready money. The two strike a bargain, and the illusion is produced that the land has am immediately realizable capital value available, for general taxation.

All that has really happened is that two individuals in opposite and complementary states of mind are in the exceptional circumstances of having respectively less and more money than they want for immediate consumption. If on the strength of this accident a public authority, afflicted as the Bolshevists were in 1917 with an attack of unscientific Socialism, were to impose a tax of anything up to 100 per cent, on capital values arrived at simply multiplying the figures of the available resources of the country by, say, the conventional 20, the result would be an income market in which would be all sellers and no buyers until the price of land had fallen to its real value for taxation – that is, its income value.

A public finance authority must never lose sight of the difference between compelling everybody to do the same thing at the same time and allowing two exceptionally circumstanced individuals to strike a bargain in which their plans are contrary. In short, it must not multiply realities by 20 to arrive at a sound balance-sheet.

Yours, &c

G. BERNARD SHAW.

In the following letter, Shaw's intuition seems to let him down, mainly because of his prejudice for Stalin and the Soviet system. William Ralph Inge (1860–1954) was Dean of St Paul's Cathedral and a close friend of Shaw. 'Gone to Canossa' is a reference to when the German Emperor Henry IV was humbled by being kept waiting for three days by the Pope in 1077.

~ 1939, August 28 ~

CAN ANYONE EXPLAIN?

Sir, A week ago Dean Inge, writing in the Evening Standard, guessed that Herr Hitler had gone to Canossa. A few days later the joyful news came that the Dean was right and that Herr Hitler is under the powerful thumb of Stalin, whose interest in peace is overwhelming.

And every one except myself is frightened out of his or her wits. Why? Am I mad? If not, why? why? why?

G. BERNARD SHAW

Shaw ends the following comments on the theatre in wartime with a quotation from Thomas Odell's ballad opera, *The Patron* (1729).

~ 1939, September 5 ~

THEATRES IN TIME OF WAR.

THE CASE AGAINST CLOSURE

Sir – May I be allowed to protest vehemently against the order to close all theatres and picture-houses during the war? It seems to me a masterstroke of unimaginative stupidity.

During the last War we had 80,000 soldiers on leave to amuse every night. There were not enough theatres for them; and theatre rents rose to fabulous figures. Are there to be no theatres for them this time? We have hundreds of thousands of evacuated children to be kept out of mischief and traffic dangers. Are there to be no pictures for them?

The authorities, now all-powerful, should at once set to work to provide new theatres and picture-houses where these are lacking.

All actors, variety artists, musicians, and entertainers of all sorts should be exempted from every form of service except their own all-important professional one.

What agent of Chancellor Hitler is it who has suggested that we should all cower in darkness and terror 'for the duration'?

'Why, brother soldiers, why
Should we be melancholy, boys?'

Faithfully,
G. BERNARD SHAW.

Here, Shaw is supportive of Stalin's move into the Ukraine and eastern Poland, seeing it more as a triumph for socialism and taking a blinkered view of the more ominous and long-term ambitions of Stalin. Vyacheslaff Molotoff (now spelled Molotov), 1890–1986, was twice Soviet Foreign Minister and Premier from 1930–1941.

~ *1939 September 20* ~

POLAND AND RUSSIA

Sir, – May I again point out that the news from Russia is good news for us as far as any war news can be called good?

The question for us is not whether Mr. Molotoff's speech resembles utterances of Herr Hitler's or not. What concerns us is whether Mr. Molotoff's statements are true or not. They are obviously true to the last syllable. We have encouraged Poland to fight by our pledge to support her; and we have encouraged ourselves by silly reports that the Polish army was unbroken and that the Poles were performing prodigies of valour. The truth, as we now have to admit, and as Mr. Molotoff notes, is that our support has so entirely failed that the Polish resistance has been wiped out, and with it the Polish army and the Polish Government, leaving Poland derelict to be picked up and put on by Herr Hitler as a shepherd putteth on his garment.

At this point, we being helpless, Mr. Stalin steps in and says: 'Not quite. If the Ukraine and White Russia are going begging Russia will occupy them, Hitler or no Hitler.' No sooner said than done. The Red Army is in occupation. Mr. Stalin, who was very explicit as to his objection to be made a catspaw to take our chestnuts off the fire, has no objection whatever to using Herr Hitler as a catspaw. The unfortunate Fuhrer is compelled to disgorge half his booty and to face yet another army saying 'Thus far and no farther.'

And instead of giving three cheers for Stalin we are shrieking that all is lost.

Mr. Stalin lately sent us a photograph of himself laughing at us. When will we learn to laugh at ourselves?

Faithfully,
G. BERNARD SHAW.

As part of the war effort, several charity exhibitions and lectures, supported by the Royal Academy, were being held at Burlington House in aid of the Red Cross.

~ 1940, January 20 ~

THE ROYAL ACADEMY

Sir, – If the most is to be made for the Red Cross by the present exhibition of pictures at Burlington House, the Academy must abandon the tradition that artists are ladies and gentlemen who must price their works in tens, hundreds, and thousands of guineas. If any but the most exceptional pictures are to be sold as well as exhibited, the lectures of Sir Joshua Reynolds must be discarded for the example of Mr. Woolworth.

I suggest that in every room in the Academy a notice should be displayed announcing that any coloured picture in the exhibition can be bought for five pounds and any plain picture for two pounds. The unsold pictures (if any) could be sold in lots by auction.

The plan has been tested in a small way with complete success at a one-artist exhibition.

Faithfully,
G. BERNARD SHAW.
4, Whitehall Court, S.W.1.

Because his previous letter (20 January 1940) had come under attack in the letters column, Shaw went deeper into the subject to explain his motives. His friend Sir William Rothenstein (1872–1945) was a well known portrait artist and had included Shaw in a special volume of portraits. Dugald Sutherland MacColl (1859–1948) was an artist of some renown and an art gallery director. Augustus John (1878–1961) was an influential artist who had painted many notables, including Shaw. Philip Wilson Steer (1860–1942) was a landscape and portrait artist and founder of the New Art Club. Ford Madox Brown (1821–93) was closely involved with the Pre-Raphaelite movement and famous for his paintings of working people. Artist Rex Whistler (1905–44) died in action in Normandy.

THE ECONOMICS OF ART.

COST OF PRODUCTION AND PRICE

Sir, – Dr. MacColl and Sir William Rothenstein must think my Woolworth suggestion over again. The cost of production of a picture has nothing to do with the price it will fetch. In competition with Sir William or Mr. Augustus John or Mr. Wilson Steer I can easily paint a picture on a larger canvas, with more expensive pigments, in a costlier frame, and in a studio with a higher rent, and ask a proportionately higher price for it. The result will be a piece of unsaleable junk, while the John, the Rothenstein, and the Steer will be snapped up eagerly for three or four figures. The prices a painter commands may dictate the rent he can afford to pay and the time and money he can afford to spend on materials and rent, to say nothing of clothes and food; but these expenses can never dictate the price at which a purchaser can be found for his pictures.

I am, of course, quite aware that if our eminent painters were to send pictures to a Woolworthized £5 exhibition the pictures would be instantly snapped up and resold at an enormous profit, in which neither the painters nor the charity would share. But I did not suggest that these famous men should do anything so thriftless. They are under no obligation to contribute to the exhibition. If they wish to contribute to the charity they can lend their pictures as an attraction at the turnstiles, but not for sale.

The problem is not how to sell a full-length portrait by a president of the Royal Academy for 2000 guineas, but to sell 2,000 other pictures which will be returned to their painters as unsaleable junk if they are priced as high as 2,000 pence, though for a modest fiver they would sell like hot cakes. A fiver in the pocket is better than 50 guineas in the air.

It may interest some of your correspondents to know that the famous wall painting of the Manchester Town Hall by Madox Brown was paid for by the square foot; and Mr. Rex Whistler did not disdain the same arrangement when he painted one of the rooms of the Tate Gallery. It was at the opening of that room that the late Henry Tonks, speaking with an authority to which I cannot pretend, said, 'The place of the artist is in the servants' hall.'

Faithfully,
G. BERNARD SHAW.
4, Whitehall Court (130), S.W.1.

Agriculture and the use of land took on a special importance with the onset of war, and the next three letters were part of a correspondence discussing that theme. Lord Bledisloe, Governor-General of New

Zealand from 1930 to 1935, was known for his scientific views of land reform. Jesse Collings (1831–1920) was a politician and an active agitator for agrarian reform. Shaw seized the opportunity to air his Socialist viewpoint and his faith in the Soviet experiments.

~ *1940, October 1* ~

USE OF LAND.

RUSSIAN THEORIES AND PRACTICE.

Sir, Nearly 60 years ago I represented the Fabian Society at an Industrial Remuneration Conference held in London under very distinguished auspices. I learnt there that the standard wage of an agricultural labourer was 13s. a week. Later on I found in Oxfordshire adult married labourers with families working as farmers boys for 8s. a week.

I laid the foundations of a reputation for perverse absurdity which I have not yet quite got rid of by saying that what agriculture needed was a minimum wage of two guineas a week for farm labourers. I was wrong. Farm labourers now expect, and sometimes get, two guineas a week; but English agriculture still cannot feed England. Years later Jesse Collings made a sensation by declaring that what agriculture needed was three acres and a cow for its cultivators. He was wrong. Three acres and a cow will no more make a man a farmer than one acre and a telescope will make him an astronomer. We were all wrong in assuming that the question was one of the remuneration of the labourer. What we should have studied, and never did, were the qualifications of the farmer. Between the extremes of Gladstone, who answered the agitation for land nationalization by nailing his colours to the old-established system of landlord, tenant farmer, and labourer, and Karl Marx, whose chronic indignation at the exploitation of the 13s.-a-week labourer kept his mind on this fringe of the subject, nothing of any importance was done until the Russian revolution in 1917.

The Bolshevist leaders tackled the problem vigorously. They knew if possible less about agriculture than Karl Marx; but they were full of principles and of a philosophy of history and a method of reasoning called the dialectic. On principle they began by seizing all the prosperous farmers and throwing them out on the roads as exploiters. Kulaks they called them. The result was that the Russian countryside, instead of becoming a paradise, became a wilderness of weeds and ruin; and Russia began to starve. Tolstoy's daughter brokenheartedly described to me what it was like in the bit of country she had known and loved. Lenin saw that this would not do. He again seized as many as he could find of the ejected Kulaks and threw them back into their farms, with orders to carry on as before until he

~ 223 ~

could think of some better plan for liquidating them. This was the New Economic Policy. But the restored Kulaks, deprived of all conviction of security and intensely resentful of their former treatment, would not carry on as before. They were so determined to leave nothing for the Government to seize that they ate their seeds and killed their livestock until nothing was left beyond their bare subsistence. They even created local artificial famines in which they themselves perished. Russia was still half starved. Clearly this would not do either. But Lenin's death hung the question up until the struggle for direction between Trotsky and Stalin ended, leaving Stalin as the winner. He found the solution in collective farming. State and cooperative, but mainly cooperative. It has been enormously successful and has mopped up the Kulaks and Moujiks as irresistibly as our factories mopped up the children of the old handloom weavers.

The moral is that, instead of wasting our energies in abusing Stalin, we must take a leaf out of his book and organise our agriculture on modern lines, as he has done.

Why is our system impossible? The answer is so obvious that no one notices it. We leave the whole vital business to individual farmers without the smallest inquiry into their qualifications. We expect each farmer to be able singlehanded not only to plough and hoe, to reap and sow, but to be an agricultural chemist, a veterinary biologist, an accountant dealing with complicated costings, a statistician, a man of business skilled in buying materials and selling products, an up-to-date reader of Lord Bledisloe and the scientific investigators, and an expert in half a dozen other capacities utterly foreign to his antecedents. And his mere reaping and sowing keeps him working in his shirtsleeves for 16 hours a day to pay his rent and mortgage interest beside keeping himself and his family fed, clothed, and lodged.

In short, his case is only to be stated to reduce itself to absurdity . He cannot even make out his income-tax return. What he needs is several partners who are experts in the scientific and commercial departments for which he has no time. No small farm could support such a managerial board. Farms of hundreds and even thousands of acres are as secondary now as industrial capitals on the same scale. When we face the necessity for cultivating these isles by the million acres we shall get a move on; and Stalin may stop laughing at us. Until then our makeshift agricultural committees, with the best intentions, can do little but provoke our farmers to resort to their shotguns by infuriating them with instructions which are sometimes idyllic and sometimes only a gratification of that craze for authority which is characteristic of people who are ignorant and stupid enough to seek it for its own sake. How should we fare in war if we depended for our weapons on village blacksmiths and for our explosives on local chemists?

Yours truly,
G. BERNARD SHAW.

Understandably, Shaw's 1 October letter aroused a number of critics who questioned his support for the methods used by Stalin. On 7 October, a Mr Gordon Fleming had written, highly critical of the Russian theories of land distribution and asking whether Shaw thought that the system was of value to their economy and labourers. John Hodge (1855–1937) was a minister in both Ramsay MacDonald and Lloyd George governments. Lord Bledisloe also wrote and suggested a system of district commissioners.

~ 1940, October 14 ~

USE OF LAND.

THE BAD FARMER AND STATE CONTROL.

Sir, – In reply to Mr. Gordon Fleming, who asks whether I contend that Stalin's treatment of Russian agriculture has enormously increased production, the answer is in the affirmative. To the second question as to whether the Russian agricultural labourer has a standard of living in excess of that enjoyed by his counterpart in this country, the reply is that the agricultural labourer, as we know him, has no counterpart in Russia, where he is an extinct species that ought never to have existed in this or in any other country. The question should have been whether it is better to be born a British agricultural labourer than a worker on a collective farm in Russia. I should say yes. Mr. Gordon Fleming is entitled to his choice.

I am not, however, concerned about Russia at present but about ourselves. The main fact to keep in the front of our minds is that, whereas Russia not only feeds herself but is making trade agreements all over the world except here, where our Foreign Secretary is engaged in a religious crusade against her, we had a narrow escape from being starved out in the Four Years War, and did not escape, at great naval expense, until our people were waiting in long queues to buy bread that was unfit for human consumption. I am not asking Lord Halifax to join the league of the Godless: I am only calling attention to the fact that agriculture under Uncle Joe is a national success and under Hodge a national failure.

In Hertfordshire, where I rusticate, I include among my neighbours two farmers whose fields are models of what well-farmed fields ought to be. I should like to set them to direct the farming of the whole county with Government capital and a staff of chemists, accountants, biologists, &c., to cooperate with them. But all our farmers are not like these. I know all about the pamphlets and the trifle of good they have done; but they are wasted on farmers who, like our politicians, do not learn by reading, and have an invincible contempt for the written word which is sometimes abundantly justified. Even the gratuitous distribution the 'Encyclopedia Britannica' to every farm in the county would not appreciably shorten our queues or lengthen our rations if the counter-blockade got the better of our Navy.

The truth is we are trying to run the agriculture of a population of 40,000,000 on the scale of a village. I live half my time in a village; but I put my money into big industry, garden cities, and Government loans.

Faithfully,
G. BERNARD SHAW.

The following reply to a letter by Sir Arthur Keith (1866–1955), a Scottish anthropologist and anatomist who specialised in the study of human fossils, is sarcastic. Keith had written to say that farms are for the rearing of happy and healthy Englishmen and not for economic reasons. The reference to Marcus is a joke about Mark Tapley in Dickens's *Martin Chuzzlewit*, a 'whimsical rustic' beloved by all.

∼ *1940, October 21* ∼

USE OF THE LAND IN BRITAIN.

HIGH EFFICIENCY OF LABOUR.

THE IMMEDIATE NEED.

Sir, I congratulate Sir Arthur Keith on having crowned his eminence as our foremost anthropologist by his discovery of a human species, the Marcus tapleyensis, hitherto regarded as fabulous.

I have been looking for him since my arrival in England 70 years ago without discovering a single specimen. Will Sir Arthur oblige with the gentleman's address?

Faithfully,
G. BERNARD SHAW.
4, Whitehall Court, S.W.1.

A Times article commented upon a new book on King George V that had mentioned the problems that the king had suffered with regard to spelling, – making light of his inadequacies. Apparently, at the age of eight the King could hardly spell three-letter words, and he was 27 before he mastered difficult ones. (Today, the affliction might have been recognised as dyslexia.) Shaw also used his letter to explain once more his ideas on phonetics.

A KIN'S SPELLING.

LETTERS AND SOUNDS.

Sir, – I am shocked by the levity and *lèse-majesté* of the leading article 'A King's Spelling' in your issue of March 28. You have failed to appreciate either the gravity of the subject or the laudable and sensible attempts of our Sovereign's royal father to spell the English language as it ought to be spelt.

He was, however, attempting the impossible. The English language cannot be spelt, because there is no English alphabet. We make shift with a Latin alphabet which has only five vowels. The vowels we use, mostly diphthongs, are innumerable: no two inhabitants of these isles use the same set; but the sounds they utter are so far recognizably alike as to be intelligibly represented by 18 letters. The consonants, as to which there is much less difference of utterance, require 24 letters.

Our attempts to make a foreign alphabet of 26 letters do the work of 42 are pitiable. We write the same vowel twice to give it a different sound, and thus get five additional vowels. We couple two different vowels, or even triple them, in various permutations, which give us much more than 18 vowel spellings. We also double the following consonant (compare 'table' and 'dabble', for instance) or make two consonants represent simple sounds like the consonants in 'thee' and 'she', for which the Latin alphabet does not provide.

These devices would make our alphabet phonetic enough for practical purposes if we used them consistently; but as our use of them is not consistent no one can pronounce a line of English from English writing or print. Still, it may be said that all we have to do is to make our usage consistent and the problem of spelling is solved Those who think this a satisfactory solution overlook the stupendous fact that it takes twice as long to write two letters as to write one. When it is pointed out to them they protest that the fact is perfectly obvious to them. But stupendous! How? Why? Could any fact be more trivial?

Let us see. The issue of *The Times* in which the article headed 'A King's Spelling' appeared was reduced by the war rationing of paper to half the usual size. The leader page, including the article, contained 54,369 letters. Each of the pages in the smaller type used for advertisements contained 88,200 letters. As there were 10 pages we have to multiply these figures by 10. Averaging them we get 712,845 letters as the content of a typical war-rationed 10-page issue of *The Times*. For a normal peace issue of *The Times* we must more than double this figure, which means that every 24 hours in the office of *The Times* alone a million and a half letters must be separately and legibly written or typed on paper, that someone reading from the paper must monotype them on a machine which arranges and casts them in metal, to be finally printed on huge rolls of paper by another machine the wear and tear of which is in proportion to the area of paper covered by the letters. This colossal labour has to be repeated every working day in the year: that is 310 times, which gives us an annual task of writing, setting-up, and printing-off four hundred and sixty-five millions of letters.

This for a single newspaper. But there are the other daily papers, the Sunday papers, the weekly reviews, the magazines, and publications of all sorts, which make the figures astronomical and indeed incalculable. In view of this, what are we to think of our device for making every letter serve two purposes by doubling it? It is easy to say 'It takes only a moment to write a letter of the alphabet twice instead of once.' In fact it takes years, wears out tons of machinery, uses up square miles of paper and oceans of ink. By shortening a single common word instead of lengthening it, we could save the cost of destroyers enough to make an impregnably guarded avenue across the Atlantic for our trade with America.

It may interest you to learn that your leading article contains 2,761 letters. As these letters represent only 2,311 sounds, 450 of them were superfluous and could have been saved had we a British alphabet. The same rate of waste on the 465,000,000 letters printed annually by *The Times* gives us 94,136,952 superfluous letters, every one of which has to be legibly written or typed, read and set up by the monotypist, cast in metal, and machined on paper which has to be manufactured, transported, and handled. Translate all that into hours of labour at eight hours a day. Translate the labour into wages and salaries. I leave the task to *The Times'* auditors, who, after staggering the proprietors with it, should pass it on to the Auditor-General to be elaborated into an estimate of the waste in the whole printing industry of the nation.

It is, I suppose, for lack of such an estimate that we do not think it worth while to lift a finger to get an English alphabet. The King, who has to spend an appreciable part of his time in signing his name, which in southern English has three sounds, and should be spelt with three letters, has to write six (100 per cent. waste of his time), with a result so equivocal that Herr Hitler speaks of him as King Gay Org. My surname has two sounds; but I have to spell it with four letters: another 100 per cent. loss of time, labour, ink, and paper. The Russians can spell it with two letters, as they have an alphabet of 35 letters. In the race of civilization, what chance has a Power that cannot spell so simple a sound as Shaw against a rival that can?

At present we are in such pressing need of more man-power that we are driven to transfer our women from their special natural labour of creating life to the industry of destroying it. I wonder some female mathematician does not calculate how many men would be released from literary industry for war work by spelling the common words could and should with six letters instead of with 11 as we insanely do at present. Battles may be lost by the waste in writing Army orders and dispatches with multitudes of superfluous letters. The mathematicians changed from Latin numerals to Arabic years ago. The gain was incalculably enormous. A change from Latin to British letters would have equally incalculable advantages; but we, being incorrigibly brain lazy, just laugh at spelling reformers as silly cranks. It took the Four Years' War to knock Summer Time into us. How many wars will it take to call our attention to the fact that there are shorter ways of spelling enuf than e-n-o-u-g-h?

Unfortunately, as most people write little and seldom, and read and spell by visual memory, not aurally, they are unconscious of any serious difficulty, and are only amused when some spelling reformer treats them to a few stale pleasantries about Frenchmen who, having been taught how to pronounce such a monstrosity as the spelling of though (six letters for two sounds), are then left to infer the pronunciation of through, cough, plough, &c. , &c. We have endless exposures of the inconsistencies of our spelling and the absurdity of its pretence to etymology; but even professional writers who waste half their lives in blackening paper unnecessarily seem to have no grasp of the importance of our losses or the colossal figures into which they run.

Much work has already been done on the subject by inventors of phonetic shorthands, who have all had to begin by designing a 42-letter alphabet. The best of these, so far as I know, is that of our most eminent British phoneticist, the late Henry Sweet, who had mastered all the systems, from Bell's Visible Speech to Pitman's; but, like all the rest, he proceeded to torture it into an instrument for verbatim reporting, and thereby made it difficult to learn, illegible, and useless for ordinary purposes. However, it is easy to discard his reporting contractions and use his alphabet in its simplicity. In my own practice I use Pitman's alphabet in this way with a great saving of time and labour for myself personally; but it all has to be transcribed and set up in the spelling of Dr. Johnson's dictionary.

The Orthological Institute has done invaluable service in calling attention to our waste of time by too much grammar through its invention of Basic English; but though the interest for foreign students is great, no British Government will ever be stirred to action in the matter until the economics of a phonetically spelt scientific and scholarly Pidgin are calculated and stated in terms of time, labour, and money.

Yours truly,
G. BERNARD SHAW.
Ayot St. Lawrence, Welwyn, Herts.

H.G. Wells was also an original signatory of this next letter but changed his mind before publication. Gilbert Murray was the renowned classical scholar and translator of Greek drama.

BOMBING OF CITIES

MILITARY AND NON-MILITARY OBJECTIVES.

Sir, – First, may we make clear that though we are about to propose an arrangement with the Axis, it is not in the nature of an armistice or a statement of war aims or anything else that could be interpreted as a symptom of weakening on the part of the Allies. Nor is it a new departure. As a precedent we cite the dealings between our postal authorities and those of the enemy by which at last prisoners of war on both sides are receiving letters from home with certainty and regularity in three weeks after their date. This enormous improvement on the pre-existing state of things could not have been effected without negotiations which, if not precisely cordial, were governed by a reciprocal disposition to listen to reason and make a bargain benefiting the belligerents equally.

There are methods of warfare which not only cannot produce a decision but are positively beneficial to the side against which they are directed. The bombardment of cities from the air may be one of them. Its conditions are quite unprecedented. Both victory and defeat are impossible, because the vanquished cannot surrender, and the victor must run for home at 300 miles an hour, pursued by fighters at 400 miles an hour. The recent bombardments of Berlin and London, though quite successful as such, have not produced any military result beyond infuriating the unfortunate inhabitants. Some of them have been killed. If raids could be maintained nightly and each raid killed 1,000 persons, half of them women, it would take over a century and a half to exterminate us and a century and a half to exterminate the Germans. Meanwhile, as both sides are depending for victory on famine by blockade, the reduction in the number of civilian mouths to be fed would be a relief to us.

As to one specific course which the War Cabinet has been provoked into taking: to wit, the threat to demolish Rome if Athens or Cairo be attacked from the air, it forces us to ask whether Rome does not belong to the culture of the whole world far more than to the little Italian-speaking group of Benitos and Beppos who at present are its local custodians. By destroying it we should be spiting the noses to vex the faces of every educated person in the British Commonwealth and in America, to say nothing of the European mainland. We may smash it for the Italians; but who is to give it back to us? In Rome no one is a stranger and a foreigner: we all feel when we first go there that we are revisiting the scene of a former existence. As to the effect of- the threat, surely the way to save Athens and Cairo is not to defy Herr Hitler to bombard them and thus make it a point of honour for him to reply by a shower of bombs on them

He, far from the seven hills, may even echo the late Lord Clanricarde's reply to his Irish tenants, 'If you think you can intimidate me by shooting my agent you are very much mistaken.'

That we should in the same breath indignantly deny that our last raid on Berlin was a reprisal, and announce a major reprisal which must have staggered the historical conscience of the world, shows that our heads are not as clear as they might be on this subject. The more we endeavour to think it out the more we find ourselves driven to the conclusion whatever may be said from the military point of view of our treatment of Bremen, Hamburg, and Kiel, there is nothing to be said for the demolition of metropolitan cities as such, and that the Bishop of Chichester's plea for a reconsideration of that policy is entirely justified.

Yours truly,
GILBERT MURRAY.
BERNARD SHAW.

Shaw's masterly interpretation of issues raised by a letter on Handel by Hubert Langley, an actor and theatre manager, makes this next letter a gem that should be studied by music critics. Shaw was 85 and his wit and knowledge had not dimmed. In the words of Leon Hugo, writing in *Bernard Shaw: Playwright and Preacher* (Methuen, 1971): 'It was instinct with him to hear music, not as diminished sevenths or augmented sixths, but as "poetry", as an emotion, a manifestation of "intelligence" and, ultimately, as a sort of explicitly inexplicit "philosophy".' Shaw was convinced that the last act of Shakespeare's Cymbeline had been cobbled together; this led him, on one occasion, to state that a revival of the play would probably be alright if he rewrote the last act. He did so and published it as *Cymbeline Refinished* in 1937.

~ *1941, October 14* ~

HANDEL'S 'MESSIAH.'

PERFORMANCES "AS HE WROTE IT.'

Sir, – Mr. Hubert Langley's letter in your issue of September 24 was a very welcome distraction of our attention from the war and the personality of Mr. Hitler to the infinitely more important though less pressing subject and greater personality of Messiah and its composer.

But his demand for a performance 'as Handel wrote it' is not so simple a matter as he assumes. A composer in writing a score is limited by the economic conditions and artistic and technical resources at his disposal. He must take what he can get and make the best of it. Had the Albert Hall, the B.B.C. Orchestra, and the Salvation Army's International Staff band been within Handel's reach the score of Messiah would have been a very different specification. The music would not and could not have been better; but the instrumentation would have been very much richer and more effective. The money taken at the doors would have far exceeded the utmost that the room in Fishamble Street, Dublin, where the first performance took place, could hold at the prices charged for admission in those days. Suppose Handel had all this money to play with. Suppose his trumpets and horns could play chromatic scales instead of the few scattered notes of a posthorn. Suppose he had clarinets as well as oboes (hautboys), and tubas as well as trombones. Suppose he had an equally tempered modern cinema organ to which all keys are alike, instead of a comparatively simple organ in mean tone temperament in which only a few of the 12 major and minor keys were available. Suppose he could count on 60 strings instead of 20, on four horns, or eight, instead of two, on woodwind in Wagnerian groups of three instead of two, on the chords from kettle drums used by Berlioz in his Fantastic Symphony. Would his score have been anything like as poor as it stands in his manuscript? Is there no excuse for the conductors and composers who have ventured to guess how Handel would have enriched it under such conditions?

Mr. Langley may say that Mozart went beyond this. He certainly did. Take for example the bass air 'The people that walked in darkness.' It is not too much of an exaggeration to say that Handel did not harmonize it at all: he scored it in hollow unisons, perhaps with some intention of conveying an impression of darkness and void. Mozart filled up these hollows with harmonies so enchanting that every musician longs to hear them again and again. I believe Handel would have been delighted with them. And is it certain that he did not anticipate them? Elgar, who adored them, pooh-poohed the purists by reminding them that Handel was at the organ, and must have put in all sorts of harmonic variations, being a great improviser. Handel's variations are lost: but are we to throw Mozart's after them?

Handel and his contemporaries wrote trumpet parts that became impossible when the pitch rose as it did until they became unplayable. The trumpets had to be replaced by clarinets until at the first performances of our Bach Society Kosleck arrived with a new two-valved Bach trumpet on which all the impossible passages are now brilliantly played. That was a glorious restoration; but its success does not justify a deliberate reduction of our Messiah performances within seventeenth-century limits.

Only, the changes must be made by a master hand. Wagner provided Gluck's *Iphigenia* overture with a very beautiful ending to replace the conventional rum-tum *coda* which was considered *de rigueur*, and which still spoils Mozart's *Don Giovanni* overture at concert performances. Who wants to have the rum-tum back again? When Wagner wrote trombone parts for a chorus in one of Spontini's operas, the composer, instead of being outraged, sent for the parts when he was producing the opera in Berlin, and was kind enough to say it was a great pity Wagner could never become a great composer, as he (Spontini) had exhausted the possibilities of music. Wagner, when he conducted Beethoven's ninth symphony, a sacred masterpiece if there ever was one, found that certain themes which were evidently meant to be heard as principal melodies were smothered by their accompaniments. He rescored the passages to correct this. Gounod accused him of sacrilege; but Wagner's version is now played instead of that left by the deaf Beethoven. Passages in which the brass was left idle because it could not play the chromatic intervals have been reinforced by it without anyone protesting.

I could multiply instances: but enough is enough. Besides, I must confine my assent to changes made by master hands like those of Mozart, Wagner, and Elgar. Genius alone has the right to tamper with genius.

I am myself a composer: that is, a planner of performances, in the special capacity of a playwright. When I began, I had to keep production expenses within the limits of, say, £2,000 at a London West End manager's bank, and £20 in the provinces. The invention of the cinema has placed capitals running to a quarter of a million at my disposal for modern revivals of my old cheap plays. This enormous economic change enables me to do things I should never have dreamt of in the nineteenth century. A cinema production which confined itself to the old version would be an imbecility. But I do not allow the additions to be made in Hollywood by the nearest Californian barman.

Finally, take the case of Shakespear. He did not write original plays: he wrote 'additional accompaniments' to old ones. Has anyone on earth except Tolstoy, who had no ear for English word music, ever suggested that we should go back to the original Lear? Could Mr. Langley endure a performance of the old *Hamlet* after tasting Shakespears version?

Fifty years ago *The Times*, greatly daring, ventured to hint, through its music representative the late J.A. Fuller Maitland, that the Handel Festivals at the Crystal Palace, where 4,000 performers created an uproar which would have infuriated the irascible composer, were barbarous orgies which had no more to do with Handel's intentions than the Cup Ties. Naturally Costa, the once famous but now forgotten conductor, piled up all the brass and blare and percussion he could muster for these occasions. I agree warmly with Mr. Langley that these additions should be ruthlessly scrapped. At the same period Shakespear himself was known to playgoers only by horribly mutilated 'acting versions' which made Mr. Granville - Barker's uncompromising restorations of the real Shakespear seem surprising novelties even to the professional critics. I agreed with Mr. Granville-Barker as heartily as I do with Mr. Langley; but that did not prevent my reconditioning the last act of Cymbeline to an extent that would have surprised Shakespear. Some changes are inevitable: I can even imagine Mr. Augustus John touching up a Goya. It all depends on how it is done.

Yours, &c.
G. BERNARD SHAW.
Ayot St. Lawrence, Welwyn, Herts.

(In this letter of Dec 24 the operative word in Mr. Shaw's statement is 'net'. On incomes over £30,000, after the deduction of income-tax at 10 shillings. in the pound, every £2 of gross income yields £1 of net income, on which 19s. of surtax is payable, making as Mr. Shaw argues with a characteristic touch, 39s. of taxation on £1 of net income.)

Times editor.

∼ *1941, December 24* ∼

CONSCRIPTIONS OF WEALTH.

INCOME FROM INVESTMENTS.

Sir, – The Chancellor of the Exchequer, in his broadcast on the 19th instant, met the persistent demand for the further 'conscription of wealth' by pleading that incomes in excess of £30,000 are already taxed 19s. 6d. in the pound. Surely this is a wild understatement. Net incomes from investments are taxed 39s. in the pound, and are consequently ruining their unfortunate possessors. It is only the spendthrifts who get off with 19s.6d. This is conscription of wealth through taxation of capital with a vengeance.

I am driven to the conclusion that our Chancellor is not much of a financier. And why did he not mention the new security which is to prevent us from leaving our money in the bank instead of handing it over to the exchequer as it comes in? It would be a welcome step away from the present policy of penalizing investment and encouraging consumption while shouting from every platform that victory depends on saving, saving, saving.

Capitalism can defend its country; and Russia is proving that Socialism can do the same; but a policy of knocking the linchpin out of Capitalism without substituting Socialism leads not to victory but to Queer Street.

Yours, &c
G. BERNARD SHAW.
Ayot St. Lawrence, Welwyn, Herts.

Further advice to the Chancellor of the Exchequer, this time on purchase tax.

MUSICAL INSTRUMENTS

Sir, – May I beg *The Times* to remind the Chancellor of the Exchequer that musical instruments are among the first necessities of civilized life, and not luxuries to be made unobtainable by a purchase tax of 66²/₃ per cent? To exempt wireless receiving sets, and by the same stroke cut off the supply of instruments and skilled players by which the masterpieces of music are broadcast, suggests that the Government is still in the hands of gentlemen from our public schools left to believe that anyone who can read the satires of Juvenal in their original tongue, but is unaware of the existence of the symphonies of the great masters, from Haydn and Mozart to Elgar and Sibelius, is an educated man.

The simplest orchestra which can give us the eighteenth-century symphonies needs at least 32 instruments. For a full range of nineteenth century music the minimum must be put at 80. And each instrument is dumb without a skilled professional player, each of whom must have been provided with it by his parents in his or her teens. Now the parents of orchestral players are not luxurious millionaires.

Many of them come from families so closely within modest incomes that a sudden demand for £20, or even £10, is a very difficult matter. In my boyhood I had a chance of being qualified as an oboist; and I should have jumped at it if I could have obtained the £14 which was the price of a second-hand oboe 70 years ago. For want of that sum I was lost to the wood wind for ever, and had to adopt a profession in which the equipment was sixpennorth of stationery.

The notion that not only the players in the B.B.C. and London Philharmonic orchestras, but in the brass bands of the Salvation Army and the factory and colliery bands which competed every year at the Crystal Palace, the best of them being of first-rate artistic quality, are extravagant voluptuaries whose instruments may be classed with blue diamond rings and dispensed with on the smallest provocation, betrays a breath-bereaving cultural and social ignorance. I hope all the bands in London will hasten to Westminster Hall and do to the House of Commons what Joshua's trumpeters did to the walls of Jericho rather than let the Appropriation Bill pass as it stands without a protest.

Faithfully,
G. BERNARD SHAW.
Ayot St. Lawrence, Welwyn, Herts.

In a speech entitled 'Christianity and the Social Order' the Archbishop of Canterbury had made what amounted to a 'propaganda' statement that there should be a Christian basis to all our activities whether in economics or war. Shaw linked it with the news that the Nazis had taken reprisals against civilians when their troops were assassinated and the call by some correspondents that we should retaliate in kind. Vercingetorix was the chieftain of the Averni who organised the tribes of Gaul to fight against the Romans. He surrendered but was nevertheless executed.

∽ 1942, October 13 ∽

REPRISALS

GERMAN AND BRITISH METHODS,

A STANDARD TO PRESERVE

Sir, – The Fuhrer's resort to the Mosaic law and our announcement of reprisals in kind raises several questions. How are we obliged to copy him? How will our doing so 'protect' his British prisoners? May it not rather provoke him to treat them as the Romans treated their prisoners when Vercingetorix surrendered to Julius Caesar? In that case should we be bound to retaliate? If we are sniped and sabotaged in Madagascar must we shoot hostages because the Nazis do it in the countries they are occupying? Is this our answer to our brave Archbishop's demand for Christian policy? Who is to make the chains, and what is to be their weight? And as the retaliatory process is self-perpetuating how is it to be stopped before the human race is exterminated?

Faithfully,
G. BERNARD SHAW.

Poet Sir John Squire (1884–1958), former literary editor of the New Statesman, had written to complain of the more modern use of participles that was forcing changes in the English language, such as 'loaned' instead of 'lent,' 'chided' instead of the old English 'chidden', etc. It may well have been written 'tongue in cheek', but Shaw seized the occasion below.

ENGLISH USAGE

Sir, – Sir John Squire, like all poets, loves the euphonious past participles of our irregular verbs. So do I. But we must not shut our minds against the hard fact that irregular verbs are the worst enemies of any language. *The Times* does a great national service every time it regularizes one of them. I hope to see in its columns some day such regular participles as thinked and buyed, though I shall still sing 'Joshua fit the battle of Jericho' rather than spoil the line.

English usage is just what we need to get rid of: it is overloaded with unnecessary grammar; and our mad persistence in trying to spell the sounds of our speech with an ancient Phoenician alphabet costs us the price of a fleet of battleships every year in writing and printing superfluous letters. As it happens, the most civilized nation in the world, the Chinese, have taken our language in hand for business purposes, and produced an English with a minimum of grammar which has immense advantages over our academic English. It may yet become the language of *The Times*.

Meanwhile we might use an entirely new English monosyllabic pidgin. The only one I know of needs only a seventeen-letter alphabet. Current English cannot be spelt recognizably and economically with less than 42 letters.

Faithfully,
G. BERNARD SHAW.
Ayot St. Lawrence, Welwyn, Herts.

Some correspondence in *The Times* on hydro-electric schemes in Scotland drew these comments and reminiscences from Shaw.

SCOTTISH WATER-POWER.

Sir, – Your correspondents on this subject have left me with an impression that, though they may have technical experience and qualifications to which I cannot pretend, they have never been in Scotland. When I explored that very attractive country, and announced that I was ready for the desperate adventure of going north of Inverness to the utmost limit of the land, and even further into the isles, I was warned even by Scotsmen to equip myself for those arctic regions with clothing of Eskimo warmth.

When I arrived, what did I find? A climate like that of the south of Ireland, in which fuchsias were trees rather than plants. To go there from the Forth was like going from Leningrad to the Crimea. From Thurso, basking in the warmth of the Gulf Stream and the sun, I looked across the water to Orkney, and estimated the journey thither as about half an hour in a rowing boat. Why not a bridge? I asked, thinking of the one in Sydney Harbour. But when I embarked in a tough little steamer older than myself, but fiercely engined, the terrible tides of the Pentland Firth swept us eastward nearly to John o' Groat's House and back again into Scapa Flow before I could land after a journey of more than three hours. Four times a day that tide swept past, with power enough to electrify all Europe, and shut up the coalmines in which Englishmen live the lives not of men but of moles.

When I returned to the mainland and explored the coast westward I found the Kyle of Tongue and other inlets into which the tide rushes, in and back, inviting us to capture and harness it. When I asked why this was not done I got two answers. It would not pay to do it because there are no factories and mills and cities of people up there to use the power. I asked whether the River Severn had waited for the cloth mills to be built on its banks before it began to flow – whether it was the power that came to the business or the business to the power. Make the power available and you will presently have a crowded northern Riviera using it. The Scots, being a reasoning people, saw my point, but also saw that the job was of a size that only the Government could tackle, and that our form of government, which is unable to build a bridge across the Severn that has been urgently needed for a hundred years, would take at least a thousand years to build a bridge to Orkney, much less harness the Pentland flow and ebb. The second reply was that of the engineers. The thing was impossible, they said. Their turbines could capture so little of the power that the game would not be worth the candle. Having no technical knowledge I had nothing more to say except that if they did not know how to capture enough of the power, they had better find out; for the power is there in monstrous excess; and since they have been able to advance from the engine of Stephenson's Rocket to that of an aeroplane with a speed of 400 miles an hour there is a reasonable probability of their getting more than an ounce of power from the weight of a thousand rushing tons of sea-water.

Perhaps some of your correspondents who know more about it than I do would tell us how this matter stands at present. The astrophysicists, who used to depress us by telling us that the sun is cooling, and that we shall all be frozen to death, now tell us that the power of the tides will retard the motion of the spheres and finally stop them, when they will all crash together into a single mass of such inconceivable heat that no form of life known to us could endure it for the billionth of a split second. That will be a pleasanter end than slow freezing; and in the meantime it gives us some notion of the enormous power we are at present wasting.

Faithfully,
G. BERNARD SHAW.

A Captain Richard Pilkington wrote to *The Times* letters column suggesting that the English use more American terms – such as 'fone' instead of 'phone' – to modernise and simplify their language, but was concerned that some 'die-hards' might object.

'FONE'

Sir, – Captain Pilkington, in your issue of Monday last, is concerned with the feelings of old-fashioned people when they see the name of the instrument which is called in Germany a farspeaker spelt with four letters instead of five. Has he considered its effect on the cost in manual labor? in wear and tear of printing and typing machinery? in paper? and in bulk and weight of books and newspapers? and in the number of plays a Shakespear can write in his lifetime? The saving of a single letter in the spelling of a common word would pay for a world war in a few months.

If we had a British alphabet of 42 letters instead of persisting in using a prehistoric one of 26 letters we could spell phone with three letters instead five, and the much commoner word though with two letters instead of six. The saving would pay for half a dozen wars if we could find nothing better to spend it on.

Faithfully
G. BERNARD SHAW.
Ayot St. Lawrence, Welwyn, Herts.

War time Budgets usually brought painful news for taxpayers. Shaw seized the opportunity to air once again his oft-stated views on taxation and to underline his conviction in socialism (or Shavianism) as the only solution to many of the problems. The Vicar of Bray was a well-known English ballad that referred to a vicar from the village of Bray who would change his creed according to circumstances. Jean Louis Darlan (1881–1942) was an admiral in the French navy under the Vichy government who negotiated secretly with the Americans and became Head of State in French Africa, but was assassinated after one month in office. Sir John Anderson was Chancellor of the Exchequer at this time.

THE COMING BUDGET.

TAXES AND THE VICAR OF BRAY.

Sir, – Now that the Budget in preparation for April threatens so many of us with financial ruin, and foreign policy is so much concerned with revolutionary changes which our diplomatists, against all their traditions, are bound to encourage and assist, may I call the attention of the Chancellor of the Exchequer and the Foreign Secretary to certain vital considerations much obscured at present by popular sentimental ignorance of political science.

When an institution is found to be unjust and anti-social, the popular reaction to the discovery is not to alter or discard the institution, but to injure those who profit by it. And when an obnoxious Government is overthrown the first impulse is to liquidate all its functionaries and replace them with congenital revolutionists. Both policies are disastrous. Their results in Russia in the few years which followed the revolution of 1917 were terrible enough to warn us off any attempt to repeat them here. Nevertheless it seems quite probable that we shall repeat them all, and learn from experience, at an appalling cost, what we are incapable of learning from history.

We are, for instance, facing an irresistible drift of economic changes from absolute private property ('real' property) to public property, from Cobdenist private Capitalism to Fascist State-aided Capitalism, from Freedom of Contract to State-regulated trade, from Competition to Cooperation and Communism, and from the wildest and most disruptive inequalities of income to a more stable equality. Such changes, unless very carefully, wisely, and gradually guided, may smash up civilization. Yet the first notion of their advocates is to reduce every exploiter or beneficiary of private property and private enterprise to destitution. The Bolshevists, convinced that private property in land is a baneful institution, took the successful farmer, the Kulak, by the scruff of his neck and threw him out into the lane to beg. The inevitable result followed: the farm ceased to produce anything but weeds and desolation; and Russia began to starve. Lenin soon had to pick up the Kulak out of the ditch – what was left of him – and pitchfork him back into his farm with instructions to cultivate and exploit it for all he was worth until the Soviet was ready to take on his job.

The moral is clear. It may be finally desirable to get rid of landlordism; but while we have landlords let us have rich ones, and encourage them to become richer, rather than poor and persecuted ones. And what applies to private farming enterprise applies to all enterprises. Lenin had to rehabilitate the trader just as he had to rehabilitate the Kulak. Collective farming and collective trading may come in time; but meanwhile the more private farming and trading flourishes the better for everybody. Dukes are better landlords than needy freeholders.

Now for foreign policy. We are 'liberating' foreign countries just now all over Europe, and our first notion of liberation is to persecute or execute all the law-abiding agents of the Governments we have overthrown. No public man in the world was so execrated as the late Admiral Darlan, who was assassinated at the depth of his unpopularity. Yet he was the only public man in Europe upon whom Europe could depend absolutely. He was the Vicar of Bray, the backbone of all civilization, the citizen who will obey and faithfully serve the established Government of his country no matter how often it changes. When I was in Russia in 1931 I was shown in Moscow an astonishing exhibition called a Revolutionary Museum, glorifying all the rebels and political assassins of the last 100 years, some of them old comrades of my own. The curator who showed me round was very proud of them and of the exhibition. I asked him, 'Do you want Stalin to be assassinated? Do you want the Soviet Government overthrown? Do you not know that the first business of a successful revolution is to liquidate revolutionists?' He seem surprised; but where are those revolutionary and anti-religious museums now? I have not heard of them lately. One of them, opened in a great cathedral, is now echoing with the canticles of the Greek Church.

Before the resumption of the war, in 1939, I was a prosperous playwright, taxed on a scale that would have seemed mad to Gladstone or Queen Victoria, but within my taxable capacity and leaving me able to pay my way. To-day I am a tax collector for the Inland Revenue, compelled to act as such for a commission of 6d. in the pound, which does not pay for my overhead, much less for my work in earning, which, in my eighty-eighth year, is heavier than it was in my twenty-eighth. The more I earn the faster my means vanish into the Exchequer. The more productive my work is, the smaller is my commission, so that all my business activities are directed to reducing its productiveness to a point at which my commission will be increased from 6d. to 4s. I have just been endowed for life with an income from a property valued as £150,000. The net result is that I have to pay £40,000 as well as the income of the estate to Sir John Anderson. My haunting dread is that some of my many admirers, by dying and leaving me a million or so, may consign me to an almshouse. As a man of letters, I belong to a profession in which one lives precariously from hand to mouth and acquires capital enough to provide for dependents and educate children only by windfalls that seldom occur more than once in a lifetime, and never more than two or three times in 10 times as many years. Yet when I get such a windfall I am taxed on it at the same rate as fellow-citizens with settled incomes of the amount of the windfall. My property rights are limited to 50 years after my death, and half nationalized at 25: theirs are everlasting.

And I am not alone in this special grievance. The property of inventors is limited to 14 years. Cabinet Ministers in comparative opulence may by the next General Election, or a reshuffle of the Cabinet, be reduced to hand-to-mouth salaries. Many traders are subject to still more sensational fluctuations. Formerly an attempt to adjust this was made by taxing, not on the current year's income but on an average of three years. But this concession has been withdrawn; and the wretch who makes £21,000 in one year, and a bare subsistence in the years preceding and following, is ruined by its withdrawal.

I am very far from being a millionaire; but since 1939 I have had to give the Exchequer £20,000 a year to pay for a war which would not have occurred if my advice had been taken in 1919. I now advise Sir John Anderson in framing his 1944 Budget to put his engines in reverse and operate as follows.

1. Exempt from surtax all legitimately earned incomes exceeding £20,000. The immediate effect will be that the potential earners of such incomes, instead of as at present straining every nerve to reduce their incomes to below that figure by piling up idle reserve funds, staving off not their creditors but their debtors, reducing their output, and sabotaging their own businesses, will do their utmost to redouble their activity and productivity. Their successes should not only be rewarded by the exemption but recognized by a new civil variety of the D.S.O.
2. The three years' average should be revived and made extensible in hard cases to any reasonable period.
3. Abolish the Excess Profits Tax root and branch.

These changes will be enough for one year. They will be resisted and denounced fiercely by the Diehards on the extreme Right who believe that the only way to make the rich richer is to make the poor poorer, and those on the extreme Left who are equally convinced that the only way to enrich the poor is to add the rich to their underfed ranks. The gentlemen who write to *The Times* so piteously to deplore the Excess Profits Tax will make a poor job of defending its abolition, because though strong in the facts they are weak in theory and consequently muddled in argument. Sir John must take an iron stand on the ground that to the extent to which we have left our culture and our industry to the pampered rich, we must pamper them for all they are worth, and, far from crying that nobody must profit commercially by war, make war the most profitable of all businesses until it ends in victory.

And let Mr Eden not forget, amid the shrieks for the blood of the quislings, that the British Vicar of Bray is the typical quisling, and our surest ally 'until *The Times* do alter.' The bureaux of the new continental governments must be recruited from compliant Fifth Columns, not from implacable Bitter Enders.

Faithfully,
G. BERNARD SHAW.

Shaw believed passionately in the viability of alphabetical reform and even left a substantial sum in his will for this purpose. Charles Kay Ogden (1889–1957) was a writer and linguist who developed Basic English, a simplified system for a standard English.

~ *1944, March 30* ~

Basic English and Spelling.

Sir, – May I beg the Basic English advocates and the spelling reformers to be content to do one thing each at a time. The two subjects are separable, and if they are not kept separate will struggle for precedence instead of getting something done.

Basic English is a natural growth which has been investigated and civilized by the Orthological Institute on the initiative of Mr. C. K. Ogden, whose years of tedious toil deserve a peerage and a princely pension. The only job comparable to it is that of the American, George S. Terry, who has given us tables of duodecimal logarithms. Before Mr. Ogden set to work, Chinese and British traders in Hong-Kong, and black fellows having to learn the speech of white fellows in Australia, had evolved what they called Business English, or, as the Chinese pronounce it, Pidgin English, in which all our superfluous grammar was ignored and the number of words used was reduced to the minimum necessary to make the speakers intelligible to one another. What Mr. Ogden did was to make a list of these necessary words (less than a thousand) and demonstrate how little grammar was needed to make them serve as an international language. He called the result Basic English. Any foreigner equipped with Basic English can live in England, or among Englishmen anywhere, without being deaf and dumb. Any foreigner who can live in England on these terms can pick up as much as he needs from Chaucer to Chesterton, just as we all pick it up by reading and conversation.

Other Ogdens in other countries will do the same for their own languages and produce textbooks and dictionaries as Mr. Ogden has for English. If any of these basics becomes a world-wide language it will be by natural selection. Basic English starts as a favourite; but once established here it must make its own way elsewhere.

So much for Basic English. Now as to spelling. The difficulty here is that we have no English alphabet. We make shift with an ancient Phoenician one; but it has only 26 letters representing 26 speech sounds. English speech has 42 sounds which must be spellable before the language can be written or read intelligibly. To do this with 26 letters we have to resort to combinations and permutations of the 26 letters, which is easy enough, as the possible permutations of the five Phoenician vowels greatly exceed the number of vowels we use. Our uncoordinated attempts to do this, complicated by a fad called etymological spelling, have produced the absurd spellings of which Dr. Gilbert Murray and Mr. William Barkley have given samples in your issue of March 17. They have been cited for a hundred years past without producing anything but a smile at them as literary curiosities. The notion of changing all our books and printing machines merely to correct them would seem too extravagant to be thought of seriously: the expense would be prohibitive. We could not afford it. They are only anomalies; and anomalies are a British speciality: we are rather proud of them, and are not to be intimidated by mere logic.

This self-complacency can be pricked. It may seem only a laughing matter that we have to spell the common word 'though' with six letters instead of two, as the time lost is only a fraction of a second. But multiply that fraction of a second by the number of times the word has to be written in the British Empire and in North America every hour, every day, every month, every year, every century, and its cost grows from the fraction of a farthing to pounds, tens of pounds, hundreds, thousands, millions, billions of pounds; and the cost of a change becomes unspeakably negligible. The fact that Russia, with its 35 letter alphabet, can spell my name with two letters instead of four may conceivably make it impossible for us to compete economically in the world with Russia. I am ready to bequeath all I possess (if the war taxation leaves me anything to bequeath) to establish a new 42-letter alphabet with it. I have saved years by using such an alphabet for my own works; but they all have to be transcribed and typed and set up and printed in Phoenician; so that nobody's time is saved except my own.

If only the British Government were as intelligent as I am!

Faithfully
G. BERNARD SHAW.

There had been a discussion in Parliament on the need to prepare plans for reconstruction after the war and the provision of more up-to-date children's homes for parentless children. Several letters called for an inquiry into conditions in government-run children's homes and for reform. What type of reform was debatable and Shaw joined in with the next two letters, giving comparisons and sound advice. The main correspondent was Lady Allen of Hurtwood (1897–1976), a landscape architect and campaigner for children's welfare, who stated that not enough thought was being given to training of staff and pay.

~ *1944, July 21* ~

Bringing Up the Child.

A Contrasting Method.

Connemara and Berlin.

Sir, – It is now many years since Judge Henry Neill, the American philanthropist who successfully agitated for mothers' pensions, convinced me of the importance of what he called 'maternal massarzh' in the nurture of infants.

At that time the most famous institution for infants in the world was the Kaiserin Augusta's House in Berlin. Within its green marble walls, children in beautifully tidy brass beds were tended by trained nurses under the best medical advice, the service being so perfectly regulated that every nurse knew exactly how many minutes an hour she could devote to each child in her care. At the same time infants in Connemara were tumbling about half naked on the mud floors of cabins little better than cowhouses under the eyes of mothers who knew rather less about the scientific nurture of children than about electronic physics. Out of doors the children combined sport with business by driving the family pig under the wheels of the motor-cars of British tourists, who paid on the nail more than the slain animal would have fetched alive in the nearest market.

And under the ideal Berlin conditions the infants died like flies, while in Connemara there was no mortality rate because children never died there. At least so I said. I will not pretend that the statement was capable of statistical verification; but it dramatized the facts effectively enough to drive them home. Judge Neill held that the difference was due to the fact that in Berlin the nurses tidied up the children's beds, and fed, and took their temperatures, and weighed and measured them very efficiently for carefully calculated divisions of their time; whereas in Connemara the mothers hugged them, mammocked them, kissed them, smacked them, talked baby talk to them or scolded them; in short, maternally massaged them to their hearts content.

Now neither of these methods can be accepted as civically satisfactory. The Berlin child either did not grow up at all, or grew up a nervous wreck or a disciplinarian terrorist. The Connemara child grew up humane and

~ 245 ~

healthy, but at best a noble savage. The problem is how to produce adults who are both humane and cultivated. Clearly they must have not only the Berlin discipline but the Connemara massage.

The trained nurse with no time to spare for cuddling must be supplemented by affectionate masseuses. Have we not enough motherly and grandmotherly women, married or unmarried, maids or widows, to volunteer for this service before and after they have reared their own children? What have Lady Allen of Hurtwood and all the institution champions to say to this? It is no use their hitting and countering as if there were only one end in view, and that an extreme one.

Faithfully,
G. BERNARD SHAW.
Ayot St. Lawrence, Welwyn, Hertfordshire.

Lady Nancy Astor had joined in the discussion with a letter on 22 July regarding parentless children. She agreed on the need for better pay and conditions but pointed out that the overriding need was for love and compassion, if the children were going to obtain lasting benefit.

~ *1944, August 2* ~

THE CARE OF CHILDREN.

HOSPITAL AND OTHER TRAINING.

A MOSCOW REMINISCENCE.

Sir – In reply to Lady Allen of Hurtwood, and in elucidation of Lady Astor's vital point, may I say that though we all have the best intentions we shall get nowhere unless we stop confusing mothercraft with hospital sick-nursing?

A hospital-trained sick-nurse, registered as such, should never be allowed to come within 10 miles of a healthy child. She can do nothing with children or with anyone else until she has them indoors and awake in bed; conditions which will soon make the healthiest child an invalid, but which the hospital trainee has worked in night and day for at least four years and become incurably habituated to. To the sick she is a ministering angel; to the sound she is an artificial monster. Noisy, playful children, with their clothes and hands dirty, upset her routine so annoyingly that she hates them. All children should be tirelessly noisy, playful, grubby-handed, except at mealtimes, soiling and tearing such clothes as they need wear, bringing not only the joy of childhood into the house but dust and mud as well: in short, everything that makes the quiet and order of sickness and its nursing impossible.

In Moscow in 1931 I had the privilege of being present when Lady Astor swept through the Kremlin like a flying bomb, and exploded all this maternal common sense on the astonished Stalin, who, though taken aback for the first time in his life, was wise enough to sense that there was something in it, and made a note which he presently acted on.

When shall we stop insanely staffing our child homes and institutions with hospital-trained sick-nurses exclusively, thereby doing what we can to make them child slaughter-houses? Replace the hospital trainees with naturally motherly women until we have established a training in mothercraft; and the institutions will be as healthy and happy as the homes which, by the way, are by no means always either healthy or happy.

Faithfully,
G. BERNARD SHAW.

In the last years of his long life Shaw contributed two letters to *The Times* on his personal distaste for the way capital punishment was then still being carried out. His unorthodox views were, in his opinion, as they had always been, concerned with the humane enactment of punishment before the law. See also letter of 5 December 1947 and the first letter of this collection.

The young lady referred to in this letter was an 18-year-old dancer, Elizabeth Maud Jones, who was sentenced to death with her partner, an American serviceman named Karl Hulton, for the murder of a taxi driver. She was eventually reprieved but he was hanged.

~ *1945, March 5* ~

THE SENTENCE OF DEATH.

THE STATE AND THE MURDERER.

EXACTING THE PENALTY.

Sir, – From a well-known passage in the Book of Genesis we learn that our method of executing criminals is the same as that in use at least 2,000 years ago. Is it not time to reconsider it?

We have before us the case of a girl whose mental condition unfits her to live in a civilized community. She has been guilty of theft and murder; and apparently her highest ambition is to be what she calls a gun moll, meaning a woman who thinks that robbery and murder are romantically delightful professions. She has earned her living as a strip tease girl, which I, never having seen a strip tease act, take to be a performance as near to indecent exposure as the police will allow, though after 20 years' observation of sunbathing I find it difficult to imagine anyone being entertained by the undress that would have shocked Queen Victoria.

Clearly we have either to put such a character to death or to re-educate her. Having no technique of re-education immediately available, we have decided to put her to death. The decision is a very sensible one, as the alternative is to waste useful lives in caging and watching her as a tigress in the Zoo has to be caged and watched.

Unfortunately our method of putting such people to death is so primitive that when it has to be practised on a girl in her teens every one, including the Sovereign who has to sign the death warrant and the Home Secretary who has to decide whether it shall be carried out or not, is revolted by it. They agree that the thing should be done, but not in this unnecessarily unpleasant way. The jury, moved by the girl's age and sex, recommend her to mercy, leaving her adult male accomplice pitilessly to his fate. As this 'mercy' takes the form of a dozen years of the daily torture, demoralization, disablement, and cutting-off from all the news of the world which we call penal servitude, and is far crueller and wickeder than burning at the stake, the only people who are satisfied with it are our anti-Christians who lust after vindictive punishment, and would welcome the spectacle of a burning or flogging, and the capital punishment abolitionists, who, shrinking from killing as such, but having no conception of State responsibilities, sign every petition for reprieve, and drop the case the moment the condemned person is left alive, no matter under what conditions.

Surely it is possible nowadays to devise some form of euthanasia more civilized than the rope, the drop, and the prison chaplain assuring the condemned that she has only to believe something she obviously does not believe, and she will go straight to eternal bliss in heaven. The fact that the horror of such a business will oblige the prison authorities to drug her to endure it only adds to the disgust it creates.

The matter has long been pressing. The savage superstitions of vengeance and expiation, the exhibition of executions as public entertainments, and the theory of deterrence, which depends on an impossible certainty of detection in which no criminal believes, and also makes it a matter of complete indifference whether the person we hang is guilty or not provided we hang somebody, are discredited; and as the necessary work of 'weeding the garden' becomes better understood, the present restriction of liquidation to murder cases, and the exemption of dangerous lunatics (who should be liquidated as such, crime or no crime), will cease, and must be replaced by State-contrived euthanasia for all idiots and intolerable nuisances, not punitively, but as a necessary stroke of social economy.

If the strip tease girl had been told simply that her case was under consideration, and she were presently to be found dead in her bed some morning in a quite comfortable lethal chamber not known to her to be such, the relief to the public conscience would be enormous. And the survivors would acquire a wholesome sense of public obligation to make the preservation of their lives by civilization worth while.

Faithfully,

G. BERNARD SHAW.

The Irish Government under the leadership of Eamon de Valera had tendered condolences to the German Minister in Dublin on the death of Hitler. This naturally led to a furore in the British Press. Pamela Hinkson (1900–82) was a prolific author who had spent many years in Ireland and had been educated there. She had also worked for the British Ministry of Information in Germany.

~ 1945, May 18 ~

EIRE AND HITLER.

Sir, – The correctness of the Taoiseach's action when the death of the head of the German State was reported has been vindicated by Commander A. MacDermott. But his letter does not cover the whole story. In 1943 the allies called upon the neutrals to deny asylum to Axis refugees, described for the occasion as war criminals. Portugal refused. The rest took it lying down, except Mr. de Valera. He replied that Eire reserved the right to give asylum when justice, charity, or the honour or interest of the nation required it. That is what all the neutrals ought to have said; and Miss Pamela Hinkson, as an Irishwoman, will, on second thoughts, be as proud of it as I am. The voice of the Irish gentleman and Spanish grandee was as welcome relief from the chorus of retaliatory rancour and self-righteousness then deafening us.

I have not always agreed with the Taoiseach's policy. Before the ink was dry on the treaty which established the Irish Free State I said that if England went to war she would have to reoccupy Ireland militarily, and fortify her ports. When this forecast came to the proof the Taoiseach nailed his colours to the top gallant, declaring that with his little army of 40,000 Irishmen he would fight any and every invader, even if England and the United States attacked him simultaneously from all quarters, which then seemed a possible result of his attitude and he got away with it triumphantly, saved, as Mr. Churchill has just pointed out, by the abhorred partition which gave the allies a foothold in Ireland, and by the folly of the Fuhrer in making for Moscow instead of for Galway.

Later on I hazarded the conjecture that Adolf Hitler would end in the Dublin Viceregal Lodge, like Louis Napoleon in Chislehurst and the

Kaiser in Doorn. If the report of the Fuhrer's death proves unfounded this is still a possibility.

It all sounds like an act from Victor Hugo's *Hernani* rather than a page of modern world-war history; but Eamon de Valera comes out of it as a champion of the Christian chivalry we are all pretending to admire. Let us recognize a noble heart even if we must sometimes question its worldly wisdom.

Faithfully,
G. BERNARD SHAW.

Just two weeks prior to this next letter the first atomic bombs had been dropped on Hiroshima and Nagasaki. Shaw's letter is interesting for what has so far proved to be a prophetic statement about the fate of atomic bombs (and by extension nuclear warfare in general) at a time when few would have risked so bold a forecast. Shaw's wife Charlotte was cremated in Golders Green in 1943. The prophecy of Prospero refers to Shakespeare's *The Tempest.*

~ *1945, August 20* ~

THE ATOMIC BOMB.

Sir, – Now that we, the human race, have begun monkeying with the atom, may I point out one possible consequence that would end all our difficulties?

For some years past our too few professional astronomers have been reinforced by a body of amateurs whose main activity is the watching and study of the variable stars. They have been excited several times by the sudden flaming up of what they call a new star, though it is in fact an old star, too small and cool to be visible, which has suddenly burst and blown up, leaving nothing but a cloud of star dust called a nebula. The heat energy liberated in the explosion is beyond human apprehension.

Apparently what has happened to these stars, and may happen to this earth of ours, is that the protons with their planetary electrons, and the heavier planetless neutrons of which their matter is composed, have combined, and produced a temperature at which the whole star has pulverized and evaporated, and its inhabitants, if any, have been cremated with an instantaneous thoroughness impossible at Golders Green.

What we have just succeeded in doing at enormous expense is making an ounce of uranium explode like the star. The process, no longer experimental, will certainly be cheapened; and at any moment heavier elements than uranium, as much more explosive than uranium as uranium than gunpowder, may be discovered.

Finally, like the sorcerer's apprentice, we may practise our magic without knowing how to stop it, thus fulfilling the prophecy of Prospero.

In view of our behaviour recently, I cannot pretend to deprecate such a possibility; but I think it is worth mentioning.

Faithfully,
G.- BERNARD SHAW.

Something very similar to the following suggestion of tax relief for investment in business was actually introduced in Britain in the 1980s, although no connection was made with Shaw's idea. Hugh Dalton (1887–1962) was Chancellor at this time and Sir John Anderson (1882–1958) was his predecessor.

~ *1945, October 29*

BUDGET AND SURTAX.

Sir, – It is generally agreed that until the industrial plant destroyed or perverted by the war is fully restored we should all reduce our consumption and increase our investments to the utmost point compatible with plain living and high thinking.

Yet I am taxed and surtaxed on the income I invest, while on the income I obtain from the sale of my investments I am not taxed at all. Would it not be more sensible to reverse this process, exempting me from taxation on all income received by me and at once invested in enterprises approved by the Government and taxing me instead on all income from the sale of my investments?

Neither Mr. Dalton nor Sir John Anderson and the rest of the financial critics seem to have considered this question, which to a mere playwright like myself appears glaringly obvious.

Faithfully,
G. BERNARD SHAW.
Ayot St. Lawrence, Welwyn, Herts.

Shaw had great sympathy for what we now refer to as alternative medicine. He occasionally recommended the services of Raphael Roche, an extremely unorthodox practitioner, to his circle of friends.

MR. RAPHAEL ROCHE

The death of Raphael Roche, perhaps the most noted and successful of the host of unregistered medical practitioners in London, on October 31 should not pass unrecorded. Born in 1857 of a well-known Jewish family of musicians, including Mendelssohn and Moscheles, he began as a professional pianist. As his father was a teacher of languages to royalty he got easily into practice as an organiser of the music at fashionable London dinner parties.

His prosperity as a musician had no charm for him. He had a craze for healing that proved irresistible. But he would not be called a healer. Nothing annoyed him more than to be credited with any personal gift in this direction; he pointed to his small stature, his unfashionable address in West Brompton, and his 6d. tie as proofs that his personality had nothing to do with his cures, which he attributed to his acquirement of an extraordinary knowledge of drugs. As he used the drugs only in infinitesimals he was classed as a homeopath; but this also he repudiated on two grounds: first, that the homeopaths labelled diseases and attached specific drugs to them as remedies, and second, because they held that infinitesimal and allopathic doses produced contrary effects. He maintained that all cases were different. When a patient named an ailment he replied that he knew nothing about labels and that the patient must simply describe the sensations of which he was complaining. He insisted that the drug in all doses attacked the vital forces in exactly the same way, but in the ensuing combat the infinitesimal dose was vanquished, whereas the allopathic dose was victorious and often fatal. He professed to use 1,300 drugs, and always added that most of them could be bought at the nearest oilshop. He refused to qualify because it would put him in the power of the General Medical Council. When it was objected that he could not sign a death certificate he replied that this did not concern him, as his patients did not die. When it was urged that without registration he could get only the patients that Harley Street had failed to cure, he said that this gave him all England to draw upon. His hostility to orthodox practice was implacable, and created an odd situation when his son Alexander Roche qualified as a surgeon and at once scored a brilliant success.

He disclaimed all knowledge of how or why his medicines produced the effects they did, declaring emphatically that the moment a practitioner began to theorize he went wrong. He was from first to last a complete empiric as a drug specialist. That he effected remarkable cures may be inferred from the fact that, although he charged 20 guineas for a diagnosis and two guineas a subsequent visit, he maintained a successful practice for

50 years. He was twice married, and claimed that he had kept his first wife alive for 15 years by his art.

G.B.S.

> With the atomic bomb being at the centre of attention of most news articles at this time, Shaw was able to use it to draw attention to his ideas on spelling reform. Mont Follick, an MP whose article prompted this letter, twice promoted a private members bill to introduce simplified spelling in schools.

~ 1945, December 27 ~

ORTHOGRAPHY OF THE BOMB.

SAVE AS YOU SPELL

Sir, – The atomic bomb has kept journalists for many days writing its name many hundreds of times.

The word 'bomb' has three simple sounds. The journalists have had to write it with four alphabetic signs. The extra sign is entirely senseless, and not only wastes the writer's time, but suggests an absurd mispronunciation of the word, exactly as if the word 'gun' were to be spelt 'gung'. This is a very mild specimen of that time we waste in writing: we have to write the very common word 'though,' which has two sounds, with six letters. However, as bomb is topical just now its attraction for your readers must excuse its understatement.

The saving of time by omitting the final b is usually taken to be 25 per cent.; and this is taken to be 25 per cent. per annum; but we forget the time factor, Einstein's fourth dimension. We ignore the number of cases we are dealing with, and, as the rate per cent. is exactly the same for one case out of two as for billions out of quadrillions, are landed in the wild absurdity of considering it of equal importance to the statesman. I can scribble the word 'bomb' barely legibly 18 times in one minute and 'bom' 24 times, saving 25 per cent. per minute by dropping the superfluous b. In the British Commonwealth, on which the sun never sets, and in the United States of North America, there are always millions of people continually writing, writing, writing without a moment's intermission. They must sleep, eat, move about, and play, but never all simultaneously: at every moment some of them are writing: say x millions. There are 690 millions of them; more than quarter the population of the globe. Those who are writing are losing time at the rate of $131{,}400 \times X$ per annum. I leave it to our statisticians to compute X. Even without it the result is staggering enough to justify a raging priority for a British alphabet, no matter what it costs. Including the X the figures are astronomical.

And yet our phoneticians have made nothing of this. They have wasted a century raising an empty laugh over our spelling of 'cough', 'laugh', 'enough', 'though', &c., &c., &c. They have never knocked into our heads the simple fact that a letter saved in spelling is saved not once but millions of times every day. The same is true of the digits of our arithmetical tables. France must owe its present desperate economic predicament largely to its having chosen as its ruler a certain intensely myopic president named Poincaré, who began counting in twopences the francs he had borrowed in tenpences. His brother, a mathematician, should have taught him better.

The matter has at last been brought before Parliament by Mr. Mont Follick, member for Loughborough: but he, too, puts the case only as it was put a hundred years ago by Alexander Ellis, fifty years ago by Henry Sweet, and repeated a thousand times since by generations of phoneticians without producing any political effect whatever. He offers to contribute generously to the endowment of a university chair of phonetics. But there is a very competent professor of phonetics at University College, though his chair is in urgent need of further endowment. Henry Sweet, our superphonetician, as such demanded the Oxford Chair of literature so furiously that he forced the recalcitrant university to make him at least a reader there. It was a slight to phonetics which he never forgave (he never forgave anything); but it planted the subject academically. Durham University helped. The thing is done. Even if Mr. Follick succeeds in establishing a chair at every university in the kingdom, the immense economy in writer's time, in paper, ink, and wear and tear of machinery which alone can move Cabinets to sit up and take notice, will remain unachieved.

I seem so far to be the only phonetician, economist, and man of letters who realizes how much money there is in a British alphabet with which every sound in our speech can be written with one graphic and easily written symbol without even crosses or dots. If the Phoenician alphabet were only turned upside down and enlarged by 17 letters from the Greek alphabet it would soon pay for the war.

I have appealed to every public department whose functions are in any way relevant to take this matter up; but, with the single exception of the scientific workers, they all agree politely that it is important, but not their job. They have other fish to fry. Mr. Winston Churchill recommended Basic English to the attention of the British Council; but everything that can be done for Basic English has already been done by Mr. Charles K. Ogden and the Orthological Institute (which Mr. Follick should endow); and it now needs only a phonetic alphabet to equip it for open competition as *lingua franca* in the modern world. If the British Council will not take this up, the Government should create a new council *ad hoc*.

It is useless to appeal to the education authorities. They dare not interfere with Dr. Johnson's monumental misspelling, which is now much more sacred than the creed and the catechism. I suggested to one eminent official educator that children in the elementary schools should be encouraged to spell phonetically as they speak, so that their mispronunciations should be detected and corrected. He replied that the barest hint of such a step would banish him from public life. I quite believe it. I do not propose to meddle with our classic texts, misspelt or rather unspelt as they are: what I desiderate as a professional writer is an alternative alphabet which will save the millions of hours of manual labour now wasted in a sort of devil worship of Dr. Johnson.

I again appeal to the Government as a Labour Government to appoint either directly or through the British Council or some cognate body a committee of economists and statisticians to provide a new British alphabet sufficiently phonetic to enable native speakers of English to be as intelligible to one another on paper as Somerset and Yorkshire, Dublin and Glasgow, are in conversation without writing more than one sign for each sound.

The following is a list of the cranks that must be disqualified from participation at all costs –

(1) Persons who want to force everybody to spell in the same way on the ground that their way is right and every other way wrong.

(2) Advocates of spelling reform, simplified spelling, and all attempts to make the Phoenician alphabet do the work of a British one. No Englishman will ever have himself set down as illiterate, ignorant, ridiculous, and even occasionally indecent by beginning his epistles with 'Deer Sur' and recalling the dying speech of *Bombastes Furioso* by writing the word 'bomb' in simplified spelling.

(3) Universal language and universal script merchants. The ears of a fool are in the ends of the earth; and for a universal script Bell's Visible Speech has been available for a century past. 690 $\frac{1}{2}$ million people are enough to begin with.

(4) Reporting shorthand experts, who can write 150 words a minute by code without spelling, and assume that the sole object of the new alphabet must be to enable everyone to do the same. Nobody except professional reporters want to do anything of the sort. All my works for 50 years past have been written in Isaac Pitman's phonography. I have to think out and find words and syntax for what I write; and as 1,250 words of such work in two hours or so is enough for a day, my speed, year in and year out, is about 12 words per minute. I am neither a reporter nor do I dictate; and a reporting code is as useless to me as a cyclotron. It takes years to acquire. Phonography without reporters' contractions can be acquired in six weeks.

(5) Perfectionists who will not consent to anything that cannot do everything. *Le mieux est l'ennemi du bien.*

(6) The old guard who keep on repeating the arguments of Alexander Ellis, and Isaac Pitman and ignoring the economic case which alone can move the Johnsonian mountain.

There are others, but no room for them all here. The phonetics involved are simple A.B.C.: what we need are economically and statistically minded men and women of vision, even if they are hopelessly bad spellers and cannot add up their own washing bills.

Faithfully,

G. BERNARD SHAW.

Replying here to a comment in the press about his play *Caesar and Cleopatra*, Shaw merely refined certain points he had made in his much earlier preface to the play.

~ *1945, December 31*

'CAESAR AND CLEOPATRA.'

Sir, – My play was written primarily for the sake of its subject. Shakespeare had created a Cleopatra so consummate that the part reduced the best actresses to absurdity. But he made a mess of Caesar under the influence of Plutarch, and made Brutus his hero. Goethe corrected this by declaring that the assassination of Caesar was the greatest crime in history, but did not write a play about him. The field was open for a play with Caesar as the hero, but not for the mature Cleopatra. She was available only as a child.

It happened just then that we had a classical actor of the first rank working with an actress of extraordinary witchery: Forbes Robertson and Mrs. Patrick Campbell. It was the moment for my play and I seized it accordingly. But it was not yet the moment for me as a classic author. Mrs. Campbell made fun of the play and lost an opportunity.

Meanwhile the success of my play *The Devil's Disciple* in New York had confirmed Richard Mansfield's position as the leading actor in America, and his claim as such to Caesar was clear. But neither his physique nor his very peculiar idiosyncrasy was suited to the part. He cried off, and a post-card from me inscribed 'Farewell, Pompey', ended our relation professionally, though not personally.

A playwright has to consider the talent at his disposal as well as the other limitations of the stage. He does not write a part for an Indian god with seven or eight arms and legs, however interesting it might be dramatically. Without Forbes Robertson at hand I might not have written Caesar and Cleopatra just then; that is all. It was a misfit for Mansfield.

Faithfully,

G. BERNARD SHAW.

Ayot St. Lawrence, Welwyn, Hertfordshire.

Shaw lived to see the introduction of the welfare state and the National Health Service by a Labour government. These two letters show his undiminished concern for a medical practice which, he believed, should be wholly in the interests of the public. The Labour government in power had a large majority and was committed to rebuilding the country in the aftermath of war along the lines of a social welfare state, something which Shaw had in broad principle long since been advocating. (See also letters of 19 January 1948: A Capital Levy; 19 and 30 August 1943: Rebuilding Babel; 1 May 1950: The Wages Paradox; and 31 August 1950: Story of British Communism.)

~ *1946, April 2* ~

MEDICAL PRACTICE.

Sir,-The monstrosity of the present system of private practice in medicine is that it gives the doctors a vested interest in disease which they are defending desperately. We, the victims, support them because we want doctors of our own friendly choice and not strangers planted on us by the State.

The solution is simple. In Sweden, the most civilized country in western Europe, the private doctor is paid an agreed fee for keeping the family well throughout the year. He gains nothing and has more to do when there is illness in the family. He loses nothing and has less work when all is well.

My Swedish acquaintances have found no difficulty in inducing English doctors to make this arrangement. Why not make it obligatory, and abolish payment by the job ruthlessly?

Faithfully,

G. BERNARD SHAW.

Ayot St. Lawrence, Welwyn, Hertfordshire.

Shaw was always concerned about the inherent danger of placing too much power in the hands of the General Medical Council and doctors generally. He himself had always tended to turn toward the more unorthodox healers, but his point was that with no one to call them to account and check on the efficacy of medical treatment, there was a potential danger. Lord Passfield was Sidney Webb prior to his elevation to the peerage.

~ *1946, July 30* ~

THE DOCTOR'S POWERS.

Sir, – Sixty years ago, when my friends Lord Passfield and the late Lord Olivier were resident clerks at the Colonial Office, they gave me a copy of a report on the Virgin Islands in the hope that it might find at least one reader. They might have made me a present of the islands for all the British public would have known or cared.

Two pieces of information stuck in my memory: first, there was only one pilot in the islands, and he was also Astronomer Royal; second, only one of the islands had a doctor on it, and it had the highest mortality. I shall not be at all surprised if in 1948, when the new Act comes into operation, the result may be a sharp rise in our mortality. It leaves the oldest and the youngest registered doctor or surgeon with powers which our monarchs have not possessed since 1649. They may poison us or mutilate us professionally with virtually complete immunity and considerable pecuniary gain. Believing them to be magically omniscient, we have made them legally omnipotent as well.

In the debates on the Bill the only consciousness of these privileges was shown in an amendment to extend them to healers with unascertained qualifications or none at all. The Government got so far as to see that it could not reasonably impose on its citizens a dictatorial life and death service without a guarantee that the training and instruction of the registered medical civil servants shall be abreast of modern biological science and free from private interests in sickness and mortality. The amendment was inevitably defeated; but it remains for the Government to provide the guarantee.

At present this guarantee is supposed to be control of the medical profession by a committee of the Privy Council called the General Medical Council. Its proper function is to protect patients against abuse of power by doctors. The first condition of its efficiency is that it shall be composed of laymen, all sorts of healers in private practice being excluded as clergymen are excluded from the House of Commons. It may on occasion make use of private doctors and biologists as experts and assessors; but they must have no control of the curriculum nor of the registration or de-registration of practitioners.

At present the G.M.C. consists of practising doctors exactly as if the Prison Commissioners were practising burglars and murderers. It is a

~ 258 ~

professional association of the worst type, a hundred years out of date scientifically. Its record is infamous. When, for instance, it was persecuting our most dexterous manipulative surgeon and cruelly beggaring his anaesthetist the Crown slapped its face by knighting him. I must not cumber your columns with notorious instances of its superstitions, its prolongation of expensive medical apprenticeship by disheartening rubbish which the student has to unlearn or forget at the bedside, its ignorance of the history of medical science, and its absurd amateur statistics dating from a time when uncontrolled *post hoc propter hoc* inferences, and percentages based on two or three cases, passed as mathematical certainties.

For many years I, as a citizen and a patient, have been calling for the laicization of the G.M.C. I actually succeeded in moving the Government to appoint one distinguished layman. He was immediately given another whole-time job which obliged him to resign.

I am too old to keep hammering in the case I stated in my preface to *The Doctor's Dilemma*. All I can do, with your permission, is to warn Mr. Bevan that if he does not make a clean sweep of the doctors from the G.M.C. and a thorough revision of the curriculum there will be trouble for him which may run to a breakdown of the Act.

Faithfully,
G. BERNARD SHAW.

The Nuremburg trials of Nazi war criminals were under way and ten top Nazis had been executed. On 15 October, six days before this letter appeared, Hermann Göring (1893–1946) had escaped by taking poison. Shaw was against the trials and executions on the grounds that they were uncivilised.

~ *1946, October 21* ~

NUREMBURG.

Sir, – Among the insanities that war always produces should be classed the general assumption that the suicide of Goring has been a defeat for the Nuremberg tribunal and the victorious Powers, and that the most rigorous inquiry must be made as to who connived at it by some relaxation of the manacling and spyhole inspection to which the prisoner was subjected. One would suppose that his evasion of the rope threatens us with a third world war.

This is not how it strikes me: and it is because I believe that my feeling is not altogether unrepresentative that I venture to ask you to make it known. Had the matter been in my hands I should have supplied all the condemned men with a liberal supply of morphia tablets and given them every opportunity of sparing us the disgusting job of hanging them.

Faithfully,
G.- BERNARD SHAW.

The following letter, written during the bitter-cold winter of 1947, when there arose something of a crisis over fuel stocks, bears some similarities to Shaw's earlier letter on power from the tides.

~ *1947, February 14*

POWER FROM THE TIDES.

Sir, – It is now many years since I arrived at the northern edge of Scotland and looked across the Pentland Firth to the Orkneys, estimating the sea journey at about half an hour. When I embarked on the hardy little steamboat with my car I found out what the Pentland tide rush meant. We were swirled away like corks in a millrace to John o' Groat's House and back again through Scapa Flow in three hours and a half; and I was told that it would be a fortnight before my car could be taken back to the mainland.

When I at last got back I explored the coast along to the west and found there several flumes like the Kyle of Tongue, ready-made by Nature, through which the tide rushed twice a day carrying thousands of tons of sheer power both ways.

But nobody was doing anything about it. When I asked the engineers why, they said they did not know how to capture more than a negligible percentage of water power. I told them they had better find out, as to my knowledge the Severn flow drove many cloth mills; and a flour mill owned by my father had its speedy upright and its heavy grindstones kept thundering away by a little stream compared to which the Kyle of Tongue was oceanic.

But they went on grubbing for power in coal mines; and now that the atomic bomb and Mr. Shinwell's prayers have wakened them up they are dreaming of nuclear energies, frightfully dangerous and enormously expensive. They do not seem to know that our tides, almost unique in the world, exist.

My suggestions usually take 30 years to attract any attention. By this time an engineering trip to Thurso and the Kyle of Tongue is a bit overdue.

The climate is delightful. Almost sub-tropical, thanks to the Gulf Stream. Not at all Scottish. Ask Sir Archibald Sinclair.

G. BERNARD SHAW.

> With the persistence of food-rationing in the aftermath of war, during the so-called 'austerity years', farming became of prime concern for the Labour government. These three letters form Shaw's contribution to a running correspondence in *The Times*, to which Shaw adds his ideas on Collective Farming. The Admirable Crichton (1560–82) was a legendary orator, linguist, debater and writer, but Shaw is probably alluding to the title character of his friend J.M. Barrie's 1902 play *The Admirable Crichton*, in which the butler Crichton is the only one with enough practical knowledge to save the day when his employer and his family are stranded on a desert island. Hodge was the servant of Piers Ploughman in the classic work of that name by William Langland. Parts of this letter are repeated almost verbatim in Shaw's letter of 1 October 1940.

~ 1947, March 29 ~

FARM MANAGEMENT

Sir, – I am not a farmer, but I have lived for 40 years in a village surrounded by farms (including poultry farms) through which many tenants have passed and some still survive. As a man of letters I may not steal a horse, but I may look over a hedge. My observation has convinced me that under our existing agricultural system only two classes of farmer can succeed in the business: the man who has a sensible wife and is in his shirt sleeves for 16 hours a day, and the landlord of a great estate who is wise enough to employ professional scientific advisers every season to dictate the farming operations. Gentlemen farmers with estates of moderate size and no advisers lose by agriculture and live on dividends and urban rents.

For the remedy we must look to Russia. There they began by turning out the landlords, leaving them to starve, and denying education to their children in the conviction that this was scientific Communism. The result, of which Tolstoy's daughter gave me a heartbreaking description, was agricultural ruin which would have wrecked the revolution had not Lenin promptly reversed his gears and restored Kulak proprietorship. But this, though it saved the situation for the moment, was no better than our system, and Stalin had within very few years to face the fact that individual proprietorship is incapable of dealing with land on national lines.

He found the solution in collective farming. It is obvious enough – I myself had urged it again and again – that to expect an average farmer to be not only a sower and reaper, but an agricultural chemist, an accountant, a meteorologist, a veterinary expert, a merchant and financier, and a resident housekeeper, all united in a single Admirable Crichton, is ridiculous; yet this is our practice; and in none of the letters addressed to you on the subject, nor in the public and Parliamentary discussions of it, do I find the slightest sign of any consciousness of it.

The collective farm employs not only the best brains in the country, but provides as well for Hodge a little holding all to himself, the equivalent of our three acres and a cow.

G. BERNARD SHAW.
4, Whitehall Court (130), S.W.1.

In the following answers to letters that had appeared on the subject of farming, Shaw shows a grasp of the dangers of erosion and the over-use of chemicals. Sir Horace Plunkett (1854–1932) was the Irish agriculturalist whose ideas greatly influenced the rise of the agricultural co-op movements. Sir John Russell was the former director of Rothamsted Experimental Station that carried out research into the history and development of agriculture.

~ 1947, April 11 ~

COLLECTIVE FARMING.

Sir, – I have a special respect and regard for Sir John Russell as a scientific authority on agriculture and as a friendly neighbour during his long and eminent reign at Rothamsted at the head of the Experimental Station there. What has he been able to say for our present Kulak proprietorship that is not common to all agricultural systems? He cites the risks of weather, disease, pests, and other sources of loss affecting farm production, willingness to accept whatever is left after paying all outgoings, and 'a ruthless Government' to put down any infringement of the law. Is our Kulak-cum-feudal system exempt from these difficulties and conditions? Is it free from weather vicissitudes? Is it not, like all civilized institutions, subject to a government which is not a government at all unless it is 'ruthlessly' determined to put down any infringement of the law? As to accepting what is left of the farm produce after paying all outgoings, Sir John answers for Russian collective farming as producing a surplus on which the operatives can live, whereas our system produces less than no surplus at all, leaving us dependent for our subsistence on imported food. I knew Horace Plunkett as well as anybody, and accompanied him in some of his attempts to persuade individual Irish farmers to exchange their uneconomic little holdings, eked out by harvesting in Great Britain, for solvent ones. His reward was having his house burnt, and exile to England. When such little experiments in cooperation as are possible under our system are successful their organisers waste their time in writing to me instead of to *The Times* or to Sir John Russell. On the scale of modern industry they come to nothing. The experiments on the significant scale are, negatively, the early Owenite attempts at Communist colonies (mostly in America). They relapse inevitably into capitalism or end as celibate monastic sects. Positively, Lenin's return to Kulakism failed to solve the Russian agricultural problem. It is collective agriculture and industry that is changing Asia from a tribal desert to a centre of civilization.

Sir John sums this up by declaring that 'full advisory and educational services are available to all farmers in Great Britain on at least as adequate a scale as under a collective system.' They are, provided we adopt modern collective farming. We have the necessary brains, if only we had organised collectivism. Nothing stands in the way except intellectual and political laziness and our dread and hatred of thinking as such. We have Ministers of everything except thinking, which is the only activity that can cope effectually with modern civilization.

Sir John has been a good friend to the handful of very untypical farmers who had the sense and knowledge to send their soils to Rothamsted for his analysis and advice, and he does well to stand up for them while they are still the best we can do in the way of scientific agriculture. The experimental kitchen gardeners, fruit growers, and petty farmers will not be liquidated by collective farming; but that they are capable of tackling agriculture nationally is too wild a delusion to impose on Sir John. He, like Ruskin, Sir Horace Plunkett, and myself, has had contacts enough with small-holders to know the limits of their capacity. Without subsidies they perish, in spite of such advice as the agricultural committees can give them. What we have plainly before us is Tennessee Valley reclamation, diversion and damming of rivers and digging of canals as in Russia, harnessing of tides, volcanoes, and atomic explosives, farming units of at least 20,000 acres regional and national operations utterly beyond the capitals and capacities of the holders of a few fields. Surely Sir John knows too much to imagine for a moment that they could be dreamt of by Hodge and his little landlords single-handed?

G. BERNARD SHAW.
4 Whitehall Court (130), S.W.1.

A parliamentary standing committee had been set up to consider a proposed new agricultural bill to deal with the power of landlords and the rights of tenants and the responsibilities of farmers generally. It had already sat for twenty-five days and had considered a wide range of options. In the meantime, Sir John Russell had written to deny any link between his research and collective farming.

COLLECTIVE FARMING

Sir, – Let me emphasise my entire innocence of any controversy with Sir John Russell. All his statements are true and important. The cooperative farming which he insists on is the beginning of collective farming. The individual skill and industry of the worker on the land is essential in any possible agricultural scheme.

Agriculture is a highly scientific art, demanding for its national development units of cultivation, masses of capital, and organization of labour far beyond the resources of small holders. Sir John does not question this. But, like Sir Horace Plunkett, he very sensibly concentrates on the cooperation that is within immediate reach. I agree as heartily as I did with Plunkett.

The difficulty is to induce the small man to cooperate. It is easy to convince him that he should hire his harvester instead of buying one all to himself; but if you ask him to dig an irrigation channel by which his neighbours will benefit as well as himself, he is apt to see them farther first. Experience in Ireland and in Italy has proved that this very individualist attitude has to be reckoned with, especially with the Kulak or able farmer. His income-tax accountancy, essential statistically, is, for scientific purposes, pure fiction. His agricultural chemistry goes no farther than an abuse of fertilizers and an utter indifference to erosion. National cooperation is possible for him only when it is nationally organised for him.

My purpose here is to avoid the usual doctrinaire assumption that I am contending that collective farming should at once supersede every other form of land cultivation, and that Sir John is contending that present cooperative farming can solve all the agricultural problems. That is not so. I agree with Stalin on collective farming and with Sir John on cooperative farming, just as I call myself a Communist (like William Morris) and am in practice perforce a Capitalist. Mr. Churchill must be aware that statesmanship that is not Communistic is not statesmanship. He would be extremely astonished if he were confronted in Whitehall with a turnpike, or at Westminster Bridge with a toll gate.

Of all politicians and reformers those whom I find the greatest nuisances are the boys of the Everything-or-Nothing-All-at-Once brigade.

G. BERNARD SHAW.

Herbert Read (1893–1968), later Sir Herbert, was a poet and the leading art critic of the 1930's. He had written to publicise the formation of a committee that had been set up to form an Institute for Contemporary Arts that would presumably co-ordinate artistic activities and initiate definite projects rather than leave recognition and exhibition of artists' work to chance. Sir Almroth Wright (1861–1947) was a bacteriologist; William Beal Carrell (1883–1944) was noted for his work with crippled children. Florence Nightingale (1820–1910) was a pioneer of modern nursing; Andrea del Sarto (ca. 1487–1531) was an Italian painter of the Florentine school, and Guilio Romano (ca. 1499–1546) was an Italian 'Mannerist' painter.

~ *1947, July 3* ~

CONTEMPORARY ARTS

Sir, – The letter from Mr. Herbert Read in your issue of June 26 raises a question the importance of which is not yet realized even by the few who are aware of its existence. That question is whether the extraordinary improvement shown by our vital statistics during the last hundred years has been produced by our bacteriologists or by our artists.

The late Sir Almroth Wright, our foremost bacteriologist, when I lectured at his request at St. Mary's Hospital, and dwelt on the part played by sanitation in the public health, put the matter in a nutshell by declaring his belief that the effect of sanitation is aesthetic.

Now the common belief is that the only scientific method of dealing with a disease is to find its characteristic microbe and kill it, Wright had already shown that you cannot exterminate microbes without poisoning patients. In the treatment of wounds in the 1914 /18 war he substituted salines for antiseptics; a carefully analysed peasant remedy but a very effective one. Meanwhile Carrell, in France, threw away antiseptic precautions with equally satisfactory results. Of all this nothing was said when Wright died the other day. His obituaries went back to his early anti typhoid inoculations, the success claimed for which had already been achieved in the Japanese war with Russia by providing clean drinking water for the troops and forbidding promiscuous drinking from rivers and ponds.

In short, a mass of evidence was and is accumulating to confirm Florence Nightingale's experienced view that disease is caused by dirt and squalor and ugliness. She never heard of microbes; but she saved the lives of thousands of soldiers.

My comment on Mr Herbert Read's letter is that a fresh epidemic of studio small talk about the beauty and cultural effect of the fine arts will cut no more ice than the lectures of Sir Joshua Reynolds and Ruskin's books. If this new Institute of Contemporary Arts is to have any effect it must take the field as a scientific body and engage in public hygiene and not in such shibboleths of my now remote boyhood as 'the morbidezza of Andrea del Sarto' and 'the marvellous foreshortenings of Giulio Romano.' It must face the hardest controversy with the dwindling but still numerous troops of pseudo-scientific Listerians and Jennerians who are dominating the National Health legislation of the Labour Government, and would, if they dared, impose 40 periodic pathogenic inoculations on our children and ourselves on the strength of statistics published a hundred years ago, when control experiments were unknown, and the results of two cases were described as percentages.

Are we to wait for some up-to-date parent to shoot an obsolete inoculation officer before we bring our hygiene science up to date?

G . BERNARD SHAW.

Here follows a brief sentence on the passing of Shaw's good friend Beatrice Webb, who had died in 1943. Beatrice (*née* Potter) was a keen social reformer who had written *The Cooperative Movement in Great Britain* which had become a classic. She had married Sidney Webb in 1892 and become an active Fabian and co-worker. Shaw's long friendship with the Webbs had begun in the 1890s.

~ 1947, September 15 ~

BEATRICE WEBB

She was a priceless friend and counsellor to me and to everyone else in our movement or out of it who had the privilege of personal contacts with her.

G.B.S.

Just a month after the above was written, Sidney Webb (Lord Passfield), Shaw's friend for over sixty years, also passed away. They had jointly built the Fabian Society (formed in 1884) into an influential socialist society. Sidney Webb became an MP in two labour governments and also helped to set up the London School of Economics. Together with Shaw they also set up the *New Statesman* magazine. Shaw once wrote that he considered Webb 'the ablest man in England.' 'Quite the cleverest thing I ever did in my life was to force my friendship on Webb, to extort his, and to keep it' (quoted in Laurence, *Collected Letters, 1874–1897*, p. 47). The remains of the Webbs were eventually interred in Westminster Abbey.

∾ *1947, October 16* ∾

LORD PASSFIELD.

Sir, – May I claim Westminster Abbey for the ashes of Sidney Webb, even should St. Paul's demand him as our greatest cockney?

G. BERNARD SHAW

∾ *1947, October 25* ∾

LORD PASSFIELD.

Sir,- It has been objected to the claim for Sidney Webb of a place in the Abbey that he himself directed that his ashes should lie beside those of his wife in a glade at Passfield Corner. The objection is not valid. No man, however eminent, can confer a national tribute on himself by directing or suggesting that he shall be buried in the Abbey. His direction must be within the ordinary competence of his executors.

But in Webb's case there is a point on which his wishes should be respected. The ashes of his wife are not in the Abbey; but they should be. Equally with himself, she was a great citizen, a great civilizer, and a great investigator. There can be no difficulty in transferring her ashes along with his from the Passfield glade to Westminster, where they will not only repair the oversight but commemorate an unparalleled partnership.

I am not urging this because the Webbs were my personal friends and colleagues. What are earthly honours to them now? It is to the Abbey that their ashes are due; for it owes its peculiar sanctity not to its stones but to the mighty dead it enshrines. The time has come to open its doors to great world-betterers and to famous women as widely as to kings and captains, novelists and actors.

The Dean and Chapter are fully as responsible as the Cabinet. The initiative belongs to either and both. In the present case a disagreement is hardly conceivable.

G. BERNARD SHAW.

4, Whitehall Court, S.W.1.

A certain reverend had written to oppose any attempt to place the remains of Sidney Webb in Westminster Abbey on the grounds that it was a place of Christian Worship.

~ *1947, October 30* ~

WESTMINSTER ABBEY.

Sir, – May I remind your reverend correspondent that the sanctity of the Abbey as a place of Christian worship is not peculiar to it? It is shared by every other parish church in the kingdom, whether 13 centuries old or 13 days.

Its peculiar sanctity is conferred on it solely by the valour of our illustrious dead commemorated there.

They were not all churchgoers.

G. BERNARD SHAW.

Ayot Saint Lawrence, Welwyn

Herts.

As has been noted in previous letters, Shaw had strong and somewhat controversial views on capital punishment, and in the following letter he differentiated between capital punishment and the death penalty. The quotation is from Dickens's *Bleak House*.

~ *1947, December 5* ~

CAPITAL PUNISHMENT.

Sir, – Had not the ambiguous and confusing terms capital punishment and death penalty better be dropped? The public right and power of civilized States to kill the unprofitable or incorrigibly mischievous in self defence can never be abrogated. Were it abolished verbally it would be restored or evaded by martial law in the next emergency. Punishment is a different matter. It should be got rid of altogether on the simple ground that two blacks do not make a white, to say nothing of the fact that criminals cannot help their nature and that retaliation is flatly unchristian. Why not call the subject judicial homicide, or, to avoid unpleasant associations, judicial liquidation? It would clear our minds, now so confused that discussion seems hopeless as to deterrence, there are insuperable objections to it. It must be cruel or it will not deter. It is effective only when detection is certain. This could be secured only by providing a police officer to watch every citizen, which is impossible. And it involves the very undesirable consequence that when a crime is committed it does not matter who is punished provided somebody is punished. The police are not impartial.

They must do everything in their power to obtain a conviction. As one of Dickens's characters put it, 'much better hang the wrong fellow than no fellow'.

Criminals should be liquidated humanely, not because they are wicked, but because they are mischievous or dangerous. A vitriol thrower should be got rid of as ruthlessly as a cobra or a mad dog. A man who lives by promising to marry women and deserting them as soon as he has spent all their money is a social weed to be uprooted no less than if he drowned them in their baths. Dangerous insanity, instead of exempting from liquidation, should be one of the strongest grounds for it.

To simply ostracize liquidation as something that is 'not done' is not humane when the alternative is long deterrent imprisonment, involving the waste of man and woman power by staffs of tormentors and maintenance of prisons. At present our death dreaders are quite satisfied when a murderer is reprieved. If they were really humane it would horrify them.

What is greatly needed is an institution to deal with people who, under tutelage, discipline, and support (like soldiers and 'good' prisoners) are well behaved and useful citizens, but when left to their own resources are presently in the dock or helpless on the street as beggars.
Criminals who can be reformed raise no problem and should be left out of the discussion. If they are reformable, reform them: that is all.

Most of what is being said in your columns at present has been said over and over again for thousands of years in vain. My excuse for cumbering your columns with more of it is that it may still be possible to clear our muddled heads about it.

Yours &c

G. BERNARD SHAW.

Shaw was a very experienced political agitator and a passionate advocate of socialism long before he established himself as a professional playwright, and his letters to *The Times* show that he never lost his interest in, and concern for, the very real problems arising from belief in the possibility of a Socialist society. Yet socialism, at least his very personal interpretation of what it essentially means – was the one subject where he was at the same time both astute and most liable to blunder (witness his remarks on Soviet Russia in the light of recent history), and in these letters he has given vent freely to his views across a wide spectrum of ideas and opinions. Nevertheless, his grasp of economics was second to none. Several of the following letters dealt with both aspects as the opportunities arose.

~ *1948, January 19* ~

A Capital Levy.

Scope of Existing Taxation.

More Arguments in Opposition.

Sir, – May I remind the Labour Party leaders and the Left Wing in general that a Capital Levy, like the General Strike and some other Left superstitions, is doomed to fail for the quite simple reason that there is no such available fund as capital in the Stock Exchange use of the term? On the Stock Exchange, the sole function of which is to organise and regulate the exchange of incomes for ready money, it is normally possible to sell incomes of, say, £5 a year for perhaps £100 cash down on the nail according to the security. But this possibility is inexorably limited by the previous savings in the hands of those who have enough to spare, and wish to exchange it for a permanent income, face to face with others who, having a permanent income, wish to exchange it for a lump sum which may amount to 20 or 30 times the income. On the Stock Exchange consequently a person with a permanent income of £X is said to be 'worth' £X plus £X multiplied by 20 or 40. This fiction has to come out of the current agricultural and industrial harvest or the harvests of previous years; for by no magic can the harvest of 1968 be reaped and consumed in 1948, though the right to it may be sold in 1948 to a customer willing and able to postpone consumption so far.

Such transactions are possible only in a market where there are buyers and sellers. Put an extinctive tax on savings, and the market becomes one in which there are all sellers and no buyers, bringing the price of future incomes to zero; for where there is nothing the King loses his rights. Lloyd George found that out when he let the Left Wing persuade him to tax land values instead of rents. Rents are income; and only income can yield anything to the Exchequer.

I once suggested that savings immediately invested in approved enterprises should be exempt from estate duties and capital taxation. No notice was taken; but already hard facts have obliged the Treasury to sell taxation reserve certificates free of tax on the interest, which comes to the same thing.

I shall be reminded that estate duties ('death duties') are now levied on capital. They are highly objectionable and cruel; but they are not a case in point because, as we do not all die every year, the money market can be strained to that extent without national bankruptcy. A Socialist Government cannot do everything. What it leaves to private enterprise should not be grudged and sabotaged, but encouraged and aided to reach the highest possible efficiency.

Let me add that I am not a Right Winger. I am so far to the left of the Left (having some knowledge of fundamental political economy) that I am if possible less understood on the Left Wing than on the Right.

G. BERNARD SHAW.
Ayot St. Lawrence, Welwyn, Herts.

Although the term 'Cold War' was not yet in common use, difficulties were arising amongst the victorious powers over the future of occupied Germany. Misunderstandings through differences in language and contention about words and political nomenclature were common-place. Ernest Bevin (1881–1951) was the Labour Foreign Secretary from 1945 to his death in 1951.

~ 1948, August 19 ~

REBUILDING BABEL.

Sir, – May I, as a man of letters, appeal to the Government to appoint a Select Committee to settle our political nomenclature? The matter is extremely urgent; for the present confusion of tongues is heading straight for a war which none of the Powers can afford and nobody desires.

Until we clear up our political nomenclature, our political oratory and journalist can come to nothing but the pot calling the kettle black without either of them knowing what they are talking about. We all lack a common and exact dictionary, and are at dangerous cross purposes over imaginary differences and delusive agreements that are only verbal. l myself find it impossible to make myself understood, though when I describe myself by this or that adjective I know precisely what I mean. As a citizen and one of the founders of British Fabian policy I am basically a Marxist Communist; but I cannot say so without being set down as an infantile advocate of catastrophic insurrection, with capitalism in full swing on Monday, revolution on Tuesday, and Socialism in full swing on Wednesday. I do not wish to see private enterprise made a felony: on the contrary, I look to private enterprise for experiment and invention in industry, art, and science as the proper sphere of individual talent and genius in the leisure which Socialism alone can gain for everybody. There is the alternative of State-aided enterprise, largely practised here in public utility schemes and friendly societies and the like. As these are so well spoken of here, why in the name of common sense should they under the Italian name of Fascist be denounced as murderous anti-Semitic tyrannies?

Communism and private enterprise are only methods of civilization, each with its proper sphere. Communism, like private enterprise, has to have many methods, one being distinguished as Socialism. Bread and milk could be communized like street-lighting and sewerage, and suburban travelling by rail or air made free of fares, because everybody needs them; but it would be silly to provide trombones, microscopes, cyclotrons, ounces of radium, atomic bombs, and hundred-inch astronomical telescopes for everybody. Everybody does not use them, nor could afford them if they did. They must be provided by various and mixed social methods. They cannot be sold to the public over the counter like postage stamps.

Compensation for confiscated private property is nonsense; but to nationalize or municipalize any acre or share of private property at the expense of its particular proprietor is manifestly unjust; he should be paid its market price at the expense of the whole body of proprietors, including himself, by taxation of income. But the process should be called adjustment, not compensation. The Liberal Party delayed temperance legislation for 20 years by mistaking this adjustment for compensation.

Pressingly important just now is the difference between diplomatic arrangements and human rights. Mr. Bevin, speaking colloquially, declared that we have a right to be in Berlin, and mean to stay there, following this by a flourish of implacable detestation of Communism. As this implied war on Russia, the four military commanders governing the four zones into which the military occupation of Berlin had been divided began skirmishing to the extent of every annoyance they could inflict on one another short of actual shooting. Yet if Mr. Bevin is not fundamentally a Communist he is not a civilized man.

Now, we have no divine right to be in Berlin, nor has the Soviet, the State Department in Washington, nor the French Republic. We are there as invaders and conquerors, as Mahomet and Joshua were in Palestine and William the Conqueror in England. There is nothing to prevent all or any of us from withdrawing from Berlin if such a rearrangement should seem expedient. Such withdrawals can be ranked as defeats only if they are fought for instead of negotiated.

There are several alternatives to play for. There is the unity of Germany. There is the division of Germany into two federations, western and eastern, with the western capital in Frankfurt and the eastern in Berlin. There is Germany disarmed or not. There is Germany disabled industrially by reparations, formerly called plunder, or not. England and America care not a snap of their fingers whether Germany is disarmed or not; France is mortally afraid of her anyhow; Russia is out for precautions. The three European Powers would have to borrow the cost of another war from the United States, and bilk their creditor as in 1914-18: a transaction which America could not afford.

I am stating the obvious facts, not advocating the various views one way or the other. I am insisting that negotiation is impossible unless the parties use the same words for the same things and understand what the words mean. The present Babel threatens a war that nobody wants, countered by a flood of Conscientious Objection from those who think that their rulers are backing the wrong horse, as we did in the American civil war until Karl Marx protested, in South Africa until Ibsen protested, and in Russia after 1917 until our Proletariat began setting up little imitation Soviets all over the place.

I repeat that I am not here advocating this or that policy, party, or personality. I am asking all the politicians, all the partisans, all the eminent personalities to support my demand for a Select Committee on political nomenclature, charged with the production of a political dictionary before the next General Election, on the common ground that logomachy is the very devil. Even liars need a language that will enable them to lie unambiguously. To the truthful the present impossibility of wording their messages without being misunderstood is an agony.

A dictionary will not cure our habit of mistaking association of ideas for logic, but it will do all that can be done at short notice to clear our heads.

Yours faithfully,
G. BERNARD SHAW.

In this reply Shaw continues his defence of Stalin and contrasts him with John of Leiden (*ca.* 1509–36) the Anabaptist who established himself as so-called king of New Zion in Munster, Germany. Sir Ernest Barker (1874–1960) was a renowned political scientist and author.

REBUILDING BABEL.

MR. SHAW'S REPLY.

'PERMEATION' AND THE U.S.S.R.

Sir, – Under the heading 'Rebuilding Babel' I did not intend to start several new hares to be hunted round the world for the next hundred years and never overtaken. I agree with Sir Ernest Barker, of whose authority and experience I stand in awe, that a universal language in which British supercargoes, Turkish porters, and Chinese coolies can converse intelligibly would be a convenience. I admit that glossary is more accurate etymologically than dictionary. I defer to a more leisurely occasion that question whether French should be the language of diplomacy.

But there is no time to go into these matters now. Any attempt to moot them would defeat my object and add to our habitual discoveries of How Not To Do It.

Let me give one leading example of what I am driving at. Sixty years ago the Fabian Society established the word 'permeation' in our political nomenclature at a time when to define revolutionary Socialism there was no verbal alternative to (a) instantaneous metamorphosis of Capitalism into Communism by class war, or (b) military world conquest . Through its disuse to-day it is being assumed that as Stalin holds that Marxism will finally become the standard policy of civilization his tactics must be those of Alexander and Napoleon. But in fact he, like Lenin, was converted by bitter experience of Military Communism in 1921 to the N.E.P. (New Economic Policy) which is in effect a Fabian policy beginning with Socialism in a single country and spreading to the rest of the world by permeation, example, and success.

In short, England has converted Russia, and does not know it. If Stalin could say unambiguously that he is a Permeatist in foreign affairs, and in domestic policy bound by a constitution as much as American and English statesmen are, the air would be clearer. He is a twentieth-century responsible Cabinet Minister and not a sixteenth-century Munster Anabaptist; and nothing is to be gained by treating him as one.

I repeat my point. The Berlin crisis is facing us with the alternatives of negotiation or war. Negotiation is impossible unless the parties know what their words mean and express it consistently in the same words. That is all.

Yours faithfully,
G. BERNARD SHAW.

A Mr Herbert Byard had raised a question as to the preferred use of harpsichord or piano to obtain the true sound of bass for the faithful reproduction of early music. In making the following comments Shaw once again demonstrated his great musical knowledge. Sir John Stainer (1840–1901) was organist at St Paul's, Government Inspector of Music and university examiner.

~ 1948 October 25 ~

BASSO CONTINUO.

MR. BERNARD SHAW ON BEETHOVEN.

Sir, – It would be a pity to let this correspondence drop without emphasizing the ever pressing need for remedying the weakness of the orchestral bass. I do not greatly care whether *recitativo secco* is accompanied by scrapes of the cello or by piano or harpsichord. I should rather like to hear the *tromba marina*; but I shall lose no sleep if I do not. Seventy years ago I filled up the figured basses in Stainer's textbook of harmony quite correctly. Any fool could, even were he deafer than Beethoven.

What has worried me through all these years is that I could never hear Beethoven's No. 3 Leonora Overture as he meant me to hear it: and I never shall until his florid basses can hold their own against the thunder of the full orchestra *fortissimo*. When his impetuous figuration rushes down from top to bottom of the orchestra, the first half of it rings out brilliantly and the rest is a senseless blare. When the bass should tremble and rattle, nothing is heard but a noisy growl and a thump.

I have inquired again and again how the bass could be made audible. Elgar thought it could be done by a group of Belgian trombones with five valves which enabled them to play the most florid passages *prestissimo*. But the ophicleide, a giant-keyed bugle with a peculiar tone which moved Berlioz to denounce it as a chromatic bullock, is as agile as five valves can make (and spoil) the trombone. My uncle played it, so I know.

The expense of extra players daunts many conductors: I know one who, when he pleaded to the municipality for third and fourth horns, was told to make the first and second play twice as loud. But nowadays, when Wagner in 'The Dusk of the Gods' and Strauss in 'Hero Life' require eight horns, and bass clarinets, English horns, hexelphones, and other luxuries undreamt of by Beethoven have to be available for every callow composer, the B.B.C. can afford to damn the expense.

The purists who want the original score and nothing but the score, not even the music, have no case. Elgar defended Mozart's rescoring of the

Messiah on the ground that Handel at the organ could improvise equivalent descants and harmonies (and who can believe that in 'The people that walked in darkness' he played only the written unisons and hollow octaves in the score?); but I am all for the replacement of Mozart's clarinet parts by the new Bach trumpet on which they are no longer unplayable. Trumpeters in Mozart's time were a bumptious lot; he hated them and loved the clarinet. Wagner had to rescore passages in the Ninth Symphony to bring out the parts that Beethoven evidently meant to be prominent, but which, great master of the orchestra as he was, he was too deaf to balance for himself. Schumann was no such master; nobody has yet complained of Mahler's rescoring of his symphonies. But it is the Beethoven basses above all that I want to hear; and we have not heard them yet.

Yours faithfully,
G. BERNARD SHAW.
Ayot St. Lawrence, Welwyn, Herts.

In the following letter, where Shaw is once again railing against heavy taxation that he claimed was misapplied to some sections of society, he also refers to 'Luddites', a term referring to those who are opposed to change or modernisation.

~ 1949, January 18 ~

THE AUTHOR'S GAMBLE.

BERNARD SHAW ON TAXATION.

Sir, – May I call attention to certain gambling industries that are neither understood nor distinguished from sport? I am myself engaged in such an industry, and dependent on it for my livelihood. All professional authors, playwrights, composers, painters, publishers, theatre managers, music sellers, and picture dealers live by gambling in values more desperately uncertain than the chances of any starter in a horse or dog race.

No turf book-maker would budget for such odds. But the few occasional winnings are so great, and the prestige and eminence they confer so ardently desired, that punters are never lacking. Let me illustrate. The late William Archer, foremost as a theatre critic, wrote several plays, but without success until he was an elderly man, meanwhile being too poor to travel otherwise than in the steerage, or, when he went to the theatre at his own expense, to sit elsewhere than in the pit. When at last an actor, the late George Arliss, made a huge box-office success of a play by Archer called *The Green Goddess*, Archer ended his days in comparative affluence. But he was taxed on this windfall at the same rate as if he had been equally affluent all his life.

I am an author and playwright of some note; but my first book had to await publication for 50 years during which it lay unproductive on my shelves. No publisher would gamble on its chances of being bought by the public in remunerative quantities; and I, having no capital, could not afford to plunge until I was too old to desire the publication of a juvenile effort. Meanwhile I had earned or acquired enough spare money to gamble on my own account after one English publisher and two American ones had been bankrupted at the game. The odds against me are still astronomical: of the fifty-odd plays I have written, a few have proved 'gold mines', a few more silver mines, the rest tin and pewter. A play called *Pygmalion* is performed again and again: others, in my mature *Third Manner*, are not performed at all. The film rights of the gold mines are worth in cash from £25,000 to £50,000: others hardly worth a hundred.

No human power can foresee whether a work of art will be commercially successful, nor ever will. A first-rate theatre production of a play costs at most a couple of thousand pounds. The filming of a first-rate film costs at least £50,000, sometimes more than half a million. If either 'flops', the loss may be a dead loss. I could cite instances in which box-office receipts, even with famous actors in the cast, have amounted to 16s. If this is not gambling, I do not know what gambling is.

Time was when some sense of this was shown by taxing authors not on their actual year's income but on its average for three years. It should have been 20 years; but still it was better than nothing. Unfortunately John Galsworthy, a great humanitarian author but no economist, was so moved by the plight of the authors who failed to average their expenditure, and left themselves destitute in the second two years, that he demanded the abolition of the average, which was thoughtlessly done, leaving my unhappy tribe where they were before it was instituted. Still, I can thank providence that I am not an inventor. My copyright costs me nothing, and lasts 50 years after my death. An inventor can at considerable expense obtain a patent for at most about half that period, and may die before his invention comes into lucrative use. He often, to pay for models and fees, has to sell his rights to Luddite firms which acquire them to suppress, not to exploit, them.

How we authors and inventors envy the gamblers on the turf and the Stock Exchange, the insurance companies, the pawnbrokers, the casino exploiters who, without running a tithe of our risks, are not taxed on their winnings! Why should we suffer what is virtually a tax on our capital which other gamblers incur only in the form of estate duties against which they can afford to insure? Why is property in our creations communized after less than two lifetimes, and that of simple distributors made perpetual? Why is property in turnips made eternal and absolute when property in ideas is temporary and conditional?

I do not know. WHY? is the fundamental question that nobody can answer. As well ask why the British people dread and hate intellect. But could not the Exchequer ease matters a little either by restoring and extending the old average, or making the privileged gamblers pay their fair share?

G. BERNARD SHAW.

> Much to Shaw's delight, a bill was being introduced in Parliament that related to the need for spelling reform. He had already made it known that he intended to leave a large part of his estate to support any system of spelling reform that equated with his own ideas. Sir Alan Herbert (1890–1968) was a popular author, playwright and humorist who was also an independent MP for Oxford. Sir Isaac Pitman (1813–97) was the inventor of the phonetic shorthand system. Mr Follick was an MP for Loughborough and a campaigner for spelling reform (see letter of 27 December 1945). Henry Sweet was the famous philologist mentioned earlier.

~ 1949 March 19 ~

WESTMINSTER PHONETICS

SPELLING REFORMS AS A TIME-SAVER.

Sir, – Mr. Follick and Mr. Pitman have been lucky enough to break virtually even with a pitiably recalcitrant Cabinet over spelling reform.

In the debate Sir Alan Herbert took the field as the representative of Oxford University, the university of Henry Sweet, greatest of British phoneticians. After debiting the stale tomfooleries customary when spelling reform is discussed by novices and amateurs he finally extinguished himself by pointing out that a sample of Mr. Follick's spelling saves only one letter from the conventional Johnsonese orthography. This was the champion howler of the debate. I invite Sir Alan to write down that one letter, and measure how long it takes him to get it on paper, and how much paper it covers: say a fraction of a second and of a square inch. 'Not worth saving' is his present *reductio ad absurdum*. But surely a University Member must be mathematician enough to go deeper. In the English-speaking world, on which the sun never sets, there are at every fraction of a moment millions of scribes, from bookkeepers to poets, writing that letter or some other single letter. If it is superfluous, thousands of acres of paper, months of time, and the labor of armies of men and women are being wasted on it. Dare Sir Alan now repeat that a difference of one letter does not matter?

The rest is poppycock. Simplified spelling, Rational spelling, Symphonic spelling are swept away, economically, because phonetic spelling with the present alphabet is impossible without the enormous expense of using two letters for one sound, and psychologically because without some new letters simplified spelling looks illiterate or childish. The notion that the value of the Bible and the plays of Shakespear lies in their spelling, and will vanish if it be changed, need not trouble anyone primitive enough to entertain it, seeing that both have survived the outrageous transmogrification of changing their spelling to Johnsonese. The fact that no two people have the same vowels any more than the same fingerprints does not matter provided they understand one another's speech. Oxford graduates, inhabitants of the Isle of Dogs, and most costermongers, will still call my native country Awlint, and speak, not as I do of sun and language but of san and laggij. No matter: we understand.

In short, what we immediately need is not an international language, nor an official persecution of Johnsonese, nor a New Spelling Bible or Old Spelling Shakespear, nor an alphabet of more than 40 letters, nor a revival of Bell's Visible Speech, nor any of the scores of phonetic fads that now confuse the issue and defeat reform, but a statistical enquiry into the waste of labor by Johnsonese spelling. The rest may be left to the Minister of Education, be he Labor, Conservative, Liberal, Communist, or what not. The roughest estimate will be irresistible; and until it is made public the promotion of Spelling Reform Bills by private members will be waste of time.

G. BERNARD SHAW.

Shaw was 93 and censorship was still arousing his indignation: when Parliament again debated changes in the law to strengthen censorship, Shaw produced more cogent arguments against it. Mrs Ormiston Chant (1870–1931) was an active campaigner for temperance and chastity.

THE CENSORSHIP OF PLAYS.

MR. SHAW'S REMEDY

Sir, – Political reforms are subject to considerations of duration and quantity, and should be submitted to expert statistical and mathematical examination before being proposed in Parliament or elsewhere. Otherwise precious Parliamentary time will be wasted in discussing impossible Utopian fancies.

What is a censor of plays? He is an official of infinite wisdom, infallible judgment, and encyclopedic erudition, for whom time does not exist. That is, a fiction that can never come to life. Nevertheless the Lord Chamberlain, the Pope, and others, have been appointed censors and are supposed to be functioning as such. They are not so functioning. They never read plays. If the Lord Chamberlain, or the Archbishop of Canterbury, or the Lord Chief Justice, or the Poet Laureate, or any other mortal creature were to attempt to read and judge all the plays written, have to discontinue every other activity, and, for 16 hours a day, do nothing but read plays. He would soon be so far in arrear that playwrights would have to wait years for a licence. Also he would go stark mad. But this is not what happens. The censor goes on with his ordinary work, engages a staff of clerks at schoolmasters' salaries to read and judge the pays. The clerks do not pretend to know better than Shelley, Tolstoy, Ibsen, Housman, or myself what the world needs to be taught. They simply make a list of controversial subjects that must not be mentioned, beginning with religion and sex, and disallow any reference to them. Thus in the United States, when my play Saint Joan was submitted to an unofficial Roman Catholic censorship, it came back to me blue-pencilled profusely. The word halo was forbidden as religious. Joan's remark that soldiers enjoy nursing babies was deleted because babies are sex. And so on.

Fifty years ago, when the white slave traffic was a burning question, plays demonstrating that it was an economic one: that, for instance, traffic flourished because brothels paid larger dividends than respectable hotels; that capable business women could make more money as procuresses than as ordinary commercial managers; and that young women could earn much more money in a single night as prostitutes than in a week as respectable workers even in the most dangerous trades. The play was suppressed by the Lord Chamberlain's censorship; and for lack of its instruction an Act was passed to flog male brothel keepers and prostitutes' bullies out of the country, leaving the procuresses in complete command of the situation. Incidentally I was branded as a pornographic author and suffered heavy loss and discredit in consequence. Even now managers advertise their performances of the play as 'banned for 30 years'.

The remedy is well known to every one interested except members of Parliament, who often provoke me to rank them as a select body of know-nothings. When I first fell foul of the censorship music-halls were places in which respectable people could not be seen. Songs with senselessly silly words made obscene by winks and gestures were the staple of the entertainment. The Empire promenade, campaigned against by Mrs. Ormiston Chant, was a prostitutes' parade, and the Argyll Rooms their market. All that has gone and is forgotten. In its place we have artistic variety theatres patronized by Royalty. How was this achieved? Simply by licensing the music-hall managers from year to year by the municipalities. All that is needed or possible now is the annual licensing of every theatre manager by the majorities on the county councils and city corporations, thereby transferring the care of the nation's morals from obscure underpaid clerks to the best available authorities with watch committees to warn them when managers are conducting their theatres as disorderly houses.

Meanwhile Parliament is reminiscing, not about Mrs. Ormiston Chant, but about Henry VIII and Walpole, and bandying worn-out phrases about Liberty and Licence. Where are our statisticians and mathematicians? Why are they silent?

G. BERNARD SHAW.

Ayot Saint Lawrence, Welwyn, Herts.

There had been a debate in *The Times* on how to categorise the many commonwealth citizens, guest workers and refugees who had been arriving in the country. Shaw joined the discussion by highlighting his own position – a little tongue in cheek, of course.

∽ *1949, April 26* ∽

'GUEST CITIZENS' OF BRITAIN.

MR. SHAW'S PROPOSAL.

Sir, – I am now a political nobody, subject to nameless penalties if I attend the meetings of the parish council of the village where I have resided and paid taxes for 40 years. Of my 93 years 70 have been spent in England. My many political activities have been occupied with English questions, never with specifically Irish ones. I am a Freeman of the City of London. But I am also an Irishman, honorary Freeman of the City of Dublin, and registered as a citizen of the former Irish Free State. Net result as aforesaid, I am a political nobody.

May I suggest that aliens residing permanently within the Commonwealth shall, under a new category of Guest Citizens, enjoy all the rights and privileges, and bear all the responsibilities, of natives? This could be extended to any international combination; but its application to Ireland (and perhaps India) is urgent.

G. BERNARD SHAW.

Ayot St. Lawrence, Welwyn, Herts,

Numerous articles and letters were appearing in the press at this time with regard to the possibility of atomic warfare. Shaw here offers another view.

~ 1949, December 24 ~

ATOMIC WELFARE

Sir, – Much of your space and time is being wasted on the subject of atomic warfare. The disuse of poison gas in the 1939–45 war, because it was as dangerous to its users as to their targets, makes it very unlikely that atomic bombs will be used again. If they are, they will promptly make an end of all our discussions by making an end of ourselves. Meanwhile, they are distracting attention from the far more vital and pressing subject of atomic welfare. Our present concern is with the threatened water shortage, which may leave us crying, like Coleridge's Ancient Mariner, 'Water, water, everywhere; and not a drop to drink.' This could be averted by distilling sea water, were it not that the cost of the necessary heat is greater than we can afford. Atom disintegration will some day make heat cheaper than can coal-burning. We shall carry in our pockets tiny pips, one of which, dropped into a cup of water, will instantly make it boil. Such pips would be worth incalculably more than atomic bombs, which nobody would dare to use. I have no hope of any notice being taken of these potentialities any more than my old urgings that our monster tides change the old lay to 'Power, power, everywhere; and voltage minus one.' Still, give me space for another cry in the wilderness, that my unquiet spirit, wandering among the ruins of empires, may have at least the mean and melancholy satisfaction of saying: 'I told you so.'

G. BERNARD SHAW

Ayot Saint Lawrence,

Welwyn, Hertfordshire

What to call the Thames Embankment which was at the time being cleared for the Festival of Britain event and for future development, was exercising quite a few minds, and Shaw joined in. Writer and politician Sir Alan Herbert was the MP for Oxford from 1935 to 1950.

∼ 1950, April 15 ∼

SOUTH BANK.

Sir, – South Bank is by far the best name for the new embankment: and it involves a very beneficial change of the present name The Thames Embankment, which is no longer distinctive, to North Bank. Whichever name be chosen will be written, printed, and typed every day, every letter costing a huge sum in human labor and every letter saved saving that sum. There are 16 letters in Thames Embankment, and nine in both South Bank and North Bank. In Southwark Side and Middlesex Side there are 13 letters each. South Bank and North Bank will thus effect a saving of manual labor that will soon run to millions of saved manpower.

The suggestions of Sir Alan Herbert and others of your correspondents ignore this enormous consideration, and should therefore be ignored as thoughtless flights of fancy.

G. BERNARD SHAW.

∼ 1950, April 20 ∼

SOUTH BANK.

Sir, May I ask Sir Alan Herbert for his estimate of the valuable working time he saves by spelling his Christian name with one 'l' instead of two? Yours, &c.,

G.- BERNARD SHAW.

Ayot Saint Lawrence, Welwyn, Herts.

At the grand age of 94, Shaw obviously perused *The Times* letters column with his customary vigour and did not let slip any chance to exercise his socialist views on economics.

THE WAGES PARADOX

Sir, – When I was a borough councillor 50 years ago the salary of a managing electrical engineer in the municipal service was £400. That of one in private employment was £2,000. Yet the public engineer was satisfied and his post much sought for, while his private equivalent was hard put to it to make both ends meet. What is the explanation of this paradox? Why did not all the municipal engineers renounce public service and exchange £400 a year for £2,000. The explanation is simple. The public servant was enormously more free and secure than the private one. He might live in Kentish Town and dress in pepper and salt with a soft hat. Nothing short of giving the chairman of the electrical committee a black eye, falling down dead drunk, or being convicted of travelling first class with a third-class ticket could shake his position. Nobody questioned his politics and religion (if any) nor his habits, provided they were up to a modest suburban standard of respectability. At a theatre he could sit in the pit or gallery and never in the stalls. He had neither to entertain nor dine out, and consequently was not obliged to belong to a West End club, nor keep a butler. He could live and die without ever possessing a dinner suit. His employers could not go bankrupt. In short, he had the utmost freedom any citizen who has to earn his own living can enjoy.

A privately employed engineer had to do all these things at all these risks willy nilly. If he were a son of a younger son of country rank and would rather die than have Bermondsey as his private address, or keep fewer than three servants (in my time a young married couple of country rank were expected to live in Mayfair and keep nine servants), he would be enslaved to the limit of human endurance, and often died leaving his widow very inadequately insured, if at all. It is true that the lowest incomes must be gradually raised to the basic income level by reducing the higher ones to it; but it would be the blindest mistake to do the same catastrophically with salaries and wages. The suburban professional is fairly comfortable and secure on a fifth of the salary which keeps the Mayfair one pulling the devil by the tail all the time. Pardon my depredation on your space. When the basic income and the miseries of the rich are in question, I cannot keep silent. It is very trying to be a Communist in a country where nobody knows what the word means and every political catchword means the opposite of what it says.

G. BERNARD SHAW.

An opinion on divorce law reform that was being discussed in Parliament and in the press led to a number of letters, stimulated by a letter that had several co-signatories, quoting prominent court cases. Mr Mills and Mr Tolstoy pointed to anomalies in the proposals and Shaw summed up with his usual clarity.

〜 *1950, July 14* 〜

DIVORCE LAW REFORM.

Sir, – There is a point not covered by the letters of Mr. Mills and Mr. Tolstoy, nor by the decision in Jeffreys v. Jeffreys. Mr. Mills shows that it is now easily possible for separated couples to petition successfully for divorce. Mr. Tolstoy deals with the right of separated spouses to apply for a divorce. In Jeffreys v. Jeffreys both spouses applied. The judicial decision was that the husband succeeded and the wife failed. Suppose, however, that neither party will petition, thereby condemning the respondent to celibacy or to an illicit union. Such cases are not uncommon. The motives for a refusal to sue are various. Sometimes the wife is determined that if the husband will not live with her he shall not marry her supplanter. Sometimes she hopes he will come back to her when he is tired of his new fancy. Sometimes she stands out for a greater alimony than he can afford. Sometimes, if he has a title which she covets, she charms him into marrying her and deserts him at the church door after the wedding, and spends the rest of her life as the lawful Lady So-and-So.

Sometimes appearance in a divorce court, however innocently, is regarded as an unbearable social disgrace. This is unreasonable; but it is so prevalent that commanding officers feel they will lose the respect of their men if their names appear in the Press reports of matrimonial cases. The situation is cruel in all cases, and vindictive or mercenary in some. Should not divorce of the separated be made both compulsory and secret so far as the names of the parties are concerned? In China the State has power to dissolve marriages on its own initiative even when the couple are living together and bringing up their children in perfect concord. When a thief marries a prostitute, and their children are being brought up to follow their parents' callings, should not the Home Office intervene and cancel the union? Why should a marriage licence be held more sacred than a driving licence?

G. BERNARD SHAW.
Ayot St. Lawrence, Welwyn, Herts.

〜 285 〜

The Bishop of Chichester had made a plea for positive steps to be taken to alleviate poverty and encourage development in Asia before the communists exploited the situation. One correspondent asked that he be more precise as to how this applied to Western Europe and a later letter suggested that one should perhaps make use of literature and drama to advertise the advantages of religion to combat the communist threat. The 'twopenny rope' is a reference to the custom in some temporary shelters for homeless people to stretch a rope across the room upon which the sleepers would support themselves. No beds were therefore necessary. Shaw hereby gives an analysis of 'communism' as practised in Britain.

~ *1950, August 31* ~

STORY OF BRITISH 'COMMUNISM.'

MR. SHAW ON THE NEED TO ADVERTISE.

Sir, – Now that our leading municipal statesman and one of our greatest Churchmen have declared their abhorrence of Communism, and thereby virtually declared implacable war on the U.S.S.R., may I be allowed to make a sane suggestion?

The Soviet State beats us all to nothing in the matter of advertisement, which is a more effective method of propaganda than war, however victorious, can ever be. For over 40 years the Kremlin has been flooding Europe with splendid illustrated magazines in all languages, boosting its extraordinary achievements in changing Asia deserts and Arctic icefields into flourishing cities and fertile pastures. Crowds of brightly dressed, well fed, happy looking workers are shown with their palatial dwellings and architecturally magnificent public buildings, in streets much handsomer than Bond Street or the Rue de la Paix. Veteran Stakhanovites manipulate their giant machines with an air of not having a care in the world. The pictures are in colour, in folio size, on sumptuous paper: veritable editions de luxe, produced regardless of expense and dirt cheap. The latest portrait of Stalin is so fine that I have torn it out and had it framed. Nobody who sees these publications will ever believe our tales' of a half-starved population dwelling in Belsen camps under the lash of a ruthless tyranny.

Meanwhile, what have we to show for our own Communism? Plenty. But we never show it. We are ashamed and apologetic, as we always are when circumstances force us to take a step forward and broaden the basis of Communism, on which all civilization, all Catholicism, and all enterprise, public or private, stand. I can remember when Seven Dials was a labyrinth of slums into which the police could venture only in couples, and homeless creatures slept on the twopenny rope. Now it is a radius of respectable thoroughfares. Had this been the work of the Soviets they would have blazed it and boasted of it all over Europe. Sixty years ago the wage of an English agricultural labourer was 13s. a week, or 18s. if he lived within reach of a big town. In Oxfordshire labourers with wives and children earned 8s. a week as 'boys.' I was thought mad because I said that what British agriculture needed was a 'moral minimum' wage of two guineas a week, then the wage of a skilled engineer. Labourers now demand £6 a week; and engineers are dissatisfied with double as much.

What are our young men told of these advances in the national welfare, all the work of British Communism? Nothing, except that Communism is a damnable heresy. What was it that saved Russia from ruin after 1917? Her adoption of British Communism, made constitutional and practicable by myself, Sidney Webb, and our fellow Fabians. Lenin, recognized as a great statesman by me and Mr. Churchill when every one else was denouncing him as a bloodthirsty bandit, began by kindly excusing me as 'a good man fallen among Fabians'.

When he had to govern and administer instead of theorizing, experience soon brought him to his senses; and he proclaimed his New Economic Policy, the first instalment of Russian Fabianism. It progressed by leaps and bounds: and Stalin came into the field with Socialism in a single country and collective farming, with a sop to the peasant's need for a little private property in the form of British Jesse Collings's prescription of three acres and a cow. Trotsky, the anti-Fabian hero of the civil war, was fired into political space, where he perished. Marxism, a British Museum export, was set on its feet by Fabianism, another British export. We are the spiritual fathers of modern successful Communism, protesting all the time in our ridiculous British way that we hold it in abhorrence, yet setting up despotic Soviets all over the land disguised as committees and commissions and boards. Our propaganda of plutocracy is incessant. We call it freedom and private enterprise. The future is to the countries that carry Communism farthest and advertise it most effectually. The Labour slogan used to be Educate, Agitate, Organise. As nobody disputes this nowadays, I propose the addition of Advertise, Advertise, Advertise.

G. BERNARD SHAW.
Ayot St. Lawrence,
Welwyn, Hertfordshire.

This is Shaw's final letter to *The Times*. He died on 3 November 1950, after having enriched the paper's columns with his views and comments for over half a century.

⟨∿⟩ *1950, September 8* ⟨∿⟩

British 'Communism'

To the Editor of The Times

Sir, – Literature and Drama are utterly useless for advertising. The arts concerned are photography, colour printing, and stage management.

G. BERNARD SHAW.
Ayot St. Lawrence.
Welwyn, Herts, Sept. 4.

APPENDIX A

This appendix contains additional material related to the letters collected in this volume that were also printed in *The Times*. Although originally written for publication elsewhere, one can see the willingness of *The Times* to publish any newsworthy items by Shaw. One can also detect the slight difference in style between letters written for *The Times* and those destined for other audiences.

The following letter, reprinted in *The Times*, is edited from an open letter to Dr. Max Nordau (1849–1923) first published in the *Jewish World* in answer to a charge of anti-Semitism brought against Shaw by Nordau in a recent article. Henry Irving had been knighted in 1895. The 'only Prime Minister of England who was a Jew' is Benjamin Disraeli (1804–81). The 'impossibly amiable Jew' is probably Riah in Dickens's *Our Mutual Friend*.

~ *1907, December 20* ~

MR. BERNARD SHAW AND THE JEWS

Sir – When, in introducing you to my readers, I mentioned that you are a Jew, I had no intention of appealing to anti-Semitic prejudice to discredit you. It never occurred to me that you could be otherwise than proud of being a Jew. In England we have no anti-Semites; we have Zionists. The way to create interest in a man here is to claim for him that he is a Jew. On every April 19 our Conservatives, our Imperialists, our Court party make a pilgrimage to the statue of the only Prime Minister of England who was a Jew, and heap its pedestal with primroses, his favourite flower. The foremost Peers in the House of Lords marry Jewesses, and are considered fortunate in their choice. My mention of your race can do you no harm in Germany, because everybody knows it. It will do you credit in England, because everybody will at once conclude that you are an able man, a rich man, a cultivated man, and a man of pedigree. The only Jew who is displaced in England is the Jew who is ashamed of his race. Such men are universally despised whether they are Jews or Gentiles. Our Jews are indeed rather apt to err in the opposite direction. They boast of their race as I boast of being an Irishman. Irving, our famous actor, made *The Merchant of Venice* a success by boldly making Shylock a sympathetic character in spite of Shakespeare's text. Dickens, who made a Jew the villain of one of his earlier novels, had to make amends by introducing an impossibly amiable Jew in a later work. During the Boer war it was much safer to be a Jew than a typical Englishman. All the typical Englishmen were on the side of the Boers. All the Jews were on the side of the British except the counter revolutionary Jews.

Yours Truly

G. BERNARD SHAW.

> Shaw had sent a letter to be read at a meeting of the executive committee of the Charles Dickens testimonial and *The Times* published the following extract.

∼ 1910, November 1 ∼

THE CHARLES DICKENS TESTIMONIAL.

Dickens should have a monument in London like Scott's in Edinburgh. He was a very great writer and a very great man. If the committee would ask the public to set up a really magnificent memorial, and set a limit to the provision for the family, I should be only too glad to have my name honoured by associating it with the project.

G.B.S.

> Although the following may not have been wholly drafted by Shaw, he was a willing signatory. Eden Phillpotts (1862–1960) was a prolific author and playwright.

∼ 1912, February 14 ∼

THE LORD CHAMBERLAIN AND MR.PHILLPOTTS'S PLAY.

A PROTEST FROM AUTHORS.

Sir, – A play by Mr. Eden Phillpotts, in rehearsal at the Kingsway Theatre, has been refused a licence by the Lord Chamberlain. It is held (apparently) to contain improper passages. These have been marked by the Lord Chamberlain, and if the author would consent to strike them out the play would be licensed after all, and no one outside the office (and Mr. Phillpotts himself) need ever know what sort of fellow he had tried to be. Thus, it seems, all would be well. Now we, his fellow-writers, have read this play, and find it to be the conscientious work of an artist doing his best in his own way, not necessarily our way, for no two writers who have anything to express can express it identically. Not thus would we have written, though many of us would have been proud to have written thus. To our mind, then, the play is worthy work, such as a stage of high aims should ever be ready to welcome, and we feel a warm indignation over the stigma cast by the Lord Chamberlain upon an author whom his fellow-writers, and the English-speaking world generally, have for many years held in admiration and esteem. Never in all these years of novel-writing has a word been breathed by any responsible paper or person against his fair fame, but the moment he has the ambition to write a play in the same spirit which inspired his novels he is at the mercy of an official who knows no better than to use him thus. We say only of the Lord Chamberlain that he knows no better. We do not doubt the kindliness of his intention when he offers to show us how to alter our work to his satisfaction: and we are sure he does not understand that these offers to save us from ourselves and hush the matter up are to authors the greatest insult of all.

If we do not come to the aid of this particular author who declines to accept this way out, he is helpless, and the public are left to presume that the Lord Chamberlain was right and that Mr. Phillpotts would be an unworthy author if he was allowed. Mr. Phillpotts is the victim to-day, but of course it may be any of us to-morrow. Many of us have never written plays, though most of us would like to do so: there is not perhaps another field so fine in the England of to-day for a man or woman of letters, but all the other literary fields are free; this one alone has a blind bull in it. We are not referring to the man but to his office. The dramatist's indeed is the only calling on British soil that is not free. We who sign this letter may be otherwise engaged, some of us may be old and done and no longer matter, our chance has gone by, but there are the men and women who are coming – are they, also, to be warned off? can we strike no blow for the young?

In this particular case there is, we find, one thing we can do. Miss Lillah McCarthy and Mr. Granville Barker being willing to make us a free gift of the production, we, his fellow-authors, can present Mr. Phillpotts's play at the theatre for the six afternoon performances that had been proposed. We can make no charge for admission, nor may the author be paid one penny for the work of half a year, but we can invite the public to come in free of charge and judge for themselves whether with this play, Mr. Phillpotts has forfeited their regard. All arrangements for this have now been completed, and the first performance will take place at the Kingsway Theatre on the 22nd of this month, at 2.30. Thus we can have the public verdict in this case

Yours faithfully,

WILLIAM ARCHER	W.H. HUDSON	J.M. BARRIE
HENRY JAMES	R.C. CARTON	JEROME K. JEROME
JOSEPH CONRAD	GEORGE MOORE	ARTHUR QUILLER-COUCH
GILBERT MURRAY	JOHN MASEFIELD	W.I. COURTNEY
ALFRED NOYES	ARTHUR CONAN DOYLE	ARTHUR WING PINERO

JOHN GALSWORTHY   ELIZABETH ROBINS   FREDERIC HARRISON
G. BERNARD SHAW   ALFRED SUTRO   ANTHONY HOPE HAWKINS
H.G. WELLS   I. ZANGWILL   MAURICE HEWLETT

The following letter was written to actress Esme Beringer, who presided over the 'Shakespearian Festival' organised by the Urban Club at the Connaught Rooms in London on Shakespeare's birthday, 23 April.

∽ *1913, April 24* ∽

SHAKESPEARE'S BIRTHDAY.

My dear Esme Beringer, – I wish you many happy returns of Shakespeare's birthday. But it is clear to me that when a man is not for an age but for all time he cannot decently be allowed to go on with his birthdays. There should be a statute of limitations. This thing has been going on now for over 550 years. How many more birthdays does he want?

G. BERNARD SHAW

First written on 4 February 1915, the following letter was – translated by Shaw's German translator Siegfried Trebitsch and published in several German and Austrian newspapers.

∽ *1915, April 22* ∽

LETTER TO A FRIEND IN VIENNA.

The notion that in a war with England, Ireland could be of any use to Germany was an illusion. My wife warned Princess — (*the excision of the name is presumably due to the German and not to the English censor*) very seriously not to attach any importance to the efforts of the anti-Home Rulers, who for party purposes tried to persuade the English voters that Ireland was on the verge of civil war. That was only bluff. Austria might perhaps have had a chance in Ireland, because Austria is Catholic, and understood how to rule in a popular way in Poland. The extreme Irish Nationalists, who said that they were on the side of any enemy of England, totally failed to shake the position of Redmond, the official Home Rule leader in Parliament. He offered England the support of the whole Irish Nationalist movement. And only the most complete misunderstanding of the political situation in Ireland could contemplate any other possibility, although the Irish dislike the English far more than they do the Germans.

G. BERNARD SHAW.

The following is a letter received by a Christian Barman, editor of *Architecture*, who communicated it in a report to *The Times* as part of a controversy concerning the reconstruction and widening of Waterloo Bridge. Barman had just had a letter of protest in this matter published in *The Times*, to which it was hoped Shaw would contribute his signature.

(See also Shaw's letter of 3 May – 1928.)

~ 1924, April 1 ~

Waterloo Bridge

I am unable to sign the above letter without an important qualification. The wave of enthusiasm for the inviolable beauty of Waterloo Bridge has not carried me away. The bridge is not only too narrow for the traffic now that the west side of the approach from the Strand can be set back, but for its own length and dignity. It will be enormously improved aesthetically by being widened- and the widening should be carried out without regard to the separate question of additional bridges.

The necessity for another first-rate bridge at Charing Cross is so obvious that anyone who does not see it must be dismissed as in a condition of hypnotic obsession with the existing Hungerford footbridge and its attached railway. Northumberland Avenue should stretch across the river as a matter of course, just as Oxford Street stretches across Regent Street; no argument on the subject is possible between sane people. Those who insist on complicating that simple necessity with impossible plans for reconstructing half the Abbey Division of Westminster are only holding up the traffic.

As to the railway, if it cannot or will not move to the other side of the Thames, it must be carried on top of the roadway as on Stephenson's great bridge at Newcastle. This would mean an engineering bridge as distinct from an architectural monument; but engineering bridges are offensive only when they are artistically pretentious, like the Tower Bridge. The existing railway bridge, in spite of all the nonsense written about it, does not really worry any artist, because it is perfectly neutral in point of fine art: it is a contrivance pure and simple, like a sweeping brush. Living within sight and earshot of it as I do, I object to it because it so often needs to be repaired by sledge hammers when I want to sleep, and because when the wind is unfavourable (to me) the trains startle me with their stage thunder; but its appearance has never cost me a tear or a sleepless night.

It must not be inferred from this confession that I have no artistic sensibility; all it means is that my conscience does not permit me to join in the inveterate hypocrisy which sets our art fanciers at cross purposes with public common sense. Far from feeling blighted and lacerated whenever I look at the bridge, I rather like the old thing. But it must go, and be replaced by a bridge for general traffic, whether the new bridge be a masterpiece of architecture or of engineering. The bridge is the thing; and it is the people who want the bridge, and not those who want to redecorate and redesign London, who must bring it about. They can employ an artist wholly ignorant and reckless of engineering to determine its appearance, or an engineer to construct it who knows he is not an artist and does not want to be considered one, or both; but I implore them not to attempt to combine the twain in one person. If they do, I shall have to move.

G. BERNARD SHAW.

The Times reprinted this letter from Shaw to the editor of the Berliner Tageblatt written after Arms and the Man had been produced in Berlin with cuts made by the producer at the request of a Bulgarian Minister, who complained that the play made fun of Bulgaria. The first performance of J.M. Synge's play The Playboy of the Western World in January 1907 led to one of the worst riots in theatre history.

~ 1924, October 9 ~

'ARMS AND THE MAN' IN BERLIN.

I greatly regret that my play *Arms and the Man* has wounded the susceptibilities of Bulgarian students in Berlin and Vienna. But I ask them to remember that it is the business of the writer of a comedy to wound the susceptibilities of his audience. The classical definition of his function is 'the chastening of morals by ridicule.' Athens has to submit to the mortification of its *amour propre* by Aristophanes, France by Moliere, Norway by Ibsen, Ireland by Synge, and both Ireland and England, to say nothing of the rest of the world, by me. This means that comedy is possible only in a highly civilized country; for in a comparatively barbarous one the people cannot bear to have their follies ridiculed, and will tolerate nothing but impossibly brave and virtuous native heroes overthrowing villainous opponents, preferably foreign ones. Civilized audiences enjoy being made to laugh at themselves, and recognize how salutary that exercise is for them. Civilized Bulgarians enjoy *Arms and the Man* as much as German audiences do, and indeed more, as they are more directly interested. Barbarous Bulgarians (Bulgaria, like other nations has it rustics and its barbarians) behave exactly as my own countrymen behaved when Synge's *Playboy of the Western World* was performed in Dublin: they are infuriated by what seems to them to be a personal insult. There are evidently many barbarians among the Bulgarian students in Berlin and Vienna (we are all a little barbarous at their age); but as the credit of their country's civilization is in their hands in Berlin, I appeal to them to sit and smile and applaud like the rest, even if they feel that they would like to shoot me, as many people do in England and America. They will notice that the brave and honourable Major Sergius Saranoff does not shoot Captain Bluntschli, though he sees well enough that the captain is laughing at his romanticism, and even forcing him to laugh at it himself. I want the Bulgarian students to laugh at it too.

I know, of course, that libraries and electric bells and houses with more than one floor and consequently with flights of stairs in them are no longer the novelties they were in 1885. And the days are gone by when it is possible to assassinate Stambuloff for the reason (among others) that he did not wash his hands often enough. But I can hardly believe that any Bulgarian student, however innocent, believes that the generation of Bulgarians who were just struggling out of centuries of Turkish oppression were able to enjoy all the refinements which are matters of course nowadays.

When the Bulgarian students, with my sincerely friendly assistance, have developed a sense of humour, there will be no more trouble.

Yours truly
G. BERNARD SHAW

THE LATE REV. P. H. WICKSTEED.

This is an obituary penned by Shaw in memory of the reverend Philip Wicksteed (1844–1927), scholar and political economist from whom Shaw (by his own admission) learnt most about economic theory. Stanley Jevons (1835–82) hurriedly produced his *Theory of Political Economy* when wealthy economist Fleeming Jenkins sent him a pamphlet on economics that threatened to upstage him.

Although his main bent was for literature in its highest aspect as moral philosophy, Philip Wicksteed was completely fascinated by the theory of value put forward by Stanley Jevons in his 'Theory of Political Economy' in 1870. From Adam Smith to Karl Marx the economists had been confused by the notion that labour is the source of value, trying to combine it with the obvious dependence of prices on supply and demand, and, by discriminating between use value and exchange value, to account for the hopeless discrepancy between prices and the utility of the objects valued. Jevons cleared up this muddle. He recognized that value can have no other source than utility, and substituted the conceptions of total utility and final utility for use value and exchange value, producing a theory that fitted every possible case without any of the old Ricardian confusion.

Wicksteed mastered this theory and made himself a missionary for its propagation and popularization. His first published utterance on the subject was a criticism of Marx. The Socialists felt bound to repel the attack, and put up as their champion myself, whose qualifications for the task, if I may quote my own later words, were 'a dexterous pen and a total ignorance of abstract economics'. The controversy ended in my education and conversion by my opponent, and the disappearance of the Marxian theory of value from the articles of faith of British Socialism. Consequently Wicksteed's later complete treatise on the Jevonian theory attracted no political notice and met with little resistance in academic circles, as Jevons' mathematical method and conclusion had by that time carried the day and become associated with the names of several other economists at home and abroad. Wicksteed's intention was to elucidate and popularize; but what he actually produced was a book for the sort of student who is rather attracted than repelled by subtlety and curiousness.

G.B.S.

Shaw's note of congratulation to the theatrical producer Sir Charles Cochran (1872–1951) found its way into *The Times*. *The Silver Tassie* was a play by Sean O'Casey (1880–1964) originally banned for its anti-war theme.

~~ 1929, November 26 ~~

THE SILVER TASSIE

My dear Cochran, – I really must congratulate you on *The Tassie* before it passes into the classical repertory. It is a magnificent play; and it was a magnificent gesture of yours to produce it. The highbrows should have produced it; you, the unpretentious showman, did, as you have done so many other noble and rash things on your Sundays. This, I think, will rank as the best of them. I hope you have not lost too much by it, especially as I am quite sure you have done your best in that direction by doing the thing as extravagantly as possible. That is the worst of operating on your colossal scale; you haven't time to economize; and you lose the habit of thinking it worth while.

No matter! A famous achievement. There is a new drama rising from unplumbed depths to sweep the nice little bourgeois efforts of myself and my contemporaries into the dustbin; and your name will live as that of the man who didn't run away. If only someone would build you a huge Woolworth Theatre (all seats 6d) to start with O'Casey and O'Neill, and no plays by men who had ever seen a £5 note before they were 30 or been inside a school after they were 13, you would be buried in Westminster Abbey. Bravo !

G. BERNARD SHAW.

The following is a summary of a letter originally published on 16 December 1929 in the Berlin newspaper *8-Uhr Abendblatt* following criticism of *The Apple Cart*, known in German translation as *The Emperor of America.*

~~ 1929, December 18 ~~

THE APPLE CART

The critics have afforded me quite a lot of amusement, especially those who have concluded that I have completely changed my political opinions. When and where in my whole life have I taught that all kings are of necessity idiots, and that nothing else is required for the creation of a perfect Government than to give the Parliamentary franchise to every Hans and Gretchen? If this is all, and republicanism and democracy in Germany mean nothing more, God help Germany.

The Apple Cart is a warning signal to all who continue to dream the old dreams and chew the end of the old speeches. Is present-day democracy anything more than an artificial effort to give the nation precisely what King Magnus in *The Apple Cart* calls 'the sensation of self-government', whereas in actual fact it is blown hither and thither as helplessly as it was driven into the trenches in 1911 and out of them in 1918? I will not speak of his union of England and America; that may be regarded at first sight as a joke. But it should not be forgotten that jokes – especially my jokes – have a way of coming back.

Yours truly
G. BERNARD SHAW.

The next two extracts are from letters which Shaw originally wrote to the St Albans Rural District Council about the refuse dump that was very close to where he lived.

~ 1931, June 5 ~

Wheathampstead Refuse Dump.

Sir, – In 1922–23 I had to call the attention of the district council to the nuisance caused in Ayot St. Lawrence and its neighbourhood by the Wheathampstead refuse dump. In 1927 the nuisance became acute again. It would seem that there is a four-year period in the nuisance, for I regret to say that now, in 1931, life here is again becoming unbearable. In March I was cruising in the Mediterranean, where I was very strongly reminded of the dump by the fumes of the island volcano of Stromboli, which is believed by the islanders to communicate directly with hell, and to be, in fact, one of the chimneys of that establishment. I was able to assure them that this could not be the case, as our Wheathampstead volcano, which has no crater, is a much greater nuisance.

I returned in May, and found the dump in full blast. This time, however, a much more dangerous nuisance than the smell, horrible as that is, has developed. To explain its gravity is beyond my literary powers; therefore I will ask the district council to allow me to quote the eighth Chapter of the Book of Exodus, verses 21 and 24. 'Behold I will send swarms of flies upon thee.'

What happens every four years is, evidently, that the covering-up is allowed to fall behind the dumping; and the uncovered refuse catches fire and Strombolizes us, while the unburnt stuff breeds billions of flies. That is what is happening now. The report of the medical officer leaves no doubt on the point.

We have now more unemployed than ever before, and are paying heavily for their support. The contractor has no possible excuse for not at once putting on extra men until his arrears of covering are cleared off. The district council's duty to make him do this, or to have it done at his expense, is equally clear.

G.B.S.

Apsley Cherry-Gerrard (1886–1959) described Sir Robert Falcon Scott's fatal Antarctic expedition in *The Worst Journey in the World* (1922), which was edited by Shaw.

~ 1931, July 2 ~

WHEATHAMPSTEAD REFUSE DUMP.

As the Cleansing Committee (of the Islington Borough Council) wishes me to be informed that my accuracy is doubted, may I assure its members that I do not for a moment question their statement that they visited the dump and were very well satisfied with the general arrangements carried out by their contractors. In this view they faithfully represent all the inhabitants of Islington, who, thanks to these arrangements, have got rid of their refuse by dumping it on the unfortunate inhabitants of Wheathampstead and its environs. I cannot imagine a more natural and obvious conclusion; and I hope the members of the Cleansing Committee had a delightful day on the dump and that the satisfactory arrangements included adequate refreshments on the spot.

But they are quite mistaken in supposing that my letter was written in the interests of merry Islington. Why should it have been? I do not live in that famous borough. Its smells and its flies do not torment me. The perfect satisfaction of its cleansing superintendent and medical officer is no satisfaction to me. The Wheathampstead dump is 20 miles north of Islington; and at that distance its fragrance is lost.

It is about a mile south of my house; and when the wind is in that quarter I am not reminded of Shakespeare's 'Sweet south that breathes upon a bank of violets'; I am reminded of Stromboli, of Etna, of Vesuvius, and of hell. My famous neighbour, Mr. Cherry-Gerrard, sole survivor of 'the worst journey in the world,' after the horrors of which one would suppose that no discomfort possible in these latitudes could seem to him worth mentioning, has written a letter implying plainly that there is little to choose between mid-winter at the South Pole and mid-summer at Lamer Park when the dump is in eruption. The inhabitants of Wheathampstead are seriously contemplating emigration en masse to Islington, where they can throw themselves on the rates until they have settled down as regular contributors to the old dump. Our medical officer of health, far from being

'perfectly satisfied that no nuisance is being caused)' is perfectly satisfied
of the contrary.

G.B.S.

On 11 May 1932, *The Times* quoted an extract from a tribute Shaw
wrote when a tablet was unveiled at Arnold Bennett's birthplace at
Darnley. Shaw stressed that Bennett was essentially a man of the
Potteries, that its people appeared in the pages of Bennett's stories, and
that in fact this was the first time in literature that much attention had
been paid to this class. In this he contrasted Bennett with other literary
figures such as Scott, Dickens and Trollope, but especially with
Dickens, to whom according to Shaw the Potteries 'meant nothing but
a smoky inferno, in which there was no sense of beauty, no romance,
nor any of the nobler elements in human character. Arnold Bennett
changed all that.'

~ 1932, May 11 ~

ARNOLD BENNETT.

Read Dickens's '*Hard Times*' and then read '*The Old Wives' Tale*,' and you
will see the difference he made. That difference is not to be despised, and
in insisting on it by erecting a monument to the man who made it you
and your friends have done good service, not only to the five towns, but to
the outer barbarians, who are all the better for having become acquainted
through his novels with a strain of the national stock that was known to be
useful and suspected of being sordid, but which is now revealed as being
as attractively endowed in its sense of beauty and capacity for culture as
any in England.

G.B.S.

The following was not a letter to *The Times* but an obituary tribute to
Rudyard Kipling. By the 1930s, in contrast to earlier years when items
by Shaw might be suppressed at the whim of the Editor, virtually
anything that Shaw wrote was printed.

TRIBUTE TO RUDYARD KIPLING.

Mr. Rudyard Kipling was a great story-teller who never grew up. He achieved greatness in his youth. He reached the climax of his career before he was grown up. He was a great figure in what may be called Imperialistic literature, and some of its reactions against that imperialism were extremely interesting. In some ways owing to his early education he began by being behind *The Times,* and he had very odd ways when he came face to face with the realities of war in South Africa and in other places. He did not attain the greatness of H. G. Wells. I don't think the reading of Kipling has ever changed anybody's life very much, but you may well say the same of Sir Walter Scott and others. Within his own limitations Kipling was really great.

G.B.S.

The following was written in shorthand and initially read at a meeting of the Association of Teachers of Speech and Drama at University College, London. Though not intended for *The Times* it was acquired by a correspondent and published by them.

SLOVENLY SPEECH ON THE STAGE

There are dramatic schools all over the place, and yet to-day all the professions speak English better for public purposes than the dramatic profession. About 50 years ago the clergy murdered the Liturgy so scandalously that I protested publicly against a candidate for holy orders being ordained until he knew the difference between a collect and a gargle. The only technically perfect speaker in those days was Queen Victoria whom some of our worst stage gabblers would probably describe as a ham elocutionist.

To-day the Church gives us some of our best broadcasters, headed by the two Archbishops, the vicar of Tewkesbury (the Rev. E. P. Gough), and the Rev. Pat McCormick. The political tub-thumpers, too, know their job; they may talk nothing but nonsense, but they at least articulate it clearly. And the telephone girls are wonderful: they speak so clearly that they are not only efficient but peremptory and terrifying.

If you want to hear slovenly speech that conveys nothing to the unfortunate audience and wastes the labour of the author, the theatre alone can provide you with it. . . . For my own work I prefer actors who have been trained as musicians. An opera sung by people with no ear for music is not more horrible than a play by Shakespear or Shaw spoken by people with no sense of verbal music or no trained skill in executing it. Yet such people offer you Shakespear, though they would never dream of offering you Handel or Elgar.

G.B.S.

Next is a Times column that throws light upon Shaw's early career as a playwright and that also contains several interesting quotations. As mentioned earlier, J.B. Vedrenne, manager of the Royal Court Theatre, together with playwright Harley Granville Barker, produced a series of Shaw's plays between 1904 and 1907.

～ 1938, February 15 ～

MR. SHAW AND HIS PATRONS.

'PICKING POCKETS'.

Mr. Bernard Shaw, in a foreword to a booklet published to-day to commemorate the silver jubilee of the Birmingham Repertory Theatre, says that he has been considerably indebted to patronage for his livelihood.

'The first performance of a play of mine was,' he says, 'a desperate venture, in which the late Jack Green spent all his savings. My first regular West-end production was financed by the late Annie Elizabeth Fredericka Horniman, a lady of property, who produced my *Arms and the Man* at the Old Avenue Theatre in 1894 and put me on the map as a playwright by drastically emptying her own pocket. Yet for 10 years all the money that came to me from the theatre came from Germany and America.

'When the famous Vedrenne and Granville-Barker management started in 1904 at the Court Theatre, with a guarantee from five patrons of £50 or so, I was able to contribute 10 unacted plays to its repertory. By hard swimming the partners kept their heads above water for some years: but in the end Granville-Barker and I had to act as our own patrons by paying the debts of the firm and winding it up in a condition of fictitious solvency. A later venture was started under a guarantee of £1,000, in which Lord Howard de Walden and myself went fifty-fifty. *Androcles and the Lion* was produced later on by Granville-Barker entirely at Lord Howard's expense.'

After a description of War-time theatre audiences and the uneconomic rents and salaries which crippled serous productions, Mr. Shaw declares that at the end of this period he was left in worse need of a patron than when he was given his first lift into the West End of London 25 years before.

'I discovered one in quite an unexpected quarter,' he continues, in relating his first meeting with Sir Barry Jackson, who challenged the playwright's attention by offering to stage his unacted five-part play, *Back to Methusaleh*. 'I began to scent a patron,' Mr. Shaw says, but tells how he warned Sir Barry Jackson against the penury he would probably incur by the experiment. Sir Barry Jackson refused to take the warning, and produced Mr. Shaw's plays both at Birmingham and at the Malvern Festivals – 'a feat impossible without the heavy expenditure and energetic management for artistic end which he has lavished.'

'I got on under his patronage very comfortably for years,' adds Mr. Shaw, but he says, in conclusion that, 'although the patronage system has brought me some valuable friendships, I have never liked living by picking the pockets of my friends.'

G.B.S.

The following postcard was written to a Mr Vernon Bartlett, who stood as an independent candidate at a by-election in Bridgewater. *The Times* saw fit to publish it.

~ 1938, November 17 ~

BRIDGEWATER BY-ELECTION.

Once as an election orator I could fill the streets with the overflow of people curious to see the animal, not one of whom had the smallest intention of voting for the subsequently defeated candidate. I cannot stage a come-back at 82. Besides as you are still very useful the last thing I desire is your extinction by a Parliamentary seat. I have seen too many good men go under in that way. My word of encouragement is 'Don't.'

G.B.S.

This was originally written to a Mr F.B. Seal, chairman of the Rabindranath Tagore Society and later published in *The Times*. This spelling of Ghandhi was considered correct at the time.

GHANDHI.

You may quote me as declaring that the imprisonment of Ghandhi is the stupidest blunder the Government has let itself be landed in by its right wing of incurable diehards. It and the unpardonable flogging business associated with it has wiped out our moral case against Hitler. The King should release Ghandhi unconditionally as an act of grace unconnected with policy, and apologize to him for the mental defectiveness of his Cabinet. That would do what is possible to save the Indian situation.

G. BERNARD SHAW.

This note, reprinted in *The Times*, was first sent to the American chapter of the Shaw Society which was founded in England by Dr. F.E. Loewenstein in 1941.

∼ 1950, July 2 ∼

SHAW'S 94TH BIRTHDAY.

The list of illustrious names on the foundation committee of the American Shaw Society is so staggering that I am at a loss how to comment on it or exult in it without a gross self-complacency foreign to my very diffident nature. Now that I am so old that to me the Bernard Shaw of 50 years ago is as dead as the infant of 90 years ago, I can contemplate any estimate of him quite disinterestedly, except for some wonder at the things he could do and I can no more do now than I can skate or sing or walk about.

G.B.S.

APPENDIX B

Previously Published Letters to *The Times*

Agitations = Agitations: *Letters to the Press 1875–1950*, ed. Dan H. Laurence and James Rambeau (New York: Frederick Ungar, 1985).

Art = *Bernard Shaw on the London Art Scene 1885–1950*, ed. Stanley Weintraub (University Park: Pennsylvania State University Press, 1989).

Collected = *The Works of Bernard Shaw: Collected Edition* (London: Constable & Co., 1930–38).

Drama = *The Drama Observed*, ed. Bernard F. Dukore (University Park: Pennsylvania State University Press, 1993), 4 volumes.

Ireland = *The Matter with Ireland*, ed. Dan H. Laurence and David H. Greene (New York: Hill and Wang, 1962).

Language = *George Bernard Shaw on Language*, ed. Abraham Tauber (New York: Philosophical Library, 1963).

Music = *How to Become a Musical Critic*, ed. Dan H. Laurence (London: Rupert Hart Davis, 1961).

Plays = *Collected Plays with Their Prefaces*, ed. Dan H. Laurence (London: Max Reinhardt, The Bodley Head, 1970-74), 7 volumes.

Theatre = *Shaw on Theatre*, ed. E.J. West (New York: Hill and Wang, 1958).

1898, SEPTEMBER 27 – MURDER AND THE HOME SECRETARY.

Collected, v. 22

1902, AUGUST 19 – THE IMPERIAL VACCINATION LEAGUE.
Collected, v. 22

1904, MARCH 11 – THE FAILURE . . . FOR THE L.C.C.
Collected, v. 22

1904, MAY 31 – ROYAL OPERA
Music

1904, JUNE 14 – CORPORAL PUNISHMENT IN THE NAVY.
Collected, v. 22

1904, SEPTEMBER 2 – FLOGGING IN THE NAVY.
Agitations; Collected, v. 22
1904, SEPTEMBER 14 – FLOGGING IN THE NAVY.

Collected, v. 22

1905, NOVEMBER 14 – THE QUEEN'S COUP D'ETAT.
Agitations

1906, SEPTEMBER 25 – THE SIMPLIFIED SPELLING PROPOSALS.
Language

1906, OCTOBER 31 – WOMAN SUFFRAGE.
Agitations

1907 – OCTOBER 5 – KULIN POLYGAMY.
Agitations

1909, MAY 10 – MAY 10 – THE NATIONAL . . . NEW REPERTOTY THEATRE.
Drama, v. 3

1909, JUNE 26 – THE CENSOR'S
REVENGE.
Plays, v. 3

1909, JUNE 30 – THE CENSORSHIP OF
PLAYS.
Plays, v. 3

1909, JULY 14 – MR. BERNARD
SHAW'S PLAY AND THE CENSOR.
Plays, v. 3

1909, JULY 16 – MR. BERNARD
SHAW'S PLAY AND THE CENSOR.
Plays, v. 3

1909, OCTOBER 11 – 'BLANCHO
POSNET' AND THE CENSORSHIP.
Plays, v. 3

1910, MAY 12 – GENERAL MOURNING:
AN OVERLOOKED HARDSHIP.
Agitations

1911, NOVEMBER 15 – 'THE DRAMA OF
DISCUSSION'.
Agitations

1913, JUNE 19 – MRS. PANKHURST'S
TREATMENT
Agitations

1913, NOVEMBER 8 – MR. SHAW ON
MORALS
Agitations

1913, NOVEMBER 15 – PUBLIC
MORALS.
Agitations

1914, DECEMBER 16 – PROPAGADA
IN ITALY.
Collected, v. 22

1921, MARCH 17 – SHAKESPEARE: A
STANDARD TEXT
Theatre

1921, MARCH 31 – CHALLENGE.
Theatre

1921, APRIL 14 – SHAKESPEARE: A
STANDARD TEXT
Theatre

1923 JULY 31 – HOLIDAYS IN IRELAND.
Ireland

1924, FEBRUARY 25 – 'BACK TO
METHUSELAH'.
Plays, v. 5

1924, FEBRUARY 28 – 'BACK TO
METHUSELAH'.
Plays, v. 5

1925, MAY 12 – THE MARCH OF
SMALLPOX.
Collected, v. 22

1925, JUNE 17 – MR. EPSTEIN'S PANEL.
Art

1925, OCTOBER 23 – GENERAL
MEDICAL COUNCIL.
Collected, v. 22

1925, NOVEMBER 12 – DOCTORS AND
THE PUBLIC.
Collected, v. 22

1928, MAY 3 – THAMES BRIDGES
Agitations, Art

1932, DECEMBER 20 – SIR EDWARD
ELGAR'S NEW SYMPHONY.
Music

1934, JANUARY 2 – B.B.C.
PRONUNCIATION.
Agitations

1934, JANUARY 25 – B.B.C. ENGLISH.
Agitations

1938, JULY 7 – NEWS AT TEN.
Agitations

1939, SEPTEMBER 5 – THEATRES IN
TIME OF WAR.
Agitations

INDEX

income distribution and, 85–8, 200–1
publishing and, 71, 77
taxation and, 116–17, 120–1, 134, 234, 239
wages and, 129–30
see also Communism; Fabianism; Labour Party, the
Society of Authors, 61, 62, 64, 66, 72, 74–6, 78
Society of West End Theatre Managers, 100, 101
South Bank, the (London), 283
Southwark, Bishop of, 107, 110–11
Soviet Union, 181, 199–204, 218, 270, 286, 287
  agriculture, ix, 203, 204, 223–6, 240–1, 261–3, 287
  Nazi-Soviet pact, 219
  post Second World War Berlin, 272–3
  revolution (1917), 200, 201, 218, 223, 240, 273, 287
Second World War, 220, 234
  see also Stalin, Joseph
Spain, 54, 56, 211
spelling, 56–60, 226–9, 243, 253–6, 278–9, 283
  and the alphabet, 60, 227, 228, 237, 239, 244, 254, 279
Spelling Reform Association, British, 57
Spontini, Gaspare, 232–3
Squire, Sir John, 236–7
St. Marylebone, Borough of, 28–30
St. Pancras, Borough of, xii, 4, 20–1, 30, 32
  electric lighting, 28, 29
  smallpox epidemics, 4, 5, 6, 7, 9
Stalin, Joseph, ix, 200, 219, 220, 247, 273–4, 286
  agriculture and, 224, 225, 262, 287
statistics, science of, 4, 7, 8, 10, 23
Steer, Philip Wilson, 221, 222
Stock Exchange, 270, 277
Stoker, Bram, 74, 75
Strauss, Richard, 167, 275
suffragettes, ix, 68–70, 138–41
  forcible feeding of, 112–13, 137, 140
  and super-tax, 114, 115, 119–20
  Women's Suffrage Society, 98, 99, 100
Sullivan, Barry, 163, 166
super-tax, 114, 115, 116–21, 134, 150–4
sweated labour, 43–4
Sweden, 257
Sweet, Henry, 56, 57, 60, 209–10, 229, 254, 278
Sykes, Dr. J. J. (St. Pancras medical officer), 6, 19, 20–1

Syndicalism, 128, 130, 201
Synge, J. M., 294, 295
syphilis, 14, 17, 18, 19, 182

T

Talks with Mr. Gladstone (Lionel Tollemache), 7, 8
Tate Gallery (London), 214, 222
taxation, ix, 272, 276
  on capital, 151–7, 218, 234, 270–1, 277–8
  on investments, 251, 270–1
  local, 217–18
  purchase tax, 234–5
  super-tax, 114, 115, 116–21, 134, 150–4
  war time, 234, 239–40, 241–3
Terriss, Ellaline, 26, 27
Terry, Ellen, 26, 47
theatre
  audiences, 134, 135–6
  campaign for a National Theatre, 88–91, 123, 214–16
  children on the stage, 26–8
  repertory, 88, 89–90, 107, 108, 191, 302–3
  Second World War, 219–20
  'slovenly speech', ix, 301–2
  see also censorship, dramatic; critics, theatre; dramatic works
Three Plays for Puritans (GBS plays), 3, 162–3
Times Book Club, 61, 62–7, 68, 71–80
Times Literary Supplement, 162–72
Times, The, ix, xi–xii, 32, 61, 210
  article on GBS, 302–3
  characteristics of GBS' letters, 191
  and dramatic censorship, 91, 92, 93, 110
  and the English language, 226–8, 237
  First World War and GBS, 147, 149
  GBS' final letter, 287–8
  on the Handel festivals, 233
  reprinted GBS letters and writings, 289–304
  theatre critics, 121–3, 179, 180
  see also Times Book Club
Tolstoy, Count Leo, 97, 172–5, 223, 233
translations, 172–5, 179, 180, 181
Trebitsch, Siegfried, 24, 46, 47, 181, 292
Tree, Herbert Beerbohm, 98, 99, 130, 146–7
  censorship and, 100, 108, 136, 137
Trotsky, Leon, 200, 201, 224, 261, 287
Turkey, 149, 295
typhus fever, 10, 182